International Practitioner's Deskbook Series

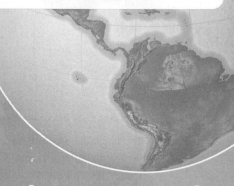

International Labor and Employment Law, Second Edition, Volume I (Europe)

Editors
Philip M. Berkowitz
Anders Etgen Reitz
Thomas Müller-Bonanni

Defending Liberty
Pursuing Justice

ABA Section of
International Law
Your Gateway to International Practice

Section of International Law
American Bar Association

Cover design by ABA Publishing.

The materials contained herein represent the opinions and views of the authors and/or the editors, and should not be construed to be the views or opinions of the law firms or companies with whom such persons are in partnership with, associated with, or employed by, nor of the American Bar Association or the Section of International Law, unless adopted pursuant to the bylaws of the Association.

Nothing contained in this book is to be considered as the rendering of legal advice, either generally or in connection with any specific issue or case; nor do these materials purport to explain or interpret any specific bond or policy, or any provisions thereof, issued by any particular franchise company, or to render franchise or other professional advice. Readers are responsible for obtaining advice from their own lawyers or other professionals. This book and any forms and agreements herein are intended for educational and informational purposes only.

Printed in the United States of America

10 09 08 07 06 5 4 3 2 1

Library of Congress Cataloging-in-Publication Data

International labor and employment law : a practical guide / editors, Philip M. Berkowitz, Thomas Müller-Bonanni, Anders Etgen Reitz—2nd ed.
    p. cm.   (International practitioner's deskbook series)
    Includes index.
    ISBN-13: 978-1-60442-111-8
    ISBN-10: 1-60442-111-8
    1. Labor laws and legislation. 2. Labor laws and legislation, International.
  I. Berkowitz, Philip M. II. Müller-Bonanni, Thomas. III. Reitz, Anders Etgen.

    K1705.I53 200
    344.01—dc22

                2008030962

Discounts are available for books ordered in bulk. Special consideration is given to state bars, CLE programs, and other bar-related organizations. Inquire at Book Publishing, ABA Publishing, American Bar Association, 321 North Clark Street, Chicago, Illinois 60654-7598.

www.ababooks.org

CONTENTS

ABOUT THE EDITORS

Philip M. Berkowitz is a partner with Nixon Peabody LLP in New York City, where he chairs the firm's international labor and employment team. He received his B.A. from the State University of New York at New Paltz and his J.D. from Northwestern School of Law. Mr. Berkowitz's extensive labor and employment experience includes discrimination and harassment, whistleblowing, wrongful dismissal, ERISA violations, executive compensation, and breach of contract and restrictive covenants. He has defended litigations in federal and state courts and administrative agencies across the United States, as well as arbitrations before the National Association of Securities Dealers, the American Arbitration Association, and the International Chamber of Commerce. Mr. Berkowitz is the senior advisor to the International Employment Law Committee of the ABA Section of International Law and is the management co-chair of the New York State Bar Association's International Labor and Employment Law Committee.

Dr. Thomas Müller-Bonanni, LL.M., is a partner with Freshfields Bruckhaus Deringer based in Germany. He specializes in labor and employment law with a special focus on mass layoffs, restructurings, outsourcings, mergers and acquisitions, and privatizations. Dr. Müller-Bonanni also has broad experience in advising on pension plans and remuneration systems, including stock options. He received his legal education at the universities of Cologne, Germany, Geneva, and Lausanne, Switzerland. Dr. Müller-Bonanni holds an LL.M. degree from New York University and was a scholar of the German Academic Exchange service. He is a regular lecturer at HR specialist seminars, both at the national and international levels, and is the author of numerous legal publications.

Anders Etgen Reitz is a senior associate of the labor and employment law group of Bech-Bruun, Denmark's leading law firm. Based at the Copenhagen office, Mr. Etgen Reitz's practice focuses on advising multinational corporations, particularly on cross-border issues. Specializing in international employment law, Mr. Etgen Reitz counsels Fortune 500 and other multinational corporations in labor and employment law issues related to doing business in Scandinavia and Europe. He has acted in numerous contentious and non-contentious cases including cases regarding incentive and stock option plans, restrictive covenant and trade secret infringements, cross-border transactions, mergers, restructurings, immigration issues, and data protection. His clients come from a broad range of industry sectors, including information technology, consultancy, private equity, banking and financial services, telecommunications, and the media. Mr. Etgen Reitz is a regular speaker at international conferences on employment law issues. He is the editor of the ABA's *International Practitioner's Deskbook Series: Labor and Employment Law in the New EU Member and Candidate States* (2007) and has written a number of articles on national and international employment law. Mr. Etgen Reitz received his master's degree in law in 2000 from the University of Copenhagen. He has pursued his international studies at Oxford and Harvard, and in 2005 he received an LL.M. in labor and employment law from New York University. Following his LL.M., he worked as a visiting attorney at Nixon Peabody LLP's New York office in the Labor and Employment Law Department. Mr. Etgen Reitz is the co-chair of the International Employment Law Committee under the ABA and editor-in-chief of the Committee's quarterly newsletter, *The International Employment Lawyer*. He is an active member of the New York State Bar Association, the Danish Bar Association, the Danish Association of Labor and Employment Law, and the European Employment Lawyers Association. Mr. Etgen Reitz is a lecturer in negotiation and dispute resolution at the Danish Bar Association's mandatory bar education. He speaks Danish and English fluently and works in English, Danish, Swedish, and Norwegian.

ABOUT THE CONTRIBUTORS

BELGIUM

Carl Bevernage is a member of the employment law, compensation benefits, and pensions practice group of Loyens. He is involved in industrial
relations law, individual employment law, and national insurance and pension plans under Belgian and European law. He specializes in civil and
criminal proceedings; arbitrations, pharmaceuticals, and medical products
law; and WTO issues. Mr. Bevernage is head of the Belgian Delegation with
the Council of European Bars, a member of the Belgian High Council of
Justice, and a member of the American Bar Association's Section of International Law and Practice and the Section of Labor and Employment Law.
He is also the senior editor of and a contributor to *International Labor and
Employment Laws* (BNA 2003) and co-president of the Belgian-Dutch Association (BENEV). He was president of the Brussels Bar Association from 1990
to 1992. He holds a law degree (Katholieke Universiteit Leuven, 1967) and
LL.M. (Tulane University, USA, 1968). He is a member of the Brussels Bar
and speaks Dutch, French, English, and German.

CZECH REPUBLIC

Gabriela Hájková is a partner with Peterka & Partners, one of the leading
Central European law firms. She has extensive experience in Czech and
European corporate, employment, and labor law and has advised both
Czech and foreign clients on a broad range of employment and labor law
matters. She took her masters in law at the Law Faculty of the Charles
University in Prague and obtained a D.E.S.S. diploma from the University
of Toulouse, France. She is a member of the Czech and Slovak Bars and is
fluent in French and English.

Eva Adamcová has been a junior attorney at law with Peterka & Partners
since 2004. She graduated from the Law Faculty of the Charles University
in Prague. During her studies, she took a one-year course at the University
of Social Sciences in Toulouse, France, where she obtained the Diplôme
d'Etudes de l'Union Européenne. She has a good command of French and
English and specializes mainly in labor law, commercial law, and European
law.

DENMARK

Anders Etgen Reitz is a senior associate of the labor and employment law group of Bech-Bruun, Denmark's leading law firm. Based at the Copenhagen office, Mr. Etgen Reitz's practice focuses on advising multinational corporations, particularly on cross-border issues. Specializing in international employment law, Mr. Etgen Reitz counsels Fortune 500 and other multinational corporations in labor and employment law issues related to doing business in Scandinavia and Europe. He has acted in numerous contentious and noncontentious cases including cases regarding incentive and stock option plans, restrictive covenant and trade secret infringements, cross-border transactions, mergers, restructurings, immigration issues, and data protection. His clients come from a broad range of industry sectors, including information technology, consultancy, private equity, banking and financial services, telecommunications, and the media. Mr. Etgen Reitz is a regular speaker at international conferences on employment law issues. He is the editor of the ABA's *International Practitioner's Deskbook Series: Labor and Employment Law in the New EU Member and Candidate States* (2007) and has written a number of articles on national and international employment law. Mr. Etgen Reitz received his master's degree in law in 2000 from the University of Copenhagen. He has pursued his international studies at Oxford and Harvard, and in 2005 he received an LL.M. in labor and employment law from New York University. Following his LL.M., he worked as a visiting attorney at Nixon Peabody LLP's New York office in the Labor and Employment Law Department. Mr. Etgen Reitz is the co-chair of the International Employment Law Committee under the ABA and editor-in-chief of the Committee's quarterly newsletter, *The International Employment Lawyer*. He is an active member of the New York State Bar Association, the Danish Bar Association, the Danish Association of Labor and Employment Law, and the European Employment Lawyers Association. Mr. Etgen Reitz is a lecturer in negotiation and dispute resolution at the Danish Bar Association's mandatory bar education. He speaks Danish and English fluently and works in English, Danish, Swedish, and Norwegian.

Michael Borring Andersen is a senior associate of the labor and employment law group of Bech-Bruun, Denmark's leading law firm. Mr. Borring Andersen received his master's degree in 2000 from the University of Aarhus. He is a lecturer in constitutional law, human rights law, and EU law at Copenhagen University and teaches labor and employment law as well. Mr. Borring Andersen is a former head of section in the Danish Ministry of the Interior. He speaks Danish and English fluently and works in English, German, Danish, Swedish, and Norwegian.

FINLAND

Jan Örndahl has been a partner with the law firm of Castren & Snellman since 1999. He heads the firm's employment law practice group, which is the largest and most recognized employment practice group within Finnish law firms. He is recognized as one of the leading experts on employment law in Finland and advises clients on all aspects of employment and labor law. He also frequently writes articles on various subjects related to employment law. Mr. Örndahl's key areas of expertise also include corporate restructuring transactions (mainly private mergers and acquisitions), transfers of business, outsourcing, and buy-out transactions. He is also a board member of several Finnish companies. Mr. Örndahl is a member of the Finnish Bar Association, the International Bar Association, and the European Employment Lawyers Association. He is fluent in Finnish, Swedish, English, and German.

FRANCE

Salli A. Swartz has practiced international business law in Paris since 1979. Ms. Swartz specializes in international arbitrations and mediations. She also regularly advises French and other European subsidiaries of major American multinational companies in connection with their business activities in Europe and the Middle East, the Foreign Corrupt Practice Act, anti-boycott laws, and the OECD Convention on Combating Bribery of Foreign Public Officials. Ms. Swartz has lectured extensively on international business law issues and teaches intellectual property at the Ecole National Superieur des Arts & Metiers in Paris and international arbitration and mediation at the French business school Hautes Etudes Commercials. She is the author of numerous articles and publications, and is co-editor and author of a chapter in *Careers in International Law*, published by the ABA in 2002. She is also the author of the chapter "Selling Products in Foreign Countries— International Sales" in *Negotiating and Structuring International Commercial Transactions*, published by the ABA in 2003. Ms. Swartz is a member of the Pennsylvania and Paris Bars, with specializations in the law of international relations and commercial law. She is admitted to practice before the French Courts, the U.S. Court of Appeals for the Federal Circuit, the U.S. Court of International Trade, and the U.S. Supreme Court, and is Finance Officer of the Section of International Law and Practice of the ABA, of which she is a member of the Governing Council. She is also a member of the ABA's Section of Business Law, is an Officer of the Mediation Committee of the International Bar Association, and is the ABA liaison to the Union Internationale des Avocats.

GERMANY

Dr. Thomas Müller-Bonanni, LL.M., is a partner with Freshfields Bruckhaus Deringer based in Germany. He specializes in labor and employment law with a special focus on mass layoffs, restructurings, outsourcings, mergers and acquisitions, and privatizations. Dr. Müller-Bonanni also has broad experience in advising on pension plans and remuneration systems, including stock options. He received his legal education at the universities of Cologne, Germany, Geneva, and Lausanne, Switzerland. Dr. Müller-Bonanni holds an LL.M. degree from New York University and was a scholar of the German Academic Exchange Service. He is a regular lecturer at HR specialist seminars, both at the national and international levels, and is the author of numerous legal publications.

GREECE

Effie G. Mitsopoulou studied law at the University of Aix–Marseille (Maîtrise en Droit) and at King's College, University of London (LL.M.). She has been a member of the Athens Bar Association since 1986. Ms. Mitsopoulou joined Kyriakides Georgopoulos & Daniolos Issaias Law Firm in 1985 and is leading KGDI's Employment and Labor Law Department. She has also worked for a number of years in the legal department of the National Bank of Greece. Ms. Mitsopoulou has handled a wide range of civil and commercial cases before all levels of the Greek courts and she is an active labor law litigation lawyer. She also advises on general labor law issues of domestic and multinational companies. Her experience enables her to deal with complex and various labor issues, such as restructuring, transfer of undertakings on an international level, negotiation and conclusion of collective bargaining agreements, and cross-border projects. Implementation of collective redundancy plans, pension plans, employee benefits, and immigration and data protection law issues are included in her practice.

Ioanna C. Kyriazi has been a senior associate at Kyriakides Georgopoulos & Daniolos Issaias Law Firm in Athens since 2006 and has extensive experience in Greek labor law. She graduated from the Faculty of Law at the University of Thessaloniki in 1998 and obtained her M.Sc. in Human Resources Management from Athens University of Economics and Business. She advises multinational companies as well as local enterprises on all aspects of labor law, including the drafting of employment agreements and collective labor agreements, the employment aspects of mergers and acquisitions, and the implementation of redundancy plans due to restructuring or closing down of enterprises (including collective dismissals and consultations and negotiations with the unions). Ms. Kyriazi also has extensive experience with employment issues related to outsourcing transactions and individual and collective labor law, maritime labor law, and social security law. She also litigates on a broad range of employment issues, incentive plans, and pension plans, including individual and collective dismissals, transfers of undertakings, European Work Councils, and discrimination law issues. She is a member of the Piraeus Bar Association.

HUNGARY

Dr. Tamás Riesz, partner, heads the employment practice of Riesz & Peteri. Dr. Riesz is recognized as one of the leading employment law practitioners in Hungary. He was involved in major restructuring projects involving a large number of employees. He has gained significant experience in employment-related litigation procedures and has valuable connections with labor authorities. Dr. Riesz has also led various negotiations between employers and trade unions on both sides. His team is one of the leading practice groups in Hungary dealing with work and residence permits. He was co-head of the working group dealing with various amendments of the Hungarian Labor Code. Before establishing Riesz & Peteri, he spent nine years at an international law firm. Dr. Riesz holds a law degree (Eötvös Lóránt University Faculty of Law, Budapest, 1994) and an LL.M. (King's College, London, 2003). He is a member of the Budapest Bar and speaks English, German, and Hungarian.

IRELAND

Kevin Langford has been a partner at the Arthur Cox firm in Dublin since 2003, having qualified as a solicitor in 1997. He previously worked as an in-house legal advisor with the Irish Business and Employers Confederation. Mr. Langford advises employers on all aspects of employment and industrial relations law. This includes representing clients in the defense of claims pertaining to unfair dismissal, wrongful dismissal, redundancy, injunctions, and trade disputes. He also advises on discrimination and equality issues and on noncontentious matters such as transfer of undertakings legislation and drafting employment contracts and staff handbooks, and provides support on the employment aspects of corporate transactions. Mr. Langford holds a law degree from Trinity College Dublin (1993) and is a member of the Society for Labour Law and the European Employment Lawyers Association. He frequently lectures and contributes articles on many aspects of employment law.

ITALY

Marcello Giustiniani is a partner and the head of the employment practice of Bonelli Erede Pappalardo, one of the leading Italian law firms. He was nominated by Chambers Global for outstanding ability in the labor sector. Mr. Giustiniani's main fields of expertise include labor relationships with top managers, stock options and investment plans for managers and other employees, workforce downscaling, collective dismissals procedures, and transfer of undertakings (including trade union consultations). He also advises companies on their day-to-day managing of personnel and sales networks. He handles precontentious and contentious labor matters and employee transfers, promoters, agents and other members of the team. Before joining Bonelli Erede Pappalardo with his associates, Mr. Giustiniani worked for 10 years for one of the leading law firms in Milan that specializes in labor law, first as an associate and then as a partner. He has been a member of A.G.I. (Italian Labor Lawyer Association) since its foundation and has been a Professor of Labor Law at the Scuola Forense dell'Ordine degli Avvocati in Milan since 2000. He is also a professor at the School of Labor Law, organized and managed by A.G.I. and by the Italian Lawyers Association in Milan. He has written extensively on employment law matters, is a freelance journalist, and is a contributor to the leading Italian business newspaper *Il Sole 24 Ore*. Mr. Giustiniani graduated with honors from the University of Milan in 1987, where he was involved in the Labor Law Institute until 2000. From 1991 to 1993 he worked as an assistant for the Institute at the Bocconi University in Milan. He was admitted to the Italian Bar in 1989.

Vittorio Pomarici is a senior associate at Bonelli Erede Pappalardo and focuses on labor and employment law matters. His work involves drafting employment agreements for top managers, stock option plans, share incentive plans, and long-term monetary incentive plans, as well as legal civil litigations opinions and pleadings. In addition, Mr. Pomarici oversees general work relations and the drafting of related agreements, as well as legal proceedings relating to extraordinary transactions, closings, and employment transfers. Mr. Pomarici worked for a prestigious law firm in Milan that specializes in labor law prior to joining Erede e Associati (which subsequently became Bonelli Erede Pappalardo) in 1998. He also worked as visiting foreign lawyer with one of Bonelli Erede Pappalardo's "best friends," Slaughter and May (London office) in 2001. Mr. Pomarici graduated from the University of Milan in 1997. He was admitted to the Italian Bar in 2002.

THE NETHERLANDS

Els de Wind is an employment law partner with Van Doorne, based in Amsterdam. She has been practicing corporate and employment law for more than 22 years. Until the Dutch merger between Van Doorne and Landwell (the correspondent law firm of PricewaterhouseCoopers) in January 2004, Ms. de Wind was an employment law partner with Landwell, a member of Landwell's Global Executive Board, and head of the Global Employment Law Practice of Landwell and PricewaterhouseCoopers. She has a background of working with specialists, such as HR consultants and tax advisors, and has managed large international projects for multinationals. Her practice is local Dutch but also very much global. Ms. de Wind frequently speaks at seminars and conferences in the Netherlands and elsewhere in the world on HR and cross-border employment law issues, and has published various articles and book contributions in this field. She is a member of various Dutch and international professional associations, including the Dutch Employment Law Association, the Amsterdam Employment Lawyers Association, the European Employment Lawyers Association (where she represents the Netherlands on the Board), and the International Bar Association (where she currently holds the position of Vice-Chair). She is also an active member of XBHR. Ms. de Wind holds a Masters of Law from the University of Nijmegen, the Netherlands; Private International Law and Public International Law Summer School Certificates of the Hague Academy of International Law; and an LL.M. International and Comparative Law from the Free University Brussels. She is fluent in Dutch, English, French, and German.

Anneke Meulenveld has been practicing labor and employment law with Van Doorne, Amsterdam, since 2006. Ms. Meulenveld works both in the international and national fields of employment law. She graduated from the University of Utrecht and the University of Amsterdam. Together with Els de Wind, she has written various articles and book chapters on Dutch employment law. She is fluent in Dutch and English.

NORWAY

Trond Stang has been a partner at the law firm Schjødt in Oslo since 1990, and heads the firm's labor and employment law group. This group advises clients on employment and labor law matters and all aspects of workforce reductions, outsourcing, and business acquisitions, and assists employers in legal issues relating to competition clauses, compensation agreements, option agreements, and employment contracts in general. From 1980 to 1986 he worked as legal counsel in the Ministry of Petroleum and Energy and from 1986 to 1987 as an associate at the law firm Sunde before joining Schjødt. He holds a law degree from the University of Oslo (1980). He is a lecturer in both labor and employment law and petroleum law. He is a member of the Norwegian Bar Association and speaks English and the Scandinavian languages.

POLAND

Aleksandra Minkowicz-Flanek has been a senior associate at the law firm of Salans D. Oleszczuk Kancelaria Prawnicza Sp. k. in Warsaw since 2001. She heads the labor and employment practice and also focuses on corporate and public procurement issues. Ms. Minkowicz-Flanek participates in projects involving mergers of companies, transfers of enterprises, negotiating and drafting collective agreements, employment due diligence analysis, and preparation of contracts related to employment issues in individual and collective employment relations (such as contracts with key executives, noncompete agreements, and termination documentation). She publishes and speaks at conferences on a regular basis. She also runs training courses for clients' employees in the field of labor law. Ms. Minkowicz-Flanek was admitted as a legal adviser in 2007. She graduated from Warsaw University (Master of Laws, 1999) and completed postgraduate studies in Intellectual Property at Warsaw University (2003). She speaks Polish and English.

PORTUGAL

César Sá Esteves is a partner with Simmons & Simmons and is head of the employment practice in the Lisbon office. He became a member of the Portuguese Bar in 1994. Mr. Esteves is a postgraduate in both business law and pharmaceutical law. He has been the Portuguese representative on the Executive Board of the European Employment Lawyers Association since 2001. He has contributed to several publications on European and Portuguese employment law and is a regular speaker at seminars and public conferences on his practice areas. Mr. Esteves has extensive experience in all areas of employment, both contentious and noncontentious, and advises on a wide variety of employment issues relating to restructurings, mergers and acquisitions, redundancies, business transfers, collective disputes, international reassignment issues, and the establishment of employee benefits and incentives, including stock option plans. He also has particular experience in dealing with senior executive work and appointments and severance packages, and advises on social security and pension matters, as well as on immigration issues.

Maria de Lancastre Valente is an associate at Simmons & Simmons Rebelo de Sousa and is a registered member of the Portuguese Bar Association. She has experience in all matters related to employment law (including contentious-related), focusing particularly on restructurings, redundancies, business transfers, and international reassignment issues, as well as on employee remuneration and benefits packages. She also has experience regarding senior executive appointments, severance packages, and other related work, having acted for major companies operating in the financial sector, the pharmaceuticals industry, and the telecommunications, media, and technology sector. She also advises on social security and immigration matters. She is a postgraduate in Employment Law and is a regular contributor to both Portuguese and international publications.

SLOVAKIA

Tomáš Rybár is a partner with Čechová & Partners law firm. He is regularly involved in various employment and labor law issues, including employment contracts, dismissals, employee representation, noncompetition, personal data, safety at work, and liability. His professional areas include contract law, mergers and acquisitions, European law, healthcare law, administrative law, financial law, unfair competition, information technology, and data protection law. During his practice he has been involved in a number of significant privatization and mergers and acquisitions transactions and has led several due diligence exercises. He has also advised in the process of preparation of laws reforming the Slovak healthcare system and drug policies. He received his Master of Laws degree at Comenius University in 2001 and completed the Course of European Integration and Law (Institute for European Politics, Berlin, 1999–2001). He is a member of the Slovak Bar Association and its Foreign Affairs Committee. He is also a member of the Executive Committee of the International Association of Young Lawyers and is its National Representative in Slovakia, and he is a member of Team Europe, a group of experts on EU affairs organized by the European Commission. He speaks Slovak, Czech, and English.

Branislav Hazucha is an associate at Čechová & Partners law firm. He has extensive experience in Slovak employment and labor law. He has advised foreign and Slovak companies on numerous labor law and other regulatory issues, including regulation of drug policies, telecommunications, postal services, energy, and financial markets. During his work for the Institute for Approximation of Law at the Office of the Government of the Slovak Republic, which specializes in bringing Slovak law in line with EU law, he participated in legislative processes of several key Slovak laws, including the Labor Code and the Civil Service Act. In addition to practicing law, he teaches in the LL.M. Program in International Economic and Business Law at the Kyushu University Graduate School of Law. He holds the Master of Laws degree from Comenius University (1999) and doctoral degrees from Trnava University (2001) and Kyushu University (2005). He is an associate member of the Slovak Bar Association and speaks Slovak, Czech, English, and Spanish.

SPAIN

Vicente Calle is a partner with the Spanish law firm Garringues. He received his law degree from Complutense University in 1989. Mr. Calle's practice consists primarily of labor law, and he is a specialist in major restructuring operations. He belongs to the Madrid Bar Association and is fluent in Spanish and English.

SWEDEN

Olle Jansson, partner with Cederquist, is recognized as one of the leading commercial labor and employment lawyers in Sweden with long-standing and in-depth experience in the field. After service with the Labor Court, Mr. Jansson has practiced labor law, representing employers from all industries. His work for domestic and international corporate clients in labor matters focuses on business transfers, reorganizations, staff reductions, union relations, protection of trade secrets, and key managers' contracts. His practice includes contentious and arbitrary matters. Community law and cross-border matters are other areas of Mr. Jansson's labor, corporate, and commercial practice.

SWITZERLAND

Ueli Sommer is a partner in the Corporate & Commercial Team of Walder Wyss & Partners, one of the leading law firms in Switzerland. Mr. Sommer heads WW&P's employment practice group. He has many years of experience in all aspects of employment law and focuses on compensation plans and participation plans. He also advises international companies and private individuals on immigration and choice-of-domicile issues. He supported many companies and high-level executives in regard to the conclusion and termination of employment agreements and termination arrangements. Mr. Sommer was educated at Zurich University (lic. iur. 1995, Dr. iur. 1999) and at the University of New South Wales in Sydney, Australia (LL.M. 2001). He worked as a district court clerk before joining WW&P in 1999. In 2001 and 2002, he worked as a foreign associate for Allens Arthur Robinson in Sydney. Mr. Sommer is registered with the Zurich Bar Registry and admitted to practice in all of Switzerland. He is a member of the International Bar Association (IBA) and the American Bar Association (ABA). In regard to the latter, he is also a member of the Steering Committee of the International Employment Committee. He publishes regularly in legal journals and speaks at national and international congresses. Mr. Sommer is also a board member of the Australian Swiss Chamber of Commerce and Industry (ASCCI). He speaks German and English.

UNITED KINGDOM

Kathleen Healy is a partner in the Employment, Pensions and Benefits Department of Freshfields Bruckhaus Deringer and is based in the firm's London office. Ms. Healy is co-head of the employment team in London and has a broad employment practice, advising on a full range of employment issues, including general advisory, litigation, and transactional matters. Ms. Healy also advises on the employment and corporate governance issues associated with the hiring and firing of senior executives. She has a particular interest in collective consultation issues, industrial relations, and TUPE, and is a co-author of *Informing and Consulting Employees: The New Law* (Oxford University Press, 2005), on the Information & Consultation of Employees Regulations 2004.

UNITED STATES

Philip M. Berkowitz is a partner with Nixon Peabody LLP in New York City, where he chairs the firm's international labor and employment team. He received his B.A. from the State University of New York at New Paltz and his J.D. from Northwestern School of Law. Mr. Berkowitz's extensive labor and employment experience includes discrimination and harassment, whistleblowing, wrongful dismissal, ERISA violations, executive compensation, and breach of contract and restrictive covenants. He has defended litigations in federal and state courts and administrative agencies across the United States, as well as arbitrations before the National Association of Securities Dealers, the American Arbitration Association, and the International Chamber of Commerce. Mr. Berkowitz is the senior advisor to the International Employment Law Committee of the ABA Section of International Law and is the management co-chair of the New York State Bar Association's International Labor and Employment Law Committee.

Anders Etgen Reitz is a senior associate of the labor and employment law group of Bech-Bruun, Denmark's leading law firm. Based at the Copenhagen office, Mr. Etgen Reitz's practice focuses on advising multinational corporations, particularly on cross-border issues. Specializing in international employment law, Mr. Etgen Reitz counsels Fortune 500 and other multinational corporations in labor and employment law issues related to doing business in Scandinavia and Europe. He has acted in numerous contentious and noncontentious cases including cases regarding incentive and stock option plans, restrictive covenant and trade secret infringements, cross-border transactions, mergers, restructurings, immigration issues, and data protection. His clients come from a broad range of industry sectors, including information technology, consultancy, private equity, banking and financial services, telecommunications, and the media. Mr. Etgen Reitz is a regular speaker at international conferences on employment law issues. He is the editor of the ABA's *International Practitioner's Deskbook Series: Labor and Employment Law in the New EU Member and Candidate States* (2007) and has written a number of articles on national and international employment law. Mr. Etgen Reitz received his master's degree in law in 2000 from the University of Copenhagen. He has pursued his international studies at Oxford and Harvard, and in 2005 he received an LL.M. in labor and employment law from New York University. Following his LL.M., he worked as a visiting attorney at Nixon Peabody LLP's New York office in the Labor and Employment Law Department. Mr. Etgen Reitz is the co-chair of the International Employment Law Committee under the ABA and editor-in-chief of the Committee's quarterly newsletter, *The International Employment Lawyer*. He is an active member of the New York State Bar Association, the Danish Bar Association, the Danish Association of Labor and Employment Law, and the European Employment Lawyers Association. Mr. Etgen Reitz is a lecturer in negotiation and dispute resolution at the Danish Bar Association's mandatory bar education. He speaks Danish and English fluently and works in English, Danish, Swedish, and Norwegian.

INTRODUCTION

The field of international labor and employment law is developing rapidly and changing to fit the needs of increasingly global businesses. Human resources play an increasingly important role in international business transactions. Counsel for multinational companies increasingly recognize the importance of having a global perspective in labor and employment law. They are searching for sources of practical assistance.

This book is meant to help fill that role. Part of the ABA's International Practitioner's Deskbook Series, it is presented in the friendly, usable format of a two-volume handbook—one volume covering the major jurisdictions of Europe and one volume covering the most important jurisdictions in the rest of the world.

Our aim has been to provide helpful, practical guidance to international corporate lawyers who confront labor and employment problems in structuring corporate transactions. Thus, we focus on practical issues: establishing a facility; hiring a workforce; drafting employment contracts; terminating or replacing employees; providing wages and benefits; dealing with unions; carrying out workforce reductions; selling the business; and paying severance. We also treat issues regarding discrimination and harassment, wrongful dismissal, and key labor issues on the horizon. It is our hope and expectation that we will revise this book periodically.

Our contributors are leading labor lawyers in numerous important jurisdictions.

We have sought to distinguish this book from others in the area of international labor and employment law that tend to be encyclopedic in scope and approach. We have focused not only on what the laws provide, but also on the perspective of on-the-ground counsel who have extensive day-to-day experience with these issues. We are aware that we have not treated every pertinent jurisdiction. We have focused, in this volume, on what we perceived to be the largest economies. We may have been somewhat arbitrary in making these determinations, and we hope to include other jurisdictions in a future volume.

We are very grateful for all of the contributors' hard work in finalizing this volume. We are particularly grateful for the assistance of Paulina Fernández Izquierdo in co-editing many of these chapters and to Susanne Louise Petersen and Britta Boserup for assistance in organizing the project. Finally, we are grateful to the ABA for permitting us to contribute to its exciting International Practitioner's Deskbook Series.

Philip M. Berkowitz
Thomas Müller-Bonanni
Anders Etgen Reitz
March 2008

CHAPTER 1

LABOR AND EMPLOYMENT LAW IN BELGIUM

CARL BEVERNAGE

Preliminary remark: Under Belgian employment law, a distinction is made between blue-collar workers (employees performing manual work), hereafter referred to as "workers," and white-collar employees (employees performing clerical or managerial activities), hereafter referred to as "employees."

SECTION I

My client wishes to establish a manufacturing facility in Belgium and will need to hire a workforce. What are the key issues involved?

Employment Contracts: Who Receives Them and What Must They Include?

Written Agreements

In principle, the employment agreement does not require any special written form; it may even be verbal. However, under certain conditions or if the parties want to include special clauses, a written agreement is legally required prior to the beginning of the employment duties.

Contracts for a Fixed Term or a Specific Task
A written agreement is mandatory if the employment is for a fixed term or a specific task. If no such document exists, the agreement will be deemed open-ended. Up to four successive fixed-term contracts are permitted, each having a minimum duration of three months, for a total duration of no more than two years (or up to three years with the prior authorization of the Labor Inspectorate). Beyond these time periods, successive fixed-term contracts are considered to constitute an open-ended contract.

Part-Time Employment

A part-time contract must stipulate in writing the agreed working hours and work schedule.

Particular Employment Contracts

Seasonal employment contracts, student contracts, replacement contracts, and apprenticeship contracts are subject to specific rules. The following clauses should be in writing:

Trial Period

For workers, the minimum trial period is seven days and the maximum is 14 days. For employees, the minimum is one month and the maximum is six months or, if the employee's gross salary exceeds €34,231 (as of January 1, 2008), 12 months.

During the trial period, the agreement can be terminated by either side without any notice period for the worker and with a seven-day notice period for the employee. However, if the termination occurs within the first seven days for a worker or the first month for an employee, the notice will become effective at the end of this period.

Noncompete Period

By a noncompete clause, the worker or employee undertakes not to perform any activities similar to those performed with this employer, either for his or her own account or for a competitor, and either as a salaried worker or employee or in a self-employed manner, after the termination of the employment contract. The validity of this type of clause is subject to several conditions, such as the worker's or employee's salary, the duration and geographical scope of the limitations, and the activities to which the limitation applies.

The clause must stipulate that the employer will pay a lump-sum indemnity amounting to at least half the worker's or employee's gross salary for the duration of the noncompete period, unless it concerns a sales representative. A worker or employee who violates the clause will have to reimburse the indemnity received and pay in addition an equivalent amount. The employer may waive the application of this clause within 15 days of the termination after the employment contract and not pay the indemnity.

Agreed Notice Period

White-collar employees earning more than €57,162 gross per annum may agree upon an alterative notice period to be observed by the employer. The agreed-upon notice period should amount to at least three months for each five years of employment. This type of clause is not included in all contracts but is still applied quite regularly.

Notice periods for blue-collar workers may be determined in collective bargaining agreements.

Language

The language to be used in employment relationships (e.g., employment contracts, notice letters, and work regulations) depends on which geographic region in Belgium the place of work is located or the worker or employee is connected. The place of work is not necessarily the same as the registered offices. For sales representatives, the place where they receive their orders is decisive.

Geographic Region	Language to Be Used in Employment Contracts and Social Documents
Flemish Region	Dutch
Walloon Region	French
Brussels Region	Dutch or French depending on the language spoken by the worker/employee. Foreign-language-speaking workers/employees should also be addressed in Dutch or French, but a translation can be provided.
German Region and communes with special language facilities	Dutch, French, or German depending on whether the commune is located in the Flemish, Walloon, or German Region

In the Flemish and Walloon Regions, documents drafted in the wrong language are deemed null and void. In the Brussels and German Regions as well as in the communes with special language facilities, a document drafted in the wrong language can always be replaced with a document in the correct language.

Changes to the Terms and Provisions

The employer and the worker or employee have the possibility to convene at any time to modify the terms of their employment relationship in mutual agreement. The employer is considered to have a right to unilaterally modify the contract, the *ius variandi*. This right, however, is not absolute. The employer is not entitled to make important changes to the essential terms of the employment contract. Salary, job content, place of work, and working hours are considered to be essential terms.

In principle, a clause in the contract entitling the employer to unilaterally change essential terms is void, unless these changes are justified by the nature of the employment relationship. Clauses that apply only to the modification of secondary terms are valid.

If the employer unilaterally makes important changes to terms deemed essential to the contract, the modifications might be construed as a constructive dismissal, entitling the worker or employee to an indemnity-in-lieu-of-notice corresponding to the notice period that should have been served.

Wages and Benefits

Minimum Wage Requirements

Minimum wages are imposed nationwide. As of May 1, 2008, the guaranteed minimum monthly income for full-time employment amounts to €1,371.88 gross for workers and employees of 21 and a half years of age or older (with a seniority of six months within the company). Furthermore, most Joint Committees (representative bodies organized at sector or industrial level, composed of an equal number of union representatives and employer association representatives) impose sector minimum salaries based on job description and age group or seniority.

Statutory Benefits, Fringe Benefits

Vacation

Employees and workers are entitled to an annual vacation of 20 or 24 working days, depending on whether they work five or six days a week.

Employees receive their regular salary during their vacation, and in addition they receive 92 percent of their monthly salary ("double vacation pay"). These allowances are paid directly by the employer.

Workers' vacation pay is funded and paid through the social security system, for which the employer contributes 14–15 percent on 108 percent of the gross salaries.

The right to vacations is accrued on the basis of the performances during the calendar year immediately preceding the calendar year during which the vacations are taken.

Sick Pay

During the first 30 calendar days of their illness, employees are entitled to a guaranteed salary equal to their normal salary, at the cost of the employer. Employees who are still in their trial period, whose contract has a fixed term, or who were hired for a specific task of less than three months are not entitled to this guaranteed salary during the first month of this contract.

Workers are entitled to 100 percent of their normal salary during the first 14 days of their illness; afterward, this percentage is reduced. During the trial period or the first month of employment, no guaranteed salary is due.

Fringe Benefits

The employer may decide to grant additional benefits, such as luncheon vouchers (which under certain conditions are exempted from social security taxes); personal use of a company car, cell phone, or laptop; health insurance; complementary insurance plans and pension plans; performance bonuses; or stock options.

In most industries, the employer is obliged by collective bargaining agreement (CBA) to pay the worker or employee an annual bonus of one month's salary as an end-of-year premium. In certain industries, the employer's affiliation with a sector pension plan is mandatory.

Labor Unions

Belgium counts three national union confederations: the Christian-Democrat Union (A.C.V.-C.S.C.), the Socialist Union (A.B.V.V.-F.G.T.B.), and the Liberal Union (A.C.L.V.B.-C.G.S.L.B.). Only these unions meet the criteria to be considered to be representative, meaning that they can represent workers and employees in the National Labor Council as well as on sector and company levels.

At the company level, the unions are represented by the union delegation. A delegation should be set up according to a collective bargaining agreement if requested by one or more representative trade unions. The members are appointed by the unions at their discretion. In most industries, the threshold to appoint the delegation is 50 workers or employees within the company. In principle, the union delegates represent only unionized workers and employees.

The tasks of the union delegation may be described as follows:

- Dealing with grievances related to employment relations and conditions, such as salary and working hours;
- Carrying out negotiations for collective bargaining agreements at company level (the agreement itself will, however, have to be signed by a full-time trade union official external to the company);
- Monitoring the application of several regulations, such as social legislation, CBAs, and individual employment contracts;
- Representing the employees in individual and collective disputes with the employer.

If no works council (see next page) has been elected in the company, the union delegation takes over certain of its powers and competences.

Collective Agreements

A collective bargaining agreement (CBA) is an agreement between one or more representative union organizations and an employer or its representative organization, determining collective or individual rights and obligations of the workers or employees.

A certain part of Belgian labor law, to be respected by employers, is determined in CBAs. CBAs may be applied either nationwide, within the applicable Joint Committee, or at the company level.

An employer must not be legally forced to apply CBAs at company level, but it shall in principle have to comply with all sector- or national-level CBAs. In the CBA, the following provisions should be included:

- The name of parties and, if applicable, the Joint Committee;
- The identity and capacity of representatives concluding the agreement;
- The scope of application of the CBA;
- The term of the agreement and the start date;
- The execution date;
- Signatures of all parties.

After execution, the CBA will be registered with the Ministry of Labor. In the event not all formal requirements have been fulfilled, the Ministry will send the CBA back to the employer or Joint Committee in order to amend the agreements in accordance with all legal obligations.

In the event a collective dispute arises, employee representatives or the employer may request mediation from the Joint Committee. It is, of course, always possible for workers or employees to bring their case before the courts in order for their rights to be respected.

A CBA may be made for an indefinite or definite period of time. If the CBA is for an indefinite period, the agreement will state the notice period required and the format for the notice letter.

Changes should be made by mutual consent with all parties.

Works Councils

Under the Act of September 20, 1948 and the Act of June 10, 1952, a works council must be established in each "enterprise" employing 100 persons or more on average. A works council may be established in a company with fewer employees if the employer so agrees.

The works council is, in principle, composed of an equal number of employer representatives, who are chosen by the employer from management personnel, and employee representatives, who are elected from lists of candidates drawn up by the "representative" trade unions in a quadrennial nationwide election. The last social election took place in 2008. The next election will take place in 2012.

The works council has an advisory role and is entitled to receive annual, periodical, and occasional information regarding the operations of the company. It should be consulted prior to any decision or disclosure on specific matters such as the restructuring of the company, outsourcing or insourcing, a layoff, and the closure of a division of the company. However, the works council must not interfere with the actual management of a business.

New legislation on worker's representation in small companies has recently been implemented in the Act of April 23, 2008.

Within the code of conduct of the members of the works council, specific provisions related to confidentiality may be stipulated. However, any worker or employee is in any event considered to respect the confidentiality of confidential data.

Again, in the event no works council has been established, the tasks of the works council will be executed by the union delegation, if applicable.

In the event the company is part of a European group of companies, a European Works Council may be established.

SECTION II

My client is acquiring an existing business in Belgium. How do I assess the existing workforce and consider changes?

In this section, the term "employees" refers to both white-collar employees and blue-collar workers.

Share Deals Versus Asset Deals

Share transactions (the sale and transfer of the shares of the target company) have no impact on the existing employment contracts. Legally, the employees will have the same employer after the transaction.

In the event of an asset deal (a sale and purchase of some or all of the assets and liabilities of the employer-company), the existing employment contracts will transfer to the purchaser by operation of law if the asset transfer satisfies the criteria of (partial) "transfer of undertaking" within the meaning of the European Acquired Rights Directive (No. 2001/23/EC) and CBA No. 32*bis,* as amended, which implements the directive in Belgium.[1] All existing employment contracts are transferred without the employees' consent. The transfer as such may not be considered by them as a breach of their employment contract tantamount to a termination.

If the sale of assets does not satisfy the criteria of a (partial) transfer of undertaking, the existing employment contracts will stay behind with the transferor.

Due Diligence Requirements and Considerations

In both share and asset deals, a complete due diligence is recommended since in both cases, the purchaser will have to take into account the existing rights and obligations of the employees.

The purchaser will have to audit all areas related to labor and employment law, social security law, and supplementary pensions. This will include reviewing standard employment contracts, checking payment of social security contributions, and reviewing supplementary pension schemes.

Conducting a due diligence may raise data protection and confidentiality issues. Confidentiality will usually be regulated by contracts and by the legal obligation to perform contracts in good faith. Data protection is regulated by the Data Protection Act (DPA) of December 8, 1992. The systematic processing of personal data—any information (characteristics, behavior, conduct, statements, etc.) relating to an identified or identifiable individual—is permitted only when based on one of the specific grounds mentioned in the DPA.

In conformity with the DPA, the applicant or the employee must unambiguously give consent to the data processing, or the processing must be necessary for the purposes of the legitimate interests pursued by the employer. Furthermore, personal data must be processed fairly and lawfully and must be collected for specified, explicit, and legitimate purposes. The Privacy Commission must also be notified before processing begins.

These provisions could lead to constraints when conducting a due diligence. It is therefore advisable for the vendor not to supply personal data attached to the names of employees, and for the purchaser not to mention any personal data directly linked to the identity of employees in a due diligence report. This will ensure that no information is processed relating to an identified or identifiable individual.

General Description of Statutory Regulations
Concerning Business Acquisitions

Business acquisitions are regulated by European Acquired Rights Directive No. 2001/23/EC and CBA No. 32*bis,* as amended. Furthermore, several other acts or national CBAs influence the legal consequences of such a business transfer.

Transfer of Rights and Obligations of Employees

In case of asset deals that qualify as a transfer of undertaking, the purchaser will automatically take over all personnel linked to the transferred business, as well as their rights and obligations as per the individual employment contracts (including salaries, fringe benefits, and seniority), CBAs, work regulations, and customary practice.

Employees' rights to old-age, disability, or survivors' benefits, under supplementary company or intercompany pension schemes outside the statutory social security schemes, are in principle not automatically transferred to the purchaser. Specific rules apply, however.

A change of ownership will also have important consequences for the establishment and composition of works councils, work safety committees, union representation, and European Works Councils. These particular consequences are not regulated by CBA No. 32bis, but by several acts and CBAs containing the basic principles of the different organizations.

Transfer of Rights and Obligations Toward the Government and Toward Third Parties

Rights and obligations toward the government (for example, reductions of social security contributions for long-time workers) are not transferred to the new owner. The seller must notify the social security authorities of the transfer and must request a certificate releasing the purchaser of liability for payment of social security contributions existing at the time of the transfer. This certificate is to be attached to the transfer act.

The rights that employees have toward third persons that are not their direct employers are not transferred. However, if the final costs of the benefits granted by a third person (e.g., a parent company) to the employee are borne by the employer, the rights of the employees to this benefit will be transferred.

Joint Responsibility

Both the seller and the purchaser are responsible in solidum for the payment of debts existing at the moment of the transfer or arising from the employment contracts existing at the moment of the transfer. This means that an employee can turn to the previous owner as well as to the purchaser for the full amount that is due to him.

Under Belgian doctrine, a controversy exists concerning the joint responsibilities of debts toward employees that arise after the date of transfer. It is therefore advisable for the seller to ensure that the purchaser will insert a provision in an agreement with the transferred employees that the purchaser will be solely regarded as debtor and that the seller is dismissed from all responsibility.

Carrying Out a Workforce Reduction

With the exception of the protection against dismissal as regulated in CBA No. 32bis and the statutory rules on layoffs, no particular regulation exists in Belgian law regarding workforce reductions. While selecting the employees to be laid off, however, the employer should bear in mind the legislation prohibiting discrimination (see Section V).

Protection Against Dismissal

The transfer of a business or part of a business shall not in itself constitute grounds for dismissal by the previous or new owner. This protection does not stand in the way of dismissals that may take place for economic, technical, or organizational reasons entailing changes in the workforce, or for a dismissal for serious cause. An employee can be dismissed for any reason besides the transfer, within the boundaries of Belgian labor and employment law.

The protection against dismissal can be invoked against the previous or the new owner. If an employee who was dismissed preceding a business acquisition can provide evidence that the sale was the motive for the dismissal, this employee can turn to both previous and new owner to claim damages caused by the unlawful dismissal.

Neither European Directive No. 2001/23/EC nor CBA No. 32*bis* provides for a time limitation on the protection. The protection can be invoked whenever there is a causal connection between dismissal and business acquisition, without any limitation in time.

CBA No. 32*bis* does not provide for any lump-sum severance to be paid by the employer in case of dismissal. An employee seeking severance pay beyond what was provided by the general rules of dismissal under Belgian employment law would have to prove that the dismissal caused moral or material damages under the general rules of law of obligations and of Belgian employment law.

Layoffs

In execution of the EEC Directive of February 17, 1975 on the approximation of the laws of the Member States relating to layoffs, the National Labor Council enacted CBAs Nos. 24 and 24a on the topic. Layoffs are defined as covering any dismissal of one or more employees for reasons not related to the individual employees concerned (economic or technical reasons in the broad sense), where over a period of 60 days the number of employees dismissed is

1. at least 10 in technical work or production units that, during the calendar year preceding the dismissals, employed on average more than 20 but fewer than 100 workers;
2. at least 10 percent of the number of workers in technical work or production units that, during the calendar year preceding the dismissals, employed on average at least 100 but fewer than 300 workers;
3. at least 30 in technical work or production units that, during the calendar year preceding the dismissals, employed on average at least 300 workers.

Any employer that is contemplating layoffs is obligated to inform the employees' representatives and start consultations with them on the matter. The information and consultation procedure prior to any decision is done with the works council, if any, or with the union delegation, if any. In the absence of any of these bodies, all employees are informed and consulted. Typically, external trade unions are part of the process. These consultations must cover possible ways and means of avoiding layoffs or limiting their number, and mitigating their consequences.

To this end, the employer must supply the employees' representatives with all relevant information and in any event give them in writing the reasons for the intended layoffs, the number of employees likely to be let go, the number of workers normally employed, and the period over which the layoffs are planned to be carried out, so that the representatives and employees will be able to formulate observations and proposals.

The subregional Employment Office must be notified of any projected layoffs, even those associated with the closure of a company (not ensuing from a court ruling) at least 30 days before the employees concerned are given their notice of dismissal. The subregional Employment Office may extend this 30-day waiting period to 60 days, but the employer may appeal this decision to the Management Committee of the subregional Employment Office.

The employer pays an additional special indemnity for layoffs, which is fixed at half the difference between the monthly salary (with a ceiling of €2,904.45) and the unemployment benefits. This indemnity is paid each month for a maximum of four months.

Furthermore, all enterprises that proceed with a layoff must set up an "employment cell" to assist workers in the active search for another job, and all dismissed workers who are older than age 45 and have at least two years' seniority must register with this cell. For a six-month period, workers continue to receive their current salary and benefits, known as a reinsertion indemnity. If the regular notice period is less than six months, then the unemployment office will reimburse the employer for part of the reinsertion indemnity. An employee severance indemnity in excess of six months' remuneration is reduced by the reinsertion indemnity.

Special provisions apply in case of closing of an enterprise.

Reorganizing the Workforce

As stated above, the purchaser will automatically take over all rights and obligations of the business's personnel according to the individual employment contracts (including wages, fringe benefits, and seniority) as well as per CBAs, work regulations, and customary practice, if any, even if different rules and different CBAs are applicable within the buyer's company.

Belgium did not use the option given by Article 3.3 of Directive No. 2001/23/EC to limit the period for observing the terms and conditions agreed in a CBA to one year.

Following the provisions of the Act on CBAs and Joint Committees of December 5, 1968, the new employer is bound by a CBA until its date of termination or expiry. Furthermore, an individual contract of employment that has been implicitly modified by a CBA remains so even after the CBA ceases to have effect, unless there is provision to the contrary in the CBA itself. However, once a CBA has expired, the individual parties are free to change the provisions of an individual contract of employment by mutual agreement. The intention to change must be clear and real; a written record is therefore required. Obviously, only individual contracts existing during the period of application (and at the time of sale) are involved. A CBA that has expired cannot be incorporated into an individual contract of employment that comes into existence later. Also, the normative provisions of an earlier CBA that were incorporated into the individual contract of employment lapse when a new CBA is in force.

Change of Employment Conditions

If the employment contract or the employment relationship is terminated because the sale of the business involves a substantial change in working conditions to the detriment of the employee, the employer shall be regarded as having terminated the employment contract or the employment relationship.

This principle is often a challenge when attempting to harmonize the employment conditions of several groups of personnel coming together following a business acquisition. Belgian doctrine and jurisprudence also limit unilateral modifications of the employment conditions of transferred employees (see "Employment Contracts" in Section I).

Once the business has been acquired, the employment conditions of the transferred employees can be modified within the same limits that the previous owner had to respect. The transfer as such, however, cannot be the reason for the modification of the employment conditions.

Once the acquisition is complete, the purchaser and the transferred employee can mutually decide to change certain employment conditions. The purchaser will have to respect the hierarchy of sources.[2]

The employee can also implicitly accept the modified conditions by working under the new employment conditions for a sufficient amount of time without registering any objections.

Furthermore, the new owner can, just as the previous owner could, use its ius variandi to modify employment conditions of the transferred employee.

In the event of an ownership change following a bankruptcy order or an arrangement with creditors decreed by the court, special provisions apply.

Changing the Wage and Benefits Structure

See "Reorganizing the Workforce" previously. In addition, the purchaser is not obliged to take over old-age, disability, and survivor's benefits payable under plans supplementing the official social security system. However, according to the Act of 1968 on CBAs, new employers are still bound by CBAs after such a transfer. As a consequence, if a benefit plan is regulated by a CBA, the new employer will therefore have to establish an equivalent plan in overall terms. It should also be taken into account that any supplementary regime can be part of the salary package and therefore cannot be substantially modified unilaterally without risk of breach of contract.

Consulting with Labor Unions or Works Councils

When acquiring an existing business in Belgium, both the purchaser and the seller will have to comply with certain obligations of information and consultation prior to the actual completion of the deal.

If There Is a Works Council Within the Employer's Company

In Belgium, the information and consultation obligation is regulated by CBA No. 9 of March 9, 1972 and by Royal Decree of November 27, 1973. In case of merger, concentration, acquisition, closure, or any other important change in structure on which the company is bargaining, the works council should be informed of the economical, financial, and social consequences before any information is made public.

The works council should also be consulted prior to the transfer on the consequences of the transfer concerning the employment of the personnel, the organization of work, and the employment policy in general.

If There Is No Works Council Within the Employer's Company

The information must in principle be given to the employees' representatives within the works council. If no works council exists within the company, the union delegations must be informed and consulted.

If There Is No Works Council and No Union Delegation Within the Employer's Company

If the company does not have a works council or union delegation, article 15*bis* of CBA 32*bis* must be applied. This article provides that the employees who will be affected by the proposed transfer must be informed of the date or proposed date of the transfer; the reasons for the transfer; the legal, economic, and social implications of the transfer for the employees; and any other factors that may affect the employees. Both purchaser and seller are bound by this obligation.

Although both purchaser and seller are only obliged to inform their own employees, it is advisable that the purchaser approach the seller's employee prior to the actual transfer to establish a relationship of trust with the employees' representatives and the unions of the transferor.

Format for Informing Employees

Neither CBA No. 32*bis* nor CBA No. 9 nor the Royal Decree of November 27, 1973 determines how the information should be given to the employees' representatives. It is advisable that this information is best given in writing, followed by a meeting with a discussion period. Meetings with the works council or union delegation should be entered into their minutes.

Since neither the Directive nor any Belgian regulation determines the timing of delivering such information, this moment should be carefully chosen. The information should be delivered to the employees as early as possible, before it is made public, but not so early as to jeopardize ongoing negotiations. The release should also be timed so that the employees' representatives can convene regarding measures to be taken.

After the Deal: General Information Obligations of Every Employer

According to Article 15 of the Act of September 20, 1948 on the organization of industrial life, the works council has the right to receive the following economic and financial information:

- At least every trimester, information on productivity and general information concerning company activities;
- At regular intervals and at the end of the company's financial year, information, reports, and documents on the financial status of the company.

According to the Royal Decree of November 27, 1973, the following information must also be provided to the works council:

- Within two months after the election of the work council members, basic information on the production and productivity of the company, financial structure of the company, positions of the company with regard to the competition, costs of personnel, and so forth.
- Annual updates on the state and evolution of the company during the last year and about the objectives of the following years.
- Periodical (at least every three months) reports on the market, production, cost of supplies, and similar measures.
- As-needed notification of any event or internal decision that might have an important impact on the company.

If no works council has been established within the company, this information must be given to the union delegation (article 24 CBA No. 5).

Consulting with the Government

Belgian law does not require consultation with the government on business acquisitions as they relate to employees.

❸ SECTION III

My client wishes to sell its existing facility. What restrictions do we need to consider?

See Section II.

❸ SECTION IV

My client wishes to replace its senior manager(s). What restrictions do we need to consider?

This section applies only to white-collar employees and to board members who have an employment contract with the company. The termination of a blue-collar worker's contract is subject to a different set of provisions, in terms of, for example, the duration of the notice period or abusive dismissal.

The Notice Period or Indemnity in Lieu of Notice

In principle, any open-ended contract can be terminated unilaterally by means of a notice period or the payment of an indemnity in lieu of notice without any procedures or prior authorization.

The notice should be in writing, stating the beginning and the duration of the notice period. If the employer wants to terminate the contract, the termination letter should either be sent by registered mail or be served on the employee by a bailiff. An employee who wishes to terminate the contract may simply give a written notice to the employer. If these formal requirements are not observed, the notice period is deemed null and void, in which case the party whom the notice is served on is entitled to an indemnity in lieu of notice corresponding to the salary for the notice period.

The length of the notice period for employees depends on their annual salary including benefits.

- If the employee earns €28,580 gross or less per annum, the notice period amounts to three months for every commenced five-year period of seniority. If the notice is given by the employee, the notice period is reduced by half but it may not exceed three months.
- If the employee earns more than €28,580 but less than €57,162 gross per annum, the notice period is determined by mutual agreement between the employer and the employee when notice is given. If the parties fail to reach an agreement, the notice period is determined by the employment tribunal and based on the employee's potential difficulty in finding a suitable new job. Often the notice period is calculated by a formula, though such formulas are not legally binding. If notice is given by the employee, the notice period must not exceed four and a half months.
- If the employee earns more than €57,162 gross per annum, the employee and employer may contractually agree upon an alternative notice period. If notice is given by the employee, the notice period must not exceed six months.

In practice, employees in a managerial position are often made redundant through a severance payment. They will be served a notice for the legal minimum notice period and are invited to negotiate the terms and conditions of the termination. Often these negotiations will result in the signing of a settlement agreement, granting additional indemnities and benefits in exchange for confidentiality, nondisparagement clauses, and a waiver of all rights to make additional claims.

When an employee is made redundant, it should always be verified whether the employment contract contains a noncompete clause. If the application of such clause is not waived by the employer, an indemnity will be due, whether or not the employee performs competitive activities after the termination of the contract.

Restrictions on Termination

Protected Employees

In principle, the termination of an employee is not subject to any procedures or prior authorization. The termination does not have to be motivated in writing, nor does the employer have to explain the reason(s) for the termination. However, certain employees are protected against dismissal:

- Employee representatives (or nonelected candidates) in the works council, the Committee for Prevention and Protection at the Workplace (CPPW) and the union delegation;
- Pregnant employees or employees on maternity leave;
- Employees on paternal leave, adoption leave, educational leave, time credit and career break, or parental leave;
- Employees entitled to breaks during the work day to nurse their newborn;
- Employees entitled to be absent from work to perform their political mandate;
- Employees who have made remarks with regard to changes to the works regulations;
- Employees who have requested to stop working the night shift to return to the day shift;
- Employees occupying the position of Prevention Advisor;
- Employees who have filed a complaint regarding discrimination in the work place, equal treatment of men and women, violence, harassment, or inappropriate sexual behavior.

In addition, employees are protected against dismissal if the employer has introduced new technologies without respecting the information and consultation procedures.

The protection against dismissal means only that the dismissal must not be related to the above situations. A dismissal for unrelated reasons or for serious cause remains possible.

Members of Works Councils

Members or candidates of a works council or CPPW may be dismissed only for serious cause, accepted as such by the Employment Tribunal prior to the termination or for economic or technical reasons acknowledged by the Joint Committee prior to termination. "Serious cause" generally means a major violation of a contractual undertaking or of the principle of good faith, rendering continuation of the professional relationship between an employer and employee immediately and permanently impossible. Serious cause justifies a termination on the spot without notice or indemnity. In the event of a dismissal without observing these procedures, the employee may request to be reinstated.

Members of the union delegation may be dismissed only if a specific notification procedure to the trade union is observed.

Sanction in Case of Violation

A dismissal in violation of the protection entitles the employee to an indemnity amounting to several months of salary, or even several years if the employee is a representative in the works council or CPPW (the indemnity increases if the employee's request for reinstatement is refused).

Job Protection in Agreements on Sector or Company Level

Agreements made at a sector or company level may offer additional job protection, such as procedures to be complied with prior to the dismissal or the prohibition of layoffs during a certain period of time. Dismissals executed in violation of such agreements may give rise to the payment of indemnities as determined in the agreement or by the employment tribunal.

Wrongful Dismissal

In reaction to their dismissal, white-collar employees may claim an indemnity for wrongful dismissal. (Blue-collar workers are protected against wrongful dismissal by a specific provision. They may, however, opt to invoke the general theory on abuse of rights, which forms the basis for white-collar employees' claims.) The burden of proof rests with the employee. He or she will have to demonstrate that the company has conducted the dismissal in a wrongful manner. In addition, the employee will have to prove that the dismissal or the circumstances attendant upon the dismissal have caused a damage that is additional to the loss of employment, and that there is a causal connection between the wrongful dismissal and the damage.

Employment courts are traditionally reticent when faced with claims regarding wrongful dismissal. They might be tempted to grant additional damages under very special circumstances, for example when the dismissal has caused a considerable amount of bad publicity created by the employer. Additional damages might also be awarded in case of a complete absence of any grounds for the termination, especially if the employee had been enticed away from his former employer under false promises.

Specific Obligations in Case of Termination of the Employment Contract

Outplacement Training

Employees age 45 or older are entitled to outplacement services unless the contract was terminated for serious cause or the employee had been employed less than one year. The employer has the obligation to inform the employee of his right to the outplacement training. Some Joint Committees provide these services without any additional expenses for the employer. In those cases the training will be provided by an institute that is financed by employers' contributions to the Joint Committee.

Time Off to Search for a New Job

During the notice period, employees are entitled to one day off per week to look for a new job, even if the employee has taken the initiative to terminate the agreement. Employees earning more than €28,580 gross per annum are entitled to an entire day per week only during the last six months of the notice period. Before that, they are granted half a day per week.

Prepension

Employees age 58 or older (the age minimum may vary depending on the industry) who are fired may be entitled to a prepension. Prepension is a form of extended unemployment, not to be confused with early retirement. In addition to their unemployment benefits, prepensioners receive an additional indemnity at the expense of the employer, amounting to at least 50 percent of the difference between the unemployment benefits and the employee's last salary.

SECTION V

What prohibitions exist against discrimination on the basis of age, race, gender, disability, pregnancy, and other factors? What are the rights of employees, applicants, or former employees who believe that they have been discriminated against?

For years, discrimination was not given major attention in Belgium. However, under the guidance of European Union legislation, recent legislative provisions have been adopted in this respect.

The principal Belgian antidiscrimination legislation is laid down in the Antidiscrimination Acts of May 10, 2007 concerning all aspects of "social relations," including employment relations. The Act of August 4, 1996 also contained special provisions related to harassment, including that based upon discrimination.

No distinction may notably be made between employees on the basis of the following particular criteria: age, health, gender, sexual orientation, financial situation, language, health, social status, full-time or part-time occupation, and employment agreements of definite and indefinite duration.

Referring specifically to employment relations, every form of direct or indirect discrimination regarding "the conditions of access to employed work, unpaid work, self-employed activities, including criteria of selection and hiring, irrespective of the type of activity and level of professional hierarchy, including possibilities of promotion, conditions of employment and work, including dismissal and remuneration, as well in the private as the public sector" is forbidden.

Some rather limited discrimination cases have been brought before the courts. Currently, one is pending before the European Court of Justice related to the question whether a building company employer may decide not to hire employees of another ethnic origin because its clients would not accept these employees working in their residences. This case is still pending.

Any stipulation in opposition with the aforementioned acts is considered to be null and void. Moreover, specific protection measures have been enacted to protect an employee who has claimed discrimination. If an employee is dismissed for having filed a discrimination claim, a compensation of six months would be due. Any victim of discrimination, if proven, may claim some compensation.

Any person may introduce a discrimination claim before the Labor Court, which may decide to order that any behavior breaching the legislation be ceased immediately and to order preventive measures.

Belgium has enacted specific regulations related to the burden of proof, meaning that a victim should bring forward some evidence of the discrimination. If facts are established from which it may be presumed that there has been direct or indirect discrimination, the burden is on the respondent to prove that there has been no breach of the principle of equal treatment.

Trade unions and organizations having a legitimate interest to fight discrimination may also start claims, even in the event the discriminated victim is not part of the trial.

SECTION VI

On the Horizon: What key labor and employment law developments should an employer doing business in Belgium anticipate occurring in the coming years?

Tax Breaks on Bonuses

Trade unions and employer federations at the national level have brokered a CBA-deal determining the application of social security and tax breaks for bonuses that the employer may decide to grant, up to €2,200 gross. New legislation enacting this agreement contains several conditions:

- The bonus plan must be set up by means of a collective bargaining agreement at company level or, in the absence of any trade delegation for the categories of employees concerned, by means of a so-called "participation act" (*acte d'adhésion*) adopted according to a procedure mirroring the procedure required for amending the work regulations within companies without a works council.
- The plan must be based on clear collective targets that are easy to define and to measure. These targets cannot be of an individual nature and can be modified in time following a method of control to be agreed upon.
- The plan must include a method of control and follow–up.
- The plan must apply to all employees or to certain categories of employees.

- The nonrecurring bonus cannot replace other forms of remuneration but can replace an existing bonus scheme based on results.
- The plan must set forth an amicable procedure for settling any dispute.

Given the low maximum bonus amount and the organizational constraints (collective bargaining agreement, collective goals), the proposed measure will certainly not replace the traditional remuneration planning. This is all the more true for the best-remunerated employees.

However, if a company currently has a bonus plan that covers a great number of participants, this alternative is a powerful and cheap tool that can easily be implemented—despite the need for a collective bargaining agreement at company level—given the fact that its scope is not limited to senior executives.

Employee Representation

Belgium has been ordered by the Belgian European Court of Justice to implement the Directive 2002/14/EC of the European Parliament and of the Council of March 11, 2002 establishing a general framework for informing and consulting employees in the European Community. Social partners are disputing the way in which the directive should be implemented. The trade unions have recommended that employee representation bodies should be established within companies employing at least 20 employees, instead of the current 50. Meanwhile, the Act of April 23, 2008 has been adopted in this respect.

For the time being, a Committee for Prevention and Protection at the Work Place shall be set up in every company that employs at least 50 employees on average and a works council shall be set up in every company that employs at least 100 employees on average.

❦ NOTES

1. A "transfer of undertaking" is defined as "a transfer of an economic entity which retains its identity, meaning an organised grouping of resources which has the objective of pursuing an economic activity, whether or not that activity is central or ancillary." European Acquired Rights Directive No. 2001/23/EC, Article 1.1(b).

2. The hierarchy of the sources of law as specified by the Act on CBAs and Joint Committees of December 5, 1968 is as follows (Article 51):

1. Mandatory legal provisions
2. CBAs that have been decreed generally applicable, in the following order of precedence:
   a. CBAs concluded within the National Labor Council
   b. CBAs concluded within a Joint Committee
   c. CBAs concluded within a Joint Subcommittee
3. CBAs that have not been decreed generally applicable, where the employer is a signatory thereto or is a member of an association that is a signatory thereto, in the following order of precedence:
   a. CBAs concluded within the National Labor Council
   b. CBAs concluded within a Joint Committee
   c. CBAs concluded within a Joint Subcommittee
   d. Agreements concluded outside any joint body

4. Written individual contracts of employment
5. CBAs concluded within a joint body but not decreed generally applicable, where the employer, although not a signatory thereto nor a member of an association that is a signatory thereto, operates in an industry covered by the joint body within which the agreement was concluded
6. Work rules
7. Supplementary legal provisions
8. Oral individual contracts of employment
9. Custom

CHAPTER 2

LABOR AND EMPLOYMENT LAW
IN THE CZECH REPUBLIC

EVA ADAMCOVÁ
GABRIELA HÁJKOVÁ

SECTION I

My client wishes to establish a manufacturing facility in the Czech Republic and will need to hire a workforce. What are the key issues involved?

Employment Contracts: Who Receives Them and What Must They Include?

The basic legislation governing employment relationships is the Labor Code of 2006[1] and the Employment Act of 2004.[2]

The provisions of the Labor Code cover all employment relations between an employer and an employee in the entrepreneurial sphere. The Labor Code is based on the principle of contractual freedom, which may be characterized as "whatever is not forbidden is allowed." Contractual freedom may thus be reflected mainly in the contents of an employment relationship and in an agreement on individual working conditions based on the needs of both the employer and the employee.

In the private sector, an employment relationship is created solely by means of an employment contract. However, for managers and key employees, their employment contract may provide that they may be terminated without notice if they are also granted the right to leave without notice.

If an employee is dismissed from a position, the employment relationship is not terminated. Other work must be offered to the employee. If no work is offered or if the work offered is rejected by the employee, a basis for serving notice arises.

Under Czech law, a person who is a director of a corporation may not be employed in an employment relationship with that corporation unless the activities to be performed in each role are separate and distinct.

Mandatory Requirements

In an employment contract, the employer and the employee are to agree upon the following elements: type of work, place of work, and date of commencement of work.

The Labor Code establishes the employer's obligation to inform the employee in writing of his or her basic rights and obligations arising from the employment relationship.

However, if all the elements of an employment contract are not stipulated validly in the contract, but the employee has already started working for the employer with the consent of the employer, a relationship between an employer and an employee subject to the Labor Code (in particular, that the employee is entitled to receive remuneration for the work performed) is created and the employee has all the rights following from an employment relationship (e.g., paid vacation). Despite this, contractual freedom is considerably limited by the reasons defined by the Labor Code.

The parties may not (1) derogate from the provisions that are explicitly designated or that indicate that no derogation is acceptable, (2) derogate from the provisions stipulating liability, unless the derogation is in favor of an employee, and (3) derogate from the provisions reflecting EU regulations, unless the derogation is in favor of the employee.

Form of the Employment Contract

Under the Labor Code, an employment contract must be concluded in writing, with a copy to each party. Nevertheless, even if not in writing an employment contract is not automatically deemed invalid.

Language

The Labor Code does not contain any provision related to the language used in the employment contract, thus the choice of language lies upon the contractual parties.

Changes to the Terms and Conditions

The Labor Code stipulates that the content of an employment contract may be modified only with the agreement of both employee and employer. Any modification of the employment contract must be in writing.

The Labor Code specifies certain cases where an employer may assign an employee to perform other work at the employer's own discretion and without the preliminary agreement of the employee: for example, to protect employees in poor health or who are pregnant or breastfeeding, or in extraordinary circumstances such as a breakdown or malfunction of machinery, unfavorable weather conditions, natural disasters, or other accidents representing a general menace. In cases other than those prescribed by the Code, it is not permitted to assign an employee to perform other work without the employee's consent.

An employer may assign an employee to a place of work other than the one agreed upon in the employment contract, within the premises of the employer, subject to the employee's consent, and only for a reason inseparable from the employer's operational needs.

An employer may also send an employee on a business trip, which is defined by the Code as a time-limited transfer of the employee to another place of work. The employer is entitled to send its employee on a business trip for the necessary period on the basis of an agreement with the employee.

Fixed-Term Employment

Following the implementation of Council Directive 1999/70/EC concerning the framework agreement on fixed-term (temporary) work, a fixed-term employment contract may be concluded or extended for a total of two years from the beginning of the employment relationship. However, if a period of six months from the termination of the previous employment relationship has elapsed, the previous employment relationship is not taken into account.

There are some exceptions to the above rule, namely (1) cases where a special law requires the conclusion of an employment relationship for a definite period as a condition for the creation of other claims; (2) cases regarding the replacement of an employee for a period when the employee is unable to perform work; (3) cases of serious operational reasons on the part of an employer or reasons based on the peculiar nature of the work.

If an employer agrees to an employment contract for a fixed-term without fulfilling the above conditions, and the employee gives written notice that he or she wishes to continue the employment relationship, the employment relationship continues for an indefinite period.

Should an employer breach the rules relating to the creation of an employment relationship (including the above rules relating to the term allowed for fixed-term employment), a fine may be imposed by the employment inspection authorities.

Wages and Benefits

Minimum Wage Requirements

In the Czech Republic remuneration within the private sphere is governed by the Labor Code.

The amount of the minimum wage is fixed by the Labor Code. Under the Code, the minimum wage in the Czech Republic is set at CZK 7,955 (about US $500) per month and the minimum hourly rate is set at CZK 48.10 (about US $3). However, a collective agreement can stipulate a minimum wage that is higher than the amount of the statutory minimum wage specified by the Labor Code.

Statutory minimum wages cover all employees, irrespective of whether they are under a contract of indefinite or fixed duration or a temporary employment relationship.

An employer can pay a part of the wage to an employee in kind, except where the minimum wage is concerned. Payment of wage in kind is subject to the consent of the employee and the conditions agreed with the employee.

Contributions to social and health insurance and the state labor policy are deducted from the pay. Each employer is legally responsible for deducting these contributions and estimated tax. Since January 1, 2008, the progressive taxation of personal income has been replaced by a single 15 percent tax rate (dropping to 12.5 percent from January 1, 2009) and the so-called "super-gross wage" (the gross wage plus the employer's portion of the social security and health insurance contributions) has been introduced. The employee's income tax base is thus calculated as the gross wage (without deducting the employee's portion of the social security and health insurance contributions) plus the amount of social security and health insurance contributions paid by the employer. At the same time, the employee's maximum annual assessment base for the calculation of their social security and health insurance contributions has been set at 48 times the average wage.

Special Benefit Requirements

In the Czech Republic, employees have the right to benefits granted by law (e.g., time off for vacations and on public holidays). Other benefits, for example pensions or unemployment insurance, may be negotiated between the employer and the employee.

Working Hours

The maximum statutory length of working hours is 40 per week (except for the following: 37.5 hours for employees working underground and with a three-shift arrangement; 38.75 hours with a two-shift arrangement.[3]

In general, an employee is entitled to have a minimum "rest period" of 12 hours between the end of one shift and the start of a subsequent shift and one continuous rest period of 35 hours per week (where "week" means seven consecutive calendar days). If the rules on working hours are not complied with, the employer may be fined.

After six hours (four and a half hours for workers under 16) of an employee's continuous working day, an employer is obliged to allow an employee to take at least a 30-minute break, which is not included in the employee's hours of work.[4]

An employer is obliged to keep records of each employee's working hours, overtime, emergency work, and night work.[5]

Overtime exceeding the limit of 40 hours per working week is permitted only under certain conditions and receives higher remuneration.

Paid Vacation Time

The basic length of the annual paid vacation is four weeks per calendar year. For employees of employers who are not engaged in business activities, the basic length is five weeks; for pedagogical and academic employees of universities, paid vacation is eight weeks.

Both a collective agreement and internal regulations may stipulate that employees of employers who carry out business activities may have their vacation time extended by additional weeks or days without limitation.

An employee is entitled to full compensation during the vacation period, and is also entitled to any benefits in kind.

Holidays

In addition to paid vacation, an employee has the right to time off on the 13 holidays that are provided by the law.

Labor Unions

Establishment/Recognition Requirements

Czech trade unions—legal entities independent from the state—are legally entitled to act on behalf of the employees in labor relations, including collective bargaining. They may operate at one employer's level (the basic trade union) or at a regional level (regional trade union) by means of their members—the employer's employees. Their establishment must be declared to the Ministry of the Interior of the Czech Republic, but no other barriers or requirements can be imposed in relation to their existence. The number of trade unions is not limited and there may be several within one employer.

Trade unions are established on the basis of industry or professional principle. Industry-based trade unions associate employees of the relevant industry segment regardless of their profession. Profession-based trade unions associate employees of the relevant profession. Different trade unions are associated in confederations (such as the Czech-Moravian Confederation of Trade Unions, the biggest industry-based confederation operating throughout the country).

Trade unions negotiate collective agreements on wages, hours, vacation, and other employment terms and conditions as well as on regulations on health and safety at work and on employment. They have, for these purposes, specific rights, such as the right to information, to consultation, to participate in decision-making processes, to participate in legislative procedure, and to strike. In accordance with the basic principle of contractual liberty, the new Labor Code has widened the extent of the issues that may be dealt with in a collective agreement.

Exclusive Bargaining

A trade union has an exclusive position among employees' representatives. While the works council and employees' representatives for health and safety at work (ERHS) act only as intermediaries between the employer and its employees in the information and consultation process, trade unions are true participants in labor relationships. This position grants them the right to act on behalf of the employees, including in the collective bargaining process, negotiating collective agreements, and monitoring compliance with employment regulations. For these purposes, they are entitled to further information and consultation.[6]

An employer must inform and consult the trade union, works council, or the employees directly if no such organizations exist at the company, on measures to be adopted concerning its financial situation. If the measures concern all or a large number of employees, the employer is obliged to provide information, consult, receive approval, or reach an agreement with all trade unions present at the employer. This mainly concerns layoffs and the scheduling of collective vacation (when all employees take a vacation at the same time, usually due to organizational reasons).

Collective Agreements

Duty to Bargain

Only trade unions can negotiate and sign collective agreements on behalf of the employees. They represent all the employees, including those who are not their members. Collective agreements are drawn between one or more employers or employer associations and one or more trade unions. Employees have the right to information on the collective bargaining process and the right to submit any proposals.

Employers are also entitled to the right of association (for example, in the Confederation of Employers' and Entrepreneurs' Associations of the CR, *Konfederace zaměstnavatelských a podnikatelských svazů ČR*, or the Confederation of Industry of the Czech Republic, *Svaz průmyslu a dopravy ČR*).

Collective agreements can thus be distinguished as follows:

- *Individual undertaking:* between one or more employers and one or more trade unions. This allows the parties to conclude a "collective group agreement" within a group of companies in a concern.
- *Higher level:* between one or more employer associations and one or more trade unions (or its organizational unit, i.e., its basic organization provided it is a legal person). Since July 1, 2005 (the effective date of Act 2/1991 on collective bargaining), collective agreements may be negotiated at industry level between employer associations and trade unions. This type of collective agreement is obligatory for the relevant employer even if a trade union has not been established in its company. The contractual parties can mutually propose to publish within the collection of laws (*Sbírka zákonů*) confirmation from the Ministry of Labor and Social Affairs that a collective agreement of a higher level is compulsory for all employers operating in the relevant industry. Such a collective agreement is also sent to all employment offices (*Úřady práce*) and is accessible on the Internet so that all employers can become acquainted with it.

Collective agreements may also be negotiated on behalf of employees who are not members of a trade union. If several trade unions are present at the employer, the employer negotiates on the conclusion of a collective agreement with all of them.

To sum up, a collective agreement binds

- Employers who are members of an employers' association that is a contractual party to a collective agreement of higher level;
- Employers who resigned membership of an employers' organization during the effectiveness of the collective agreement;
- Employees on whose behalf a trade union concluded the collective agreement;
- The trade union that concluded the collective agreement at a higher level.

A collective agreement of an individual company is invalid if it offers employee rights and obligations that are less than a collective agreement of higher level. Obligations arising from a collective agreement of higher level apply directly to the employers and members of employers' associations that concluded the collective agreement for their employees.

Form Requirements

A contractual party has to respond in writing to a proposal from the other party to conclude or amend the collective agreement within seven days.

A collective agreement must be concluded in writing and signed by all parties, otherwise it is invalid.

Dispute Resolution

Any dispute regarding the conclusion and execution of a collective agreement can be resolved by means of a mediator, an arbitrator, a strike, or exclusion.

Mediation

A mediator is appointed upon the agreement of the parties or, if no agreement is reached, by the Ministry upon the proposal of one party. If the dispute is not resolved within 20 days, proceedings before the mediator are unsuccessful. Parties can then ask the Ministry to appoint a new mediator.

Arbitration

Following unsuccessful proceedings before a mediator, the parties can, upon written agreement, ask an arbitrator to resolve their dispute. An arbitrator informs the parties in writing of its decision within 15 days. An arbitrator may declare that a collective agreement has been concluded. It is possible to appeal this decision in court.

Strike

If a collective agreement is not concluded after proceedings before a mediator and the parties do not submit the dispute to an arbitrator, a strike can be called.

Exclusion

Exclusion, or work slow-down or stoppage, is the ultimate instrument of dispute resolution regarding the negotiation of a collective agreement (on the presumption that the dispute has not been resolved by a mediator and has not been submitted to an arbitrator).

Changes and Termination

A collective agreement can be established for a definite or indefinite period with a termination period of six months starting from the first day of the month following the delivery of written notice. A collective agreement cannot be terminated in its first six months. This means that under Czech law, a collective agreement for an indefinite period is effective for at least 12 months.

If the parties have agreed to allow amendments to a collective agreement or if the agreement has been terminated, the parties must initiate a bargaining process at least 60 days prior to the expiration of the collective agreement or prior to the date of the amendment as agreed.

Works Councils

Mandatory Requirements

Works councils and ERHSs can be elected if there is no trade union at an employer's undertaking, regardless of the number of its employees. They are employees' representatives *sui generis*. Unlike trade unions, they are not a legal person and are simply intermediaries between the employer and its employees. They ensure that the employees are informed and consulted. They are not entitled to negotiate collective agreements on behalf of the employees.

Function and Frequency

A works council has at least three and at most 15 members. The number of ERHS depends on the total number of employees and the risk factor of the work performed (but at least one representative for every 10 employees). The term of office is three years.

Elections are organized by an employer no more than three months after the delivery of a written proposal signed by at least one third of all the employees. The election commission is composed of three to nine employees. The quorum is one half of the employees.

The works council and ERHS cease to exist when a collective agreement is concluded. However, unlike the previous labor code, when a trade union is established at an employer's undertaking, a works council does not cease to exist automatically but executes its function until the end of the term of office or until the conclusion of a collective agreement.

National/Regional Group

As of May 1, 2004 (entry of the Czech Republic to the EU), a European Works Council can be established in multinational companies that have at least 1,000 employees with at least 150 employees in two EU member states. The council's goal is to ensure that the employees are informed and consulted at a supranational level and to guarantee representation of all employees.

The relevant provisions of the Labor Code implement Council Directive 94/45/EC on the establishment of a European Works Council or a procedure in Community-scale companies or related companies for the purposes of informing and consulting the employees.

The Labor Code guarantees the right of employees in businesses operating in two or more EU member states to supranational information and consultation by means of a European Works Council or by means of an agreement on other proceedings regarding supranational information and consultation.

A special negotiation body is established in this regard, the bargaining committee, whose members are employees of the employer or a group of employers operating in EU member states. The bargaining committee negotiates with the management on the establishment of a European Works Council or other proceedings. A European Works Council is established on the basis of negotiation between the bargaining committee and the management or according to Section 296 of the Labor Code.

SECTION II

My client is acquiring an existing business in the Czech Republic. How do I assess the existing workforce and consider changes?

Share Deals Versus Asset Deals

Share Deals

A share transaction (i.e., a transfer of a company's shares usually based on a share purchase agreement) has no impact on the employment relationships of the company. A change in the employment contracts or the termination of an employment relationship is possible under the same conditions as before the transaction. The purchaser is obliged to comply with the rights stipulated in the current collective agreement and remains subject to the same protective labor laws as prior to the share transfer.

An employer is not obliged to inform the employees' representatives of the intended share transaction; however, doing so is common practice.

Asset Deals

An asset deal (i.e., a sale and purchase of some or all of the assets of an employer company) under certain conditions implies the transfer of existing employment contracts, or more precisely the transfer of the rights and obligations of the employment relationship.

The situations in which the transfer of assets will imply the transfer of existing contracts are stipulated by the Labor Code, which implements European Directive 2001/23/EC. Under the general provision of the Labor Code, existing contracts are subject to the transfer when a business or part of it is transferred or the employer's tasks or activities (or parts of them) are transferred to another employer. The transfer of tasks or activities of one employer to another means in particular the transfer of manufacturing or services. Transfer of tasks or activities is not subject to the transfer of property rights to things ensuring tasks or activities (e.g., manufacturing line). Thus, the transfer of existing contracts may be based on the conclusion of a lease agreement.

The rights and duties are transferred to the purchaser in full. The purchaser is obliged to provide to all transferred employees the same conditions as before the transaction. Therefore, the purchaser should review the employment contracts, with special attention to items such as the salary and vacation. In addition, under some circumstances the purchaser will be obliged to compensate an employee for the damage caused by an employment accident that occurred during employment with the previous employer.

The transfer of rights and duties includes the rights and duties under a collective agreement (see Section I). Thus, the purchaser is obliged to satisfy the claims of employees as stipulated in the collective agreement.

Consequently, whether a shares transaction or asset deal, the purchaser is recommended to execute due diligence.

Carrying Out a Workforce Reduction

An employer can terminate an employment relationship by a notice of termination only on the grounds stated in the Labor Code. A notice of termination issued for any other reason would be invalid and an employer would have no chance of success in case of a dispute.

In the case of a serious violation of labor legislation by an employee, the employee's contract can be terminated immediately without notice. The same option is available when an employee is sentenced to at least one year's imprisonment for a criminal offense.

Reductions for Organizational Reasons

An employer is entitled to execute changes in the company of an organizational, financial, or technological nature, which may result in a reduced workforce. Thus, an employer may elect to divide premises, change the internal structure, or change the tasks. An employer is also free to decide to reduce the total number of employees.

Should an employer terminate the employment relationships for any of these reasons (hereinafter "organizational reasons"), it is not limited by provisions protecting certain groups of employees, such as pregnant women, from termination. In cases where it is not possible for objective reasons, for example the dissolution of an employer, to insist on the protection of an employee, the employer is entitled to give notice of termination to a protected employee.

If an employment relationship is terminated for organizational reasons, the employer is not obliged to offer a dismissed employee other work or to provide assistance in finding new employment. Further, the employee is entitled to compensation for loss of employment, whether or not the employee finds new employment. The compensation is triple the average monthly salary.

Layoffs

Layoffs occur where, within a period of 30 calendar days:

- In an establishment with more than 20 but fewer than 100 employees, more than 10 employees are dismissed;
- In an establishment with more than 100 but fewer than 300 employees, 10 percent of the workforce is dismissed;
- In an establishment with at least 300 employees, at least 30 employees are dismissed.

In the event of a layoff, an employer is obliged to inform the employees' representatives (including trade unions and work councils, if any) of the reason for the layoff, the number of dismissed employees and the specific employees slated for dismissal, the compensation for the dismissal, and the duration of the layoff, if temporary.

The purpose of negotiations between the employer and the employees' representatives is to reach an agreement on these issues. However, the approval of the employees' representatives is not necessary for the transaction.

An employer is obliged to inform the labor authorities of its intention to execute a layoff. It must also deliver to the labor authorities written notification of the results of negotiations with the trade union or work councils. Employment contracts cannot be terminated until 30 days after the employer has delivered this notification. If the employer does not inform the labor authorities, the employment contracts are considered to remain in force.

The conditions for executing organizational changes are the same for a share deal and an asset deal.

Reorganizing the Workforce

The extent to which an employer may reorganize the workforce depends on the stipulations in the employment contracts, particularly regarding the place of work and the type of work. For example, if the type of work is broadly defined, the employer has wide discretion to transfer an employee to another position within the scope of the stipulated type of work.

More radical changes exceeding the rights and obligations stipulated in an individual contract are possible only by amending the employment contract; that is, the employer needs to obtain the approval of the employees. For example, in the event of a relocation of business premises an employer would have to negotiate amendments to employment contracts concerning the change in the place of work.

Changing the Wage and Benefits Structure

In an asset deal, the rights and obligations arising from the employment relationships are transferred to the acquiring employer in its full scope. This means that the acquiring employer will be obliged to remunerate all the transferred employees under their existing employment contracts and collective agreements.

Therefore, the acquiring employer is authorized to change the wage or benefit structure only with agreement of his employees.

The same principle applies to share transactions.

Consulting with Labor Unions or Works Councils

Share Transactions

There is no obligation on the employer to inform the employees or employees' representatives of a change in share ownership. The sale of shares takes place at shareholder level and does not affect the employer company from the point of view of an employer.

Nevertheless, it is quite usual to inform the employees in advance of a change in the ownership structure. There is no obligation to provide the employee representatives with a copy of the sale and purchase agreement.

Asset Transactions

In the event of an asset transaction both the current employer and the acquiring employer have an obligation to inform the trade union or works council or other employees' representatives of the transaction and the reasons for it. They are also obliged to negotiate with employees' representatives regarding the following aspects of the intended transaction:

- The proposed date of the intended transaction;
- The legal, economic, and social consequences of the transfer for an employee;
- The related planned precautions for employees.

Both employers are obliged to deal with these aspects for the purposes of reaching mutual agreement. In the event that the employers do not inform either employees or employee's representatives of the aspects related to the transaction, the labor authorities can impose a penalty on them.

Neither a share transaction nor an asset transaction results in termination of a collective agreement. In the event of a share transaction, a current collective agreement will remain valid. In an asset transaction, the rights stipulated in the collective agreement are transferred along with the employees. Thus, the acquiring employer is obliged to satisfy rights arising from the collective agreement for as long as it is in force. It is, however, arguable whether this obligation applies if there is no trade union at the acquiring employer.

Consulting with the Government

An employer is not obliged to notify or consult with the government regarding an asset or share transaction. It is, however, obliged to notify the labor authorities in advance of a layoff.

SECTION III

My client wishes to sell its existing facility. What restrictions do we need to consider?

Assessing Employment Contracts

To assess employment contracts, the buyer will usually execute due diligence, checking the following in particular:

- The number of employees, in particular whether there are some "hidden" employees such as employees assigned by agency work;
- Special arrangements or special working conditions;
- The benefits that are granted to the employees (accommodation, preferential loans, contribution for pension, additional insurance, etc.);
- Employee wages and bonus plans;
- Company obligations arising from job-related injuries and illnesses;
- Company obligations regarding legally required employee education;
- Complaints of employees or other persons on the nonfulfillment of some of the employer's obligations.

Based on the results from executed due diligence, the seller will negotiate the purchase price with the buyer.

Consulting with the Government

An employer is not obliged to notify or consult with the government regarding an asset or share transaction. It is, however, obliged to notify labor authorities in advance of a layoff.

Consulting with Labor Unions or Works Councils

The information and consultation requirements are the same as for the acquisition of an existing business. (See Section II.)

Negotiating with the Purchaser: Special Labor Issues

Since all the rights and duties arising from labor law relations are transferred to the new owner, the seller is not obliged to settle any employee claims before the sale, unless agreed otherwise with the buyer in the purchase agreement. It is commonly agreed in the purchase agreement that the seller undertakes to indemnify the buyer against all labor-related liabilities arising prior to the transfer of the enterprise.

SECTION IV

My client wishes to replace its senior manager(s). What restrictions do we need to consider?

Employment Contracts

The removal of a senior manager in the Czech Republic depends on the manager's position in the company. The two main options are as follows:

1. the senior manager is an executive of the company, fully entitled to act on its behalf; or
2. the manager is an employee of the company.

Manager as an Executive of the Company

Chief executives in Czech companies are defined as persons authorized to act and sign on behalf of a company (directors of a corporation/members of a board of directors). Their relationship with the company is based on the Commercial Code and, unless a specific contract of service has been negotiated, it is considered a mandate contract. Since these contracts are negotiated on an individual basis, they are not governed by the provisions of labor law. Therefore, the conditions of termination, such as severance pay or noncompetition clauses, must be specified in them. The removal of executives is voted upon by the shareholders in a general meeting.

Manager as an Employee of the Company

All other managers are employed under ordinary employment contracts governed by Czech labor law. Thus, they must be given notice of termination.

Statutory Protections

To be valid, the termination notice must be in writing and must contain a specific cause allowed by the law. Once the notice is given, the cause cannot be modified. The possible grounds are listed below:

- Plant or company closure;
- Relocation of the employer;
- Layoff;
- The employee's poor health or failure to meet legal requirements for the exercise of the job.

In addition to these requirements, it is strictly forbidden to give notice to a pregnant employee or a person on parental leave, to a person temporarily unable to work, or to someone who has been released to exercise a public function (such as being elected as a member of Parliament or a municipal council).

Period of Notice

The notice period is the same for both the employer and the employee and must be at least two months (subject to modification in the employment contract). The time limit starts to run on the first day of the month following the month in which the notice was given (e.g., notices given on January 1 and January 31 both expire on March 31).

Any notice must be discussed with the trade union, if there is one in a company. If the employee is a trade union member or was a member within the last year, the notice must be approved by the union. If the union refuses to approve the notice, the case is submitted to the court.

Common Contractual Protection

Managers directly subordinate to an executive member of a board of directors, as well as lower-level managers, can be considered as "leading employees" under the Labor Code. If such a clause is present in their employment contract, they can be subject to immediate dismissal from their positions (and also have the right to leave without notice). However, this does not mean they are no longer employed. They must be offered a position commensurate with their qualifications in the same company. If the employer is unable to satisfy this requirement, grounds for termination are present and ordinary notice may be served.

Concerning severance pay, managers under employment contracts are covered in case of notice and even in case of agreement on contract termination, if the termination cause is one of those applicable to notice. When the cause is termination of activity, relocation, or layoff, the terminated employees are entitled to at least three times their average monthly pay. When the cause is related to medical issues (permanent inability, work injury, etc.), the indemnity equals annual pay.

🌐 SECTION V

What prohibitions exist against discrimination on the basis of age, race, gender, disability, pregnancy, and other factors? What are the rights of employees, applicants, or former employees who believe that they have been discriminated against?

Areas of Protection

Basic principles concerning discrimination and equal treatment are regulated by the Chapter of Fundamental Rights and Basic Freedoms, which is a part of the constitution of the Czech Republic, by the Labor Code and Act 435/2004 Coll. on Employment.

The Antidiscrimination Act on equal treatment and on legal instruments of protection against discrimination (*Zákon o rovném zacházení a o právních prostředcích ochrany před diskriminací a o změně některých zákonů*), currently in the process of adoption (scheduled to be in force at the end of 2008), is intended to ensure equal access for all people in employment and other areas, without any discrimination on the basis of race, ethnic origin, nationality, gender, sexual orientation, age, health, or religion.

Statutory Rules

The Labor Code expressly stipulates that employers must ensure equal treatment for all employees with regard to working conditions, salary and wages, and perquisites of monetary value. Therefore, men and women should be paid equally for the same job or for a job of the same value. Equal treatment must also be ensured for vocational training and opportunities for career advancement. Employers must provide the same opportunities to all employees and not make unreasonable differences between them. Equal treatment is to be understood in particular as prohibition of discrimination for reasons stated by law.

The Act on Employment regulates discrimination and equal treatment when exercising the right on employment. According to this Act, an employer must provide equal treatment to all persons exercising their rights to employment.

The Labor Code prohibits any form of discrimination in labor relations. However, it does not regulate any terms concerning the discrimination and only refers to the Antidiscrimination Act, which has not been adopted so far. This Act defines terms such as "direct discrimination," "indirect discrimination," "harassment," "indirect harassment," and "persecution." Under this Act an employer's behavior that seems neutral but that results in discrimination against a group or an individual is prohibited. However, some different treatment in labor relations is permissible. For example, it is not discrimination if a certain group of employees working for one employer has longer vacation than others if the difference is due to the difficulty of their work.

Sanctions and Remedies

In the case of a breach of rights and duties in an employment relationship or in the case of discrimination, an employee is entitled to assert his or her rights before the court. The employee may ask the court to compel the employer to restrain from discrimination, remove the consequences of such discrimination, provide adequate satisfaction, and pay adequate financial compensation.

The amount of potential compensation for the injury is fixed by the court, which considers the gravity of the injury as well as the circumstances under which the breach of rights and duties occurred.

Burden of Proof

Concerning proof of discrimination, an employee has the benefit of the doubt, meaning there is a presumption that a violation of an employee's rights has occurred as alleged. Thus, the burden of proof rests with the employer.

⊕ SECTION VI

On the Horizon: What key labor and employment law developments should an employer doing business in the Czech Republic anticipate occurring in the coming years?

As of January 1, 2007, new and complex legislation on employment has taken effect in the Czech Republic. The new Labor Code has replaced the code that had governed employment relationships for 40 years. The new legislation is intended to give contractual parties wider freedom over employment relationships. Under the previous legislation, provisions had to be strictly adhered to with no possibility of settling employment relationships differently.

This principle has been partly overridden by the new Labor Code; however, contractual freedom is still largely limited. Nevertheless, the new Labor Code has brought several fundamental changes:

- The obligation to offer new work to an employee who has been given notice no longer applies.
- The notice period has been reduced from three months to two.
- Employment is created only with an employment contract. Managers may be appointed to their positions but an employment contract is still required.
- A noncompetition clause is not restricted to managers but may be negotiated with any employee.

Given that a number of technical and legal inaccuracies have come to light since the new Labor Code came into effect, the government prepared an amendment that came into force on January 1, 2008. The purpose of the amendment is to liberalize the labor market and eliminate vague wording and inaccuracies in the new Labor Code. Moreover, the Constitutional Court partially implemented a proposal by several members of Parliament by striking out 11 provisions (or parts of them) of the Labor Code. The Constitutional Court mainly struck out unclear parts of the Code and reduced trade union powers.

A substantial revision of the Labor Code is also being prepared by an expert commission from the Ministry of Labor and Social Affairs. Legislation regarding employee's accident insurance should come into force on January 1, 2010. Presently, an employer must be insured to cover liability for damage caused by an accident at work or an occupational disease. The new legislation would transfer the employee's accident insurance to the social security system. As discussed in Section V, the Antidiscrimination Act has not been adopted yet. This Act is intended to come into effect by the end of 2008.

As discussed in Section V, the Antidiscrimination Act is in draft form, meaning that in the meantime the Czech Republic does not yet have antidiscrimination legislation. This Act is intended to come into effect by the end of 2008.

❸ NOTES

1. Act No. 262/2006 Coll., as amended.
2. Act No. 435/2004 Coll. on Employment, as amended.
3. "Three-shift arrangement" is the work system where employees change in three shifts within 24 consecutive hours; "two-shift arrangement" is the work system where employees change in two shifts within 24 consecutive hours.

4. Special conditions apply to a breastfeeding mother, who is entitled to two 30-minute breaks per shift until the child reaches the age of one year, and one 30-minute break per shift for the next three months.

5. "Emergency work" means time when an employee is prepared to work, or on call, in case of an emergency. Such situations are common in health services.

6. Under Labor Code § 38 an employer must submit to a trade union a report on new labor relations; under § 61(5) an employer must inform a trade union of the termination of labor relationships other than by notice or immediate termination; under § 61(1) an employer must consult with a trade union on notice or immediate termination of labor relations in advance; under § 46, if the employer wishes to transfer an employee to work other than stipulated in the labor contract, and the employee does not agree, the employer must consult the trade union.

CHAPTER 3

LABOR AND EMPLOYMENT LAW
IN DENMARK

ANDERS ETGEN REITZ
MICHAEL BORRING ANDERSEN

SECTION I

My client wishes to establish a manufacturing facility in Denmark and will need to hire a workforce. What are the key issues involved?

Employment Contracts: Who Receives Them and What Must They Include?

Mandatory Requirements in Brief

In general terms, an employee is a person who personally carries out work on the instructions of his or her employer in exchange for payment. The employment relationship is characterized by the employee's performance of work under the employer's supervision and at the employer's risk and expense.

Most Danish mandatory regulations on the labor and employment law area are ruled by the Danish Salaried Employees Act (*funktionærloven*).[1] The Act contains an exhaustive list of the persons considered salaried employees and therefore covered by its provisions:

- (a) shop assistants and office workers employed in buying and selling activities, in office work or equivalent warehouse operations;
- (b) persons whose work takes the form of technical or clinical services (except handicraft work or factory work) and other assistants who carry out comparable work functions;
- (c) persons whose work is wholly or mainly to manage or supervise the work of other persons on behalf of the employer;
- (d) persons whose work is mainly of the type specified in (a) and (b).

Employment relationships are regulated under Danish law by the Danish Constitution, general and specific legislation (applicable to all employment relationships or only to a certain group of employees), collective agreements (for the private as well as the public labor market), individual employment contracts, customs, and case law. Most employees are covered by collective agreements and/or the Danish Salaried Employees Act.

Although the employment relationship must comply with the mandatory requirements deriving from the referred sources of law, the principle of freedom of contract is largely recognized in Denmark.

Form of the Employment Contract

The implementation of Council Directive 91/533 EEC of October 14, 1991 on an employer's obligation to inform employees of the conditions applicable to the contract or employment relationship created the employer's obligation to provide the employee with a statement of employment terms.

The Directive was implemented into Danish law by Act No. 392 of June 22, 1993 on the employer's obligation to inform employees of the conditions applicable to the employment relationship as amended by the Danish Employment Contracts (*ansættelsesbevisloven*).[2] The Act applies to employees who are hired to work for more than one month and whose weekly working hours are above an average of eight hours.

List of Required Information

In Denmark, an employment contract must meet certain mandatory requirements. Section 2 of the Employment Contracts Act provides that the employer must inform the employee of any material term of contract and ensure that the following information is provided in the employment contract:

- The name and address of both the employer and the employee;
- The place where the work is to be performed;
- A description of the work to be performed and the position the employee will occupy;
- The date of commencement of the employment;
- The expected term of employment (for fixed-term contracts);
- The employee's right to paid vacation;
- The period of notice in the event of termination;
- The salary and any other remuneration the employee may be entitled to, and the date and place of payment;
- Normal daily or weekly working hours;
- Reference to any applicable collective agreement.

Language

There are no general language requirements in Denmark. However, some statutes provide that certain specific information must be made available to the employee in Danish. For example, according to Section 3 of the Danish Stock Option Act (*aktieoptionsloven*),[3] information about stock compensation plans must be provided to the employee in a separate written document that must be in Danish.

Timing Issues

The employment contract or information regarding the employment relationship must be provided to the employee in writing no later than one month after commencement of the employment. Failure to provide the employee with this information may result in the payment of compensation, which according to existing case law usually amounts to between DKK 5,000 and DKK 10,000, depending on the individual circumstances.

Changes to the Employment Terms

Unilateral changes to the terms and conditions of the employment contract are as a general rule unlawful.

Fixed-Term Employment

In general, there are no rules in Danish law specifying the length of an employment contract. According to the Danish Salaried Employees Act, when the length of the employment contract is not provided, the employment contract is assumed to be for an indefinite period and it may be terminated by notice by either party.

The Danish Temporary Employment Act (*lov om tidsbegrænset ansættelse*),[4] which implements Council Directive 1999/70 EC of June 28, 1999 concerning the framework agreement on fixed-term work, protects persons employed under a fixed-term contract or a contract by task from discrimination arising from the use of successive fixed-term employment contracts or relationships. The parties may agree on an employment contract that is to last for a fixed term (a fixed-term contract) or for the period it takes for a certain job to be accomplished (contract by task). In these cases, the contract will terminate, without any notice period, when the agreed period expires or the task is accomplished without any notice period.

The length of an employment relationship may vary depending on the parties' agreement in the contract, what the applicable collective agreement provides in that respect, and any statutory period applying to a certain type of employment.

When a fixed-term employment contract expires, the employment relationship may continue if the parties agree on a new contract or if the employment relationship remains unchanged. In the first case, if the parties agree to renew the employment contract, the employee's seniority must be calculated from the beginning of the original contract. To protect the employee's rights and benefits, the Danish Temporary Employment Act and some collective agreements prohibit extending fixed-term contracts with the same employee several times, unless the contracts are objectively and fairly reasoned or are necessary to complete a job.

In the second case, if the employer keeps providing work to the employee and the employee keeps performing his or her tasks, thereby keeping the employment relationship unchanged, the parties will be considered to have tacitly (by their actions) entered into a new employment relationship for an indefinite period of time, which will be valid until terminated by either party. The new employment relationship will be deemed to have been entered into as from the date of commencement of the fixed-term contract.

Wages and Benefits

Minimum Wage Requirements

Danish law does not establish a minimum wage requirement. The parties may freely determine the amount that the employee will be paid for his or her work, per hour, per piece of work done, or on a fixed basis. The only limitations to this freedom are set out in Section 55 of the Training Scheme Act (*erhvervsuddannelses-loven*), which provides that the payment to trainees must correspond to the custom and practice in similar jobs and in the applicable collective agreement where a minimum wage is provided.

Payment may be made in money or in kind on a previously determined schedule, such as bimonthly, monthly, or after the work is completed.

A written salary statement detailing taxes and other deductions and year-to-date totals must be given to the employee before or on the date of payment.

Special Benefit Requirements

Working Hours

Council Directive 93/104/EC of November 23, 1993, concerning certain aspects of the organization of working time as amended by Directive 2000/34/EC of June 22, 2000, was implemented in Denmark by the Act to partially implement the Working Time Directive (*arbejdstidsdirektivloven*)[5] establishing a maximum limit of 48 working hours per week.

The applicable collective agreements may provide for a shorter maximum limit, generally ranging from 37 hours per week for the day shift and 35 hours for the night shift.

Under the Danish Working Environment Act (*arbejdsmiljøloven*),[6] employees are entitled to an uninterrupted period of rest of 11 hours for every 24-hour period, which can be extended only in very specific cases determined by law.

Vacation

All employees have a right to five weeks' vacation each year. Salaried employees are entitled to paid vacation and a supplement of 1 percent of their annual salary. Blue-collar workers receive a vacation allowance equal to 12.5 percent of their annual wage.

In addition, most employers offer one additional annual week of vacation.

Sick Pay

Pursuant to Section 5 of the Danish Salaried Employees Act, salaried employees are entitled to full payment during sickness.

By contrast, pursuant to the Danish Sickness Benefit Act (*sygedagpengeloven*),[7] blue-collar workers not covered by a collective agreement who fall sick are not entitled to their normal salary during sickness but rather to a sickness benefit. The employer must pay the sickness benefit to the employee for the first two weeks; thereafter, the employee's municipality of residence will reimburse the employer for the payment. In any case, the maximum weekly reimbursement is DKK 3,415 (as of 2007) and for a maximum of 52 weeks in an 18-month period.

Pension Plans

In Denmark, employees who reach the age of 65 are entitled to an old-age pension and to an additional pension allowance called the Labor Market Supplementary Pension (ATP). Both the employees and the employers contribute to the ATP fund. People between the ages of 60 and 65 may apply for a postservice benefit, whereas employees below that age who are unable to work because of a permanent and severe disability are entitled to an early-retirement pension.

Nevertheless, employers often choose to set up and administer private pension plans to which both the employer and employee contribute, with the possibility of deduction for tax purposes.

Health Insurance

All persons working in Denmark and registered with the National Registration Office receive free medical care. Nevertheless, many companies have introduced additional insurance plans for their employees.

Labor Unions

Formation/Recognition Requirements

In the Danish labor market there are local and industrial labor unions. A local labor union is the association of members of a specific trade within a certain geographical area. An industrial labor union is basically a coalition of several local unions within the same industry.

Exclusive Bargaining

Exclusive bargaining is not a concept known under Danish law. However, labor unions are entitled to participate in the negotiation and drafting of future Parliament acts that relate to the labor market and have the right to negotiate collective agreements containing more favorable terms and conditions for their members. Further, they participate in the resolution of conflicts among the parties to an employment contract.

Collective Agreements

Duty to Bargain

Collective agreements are bargained at a local and a national level. Collective agreements to regulate specific local issues, often for a single enterprise (in which case the term "local agreement" [lokalaftale] is also used), are normally agreed between a local union and an employer or a local employers' organization. If an industrial collective agreement is in place, a local union that wishes to contract with an individual employer generally must obtain the industrial labor union's consent and must state in the local agreement that the industrial union is not a party to the agreement. At the national level, collective agreements (overenskomstaftaler) are mostly entered into between an industrial labor union and the corresponding employers' association.

In Denmark, national employee and employers' organizations are allowed to associate into bigger and more complex groups with the capacity to conclude collective agreements with binding effect on their members. The most important of these groups are the Danish Confederation of Trade Unions and the Danish Employers' Confederation.

Form Requirements

The content of a collective agreement is not regulated by law. The parties are thus free to determine which matters to regulate with the advantage of adapting the content of the collective agreement to the different needs of the various trades, the only restriction being that the parties may not agree on terms and conditions that do not provide for at least the same level of protection afforded to the employees by law. Naturally, the parties may agree on terms and conditions more beneficial to the employees than those guaranteed by law.

As a general rule, collective agreements specify minimum standards for employment contracts and set rules regarding the union's functioning, such as the members' obligations toward the union itself.

Mechanisms of Dispute Resolution

A very important feature of the collective agreement is that it requires that disagreements be resolved without interrupting the workflow. Employees may take collective action only under circumstances as specified by law. Under Section 5 of the Standard Rules for Handling Industrial Disputes (*norm for regler for behandling af faglig strid*),[8] employees are allowed to stop working when the employer has not paid their wages on time and when necessary to safeguard their honor, life, or welfare. Employees may also refuse to perform work if the work in question corresponds to employees taking part in a legal strike or to performing the work of employees who are legally locked out.

If a dispute arises between employees and an employer and their relationship is governed by a collective agreement, their dispute has to be resolved by conciliation or industrial arbitration. The parties are obliged to mediate or negotiate their disputes. If after going through the negotiation or mediation process the parties do not reach a satisfactory agreement, both parties are entitled to bring the dispute before a board or court of arbitration for a final award. There is no right of appeal, and the ordinary courts have no jurisdiction on matters relating to the interpretation of collective agreements.

Changes and Termination

Collective agreements normally contain rules on their termination. Once the specified period of validity expires, either party may terminate it by giving notice. The notice period may vary from one collective agreement to another, but is typically three months.

For changes to collective agreements, see "Carrying Out a Workforce Reduction" in the next section.

Works Councils

National Works Councils

If an organization is covered by a collective agreement subject to the Danish Confederation of Trade Unions and the Danish Employers' Confederation's Agreement on Cooperation (*samarbejdsaftale*), it must establish a works council if it employs more than 25 employees. In the private sector this is necessary only if the employer or a majority of the employees request it.

The works council is composed of an equal number of representatives from the management and from the employees. Employee representatives are chosen by the employees, and the management chooses its own representatives.

The works council has to be informed on a current basis of managerial affairs, including changes in the work organization, and in general of the development of activities and financial situation of the enterprise.

If the enterprise is not covered by a collective agreement, the Danish Information and Consultation of Employees Act (*lov om information og høring af lønmodtagere*)[9] applies. The Act implements Directive 2002/14/EC of March 11, 2002 establishing a general framework for informing and consulting employees in the EU. The Act states that enterprises employing at least 35 employees are obliged to inform and consult the employees. The employees choose their own representatives, who are informed and consulted on behalf of the employees (see Section 6 of the Act) in all essential matters, such as threats to employment and potential changes in work organization, and in general on the development of the activities and financial situation of the enterprise. In special cases where information and consultation may damage the enterprise, it is not obliged to consult and inform the employees (see Section 5 of the Act).

Employee Representatives on the Board of Directors

Danish corporation law empowers the employees to exert influence on the operation of the corporation. An organization that has employed an average of at least 35 employees for the past three years must permit employee representatives on the board of directors. The employee representatives have the same rights and obligations as the other board representatives.

National or Multinational Organizations

The Danish Act on European Works Councils (*lov om europæiske samarbejdsudvalg*)[10] implements Council Directive 94/45/EC on European Works Councils. According to Section 4 of the Act, multinational organizations operating in Denmark that employ at least 1,000 employees, with a minimum of 150 employees working in at least two EU member states and EAA countries (excluding the United Kingdom), are obliged to set up a European Works Council.

The objective of the Act is to improve the employees' possibilities of information and consultation on matters affecting related companies or company divisions located in several countries.

The European Works Council has the right to meet with the central management once a year, to be informed and consulted on the basis of a report drawn up by the central management about the progress and prospects of the Community-scale company or related companies. The local managements are to be informed accordingly.

Section 23(2) of the Act provides that the meeting must relate in particular to the structure, economic and financial situation, probable development of the business and its production and sales, current and probable trend of employment, investments, and substantial changes concerning organization, introduction of new working methods or production processes, transfers of production, mergers, cut-backs or closures of companies or important divisions, and layoffs.

Where there are exceptional circumstances that considerably affect the employees' interests, particularly in the event of relocations, the closure of establishments or divisions, or layoffs, the selected committee or, where no such committee exists, the European Works Council has the right to be informed. The committee or Council has the right to meet, at its request, with the central management, or any appropriate level of management within the organization, so as to be informed and consulted on such measures.

This information and consultation meeting must take place as soon as possible on the basis of a report drawn up by the central management or any other appropriate level of management, on which an opinion may be delivered at the end of the meeting or within a reasonable time.

Employee Representatives in Related Companies

Employees in a parent company and its subsidiaries in Denmark have the right to choose a number of board members of the parent company, if:

- The subsidiary is a public limited company (*aktieselskab*) or private limited company (*anpartsselskab*);
- The parent company holds the majority of the voting rights;
- The parent company and the subsidiaries all together on average employ at least 35 employees.[11]

In that way the employees may exert influence on the management of the parent company.

Labor Unions/Nondisclosure Issues

The Danish Act on European Works Councils establishes that it does not apply to those enterprises that have a collective agreement with obligations and rights that at least match the provisions of the Directive on Works Councils. However, the provisions of Chapter 6 of the Act apply in all cases to Community-scale organizations and to foreign subsidiaries and establishments.

Chapter 6 of the Act states that the members of the special negotiation body may be obliged to observe confidentiality in certain circumstances for the purpose of protecting the company's interests. The duty of confidentiality remains effective even after expiry of the members' terms of office.

SECTION II

My client is acquiring an existing business in Denmark. How do I assess the existing workforce and consider changes?

Share Deals Versus Asset Deals

In the case of a business sale or acquisition, it is relevant to distinguish between a purchase effected as a stock (share) or as an asset deal.

Generally, in a stock deal, even where the stockholders change, the employer's identity before the transfer remains the same after the purchase and, as a result, the existing employment relationship between the employees and their employer is not changed. Similarly, the existing relationship between the employer and the labor unions is not changed. The parties to any individual and collective employment agreements will be the same as before the transfer.

However, an asset deal unleashes a series of obligations on both the new and the previous owner, the most important being that all the rights and obligations under individual and collective employment agreements binding upon the original owner will transfer without changes to the buyer after the transfer. The buyer will replace the seller as a party to any agreement to which the latter is bound with a very limited possibility of modifying the terms and conditions contracted therein. Different criteria are used to identify an asset deal, the change of the employer and the unchanged identity of the entity being the most essential criteria.

The Danish Act on Employees' Rights in connection with business transfers (*virksomhedsoverdragelsesloven*)[12] implements the main rules laid down by Council Directive 77/187/EC of February 14, 1977 on the approximation of the laws of the member states relating to the safeguarding of employees' rights in the event of transfers of businesses or part of businesses (the Acquired Rights Directive).

The Act and the Directive refer only to business transfers effected as an asset deal.

Due Diligence Requirements and Considerations

The Danish Data Protection Act (*persondataloven*),[13] which applies to the transfer of a business with an existing workforce, provides that ordinary nonsensitive employee data (e.g., education and field of activity) may be processed and disclosed without the employee's consent. Sensitive information (e.g., health information and labor union membership) may be processed and disclosed only with the employee's consent. If the employee's consent cannot be obtained, the seller of the business must anonymize the sensitive information before carrying through the due diligence investigation.

It is important that the seller inform the buyer of all the rights and obligations that will be transferred to him. However, the seller's failure to notify the buyer of any right or obligation will have no effect on the rights of any employee against the buyer and/or the seller with respect to that right or obligation.

The transfer of a business must not be detrimental to its employees. Employees are entitled to preserve the seniority earned while working under the original owner. When calculating the length of service of the employees transferred to ascertain any rights of a financial nature, such as severance benefits or salary increases, the buyer must also take into account the period during which the employees worked under the previous owner.

Carrying Out a Workforce Reduction

Layoffs

A layoff in the event of a business sale or acquisition may be justified as necessary and inherent to the running of the enterprise if, for example, the enterprise changes its regular operations or stops or reduces its operations because of a work shortage.

For a group of dismissals to be considered a layoff, the number of employees being terminated within a 30-day period should total:

1. At least 10 in an enterprise employing more than 20 and less than 100 employees;
2. At least 10 percent in an enterprise employing at least 100 but less than 300 employees;
3. At least 30 in an enterprise employing 300 or more employees.

Statutory Protection

Layoffs are governed by the Danish Collective Dismissals Act (*lov om kollektive afskedigelser*),[14] which implements Council Directive 98/59/EC of July 20, 1998 on the approximation of the laws of the member states relating to layoffs.

Period of Notice
The period of notice in the case of a layoff is 30 days, calculated from the time the county-level labor market council is informed of the situation (which is never before the employer has established negotiations with the employee representatives). The 30-day period may be extended to eight weeks if the number of dismissals totals more that 50 percent of the enterprise's workforce and more than 100 workers are employed. This period may even be longer if stipulated in a collective agreement or if the employees' individual contractual or statutory rights entitle them to a longer period of notice.[15]

Severance Pay
If the employer fulfills its obligations under the Collective Dismissals Act, the employee is not entitled to claim severance pay in connection with a layoff, unless the employee has made an agreement on severance pay. The individual rights still apply, and if the employee is covered by the Salaried Employees Act, the employee

is entitled to severance pay if he or she has been employed by the organization for more than 12 years.[16]

However, an employer who does not fulfill the requirements of the Collective Dismissals Act must compensate the employees in question. The compensation must equal 30 days' salary counting from the date of notice. If the number of redundancies totals more than 50 percent of the employees and the company normally employs more than 100 persons, the remuneration equals eight weeks' payment from the date of notice; unless a collective agreement provides otherwise. Individual rights still apply alongside the Collective Dismissals Act. If the employer is covered by the Salaried Employed Act, the employee is entitled to salary during the notice period as provided under Section 2 of the Salaried Employees Act.

Procedural Requirements

The first step that an employer must take before deciding whether to carry out a layoff is to initiate negotiations with the employee representatives. The purpose of the negotiations is to prevent the dismissals or at least to reduce their number or limit their effect.

At the negotiation stage, the employer must provide the employee representatives with a written statement specifying:

- The cause(s) of the dismissals;
- The number of employees to be dismissed;
- The number of employees regularly working at the enterprise;
- The period of time during which the dismissals will take place;
- Any other required information.

A copy of the statement must be forwarded to the Regional Employment Council.

The layoff may not be effected until the notice period has elapsed. During this period, the employer remains obligated to pay wages to the employees.

Protected Groups

No statute specifically gives protection to labor union leaders and shop stewards against termination. However, in the case of shop stewards, case law has shown that this group of employees should be the last one to consider for dismissal, unless the reasons for termination are compelling.

Particular attention should be paid to pregnant employees, employees on maternity/parental leave, and safety representatives, because these groups of employees enjoy special termination rights under specific statutes.

Reorganizing the Workforce

Procedural Requirements

Once a buyer has identified the rights and obligations to which he is bound by virtue of the employment contracts, he might recognize the need for some material changes to the employment terms and conditions. It follows from the Danish Act on Employees' Rights in connection with business sales and acquisitions that if a buyer finds that he cannot provide the same terms and conditions of employment that the employees enjoyed under the previous owner, he must find a way to offer other conditions that must be equally beneficial for the employees in question.

It may be possible for the employer to make minor modifications or changes in the employment contract by notifying the employee in writing no later than one month after the modification or change was made.

Where the intended changes relate to the rights and obligations of the employee, the employer must obtain the employee's consent. The employee has no obligation to accept the proposed amendments to the original contract; if the employee refuses to accept the amendments, the employer's sole option will be to terminate the original employment contract and to present the employee with a new contract containing the new terms of employment. Again, the employee is not obliged to accept the new employment contract. If the employee rejects the new offer, the employee will be entitled to claim severance pay due to wrongful dismissal.

Material changes to the terms of employment may be justified where the seller is in a situation of serious financial crisis. In that case, the buyer or the seller, on the one hand, and the representatives of the employees, on the other hand, may agree on alterations to the employees' terms and conditions of employment, to the extent permitted by current law or practice, as a measure to safeguard employment opportunities by ensuring the survival of the business.

Termination Rights and Obligations

In principle, the employees have an obligation to continue working for their new employer. However, the employee has the right to terminate his or her employment contract whenever the buyer makes any unfavorable changes to the terms of employment and working conditions.

On the part of the employer, the business acquisition is not in itself a valid cause for termination, unless the dismissal is necessitated by economic, technical, or organizational changes. If the termination is not justified by any of the previous reasons, it will be considered as wrongful, entitling the employee to compensation.

The notice period in the event of termination by the employer may vary depending on the type of employment. According to the Salaried Employees Act, the period of notice to which the employee is entitled ranges from one month for the first six months of employment to three months in the case of a longer period of employment. The three-month notice period is increased by one month for every three years of employment with a cap of six months after nine years of employment.

In the event of termination of the employment by the employee, the period of notice is one month, irrespective of the length of employment.

In both cases, the notice must be given to expire at the end of a month.

Protected Groups

The Danish Act on Employees' Rights in connection with business sales and acquisitions states that after the transfer, employee representatives, shop stewards, safety representatives, and members of the works councils must be afforded the same rights as they enjoyed during employment with their former employer.

Changing the Wage and Benefits Structure

Statutory Protection

The different elements of the employees' remuneration rights originating from their employment contracts or employment relationships may not be changed even if the total amount of their wages remains unaffected.

Procedural Requirements

Generally, the transferred employees are legally obliged to accept the transfer of the enterprise. The exception to this rule occurs when the terms and conditions of the employees' contracts of employment or employment relationships are materially changed as a consequence of the transfer, in which case the employees may decline the transfer and terminate their employment.

For this reason, and to prevent the loss of key employees who may decide to terminate the employment, it is recommended to identify any terms of employment that will be materially affected by the transfer and to prepare new employment contracts (or amendments to the existing ones). Some of the anticipated changes may be reconsidered before taking any final decision.

An employee's refusal to accept the transfer may trigger specific rules on termination, including special notification requirements, especially if the number of employees to be terminated amounts to the limits established by the Collective Dismissals Act.

It is very important to consider that if the employment contract or the employment relationship is terminated because of a substantial change in the terms of employment and working conditions to the detriment of the employee due to the transfer (e.g., a pay cut), the employer shall be regarded as having been responsible for the termination, entitling the employee to seek compensation.

Consulting with Labor Unions or Works Councils

In the event of a business sale, both the seller and the buyer have certain information and consultation obligations. The seller must provide the employee representatives with specific details about the transfer and must be prepared to negotiate on any possible means to reduce its effect on the employees.

Under a collective agreement, the employer has rights and obligations both toward the employees (terms and conditions relating to salary, working time, termination, etc.) and toward the union (e.g., compromises with respect to conflict-solving mechanisms). The rights and obligations toward the employees are transferred to the buyer, who is bound by them until the date of termination of the collective agreement or the entry into force or application of a new one. However, the buyer may choose not to become a party to the agreement and thus be released from his rights and obligations toward the union. In this event he must formally notify the labor union to that effect no later than five weeks after the time when he knew or should have known that a collective agreement applied to all or a part of the transferred employees, but no earlier than three weeks after the transfer. If the buyer fails to inform the union, he will be bound by such agreement as if he had entered into it personally, until the expiry of the collective agreement.[17]

Once the collective agreement expires, the buyer, as the new employer, is allowed to modify or terminate the transferred employees' rights and obligations deriving from such collective agreement, unless it is renewed.

Consulting with the Government

As mentioned before, a written statement containing the most relevant information regarding a planned layoff must be addressed to the employee representatives, with a copy to the county-level labor council, which assists the local branch of the Employment Service.

The county-level labor council will try to find a solution as soon as possible to avoid dismissals, but not until the negotiations between the representatives and the employer have ended, except if otherwise established in a collective agreement. If the number of employees to be dismissed corresponds to at least 50 percent of employees and the total number of employees exceeds 100, the employer must not notify the council until 21 days after negotiations with the representatives have started.

Once the employer has informed the labor council about the layoff, a list containing the names of the employees to be dismissed must follow within the next 10 days. A copy of this list must be sent to the employee representatives, allowing them the opportunity to make any necessary remarks to the council.

SECTION III

My client wishes to sell its existing facility. What restrictions do we need to consider?

Assessing Employment Contracts

Common/Uncommon/Necessary Provisions

It must be remembered above all that the protection guaranteed to the employees in the case of a business sale is a matter of public policy. Consequently, the legal rules may not be derogated from in a manner that is unfavorable to the employees.

Confidentiality

The duty of loyalty is one of the basic principles in any employment relationship in Denmark. This principle involves the employee's obligation not to disclose any trade secret or information considered confidential by the employer that the employee could have acquired during employment.

As the buyer acquires all the seller's rights and obligations in respect of the transferred employees, the employee's duty of confidentiality is transferred as well, in favor of the new employer.

As regards those employees who will not be part of the transfer and whose employment contracts are to be terminated, the duty of confidentiality to their former employer still applies. Section 19 of the Market Practices Act (*markedsføringsloven*)[18] prohibits the employee's unauthorized disclosure of confidential information for a period of three years after the termination of employment.

Furthermore, the employee may be subject to an extended duty of confidentiality after termination where a confidentiality clause included in the employment contract so provides.

Data Protection

The protection of the employee's personal data in the event of a business sale is a relevant aspect to take into consideration.

The Danish Act on the Processing of Personal Data implements Council Directive 95/46/EC of October 24, 1995 on the protection of individuals with regard to the processing of personal data and on the free movement of such data. According to the Act, data must be processed in accordance with good practices for the processing of data. Data to be processed must be collected for specified explicit and legitimate purposes. It must be adequate, relevant, and not excessive in relation to the purpose for which the data is collected.

With regards to personal data, the data subject (in this case, the transferred employee) should be notified of the disclosure and transfer. Ideally, personal data may be processed only if the employee has given explicit consent.

It is important to note that the Danish Act on the Processing of Personal Data applies not only in the case where the person who determines the purposes and means of the processing of personal data (the "controller") is established in Denmark, but also when the controller is established in a third country outside of the European Community if the data is collected in Denmark for the purpose of processing in a third country.

Generally speaking, European legislation has several strict rules regarding the transfer of personal data to any state that is not a member of the European Community and that has not implemented agreements entered into with the European Community containing rules like those laid down in Directive 95/46/EC.

According to Danish law, for a transfer of data to a third country (outside of the European Community) to be allowed, the country in question must ensure an adequate level of protection. The adequacy of the level of protection afforded by a third country will be determined on a case-by-case basis, depending on the circumstances surrounding the data transfer operation. The main elements to analyze may be the nature of the data, the purpose and duration of the processing operation, the country of origin and country of final destination, the rules of law in force in the third country in question, and the professional rules and security measures that are complied with in that country.

The transfer of data to a third country may also take place on the condition that the employee has given explicit consent.

Noncompetition Clauses

According to the Salaried Employees Act, a noncompetition clause may be included in an individual employment contract between the employer and an employee holding a fiduciary position. For a noncompetition clause to be valid, it must afford the employee the right to receive compensation during its term and must be in writing.

The employee's monthly compensation during the term of the noncompetition clause must amount at least to 50 percent of his or her salary, including all the benefits to which the employee is entitled. A sum equivalent to three months' compensation will be paid right after termination, whereas the remaining compensation may be paid monthly for as long as the clause is in effect.

In the case where the employee finds a new job after termination that sufficiently matches his or her qualifications, the compensation amount will be reduced by the sum of the employer's new salary. The three months' compensation paid after termination will not be affected by this.

A number of other conditions may render a noncompetition clause invalid. Whether or not a clause is deemed effective may depend on certain time limits. It will not be effective if the employment relationship lasts for only three months. Where the employment relationship lasts for more than three months but less than six months, the clause will be valid for a maximum of six months after termination.

Finally, a noncompetition clause's validity may be jeopardized depending on the type of termination. If an employee is wrongfully dismissed or is terminated because of a serious breach on the part of the employer, the clause will not be enforceable. By contrast, the clause will remain enforceable if the employee is terminated due to gross misconduct or violation of his obligations under the clause, thereby annulling the employee's entitlement to compensation.

A noncompetition clause may be terminated by the employer at a notice of one month during or after employment. If the clause is terminated during employment and the employee ends the employment relationship within the next six months in a situation where the employer would have relied on that clause, the employer is entitled to receive compensation equal to three months' salary.

Nonsolicitation Clauses

A nonsolicitation clause may be included in an individual employment contract between the employer and any salaried employee independently of his or her position and functions. A nonsolicitation clause prohibits the employee from being employed by or doing business with any of the former employer's customers or other business connections after the employee's resignation. The clause may only be invoked if there has been a commercial relationship with the customer concerned within the 18 months prior to the date of the notice of termination.

Under the nonsolicitation clause, the employee is entitled to a compensation equivalent to 50 percent of his or her salary on the effective data of termination, payable monthly. In the case where after termination the employee finds an appropriate job that matches his or her qualifications, the compensation amount will be reduced by the sum of the employee's new salary.

The clause will remain valid even if the employee is wrongfully dismissed. However, if the employee is terminated due to gross misconduct, the right to compensation will be forfeited.

A nonsolicitation clause will not be effective if the employment relationship lasts for only three months. Where the employment relationship lasts for more than three months but less than six months, the clause will be valid for a maximum of six months after termination.

A nonsolicitation clause may be terminated by the employer at a notice of one month during or after employment.

Consulting with the Government

There is no obligation to consult the Danish government in the event of a business sale, except in the case of layoffs.

Consulting with Labor Unions or Works Councils

Procedural Requirements

According to the Danish Act on Employees' Rights in connection with business sales and acquisitions, the seller must inform and consult the employees and their representatives about the transfer.

The seller must inform the employee representatives or the employees in the absence of employee representatives, of the following:

1. The date of the transfer;
2. The reason(s) for the transfer;
3. The legal, economic, and social implications of the transfer for the employees;
4. Any measures envisaged that will affect the employees.

The seller must give such information to the employee representatives well in advance of the transfer, and in any event before the employees are directly affected by the transfer as regards their terms of employment and working conditions.

The seller is obligated to consult with the employee representatives only if employees will be affected by the transfer. In that case, the obligation to consult the employee representatives must be satisfied in good time and with a view to reaching an agreement. Even if case law and legal theory do not provide a specific moment in time that might be considered "good" to consult the representatives of the transferred employees, it is generally assumed that they must be informed in time for them to influence the decision-making process.

Moreover, most collective agreements include a duty to notify the joint cooperation committee (works council) of the contemplated transaction as soon as possible and even before the transaction is made.

Transfer/Termination of a Collective Agreement

The seller's rights and obligations under a collective agreement pass to the buyer through the transfer.

Negotiating with the Purchaser: Special Labor Issues

Use of Warranties in Transfer Agreements

The use of a warranty (a seller's guarantee that certain assertions are true) is highly recommended as the *inter partes* obligations under the Danish Act on Employees' Rights in connection with business sales and acquisitions may be derogated from.

It is important to remember that not all obligations can be handled with warranties, for instance, those toward the employees.

SECTION IV

My client wishes to replace its senior manager(s). What restrictions do we need to consider?

Employment Contracts

Employee Status

In general terms, managerial staff falls within the scope of the Salaried Employees Act under the classification of employees whose work mainly consists of supervising the work done at the enterprise on behalf of the employer. This Act places the managerial staff at the same level as other employees like shop assistants, clerks employed in purchasing and selling or in associated storage and dispatch work, and persons assisting in a technical or clinical establishment. In theory, an employee who followed an education to perform his or her work can be considered a salaried employee within the definition of the Salaried Employees Act, as opposed to a craftsperson trained by apprenticeship in a trade. Consequently, an employee whose main function is to take charge of the work done by the other workers at the company may be considered a salaried employee.

However, the employee status does not cover chief executive officers. CEOs do not fall within the definition of employees under the Salaried Employees Act and are thus not afforded the same level of protection. Most of the terms and conditions applicable to their employment contracts will depend on the contractual freedom of the parties. The only limitation to this freedom is that the parties may not agree on any terms that afford the CEOs with a lower level of protection than that guaranteed by law.

The distinction between a CEO and the rest of the managerial staff must be determined on a case-by-case basis. The categorization as a CEO will depend on the analysis of a number of factors, primarily the person's degree of responsibility and participation in the decision-making process regarding the enterprise's operations. The most obvious indications, of course, are if the person functions as chair of the board of directors and has been given the title of CEO.

In certain circumstances, even when the difference between a salaried employee and a CEO may be clear, the line between the latter and an independent contractor may be rather blurred. Again, the classification will depend on the circumstances in each case. It will be necessary to look at the different criteria, such as who will be financially liable if the operations of the enterprise fail.

Period of Notice

The period of notice applicable to salaried employees does not apply to that of CEOs in case of termination, and there is no other statute provision regulating this matter.

As a result, the period of notice applicable to CEOs may be freely determined by the parties. Where no period of notice is specified, the employment may be terminated at a reasonable notice considering the responsibilities and seniority of the CEO.

In practice, there is a great deal of variation in the agreements on notice periods, but six to 12 months is the most common notice period if the employment is terminated by the company and three to six months if it is terminated by the CEO.

Common Contractual Protection

Owing to the fact that CEOs are not covered by the Salaried Employees Act, there are no restrictions on how to terminate them, and there are no obligations to state the reasons for termination or to bargain before termination, unless this is agreed in the employment contract. Similarly, there are no regulations on severance pay, but in practice there may be an agreement on severance pay in the contract.

In practice, the CEO can consider himself or herself terminated in the event of a change of control, and will be entitled to compensation.

Procedural Requirements

It is the employees who are entitled to be informed and consulted through the employee representatives. CEOs will naturally be informed and consulted by virtue of their position.

As regards layoffs, the Collective Dismissals Act applies (see discussion in Section II).

Protected Groups

Protected groups include shop stewards, employee board members, works council members, pregnant employees, and employees with high seniority.

Shop and safety stewards enjoy a higher level of protection against termination. Termination of members of these groups must be absolutely well-founded. The same applies to employees appointed as board members.

Members of works councils in the private sector have the right to an extended notice of termination. In the public sector, members of works councils normally have the same protection as shop stewards.

Pregnancy is regulated by the Gender Equality Act (*ligestillingsloven*).[19] Termination based on the employee's pregnancy is unreasonable, and the employee is entitled to claim compensation. In practice, it is very difficult for the employer to satisfy the burden of proof that termination was not motivated by the employee's pregnancy.

The Equal Treatment Act (*ligebehandlingsloven*)[20] applies to senior employees. The Salaried Employees Act provides for a severance pay to employees with high seniority, but this does not apply to CEOs.

A violation of these restrictions may be sanctioned by the payment of compensation to the dismissed employee, and the dismissal may also be set aside as invalid.

Statutory Severance Pay Requirements

Common Contractual Obligations

There are no statutory rules entitling CEOs to severance pay. The employment contracts of CEOs usually contain clauses allowing them to receive severance pay due to seniority. The same practice is observed regarding severance pay in the event of wrongful dismissal.

Confidentiality and Nondisparagement Agreements
The use of confidentiality and nondisparagement clauses is not widespread in Denmark because Danish rules and generally applied principles already protect the employer from most kinds of disparaging statements by the employee.

Even if the CEO has not agreed to a confidentiality and nondisparagement agreement, he or she will be prevented from competing with the company in a disloyal way, per the Danish Marketing Practices Act.

Noncompetition and Nonsolicitation Clauses
Noncompetition and nonsolicitation clauses agreed with the CEOs will be effective, without entitling them to the compensation rights afforded by the Salaried Employees Act.

Stock Compensation Plans
Employee stock compensation plans are regulated in Denmark mainly by the Stock Option Act (for grants after July 1, 2004) and Section 17(a) of the Salaried

Employees Act (for grants prior to July 1, 2004). For stock option grants covered by the Salaried Employees Act, Section 17(a) states that the employees may keep granted stock, warrant plans, restricted stock units, and incentive stock option plans, regardless of termination for whatever reason. The Stock Option Act provides that an employee may only keep granted stock options, warrants, etc. if he or she is terminated for any reason other than misconduct. Forfeiture provisions contrary to the Stock Option Act will be set aside. In case of resignation or termination due to misconduct, the forfeiture provisions of the stock option plan will apply. Employee stock purchase plans are covered neither by the Stock Option Act nor by the Salaried Employees Act, and consequently forfeiture provisions will apply in all situations.

Statutory Restrictions on Dismissal Without Cause

There are no rules that protect a CEO from being dismissed without cause. A dismissal will be valid if it is decided by the company board.[21]

SECTION V

What prohibitions exist against discrimination on the basis of age, race, gender, disability, pregnancy, and other factors? What are the rights of employees, applicants, or former employees who believe that they have been discriminated against?

Areas of Protection

Employees are protected against discrimination on the grounds of political conviction, gender, sexual orientation, race, religion, and national, social, and ethnic origin.

Statutory Rules

The principle of equal treatment must be observed in any aspect of the employment, and especially in terms of remuneration. Nevertheless, differential treatment is allowed where an employee's specific characteristics constitute an occupational requirement or where necessary to match with the enterprise's express objective of promoting particular political or religious beliefs.

Direct as well as indirect discrimination is forbidden under Danish law. Affirmative action is permitted to offset intrinsic differences that may put a certain group of employees in a disadvantageous position. Harassment and sexual harassment are equally banned.

Equal treatment is particularly emphasized among male and female workers. The Act on Equal Pay for Men and Women (*ligelønsloven*)[22] and the Gender Equality Act oblige the employer to pay the same wage to men and women for doing equal work and guarantee them the same working conditions. Discrimination against female employees is also illegal on the grounds of pregnancy, marital, or family status.

Legal Effect of Nondiscrimination Policies

The legal provisions preventing discrimination at the workplace cannot be deviated by contract or collective agreement to the detriment of the employee. Any stipulation by the parties that might be unfavorable for the employer will be considered invalid. An employee cannot renounce the level of protection afforded by law.

Venue and Procedure

Employees who consider themselves discriminated against on any of the grounds protected by law have the right to bring their claim before the ordinary courts.

Danish law protects those employees who have been terminated for bringing their claims to court, entitling them to compensation.

In discrimination cases the burden of proof usually is on the employer. For instance, in the case of a woman being terminated on the grounds of pregnancy, where termination occurred during the period of pregnancy, the burden of proof rests on the employer. However, after the pregnancy, the burden of proof is shared by both parties.

Sanctions and Remedies

An employee who is discriminated against by his or her employer may be entitled to compensation. The employer may also be subject to a fine by the ordinary courts and in serious cases even imprisonment.

SECTION VI

On the Horizon: What key labor and employment law developments should an employer doing business in Denmark anticipate occurring in the coming years?

Different transitional arrangements concerning free movement of workers have been put in place for the 10 countries that joined the EU in 2004. These arrangements do not apply to Cyprus and Malta, meaning that their nationals enjoy complete freedom of movement within the European Economic Area.

In accordance with regulations enforced since May 1, 2008, a change in the Danish Aliens Act means citizens of Bulgaria, the Czech Republic, Estonia, Hungary, Latvia, Lithuania, Poland, Romania, Slovakia, and Slovenia are no longer required to obtain a residence and work permit, providing work undertaken is covered by a collective bargaining agreement. In this case, such citizens are now solely required to apply to the regional state administration for a certificate of registry no later than three months after their arrival in the country.

✪ NOTES

1. Consolidation Act No. 68 of January 21, 2005 on the legal relationship between employers and salaried employees.

2. Consolidation Act No. 1011 of August 15, 2007 on the employer's duty to inform the employee of the employment terms.

3. Act No. 309 of May 5, 2004 on the use of purchase options or subscription rights, etc. in employment relationships.

4. Act No. 370 of May 28, 2003 on fixed-term employment.

5. Consolidation Act No. 896 of August 24, 2004 to partially implement the Working Time Directive.

6. Act No. 268 of March 18, 2005 on the working environment.

7. Act No. 563 of June 9, 2006 on sickness benefits.

8. Standard Rules for Handling Industrial Disputes of August 17, 1908.

9. Act No. 303 of May 2, 2005 on information and consultation of employees.

10. Act No. 371 of May 22, 1996 on European Works Councils.

11. *Cf.* Danish Public Companies Act (*aktieselskabsloven*) § 49(3), Consolidation Act No. 649 of June 15, 2006 on public limited companies.

12. Consolidation Act No. 710 of August 20, 2002 on employees' rights in connection with transfers of undertakings.

13. Act No. 429 of May 31, 2000 on the processing of personal data.

14. Act No. 414 of June 1, 1994 on collective dismissals.

15. *See* Salaried Employees Act § 2.

16. *See* Salaried Employees Act § 2a.

17. *See* Danish Act on Employees' Rights in connection with business sales and acquisitions § 4a.

18. Act No. 1389 of December 21, 2005 on marketing practices.

19. Act No. 1095 of September 19, 2007 on gender equality.

20. Consolidation Act No. 734 of June 28, 2006 on equal treatment of men and women as regards access to employment etc.

21. *See* Danish Public Companies Act § 57.

22. Consolidation Act No. 906 of August 27, 2006 on equal pay for men and women.

CHAPTER 4

LABOR AND EMPLOYMENT LAW IN FINLAND

JAN ÖRNDAHL

SECTION I

My client wishes to establish a manufacturing facility in Finland and will need to hire a workforce. What are the key issues involved?

Employment Contracts: Who Receives Them and What Must They Include?

Basic Principles

The Employment Contracts Act (55/2001) does not prescribe any formal requirements for employment contracts. According to the Act, an employment contract may be oral, written, or electronic. However, preparing a written employment contract is a highly common and recommendable practice. The Employment Contracts Act does not include provisions regarding the language of the contract, but if a foreign language is used, the employee must understand the content of the contract.

Form of the Letter

Freedom of contract serves as the basis for the content of the employment contract. However, several employment contract-related issues are regulated by other, higher-level mandatory norms, such as laws or collective labor contracts. Consequently, these priority norms must be taken into consideration when drawing up an employment contract.

Regardless of the absence of formal requirements, the employer is obligated under the Employment Contracts Act to provide the employee with a written document indicating the key terms and conditions of the employment relationship if the contract is for an indefinite term or for a fixed term of more than one month, and if the key terms and conditions are not shown in the written employment contract. This information must be provided no later than by the end of the first salary payment period. The information must include the following: domicile or registered office of the parties of the employment contract; date of commencement of employment; duration and grounds of a fixed-term employment contract; length of trial period; place of work or explanation of the principles on which the place of work is determined; the employee's key duties; salary or explanation of how other payment is determined; salary payment period; regular working hours; vacation policy; and period of notice or an explanation of how this period is determined.

Key terms and conditions of employment may also be explained by making reference to the law or collective labor contract applicable to the employment relationship. Some companies prepare a special guidebook for new employees.

Changes to the terms of employment during the employment relationship may be made under mutual agreement, a collective labor contract, or other norms entitling the employer to make changes. In order to make essential changes to the terms of an employment contract unilaterally, the employer must have grounds for termination of the contract (e.g., financial or production-related grounds). In such a case, the employer may then always choose the milder alternative of amending the terms of employment instead. Such changes then take effect only after the applicable notice period has passed.

Fixed-Term Employment

According to the Employment Contracts Act, an employment contract may be made for a fixed term at the initiative of either the employer or the employee, but if it is at the employer's initiative, the employer must have a justifiable reason for hiring a temporary employee. Examples include needing a substitute for an employee on leave, or employing a worker for a highly seasonal activity. A fixed-term contract may not be used to circumvent the provisions imposed to protect employees against unilateral termination.

A contract made for a fixed period at the employer's initiative without a justified reason is not, however, considered invalid in its entirety. Only the condition regarding the term of the contract is invalid. In such a case, the employment contract shall be deemed effective indefinitely.

A fixed-term contract must not be terminated during the employment. It may be canceled only in accordance with the Employment Contracts Act, to be precise only upon an extremely weighty cause. Such a cause may be deemed to exist if the employee commits a breach against or neglects duties based on the employment contract or the law and these actions have an essential impact on the employment relationship in such a serious manner that it would be unreasonable to expect that the employer should continue the contractual relationship even for the period of notice. If a contract is not canceled, it will expire without termination at the end of the fixed term, or on completion of the specified work.

Wages and Benefits

Minimum Wage Requirements

Employment legislation does not specify any minimum wage. In practice, the collective labor contract applicable in each line of industry specifies the minimum wage. The collective labor contract to be applied to the work performed by the employee depends primarily on the employer's line of industry and the scope of application of the collective agreement. Secondarily, the employee's wage is determined on the basis of the provisions of the applicable collective agreement regarding wages and salaries.

However, not all sectors of industry enforce collective labor contracts. If the employment relationship is not governed by a collective agreement and the employer and employee have not agreed on the compensation to be offered for the work performance, the employee must, under the Employment Contracts Act, be paid a reasonable standard salary for the work performed.

Special Benefit Requirements

Pension

An employee's pension security consists of an earnings-related employment pension. The employer is required to arrange the employee's statutory pension security. As a rule, employers do so by taking out a pension insurance policy. Pension trusts are another, less frequently used alternative. Employers and employees jointly finance the pension security by paying statutory pension insurance contributions. The employer's and the employee's contributions are determined on the basis of wages and salaries paid. The employer's monthly pension insurance contributions are approximately 21.6 percent and the employee's around 4.6 percent of the employee's full monthly earnings.

Vacation

The employee's right to vacation is regulated by the Annual Vacation Act (162/2005). According to the Act, an employee is entitled to two days of paid annual vacation for each full vacation-credit month. If, by the end of the vacation credit year, the employment has continued without interruptions for at least one year, the employee shall be entitled to two and a half days of vacation for each full vacation credit month. When taking vacation, Saturdays count as weekdays. To be entitled to annual vacation, the employee must work at least 14 days or 35 hours a month. Employees who do not meet the vacation eligibility criteria in any working month must be paid vacation pay based on a percentage of their earnings.

Sick Pay

According to the Employment Contracts Act, an employee who is unable to perform his or her duties due to illness or accident shall be entitled to sick pay. If the employment has continued for at least one month, the employee is entitled to full pay for the time during which he or she is unable to work, for a period of up to nine weekdays but not longer than until such time when he or she becomes entitled to daily allowance under the Sickness Insurance Act (1224/2004). If the employment relationship has continued for less than a month, the employee shall be entitled to 50 percent of his or her salary in the period specified above. Employment contracts often contain provisions regarding sick pay.

Labor Unions

Establishment and Recognition Requirements

Labor unions are governed by the Associations Act (503/1989) and are the lobby organizations for registered wage earners. The key purpose of the unions must be the protection of employees' interests in employment relationships.

Organization into labor unions is primarily guided by the so-called line of industry principle, which means employer enterprises in the same line of industry, and their employees, organize into their own trade unions or associations, which sign their own nationwide collective agreements. Examples include the metal, textile, paper, and food industries. Binding of the collective bargaining agreements are divided into two categories. "Normally binding" collective bargaining agreements bind only the employers who are members of the employers association. "Generally binding" collective bargaining agreements bind all employers who operate in the relevant industry, whether they are members of the employers association or not. Generally binding agreements are notarized by the Labor Court.

Exclusive Bargaining

According to the Collective Agreements Act (436/1946), the employer's representative in the collective agreement may be an individual employer or a registered employer association. On the employee side, only registered associations are entitled to sign collective agreements. An association entitled to sign a collective agreement must have the protection of either employers' or employees' interests in employment relationships as its principal purpose.

However, parties may expressly agree in the collective agreement that the local representatives of employers and employees may agree on certain things in mutual negotiations. This is often the case with provisions regarding working hours.

Collective Agreements

About 80 percent of Finnish employees are members of some trade union. Similarly, the majority of employers are members of an employer organization. Approximately 5 percent of employees are not covered by any collective agreement.

According to the Collective Agreements Act, a collective agreement must be in writing in order to be valid. The contracting parties must also sign the agreement.

The Act on the Labor Court (646/1974) establishes the Labor Court as the sole venue for matters pertaining to collective agreements, including the right to strike. As a special court, it addresses and resolves disputes regarding collective agreements when they involve (1) the validity, currency, content, or scope of the collective agreement, and the correct interpretation of a particular stipulation of a contract; (2) the conformity of a given procedure with the terms of a collective agreement or with any of the regulations referred to above; and (3) the consequences of a procedure not conforming to the collective agreement or the regulations specified above, excluding penal or disciplinary consequences.

The Labor Court cannot process any claims based on the Employment Contracts Act, or any claims based on employment contracts. A collective agreement may specify that any disputes falling within the jurisdiction of the Labor Court be settled in accordance with the Arbitration Act (967/1992). If it has been agreed that arbitration proceedings will be used, such will be the only avenue for dispute resolution.

A collective agreement will be effective for as long as the relevant parties have agreed. The parties may agree, for example, that the agreement shall be effective for a fixed term, or until further notice. A collective agreement made for a fixed term longer than four years will, after four years, be effective until further notice.

According to the Collective Agreements Act, a party may terminate a collective agreement effective until further notice at any time at three months' notice unless the parties have agreed otherwise. Any changes to collective agreements require both parties' approval.

Works Councils

The provisions of the Act on Cooperation within Undertakings (334/2007) are primarily applied in companies with at least 20 employees in regular employment. According to the main rule specified in the act, the parties in the cooperation are the employer and the company personnel. Usually, a shop steward or a delegate represents the company personnel.

According to law, the employer and the personnel representatives may agree on setting up a special joint advisory committee, which will address matters falling within the scope of the Act on Cooperation within Undertakings in the company or in its various parts. The mandate of the special joint advisory committee is a contractual issue between its founding parties. However, as a principal rule this committee handles all cooperational issues that are related to all personnel groups of the company and that fall under the scope of the Act on Cooperation within Undertakings. Under the Act, the committee can address issues regarding the impact on personnel of changes in business activities, business transfers, and workforce reductions.

Although the employee representatives on the advisory committee, as a rule, are members of labor unions, they do not directly represent the unions in the committee but rather the personnel groups in the workplace.

According to the Act on Cooperation within Undertakings, employee representatives must not disclose any confidential information they have obtained in connection with the cooperation procedure, such as business and trade secrets; information regarding the employer's financial position that, under other legislation, is not public and that if disclosed would be detrimental to the employer and its business and contractual partners; information on corporate security and similar security arrangements that, if disclosed, would be detrimental to the employer and its business and contractual partners; and information regarding an individual's health, financial standing, and other personal information, unless the individual has expressly given his or her consent to the disclosure. The employee representatives may disclose such information to other employees to the extent necessary to achieve the committee's objectives, but must inform them of the nondisclosure obligation.

SECTION II

My client is acquiring an existing business in Finland. How do I assess the existing workforce and consider changes?

Share Deals Versus Asset Deals

When a business acquisition is carried out through a share deal, the only change is the company's ownership. This has no direct impact on employee relationships. It is not until the potential integration of the acquired company with the buyer's existing operations begins that employees may be affected.

In contrast, a business acquisition carried out as an asset deal involves a change of employer. In such a case, employees will automatically be transferred to the buyer. Finland has implemented the EU directive on business transfers. The concept of business transfer is defined in the Employment Contracts Act as "the assignment of a company, a business, an association, or a foundation, or certain active parts thereof, to another employer, where the assigned activities, whether full-time or part-time, or part thereof, remain the same or similar after the transfer." Thus, identifying an ownership change as a "business transfer" requires an overall assessment of the situation.

A key criterion in the assessment of whether a business transfer meets the criteria of the Employment Contracts Act is whether the entity in question retains its identity, as indicated by the continuation or relaunch of business activities. The business transfer must involve a financial entity that has been permanently organized and that is involved in activities not restricted to the completion of a specific item of piecework. The concept of "entity" refers to an organized whole comprising people and other production elements that enable the performance of financial activities with a separate objective.

According to the Employment Contracts Act, neither the transferor nor the transferee may terminate an employee's employment contract solely on the basis of the business transfer. If, however, grounds for an individual termination or a layoff exist, there is no impediment to termination. Before the termination of employment, both the transferor and transferee are required to explore the opportunities specified in the Employment Contracts Act for providing other employment and the necessary training. Fixed-term employment contracts transferred alongside the business transfer cannot be terminated, since they are tied to a specific contract period.

In business transfers meeting the definition of the Employment Contracts Act, the transferor and the transferee must, under the Act on Cooperation within Undertakings, disclose the following information to the representatives of the affected personnel groups: the time or planned time of transfer; reasons for the transfer; the legal, financial, and social consequences of the transfer to the employ-ees; and planned measures regarding employees.

The transferor must provide the information specified above to the represen-tatives of personnel groups in good time before the transfer is carried out. The transferee must provide the information to the representatives of the personnel groups no later than within a week of the transfer execution date. If the business transfer involves the effects on personnel referred to in the law, these effects must be discussed in a manner required by law.

The transferee is obligated to comply with the collective agreement binding the transferor at the time of transfer until the agreement is no longer in force. The transferor has a duty to comply with the collective agreement irrespective of whether or not the transferee is unionized. Similarly, the issue of whether or not the trans-feree is already bound by another collective agreement is of no consequence.

Carrying Out a Workforce Reduction

Statutory Protection

The provisions regarding the termination of an employment contract cover two areas: termination on personal grounds, and termination on production and finan-cial grounds. In addition, the Employment Contracts Act includes a general provi-sion regarding both personal and financial and production grounds. It states that the employer may terminate an employment contract valid indefinitely only for a justified and weighty reason. The Employment Contracts Act contains manda-tory regulations on protection against termination. If the employer has no suffi-cient grounds for termination, the employer shall pay compensation to the employee of between three and 24 months' salary. Shop stewards elected on the basis of a collective bargaining agreement and elected representatives receive a maximum of 30 months' pay. The employee has no right to rejoin the service of the employer.

Unless the parties agree otherwise, the employer must observe the following periods of notice: 14 days, if the employment has continued for no more than one year; one month, if the employment has continued for more than one year but no more than four years; two months, if the employment has continued for more than four but no more than eight years; four months, if the employment has con-tinued for more than eight but no more than 12 years; and six months, if the employment has continued for more than 12 years. Wages or salary must be paid for the period of notice.

Procedural Requirements

According to the Employment Contracts Act, justified and weighty grounds for termination on personal grounds include serious breach or neglect of obligations specified in the employment contract or in law that have a fundamental impact on the employment relationship, as well as essential changes related to the employee that affect his or her ability to perform work duties. When assessing the justification and the weight of these grounds, the employer's and employee's overall circumstances must be taken into account. The law also specifies those grounds that cannot be deemed justified and weighty.

An employee who has neglected or failed to fulfill the duties of the employment relationship may not, however, be dismissed before he or she has been given a warning and an opportunity to amend his or her conduct. Furthermore, prior to giving notice the employer must investigate whether it is possible to avoid giving notice by placing the employee in other work. Noncompliance with the procedural provisions regarding warning and replacement is permitted only if the grounds for termination constitute such a serious breach of the employment contract that the employer cannot reasonably be required to continue with the employment relationship.

The employer must give notice of termination within a reasonable period after becoming aware of the cause for termination. Before giving notice, the employer must provide the employee with an opportunity to be heard with respect to the grounds for termination. The employment contract will be terminated in a notice of termination delivered to the other contracting party.

According to the general provision of the Employment Contracts Act regarding grounds for layoff, the employer has justified and weighty grounds for termination if the work available has significantly and permanently decreased for financial or production reasons or for reasons related to business reorganization. However, employment contracts may not be terminated if the employee can be offered other work and suitable training as required by law. The law also specifies those grounds that cannot be deemed justified and weighty.

If an employer falling within the scope of application of the Act on Cooperation within Undertakings (see "Works Councils" in Section I) considers measures that could result in the dismissal, layoff, or change to part-time status of one or more employees for financial or production reasons, the employer must fulfill the negotiation obligations prescribed by the Act. To initiate these negotiations, the employer must provide a written notification of the initial meeting at least five days in advance. The notification should indicate at least the time and place of the negotiations, as well as an outline of the matters to be discussed. If the employer is planning to dismiss or lay off at least 10 employees for more than 90 days, or to make them part-time employees, the employer must also attach the following information: grounds for the planned measures; a preliminary estimate of the number of personnel to be dismissed, laid off, or made part-time employees; an explanation of the principles applied to determining which employees are to be dismissed, laid off, or made part-time employees; and an estimated schedule of the planned dismissals, layoffs, or shifting to part-time work.

If the planned dismissals, layoffs, or shifts to part-time work will affect fewer than 10 employees, or if layoffs affecting more than 10 employees will last no more than 90 days, the employer has fulfilled its legal obligation to negotiate after the negotiations have been conducted for 14 days from their commencement. If the dismissals, layoffs for more than 90 days, or shifting to part-time work will affect at least 10 employees, the negotiation period is six weeks. The parties may agree to change both of these deadlines.

After having fulfilled the legal duty to negotiate, the employer must, within a reasonable time, provide a general overview of the measures being considered on the basis of the negotiations.

Before the employer terminates an employment contract on collective grounds for termination, the employer must explain to the employee to be dismissed the grounds for termination, the alternatives available, and the employment services offered by the employment office as early as possible. An indefinite-term employment contract may be terminated only through a notice of termination delivered to the relevant party.

Protected Groups

Shop Stewards

The grounds for termination for shop stewards and elected representatives are defined in the Employment Contracts Act and collective agreements. According to the Employment Contracts Act, the employer can terminate the employment contract of a shop steward elected on the basis of a collective agreement and an elected representative on grounds related to the employee personally only if the majority of the employees represented by the shop steward or the elected representative give their consent.

When terminating employment on collective grounds, the employer is entitled to terminate the employment contract of a shop steward or an elected representative under the Employment Contracts Act only if the work of the shop steward or the elected representative ceases entirely and the employer is unable to arrange work that meets the person's professional skills or other suitable work, or to train the person for other work. Collective agreements provide additional protection to shop stewards against termination. A shop steward's special protection against termination also applies to the occupational health and safety representative.

Pregnancy

Employees who are pregnant or on family leave are covered by the enhanced protection against termination laid down in the Employment Contracts Act. This provision prohibits the employer from terminating employment on the grounds of pregnancy, or because the employee is exercising his or her right to family leave. To enhance said protection against termination, the law imposes a burden of proof on the employer, which means the employer must prove that there is a justified and weighty reason for the termination.

However, this special protection does not prevent the termination of employment of an employee who is pregnant or on family leave when the reason for termination is justified and weighty and in no way linked to the pregnancy or family leave. Such reasons could include the grounds for termination related to the employee personally, as laid down in the Employment Contracts Act, or financial and production-related grounds. If an employee is on family leave, the employer is not entitled to terminate the employment contract on financial and production-related grounds unless operations are fully discontinued.

Sanctions

According to the Employment Contracts Act, an employer who has terminated an employment contract without just cause will be ordered to pay compensation for unjustified termination equivalent to wages for at least three months and not more than 24 months. This compensation is paid in addition to continued salary payment during the notice period. The maximum amount of compensation to be paid to shop stewards elected on the basis of a collective agreement or to elected representatives will be equivalent to wages for 30 months. Collective agreements provide additional protection against termination to shop stewards and elected representatives. Employees whose employment has been terminated without just cause are not entitled to reinstatement.

Reorganizing the Workforce

Changing the terms of the employment relationship while the relationship is in force may be based on mutual agreement between the parties, collective agreement, or norms entitling the employer to make changes, such as changing the grounds for termination. Essential changes to the terms of an indefinite-term employment contract may be made unilaterally only with respect to grounds for termination and in compliance with the period of notice. The period of notice commences when the employer notifies the employee of changes in the terms and conditions of employment. In fixed-term employment relationships, unilateral changes take effect immediately after the employer has informed the employee of the unilateral change in the terms and conditions of employment.

Unilateral changes in the terms of employment of protected groups such as shop stewards, pregnant women, and employees on family leave may be imposed under special grounds for termination as specified previously. Even in such cases, the termination procedure described previously must be complied with.

Changing the Wage and Benefits Structure

According to the principles laid down in legal practice, the employer can decrease the wage by unilateral decision only if the employer has legal grounds for termination of the employment. After the decrease, the level of wage must meet the minimum requirements specified in the collective agreement. If collective agreements are not applicable in the field in question, the employee must receive a reasonable standard wage. See "Procedural Requirements" on page 69.

Consulting with Labor Unions or Works Councils

Employment legislation does not obligate the transferee to consult with labor unions in connection with the business transfer. Instead, the transferee must, under the Act on Cooperation within Undertakings, provide a statement to the works council or, if the company has no works council, to the representatives of the personnel groups affected by the transfer. The statement must include the following information: the time or planned time of transfer; reasons for the transfer; the legal, financial, and social consequences of the transfer with respect to the employees; and planned measures regarding employees.

The information must be delivered to the personnel group representatives no later than within a week of the execution of the transfer. After delivering the information to the personnel group representatives, the transferee must provide them with an opportunity to ask questions, and must answer these questions. Upon the request of the personnel group representatives, the employer must present the information referred to above to the entire company personnel in compliance with the in-house communication principles and practices specified in the law.

The transferee is obligated to comply with the collective agreement binding the transferor at the time of transfer. The transferor has a duty to comply with the collective agreement irrespective of whether or not the transferee is a unionized employee. Similarly, whether or not the transferee is already bound by another collective agreement is of no consequence. The transferee is obligated to comply with the collective agreement binding the transferor until the agreement is no longer in force.

Consulting with the Government

In a pure business transfer situation, neither the transferor nor the transferee is required by employment legislation to inform the employment authorities. However, if the employer proposes measures under the Act on Cooperation within Undertakings that may result in a termination of employment, layoff, or shift to part-time work, a negotiation notification required by law or the information it contains must be submitted in writing to the employment office no later than when the negotiations begin.

Furthermore, the employer is required to inform the employment office immediately of the layoff of any employee whose employment history spans at least three years with the same employer or different employers before the end of the period of notice.

● SECTION III

My client wishes to sell its existing facility. What restrictions do we need to consider?

Assessing Employment Contracts

In case of a share deal or sale of the entire business of the client, the employment contracts continue under the same terms and conditions. In case of partial sale of the client's business within the same company, the question of selection of employees becomes relevant. According to Finnish law, employees who have been mainly responsible for tasks in the transferring business will transfer. The actual tasks are decisive, not the person's position in the organizational hierarchy.

Consulting with the Government

In a pure business transfer situation, the transferor is not required by employment legislation to inform the employment authorities. However, if the employer proposes measures that may result in the termination of employment, layoff, or shift to part-time work, a negotiation notification required by law or the information it contains must be submitted in writing to the employment office no later than the beginning of the negotiations.

Furthermore, the employer is required to inform the employment office immediately of the layoff of an employee whose employment history spans at least three years with the same employer or different employers before the end of the period of notice.

Consulting with Labor Unions or Works Councils

The employment legislation does not obligate the transferor to consult with labor unions in connection with the business transfer. Instead, the transferor must, under the Act on Cooperation within Undertakings, notify the works council or, if the company has no works council, the representatives of the personnel groups affected by the transfer. The notification must be provided in good time before the execution of the transfer. It must include the following information:

- The time or planned time of transfer
- Reasons for the transfer
- The legal, financial, and social consequences of the transfer with respect to the employees
- Planned measures regarding employees

The transferee is obligated to comply with the collective agreement binding on the transferor at the time of transfer. The transferor has a duty to comply with the collective agreement irrespective of whether or not the transferee is a unionized employee. Similarly, whether or not the transferee is already bound by another collective agreement is of no consequence. The transferee is obligated to comply with the collective agreement binding the transferor until the agreement is no longer in force.

Negotiating with the Purchaser: Special Labor Issues

In business deals, the seller normally bears the costs associated with employees as well as other employee-related risks until the time of transfer. Sales contracts feature relatively extensive seller's insurance addressing this issue.

In many cases, the parties of the business deal will attempt to sign loyalty agreements with key personnel to ensure that said staff continue to work for the buyer. On occasions, the buyer obtains a commitment from a sufficient number of key personnel to continue working for the buyer as a preclosing condition.

SECTION IV

My client wishes to replace its senior manager(s). What restrictions do we need to consider?

Employment Contracts

Being a statutory entity under company law, the chief executive officer (CEO) is not considered an employee (so-called organ theory: the CEO is a company organ, like the board of directors). Consequently, the CEO is not regarded as an employee in an employment relationship governed by employment legislation. Other staff and executives are deemed to be in an employment relationship, and are therefore subject to the same rules and conventions as other employees.

Usually, the parties mutually agree on the manner and grounds of terminating the CEO's employment. The dismissed CEO is normally entitled to severance pay equaling approximately one year's wages. However, severance pay is a contractual matter between the parties. Non-CEO executives who meet the criteria specified in employment legislation for an employment relationship are covered by the termination provisions of the Employment Contracts Act. See "Carrying Out a Workforce Reduction" in Section II.

Statutory Severance Pay Requirements

The employment legislation does not recognize the concept of severance pay as such. However, if the criteria for an employment relationship are met, salary for the period of notice must be paid.

The standard practice under executive severance agreements is to pay executives severance pay. The amount ranges from pay for a few months to pay for about a year. The amount of severance pay is completely a contractual matter between the parties.

To receive severance pay, executives are commonly required to agree not to disclose the terms of the severance agreement and the employer's business secrets. Loyalty commitments and agreements on a press release announcing the resignation are standard practice.

Statutory Restrictions on Dismissal Without Cause

If the criteria for an employment relationship are met, the employer is required to comply with the mandatory provisions of the Employment Contracts Act in cases where the employment contracts of people in executive positions are terminated. According to this law, there must be a justified and weighty reason for termination. See "Carrying Out a Workforce Reduction" in Section II.

If the criteria for an employment relationship are met, an employer that has terminated an employment contract without due cause will be ordered to pay exclusive compensation for unjustified termination equivalent to pay for at least three months and not more than 24 months. Employees whose employment has been terminated without due cause are not entitled to reinstatement.

SECTION V

What prohibitions exist against discrimination on the basis of age, race, gender, disability, pregnancy, and other factors? What are the rights of employees, applicants, or former employees who believe that they have been discriminated against?

Areas of Protection

The Employment Contracts Act, the Nondiscrimination Act (21/2004), and the Equality Act (609/1986) contain provisions against discrimination in working life. The general obligation laid down in the Employment Contracts Act states that employers must not, without due cause, treat employees differently based on their age, health, disability, national or ethnic origin, nationality, sexual orientation, language, religion, opinion, family relations, trade union activity, political activity, or other similar reason. The law also states that less favorable terms of employment must not be applied to fixed-term or part-time employment contracts than to other contracts, unless there are justified grounds for doing so.

The purpose of the Nondiscrimination Act is to foster and safeguard equality. According to the Act, no one may be discriminated against on the basis of age, ethnic or national origin, nationality, language, religion, opinion, health, disability, sexual orientation, or any other reason related to the person in question. The Act covers recruitment efforts, working conditions, terms of employment, career moves, and training. Furthermore, its scope of application includes membership and activity in employee organizations.

The objective of the Equality Act is to prevent discrimination based on gender, to promote equality between men and women, and to improve the position of women, particularly in working life. The Act contains a special provision on working life, which prohibits discrimination based on gender in recruitment, working conditions, payment, and other terms of employment. Gender-based discrimination is also prohibited in the context of the termination of employment, layoffs, or reassignment of employees. Harassment and victimization targeted at an employee who has exercised his or her rights constitute discrimination. According to the law, each employee must systematically promote gender equality.

Statutory Rules

The Nondiscrimination Act contains a specific provision regarding burden of proof. This provision states that supportive evidence presented by a person who considers himself or herself a victim of illegal treatment constitutes a presumption of discrimination. To disprove this presumption, the employer must show that the nondiscrimination clause has not been violated. The Equality Act contains a similar provision regarding burden of proof.

Legal Effect of Nondiscrimination Policies

By enforcing equality guidelines, the employer can show that it has taken measures to prevent discrimination. But this does not remove liability, since the actual circumstances in each case are decisive.

Venue and Procedure

Compensation under the Nondiscrimination Act and Equality Act may be claimed in a suit filed in the district court located in the employer's domicile. Court proceedings will follow the course of procedure followed in civil cases. The period for filing a suit under the Nondiscrimination Act is determined on the basis of the nature of the case. In case of infringement of the Act, the suit must be filed within two years from the infringement. If the infringement has been continuous, the suit must be filed within two years of its cessation. In cases relating to employee recruitment, however, action must be instituted within one year of the date on which the jobseeker who claims discrimination receives notification of the recruitment decision.

The Equality Act also recognizes special periods for filing a suit. In recruitment-related cases, the suit must be filed with the court within a year from the violation of the nondiscrimination clause. In other cases, the suit must be filed within two years of the violation of the nondiscrimination clause.

Sanctions

An employer that fails to comply with the Nondiscrimination Act may be ordered to pay compensation to the injured party. Maximum compensation is €15,000. When determining the amount of the compensation, matters to be considered include the type, extent, and duration of the discrimination; the attitude of the party guilty of violating the nondiscrimination and nonvictimization provisions; and the settlement that the parties involved have been able to reach.

An employer that has violated the prohibition of discrimination laid down in the Equality Act will be required to pay at least €3,000 in compensation to the injured party. The amount of compensation must be confirmed in individual cases, depending on the type of violation. When determining the compensation, matters to be considered include the type, extent, and duration of the discrimination. Compensation must be paid irrespective of whether or not the discrimination harms the job applicant or employee.

SECTION VI

On the Horizon: What key labor and employment law developments should an employer doing business in Finland anticipate occurring in the coming years?

There are currently no major developments or expected changes of law.

CHAPTER 5

LABOR AND EMPLOYMENT LAW
IN FRANCE

SALLI A. SWARTZ

Preliminary remarks: French labor law has been changing more rapidly in the last year than it has in the last 20 years. As this chapter goes to print, pursuant to an Agreement entered into by the majority of the French labor unions in January 2008, modifications to the Labor Code are encompassed in a bill that, if adopted as drafted, will significantly alter the nature of employment agreements and their termination in France. This new approach has been called "flexicurity" and is based on the Danish model. The goal is to make the labor market more flexible while guaranteeing a minimum level of security for employees.

The Agreement provides for a new type of fixed-term employment agreement, new trial period requirements, a new method of terminating employment agreements, and several other innovations that are detailed in this chapter. Because the legislation is not enacted and the Agreement signed by the majority of the labor unions may be modified by Parliament, readers are encouraged to verify the exact state of the legislation before giving any specific advice to clients.

Before discussing the specifics of the current status of French labor law, it may be helpful to summarize its applicability to foreign nationals and to foreign companies doing business in France.

Although there are a few exceptions, the general principle is that employees who are employed by a French entity and who perform their duties in France will be subject to and will benefit from the provisions of French labor law. Employees who are employed by a foreign company but who perform their duties in France may also be subject to certain provisions of French labor law, in particular those provisions that are "public order provisions," depending upon other elements of their particular situation such as where they are paid and in which country they contribute to obligatory social security regimes.

In addition to the provisions of the French Labor Code, the terms of the national collective bargaining agreements that are applicable to the activity of the company concerned will apply. To the extent they are more favorable to the employee, they will supersede the provisions of the French Labor Code. Likewise, the terms of the employee's employment agreement, if more favorable to the employee than the Labor Code and the applicable national collective bargaining agreement, will supersede the provisions of the Labor Code and the national collective bargaining agreement.

National collective bargaining agreements will apply to newly formed companies if such companies are in a sector that has a collective bargaining agreement. If a company is not in a sector that has a collective bargaining agreement, the company can choose to apply the terms of a national collective bargaining agreement applicable to a sector that is similar to the activity of the newly formed company. A newly formed company that fails to adhere to any collective bargaining agreement may have difficulty recruiting, as new hires will want to benefit from the generally more favorable terms of a collective bargaining agreement.

SECTION I

My client wishes to establish a manufacturing facility in France and will need to hire a workforce. What are the key legal issues involved?

Employing Non-French Citizens

Residency and Working Papers

All non–European Union citizens must obtain the proper residency and working papers in order to live and work in France. This process can take several months and must be started from the country of domicile of the employee and the parent company.

Citizens of the 10 most recent members of the European Union must obtain work permits during a period of transition that is set forth in each country's treaty of admission. The maximum length of the transitional period is seven years.

The French require non–European Union citizens to obtain a visa to enter France in order to file the paperwork requesting a residency permit (*carte de séjour*) with the right to work (*permis de travail*). The paperwork is filed with the French embassy or consulate closest to the parent company's offices. It is illegal to enter France with the intention of working and residing without first filing a request for and obtaining the necessary residency and working papers.

Spouses who accompany expatriated employees will receive a residency permit but will not be granted the right to work in France, unless they have individually applied and can justify a valid job offer from a company established in France (or from a foreign company that wants to promote its business or do a market study for its products in France). Minor children will be given residency permits.

A non-EU national hired to hold the office of president or manager of a French company may be appointed without having to obtain a commercial card if such person is a national of a country that is a member of the Organization for Economic Cooperation and Development (OECD) and will neither reside nor work in France. However, if the person intends to work and reside in France, he or she will have to obtain the necessary residency and working papers.

Social Security Contributions

Many countries have entered into bilateral treaties with France providing that the employee need not contribute to part of the French social security regimes if the employee is contributing to them in his or her home country. However, in order to qualify for this exception, documents are always required and in the case of the United States, the proper form can be obtained from the United States Social Security Office upon justification of the request. Most of the double-taxation treaties allow this exception for a nonrenewable five-year period. If the employee stays in France after the expiration of the five-year exception period, the employer and employee must contribute to all of the obligatory social security regimes.

Taxes

If the employee is tax-domiciled in France (living in the country for more than 183 days per calendar year or has family ties to France, that is, if the employee's spouse and children are living with him or her in France), the French authorities could consider that the employee is a French resident for tax purposes and that person will have to file and pay taxes in France. If the employee is also a U.S. citizen, or a green card holder, that person should also file in the United States, but will receive a tax credit for taxes paid in France. Most countries have concluded bilateral tax treaties with France to avoid or diminish double taxation. Moreover, French citizens and permanent residents may be subject to the wealth tax if the person concerned has more than €770,000 in net assets in France.

Expatriate Employment Agreements

To the extent the employee will be managing or working for a French legal entity and living in France, certain provisions of French labor law will apply irrespective of whether the person has a French employment agreement, a U.S. or U.K. employment agreement, or no employment agreement at all. This means that the employee may request and should obtain the same type of benefits as if he or she was employed by a French company. These benefits will prevail over anything to the contrary written in any employment agreement concluded by the parent company and the employee. Such benefits include the paid vacation, maternity and paternity leave, dismissal procedures, and compensation or severance payable to dismissed employees as described hereunder, to name a few.

Some benefits may be waived, but those that are considered to be of public order cannot be waived. These include, but are not limited to, protection against dismissal for pregnant women and maternity leave.

Thus it would be wise, in order to avoid any future disputes when expatriating an employee, to suspend his or her current employment agreement and negotiate and conclude an employment agreement that will be applicable to the employee when employed in France. Countless lawsuits and bitter "divorces" will be avoided if this issue is resolved before the employee is expatriated.

The other issues that should be taken into consideration are home leave, relocation and moving expenses, tax issues, school expenses, and a housing allowance, to name a few.

Employment Contracts: Who Receives Them and What Must They Include?

French law does not permit "at will" employment, and there are only two types of employment in France: indefinite-term and fixed-term employment. Although offer letters are used, they are not the usual practice, and employment agreements (whether indefinite or fixed term) are almost always signed. If offer letters are used, they must include (usually in an attachment) a full description of the employee's job responsibilities, remuneration, and the other provisions discussed next.

Indefinite-term employment agreements are the norm. As the name suggests, these employment agreements do not have a term or duration. Moreover, they typically include the following provisions, most of which are required either by French labor law or by the provisions of the applicable collective bargaining agreement.

Required Information

Trial Period
The Agreement sets forth specific lengths of time for trial periods that will be applicable unless the individual employment agreement or offer letter provides for shorter periods or unless specific sectorwide agreements have been entered into before the entering into force of the Agreement.

The new trial periods, which must be specifically set forth in the employment agreement, are as follows:

- A maximum of two months for workers and employees.
- A maximum of three months for supervisors and technicians.
- A maximum of four months for executives.

A trial period can be renewed only if a national bargaining agreement so provides, and even when it may be renewed, it may never exceed a maximum duration of four, six or eight months, in each respective case.

The notice to end the trial period must be:

- Forty-eight hours during the first month of employment.
- Two weeks after one month of employment.
- One month after three months of employment.

When the trial period is ended by the employee, he or she should respect a period of notice of 48 hours.

To facilitate access to the labor market for the young, internships taken during the final year of study will reduce the length of the trial period by up to 50 percent.

Job Duties

French employment agreements detail with great specificity the obligations of the employee, although no law or regulation requires this. The reason for this practice is to protect both parties in the case of dismissal or the attempted unilateral modification of the employment agreement by the employer (see "Modifications to the Terms and Provisions" on this page). The Agreement requires that the employment agreement specifically list those employment terms and conditions that can be modified by the employer without the employee's consent. It is therefore advisable to have a complete description of the employee's duties in the employment agreement.

Notice Period for Termination

The employment agreement should provide for the duration of the notice period for termination to be given by either party to terminate the employment agreement. The term of the notice period will usually mirror the trial period, but its term cannot be renewed. Most national collective bargaining agreements provide for the duration of the notice period for termination.

Language

The official version of an employment agreement must be signed by both parties in the French language.

Modifications to the Terms and Provisions

An employer cannot unilaterally make any material modifications to an employee's employment agreement without the employee's prior written agreement to such modifications.

The following elements are usually considered by the case law to be material changes:

- The method and amount of remuneration.
- Changes in the workplace, such as a move to a different place of employment if the employee's commute time is increased significantly or otherwise rendered more difficult.
- Change in the employee's job responsibilities.
- Important modifications in the employee's working schedule.

For modifications that are not specifically listed as modifiable without the employee's consent, the employee must be given written notice of the modification and has 30 days to respond. The notice must clearly set forth the requested modification and all relevant details.

If the employee does not accept the modifications, then the employment agreement is considered to have been terminated by the employer, who must pay the employee all amounts due to such employee such as a termination compensation (if applicable) and accrued vacation pay.

Termination of Indefinite-Term Employment Agreement: Dismissal or Resignation

Only two legal justifications exist to dismiss employees: a real and serious cause (i.e., a professional reason concerning the employee) or an economic reason. Economic reasons must be proved through financial and other accounting evidence. If the employer wishes to dismiss one or more employees for real and serious cause, the employer will have to follow a highly regulated procedure and be in a position to prove the cause (fault, negligence, disagreement with strategy, to name a few). The procedure, whether for economic or personal reasons, provides for notice, a predismissal meeting, and a reasoned and detailed dismissal letter.

In addition to the reasons of the dismissal, the dismissal letter must also state whether or not the employee is expected to work during the notice period. If the employee is not required to work during the notice period, the employer nevertheless has the obligation to pay the employee's salary during such period. Moreover, if the employee has a noncompetition obligation and the employer does not require the employee to respect this obligation, the employer should take great care in waiving such obligation in a timely manner, which is usually in the dismissal letter, unless stipulated otherwise in the employment agreement. Failure to release the employee from the noncompete period will result in the employer being obligated to pay to the employee compensation during the noncompete period.

A failure to justify adequate reasons for dismissing an employee or a failure to respect the proper procedure and requisite time periods could cause the labor courts to hold that the dismissal was not lawful, in which case the employer will be ordered to pay damages to the employee in addition to whatever other amounts may be owed to the employee, such as salary during the notice period, severance pay as required by law or the national collective bargaining agreement, and accrued vacation days. The amount of damages will depend upon the seniority of the employee and can amount to several years of salary for those who have been employed for many years. If the employee has at least two years of seniority, the minimum payable in the event of nonrespect of the procedure is six months' salary.

At the end of the employment agreement, the employee is entitled to receive all final amounts due including all accrued vacation pay, severance pay, and the like. The sums due are detailed in a document entitled "Final Accounting" (*Reçu pour solde de tout compte*). The employee has six months to contest the final accounting, after which time it is binding on both the employer and employee and cannot be contested.

Employees rarely resign in France because if they do so, they are not entitled to unemployment benefits. The amount and duration of unemployment benefits vary and will depend on the current legislation, which is in the process of being modified. Moreover, union representatives and members of the work council or the personnel representatives cannot be dismissed without the Labor Inspector's authorization. And, as stated above, employees cannot be dismissed during pregnancy or maternity leave.

The procedure for layoffs is discussed in Section II under "Carrying Out a Workforce Reduction."

New Method for Terminating the Employment Agreement: Amicable, Negotiated Termination

The Agreement has created a new manner to terminate the employment relationship: by common agreement. It would appear that this new type of termination does not apply to dismissals for economic reasons, nor does it eliminate the possibility of negotiated settlement agreements after dismissal if the dismissal is contested by the employee.

During the preliminary discussions between the employee and the employer concerning the possibility of mutually agreeing upon the conditions of the termination of the employment agreement, the employee has the option of being assisted by a person of his or her choice employed by the company, or by an independent advisor, such as an attorney or a union representative. If the employee is assisted by a third person, the employer may also have an advisor present during the negotiations.

If an amicable agreement is reached and a termination agreement signed, the employee has the right to retract his or her agreement during a period of 15 calendar days following the date of the signature of the termination agreement.

One copy of the termination agreement must be sent to the Director of the Department of Labor Inspection at the expiration of the retraction period. The Director has 15 calendar days to approve or reject the termination agreement. Approval is tacit if the Director does not respond within the 15-day deadline.

Employees whose employment agreements are terminated amicably pursuant to a termination agreement are entitled to unemployment benefits and to a special indemnity of a minimum of one-fifth of one month's salary per year of seniority, except in those cases where more favorable conditions in the employment agreement or in the relevant collective bargaining agreement apply. This indemnity is due after one year of seniority and is not subject to social security contributions and income tax.

Except in case of gross misconduct, employees who lose their jobs are entitled to continue to benefit from the health care insurance that they received from their former employer during the period that they are unemployed up to a maximum period of one-third of the period of time during which they are entitled to unemployment benefits. This period, however, may never be less than three months.

The Agreement also provides that the right to professional training that the employee accrued during his or her employment is transferable to his or her new employer, provided the latter accepts.

Fixed-Term Employment Agreements

Fixed-term employment is highly regulated in France and it can only be used temporarily and for certain reasons that are defined by legislation. Such reasons are currently the following:

- To replace an employee who is out of work (for example, to replace someone who is on maternity, sick, or vacation leave);

- To replace an employee who has been dismissed due to the elimination of his or her job, pending the elimination of the job itself, that is, during company reorganizations;
- To replace an employee who has resigned pending the arrival of a new employee who has been hired pursuant to an indefinite-term agreement;
- To perform habitual seasonal work, such as agricultural harvesting work (for example, as the harvesting of grapes in the autumn) or tourist activities;
- To effectuate a specific mission, such as a financial audit;
- To supplement the workforce during a temporary increase in activity.

Fixed-term employment agreements may also be concluded when the company's main activity is, by nature, temporary, such as jobs relating to theatrical or musical performances; certain teaching, educational, or cultural activities, such as the biannual couture fashion shows; or construction work.

When such agreements are justified, their duration must be indicated in the employment agreement and such durations are restricted as follows:

- The maximum duration is 24 months when the purpose of the employment agreement is to transfer an employee abroad, or when an employee has resigned and the job will be eliminated or to assure an exceptional export order.
- The maximum duration is 18 months when the purpose of the employment agreement is to accomplish a specific and temporary task.
- The maximum duration is nine months when the purpose of the employment agreement is to replace an employee who has left when his or her replacement (hired under an indefinite-term employment agreement) has not yet arrived, or to accomplish urgent work to assure the security of the workplace.
- The maximum duration is three months when the purpose of the employment agreement is to supplement the workforce during a temporary increase in activity.

Aside from the duration of the employment agreement itself, the only other differences between a fixed-term and indefinite-term employment agreements are as follows:

- Upon the expiration of the term of the employment agreement, the employer must pay an indemnity to the employee. The amount of such indemnity is currently 10 percent of the total gross amount of remuneration paid to the employee for the duration of his or her employment. This amount is subject to social security contributions by both the employer and the employee.
- Unless the parties agree otherwise, the employment agreement may not be terminated by either party during its term unless the employer can prove the gross negligence of the employee or if a case of force majeure arises.

All of the other provisions relating to social security contributions, vacation, working hours, and other benefits as described above also apply to fixed-term employment agreements.

In addition to the above types of definite-term employment agreement, the Agreement creates a new fixed-term employment agreement for executives and engineers, which, if adopted, will be introduced on an experimental basis. This new type of employment agreement must have a minimum term of 18 months and a maximum term of 36 months and it must have a specific purpose, such as a specific project or mission. The Agreement does not provide for this type of employment agreement to have a trial period. It cannot be renewed, but the employer can (and it is hoped that it will) propose to the employee an indefinite-term employment agreement at the expiration of the term of this special type of employment agreement.

The employment agreement may be terminated at each annual anniversary date, but only for a real and serious reason. In such a case, the employer must pay to the employee an amount equal to 10 percent of the employee's gross salary. This payment is not subject to social security contributions by the employee or the employer. The employer is obligated to notify the employee two months before the term of the employment agreement if the employer does not intend to offer the employee an indefinite-term employment agreement.

Wages and Benefits

The employment agreement should state the annual gross remuneration of the employee and specify that it is payable in monthly installments. French companies pay salaries on a monthly, not weekly, basis. Although the law is silent on this issue, most collective bargaining agreements provide for employees to be paid on a 13th-month basis, meaning that the gross annual remuneration is paid in 13 equal installments. The 12th and 13th months are usually paid together at the end of December of each year. Before offering anyone employment in France, this point should be verified. In no event should the salary be expressed in monthly terms, since this could cause problems when discussing the 13th-month remuneration issue.

There are minimum hourly and monthly wages defined by law and modified from time to time by the government. Moreover, the national collective bargaining agreements define the minimum hourly and monthly wages for each category of employees: workers, technicians, and executives. These minimums are negotiated annually by the national labor unions. Employers must pay employees the relevant minimums.

In July of 2007, the government enacted a new law to encourage economic growth. This law entered into force in February 2008 and permits employees to waive all or part of their vacation days that have been accrued due to the reduction in the work week, or additional vacation days accrued to overtime worked, in exchange for an increase in salary which cannot be less than 10 percent. Other additional benefits are provided by law but they are optional. They include the release of a maximum of €10,000 invested by the employee in company investment or profit participation plans, which funds are otherwise not available due to vesting rules, and the payment of a one-time bonus of €1,000 by the employer to the employee for companies that do not have profit participation plans. Most of these benefits are valid only for the years 2008 and 2009. Consequently, before implementing any of them, readers are advised to consult local counsel to assure that the benefits are still valid and applicable.

Commissions and Bonuses

If commissions are an integral part of the employee's salary, their method of calculation, accrual, and payment should be specifically detailed in the employment agreement in order to avoid any misunderstandings. For employees who are remunerated partially on the basis of sales of products or services, issues such as whether commissions are due to the employee when the sale is made or when the monies are actually received by the employer and what happens to commissions payable on sales made before the employee leaves the company but that the employer receives after the employee has left the company need to be addressed.

The basic salary of an employee and the method of calculating commissions cannot be modified by the employer unilaterally without the agreement of the employee, even if the result is that the employee's remuneration may be increased. The employee must agree to the modification; otherwise, the French courts could hold that there has been a substantial and material modification of the employment terms that has not been agreed upon by the employee and qualify the modification as an act of constructive dismissal of the employee at the employer's cost, with all of the resulting financial consequences.

Bonuses, if provided in the employment agreement or if granted to the employee on a regular annual basis for several years, will be considered by the French courts to be an integral part of the employee's remuneration and therefore due to the employee. When considered to be part of the salary, bonuses are deemed to be acquired advantages and cannot be eliminated by the employer unilaterally. Thus, when drafting bonus clauses, it should be made very clear that the employer may grant these on a fully optional basis.

Social Security and Other Withholdings

The employer is obligated to withhold and then pay to the appropriate French administrative entities obligatory French social security and other contributions. The amounts of such withholdings will vary depending upon the salary and level of the employee, but generally range from 15 percent to 28 percent of the employee's gross salary. The contributions cover health care, unemployment, and retirement benefits.

In addition to the amounts withheld from the employee's salary, the employer is also obligated to contribute to social security regimes. The employer's contribution will depend upon the level of the employee's job, but as a general rule, the obligatory employer contributory regimes amount to approximately 48 percent to 52 percent of the employee's gross remuneration.

Working Week and Vacations

The official French working week has been fixed by law at 35 hours. This legislation requires the payment of overtime or compensatory time off unless the employment agreement specifically provides otherwise. Top-level executive employees can be excluded entirely from the 35-hour-work-week legislation, but this requires careful wording in the employment agreement (as well as the employee's agreement thereto). Before attempting to draft any exclusion to the 35-hour-work-week legislation, an employer should obtain legal advice as the legislation is complex and noncompliance can be more expensive than the cost of legal advice.

French law grants all employees a minimum of five weeks' paid vacation per year or 30 days (jours ouvrables), which are defined as Monday through Saturday. In addition, employees in companies that negotiated a reduction in the workweek from 39 to 35 hours may have several additional weeks' vacation. Furthermore, employees are entitled to 11 official legal holidays, including New Year's Day, Labor Day (May 1), V-E Day (May 8), All Saints Day (November 1), Armistice Day (November 11), and Christmas Day (December 25). The government often declares other holidays, such as the Catholic holiday of Pentecost.

Additional Health Insurance

Although not obligatory, most companies will offer a group plan for additional health insurance to increase the amounts reimbursed to the employee under the general governmental social security plan. The cost of the additional insurance is shared by the employee and employer, and the employee's share is withheld from his or her monthly salary.

The type of plan and its cost should be mentioned in the employment agreement.

Transportation

For companies that are located in the greater Parisian region (Ile de France), the employer must share the cost of a monthly public transportation ticket equally with the employee. The employee's share is deducted from his or her monthly salary. This may be mentioned in the employment agreement for purposes of clarity, but as a general rule, since it is obligatory, most French employment agreements do not mention it.

Meals

For companies that employ more than 25 employees who habitually eat their meals on the premises, the employer must either make cooking facilities and a place to eat available to the employees (such as a company-run cafeteria, or kitchen with microwave, sink, utensils, etc.) or the employer must share in the cost of meal tickets that the employer will purchase and then remit to the employee, usually on a monthly basis. The employee's share of the meal tickets is deducted from his or her salary.

Expenses

If the employee will be reimbursed for expenses incurred while carrying out his or her functions, the employment agreement should specify what type of expenses will be reimbursed, the documentary proof of expenses that will be required to obtain reimbursement, and the method of reimbursement (e.g., monthly by check, quarterly by bank transfer).

Automobile

If a company car is put at the disposition of the employee, the employment agreement will need to specify what expenses will be paid by the employer (insurance and maintenance, for example), what expenses will be shared (gasoline for personal use, for example), and what expenses, if any, will be borne solely by the employee. If the personal use of the car by the employee is authorized, the details of such use should be detailed in the employment agreement (use on vacations, for example).

Housing

If a housing allowance is included in the employee's compensation package, the amount of the allowance should be specified. Moreover, the employment agreement should also detail which party will pay for telephone and utilities.

Taxation of Advantages in Kind

It should be noted that when an advantage in kind is granted to an employee, such as the use of a company car or company-paid housing, social security contributions are payable on the monetary value of the advantages and the employee's salary is grossed up to include the monetary value of such in-kind advantages for tax purposes. When the benefit is monetary, such as a cash payment for housing or an education allowance, such amounts will be subject to social security contributions and taxed as part of the employee's compensation package. Whether in kind or monetary in nature, the advantage will be indicated on the employee's pay slip.

Labor Unions

All of the national labor unions may organize union chapters within companies to assure the representation of the interests and well-being of its members.

Each union is allowed only one chapter per enterprise or establishment. The law does not subject the creation of a company union chapter to any kind of particular procedure. The unions collect contributions and display information and leaflets in the company. The company must put at their disposal a place in the company where they can meet during the employees' working hours.

Collective Agreements

Collective bargaining agreements are negotiated between employers and labor unions per sector of activity at the national level. Such agreements generally provide for employee benefits that exceed the legal minimums with regard to dismissal indemnities, retirement benefits, consideration for noncompetition obligations, working hours, additional medical benefits, and the like. Collective bargaining agreements are negotiated frequently and there are often amendments that apply to certain categories of employees, depending upon the scope of the negotiations.

Works Councils

The election of personnel representatives (*Représentants du Personnel*) is obligatory for establishments employing at least 11 employees. In establishments that have fewer than 11 employees, the employer and employees can decide to institute personnel representatives.

Works councils (*Comités d'Entreprise*) are obligatory for companies that employ more than 50 employees and are formed by elections of the employees, which are generally organized by the union representatives in each company with the employer. As is the case with personnel representatives, companies that employ fewer than 50 employees can agree to establish works councils pursuant to a collective agreement.

The powers of the works council are large. It has either decisional or consultative authority with regard to all matters that affect the organization of the company, including internal regulations, reorganizations, sales of assets and shares, mergers, collective dismissals for economic reasons, health and safety regulations and issues, working hours, the introduction of new technology, and all other matters that could affect the remuneration, health, safety, and working conditions of the employees. The president of the company is the president of the works council and presides over the meetings of the works council. Minutes of the meetings of the works council must be signed by the works council representatives and the employer representative and are displayed in the company. In certain instances, such as works council meetings to deliberate on collective dismissals, the minutes must be filed with the Labor Department.

Large companies that have offices in several countries in the European Union can establish European-wide works councils.

Disputes

All employee-employer disputes are heard by the Labor Courts (*Conseil de Prud'homme*). Such labor courts comprise elected representatives of the employees and the employers; the judges are not professionally trained, although the persons elected to serve do take part in professional training for such purpose. Decisions may be appealed to the Appellate Courts and to the Supreme Court (*Cour de Cassation*).

The first step in any litigation is the filing of a summons, which is done by the plaintiff on forms available at the court. Although plaintiffs and defendants may represent themselves in court, usually the parties are represented by attorneys. Employees are sometimes represented by union representatives.

The first hearing is a conciliation hearing during which the judges attempt to get the parties to settle. Normally the employer must be present in person, although recent practice has permitted the employer to be represented by its attorney, who must have a power of attorney explaining why the employer cannot be present. The Agreement has reinforced the presence requirement in order to reinforce the conciliation function of the judges.

The parties then exchange pleadings and evidence, which can take 12 to 18 months depending upon the deadlines fixed by the judges and the delays requested by the parties. There is one final hearing and the judgment is rendered several months thereafter depending upon the court backlog.

SECTION II

My client is acquiring an existing business in France. How do I assess the existing workforce and consider changes?

Unless otherwise indicated, the laws and regulations discussed in this section apply to both share and asset sales.

Due Diligence

During asset or share acquisitions, the purchaser will conduct due diligence, which should include a review of the employment agreements, salaries, and benefits granted to employees by the company, including those that are granted by employment agreement, by the national collective bargaining agreement, and by the internal regulations of the company.

Where personally identifiable data is collected (such as name, age, and salary), it is subject to strict regulations concerning its use. Such data may not be retained or distributed unless the French data protection agency (*Conseil National d'Informatique et Libertés*, or CNIL) has agreed to such dissemination. Normally, due diligence and the ensuing report should not violate French data protection rules, but when doing due diligence, companies and their counsel should be particularly attentive to this potential problem and not collect or disseminate personal data without verifying the validity of the dissemination.

A word about diversity: Most American companies seek to have a workforce that is diverse in terms of gender, race, age, religion, and other criteria. When acquiring businesses and companies in France, such American companies may attempt to obtain information on the diversity standards of the target company. Since French data protection laws prohibit the collection of data pertaining to race, religion, and other diversity criteria, such information will not exist. Attempting to obtain such information could violate French data protection regulations, unless the CNIL has been informed of the manner in which such data will be collected, retained, and used and has approved of the procedures.

Consultations Before the Acquisition or Sale

Under French law, whenever an acquisition or a sale of a major part or all of the assets or shares of a French company is planned, management of that company (or both companies if both companies are French) must consult and inform the labor representatives of the French company. In companies having more than 50 employees, the organ that must be consulted is the work council. The unions are represented through the members of the works council and need not be consulted separately. In companies that do not have a works council, the personnel representatives must be consulted.

The consultation process involves a minimum of two separate meetings. The purpose of the first consultation with the works council is to present and explain the envisaged acquisition or sale. The purpose of the second consultation with the works council is to detail the transfer and explain any effect it may have on employment. If the effect on employment will result in dismissals, management must draft a social plan for approval by the works council.

Although the consultations with the works council or the personnel representatives cannot prevent the acquisition or sale from occurring, the consultation procedure can slow down the operation and there may be calls for strikes.

Carrying Out a Workforce Reduction

With regard to asset acquisitions, under both European and French law, all employees employed by a part of a division or business that is acquired are automatically transferred to the acquiring company. Thus, unless the seller undertakes to reduce its workforce before the date of the acquisition, all of its employees will automatically become employees of the acquiring company upon the effective date of the acquisition or sale. If the acquiring company is located in a European Union country, the above will apply to both the selling and acquiring entity. In share transfers, since only the identities of the shareholders change, the status of the employees remains the same.

The reduction of the workforce is not simple, as an employer cannot easily dismiss employees in France. The requirements set forth below apply to all employees, including management-level employees and board directors who are also employees, but not to presidents, managers, or board directors who are not employees of the company.

In workforce reductions following an acquisition or sale, the usual justification is economic reasons since it is difficult to justify the dismissal of more than a few employees for professional reasons. Under French law, dismissals for economic reasons may be justified only if the employer can prove one or several of the following: financial difficulties, changes in technology that result in a reduction in the workforce and that are necessary to preserve the competitive nature of the company, and the restructuring of the company in order to maintain its competitive nature.

The precise dismissal procedures to be followed will vary depending on the number of dismissals to be made within any 30-day period as well as on the total number of employees employed by the employer. The procedure to dismiss fewer than 10 employees over less than 30 days in a company that employs fewer than 50 employees and that does not have any personnel or union representatives is less complex than the procedure to dismiss more than 10 employees in 30 days or more in a company that employs more than 50 employees.

To take the most complex example, in a company that employs more than 50 employees (and thus has a works council) and that wants to reduce its workforce by more than 10 employees over a period of 30 days, the following procedure must be followed (failing which the dismissals could be declared illegal by the courts):

First Meeting of the Works Council

Management must convene a meeting of the works council and present to the works council the draft social plan that covers the issues set forth above. The purpose of the first meeting is for management to explain the draft social plan and to answer questions. During this meeting, the members of the works council may object to all or certain parts of the draft social plan and may make a number of suggestions and requests to management, such as the addition of elements to the package that is being offered (for example, the payment of moving expenses if the employee finds a job in another region).

Companies that wish to dismiss more than 10 employees over a 30-day period and companies that have works councils must prepare a social plan. It must include the following:

- Justification for the reasons for the dismissals (i.e., technological, economic, financial, structural). If the reason is economic/financial, the company will have to produce proof of the financials and why the dismissals are the only solution.
- The number of dismissals envisioned and the types of positions concerned by the dismissals.
- The criteria for choosing which employees will be dismissed.
- The proposed timing of the dismissals.
- The possibility of reducing the number of hours worked in order to preserve employment in the event the company has not already complied with the regulations concerning the 35-hour work week.
- The efforts that have been and will be made to find jobs for the employees to be dismissed, including the possibilities of employment within the company's corporate group, if applicable, as well as the provision of outplacement opportunities.
- The financial package(s) offered to the employees.

The criteria for the choice of who will be dismissed must be objective so as to avoid the employer making "arbitrary" choices, although one of the criteria may be job performance. Usually, the criteria chosen are seniority with the company, age, number of family members who are supported by the employee, and type of job (for example, if people in a certain job category are being replaced by machines, or if an entire department or branch of the company is being eliminated). The employer may choose the criteria that will apply and may apply them in any order.

The works council has the right to appoint an independent expert (who is usually an accountant or a financial expert) to assist it in evaluating the economic or financial reasons for the suggested dismissals. The employer is responsible for the payment of the expert's fees and may not object to the appointment of such an expert. Moreover, the employer must make available to the expert the same documents that it must make available to the statutory auditor. The expert may visit the premises and interview employees.

The draft social plan must also be remitted to the Labor Inspector, who is responsible for ensuring that the proper procedure is being followed and that the draft social plan is a responsible one in light of job preservation and avoidance of unemployment in the geographic region for which he or she is responsible.

Minutes of all of the meetings of the works councils are drafted and signed by the representatives of the works council and management. The minutes should reflect the discussions that occurred and should note any suggestions and objections raised by the works council.

Expert Report and Second Meeting of the Works Council

If no expert has been appointed, the second meeting of the works council must take place within 15 days (unless agreed otherwise) after the date of the first meeting if fewer than 100 people are to be dismissed, 21 days if 100 to 250 people are to be dismissed, and 28 days if more than 250 people are to be dismissed. If an expert is appointed (which is generally the case), instead of two obligatory meetings of the works council, there will be three. The expert will have between 15 and 21 days from the date of the first meeting of the works council to remit his or her report. This report must be distributed to the members of the works council and to the management at least eight days before the second meeting of the works council.

Management must make available to the expert the same financial documents as those that are available to the statutory auditors.

The Second or Third Meeting

During the second meeting if no expert has been appointed, or the third meeting if one has been appointed, management and the works council are supposed to agree on the content of the finalized social plan, including the amount and scope of the package(s) offered, the efforts that will be made to find jobs for the dismissed employees, the criteria by which the employees will be chosen, and the timing of the dismissals.

The works council must agree to the definitive social plan in the written minutes of the final meeting of the works council convened for such purpose. If management and the works council do not agree, the minutes should reflect the works council's objections to the draft social plan and its suggestions. Further meetings may be convened and held in order to continue the negotiations.

Moreover, the Labor Inspector, with whom the minutes of each meeting must be filed, may intervene and make suggestions in order to get the parties to agree.

If no agreement is reached and the draft social plan is not approved, management may not proceed with the dismissals legally. No dismissals may occur before the social plan is finalized and approved by the works council. If dismissals do occur before the social plan is approved, the employees can usually obtain a court order reinstating them.

If and when the social plan is approved by the works council, it must be filed in its finalized and approved form with the Labor Inspector and the Departmental Labor Administration. The social plan is then binding on the employer and the employees may no longer object to its being put into place.

Establishing Uniform Benefits for the French Legal Entity

The major issue in acquisition (aside from dismissals rendered necessary following the reorganization of the workforce) is the harmonization of employee benefits.

If the benefits afforded by the acquired company are more favorable than those granted to the employees of the acquiring company, there will be a problem because the acquired company's advantages cannot be reduced or eliminated without the employees' agreement. It is irrelevant whether the acquired advantages are granted by a national collective bargaining agreement or by virtue of contractual provisions.

This situation will undoubtedly come up during the obligatory consultations with the works councils of the two companies (provided they are both in the European Union) and should be addressed at that time. The financial factor should be considered when an acquisition is being considered.

When the employees of the acquired company have less favorable benefits than the employees of the acquiring company, provided that both companies are in the European Union, then the employees of the acquired company will automatically benefit from the advantages granted by the acquiring company to its employees.

The only way to minimize the generalization of the most advantageous benefits to all employees (i.e., those of both the acquired and acquiring companies) is to negotiate with the employees through the works council or the personnel representatives. Such negotiations may take place either before or after the acquisition, but, as stated above, it is more than likely that they will occur during the obligatory preacquisition consultations with the works council or the personnel representatives.

Establishing Benefits That Are Uniform with the Parent Company

There is no prohibition against granting employees of a French legal entity the same benefits as those enjoyed by the employees of the parent company. However, in light of the obligatory nature of many benefits that must be granted to employees of a French legal entity and the difficulty of eliminating advantages that are enjoyed by employees of a French company, management of the parent company should take great care when examining the issue of benefit grants.

For example, stock option plans are treated very differently by the French tax and social security authorities than they are in the United States. Without getting into all of the details of the differences, it should be noted that as a general matter, most U.S. companies that acquire a French entity need to create a separate French stock option plan or subplan in order to comply with a certain number of French requirements, such as vesting periods. Moreover, the tax treatment of stock options under current French tax law makes such plans less of an incentive for hiring and retaining key employees than U.S. plans do. Although this may change, U.S. management should not assume that the creation of a stock option plan for French employees will be an important incentive for France-based employees, although there may be certain individual situations when French stock options could make sense.

Internal regulations and policies of the U.S. company, such as ethics reporting, hotlines to report violations of company policy or law, drug testing, privacy of e-mail, and the like, as well as legal regulations, such as the Foreign Corrupt Practices Act, the Equal Employment Opportunity Act, and other regulations that may apply to employees of a foreign-based subsidiary of a U.S. company, may not be capable of direct "as is" application to employees of a French subsidiary.

The first problem with attempting to apply a U.S. company's policies to a French entity is that a unilateral modification, if significant, of an employee's contractual terms after the employment agreement is signed may be lawfully rejected by the employee. Thus, the introduction of constraints such as obligatory drug testing after the employment agreement is concluded could result in the constructive dismissal, at the employer's cost, of an employee who refuses to accept the modification. Another common problematic area is the treatment of whistle-blowers. Under French data privacy regulations, whistle-blower protection is highly regulated and cannot usually be introduced without consultations with the works council and with the CNIL. However, the CNIL has unofficially stated that whistle-blowing provisions of the Sarbanes-Oxley law may be acceptable.

The second problem is that some internal policies are not required because they are already provided by French law. This would be the case, for example, for sexual or psychological harassment and racial or gender discrimination, which are prohibited by French law.

Thus, French counsel cannot simply translate internal policies or regulations in an attempt to have them apply prima facie to employees of French subsidiaries of U.S. companies.

To avoid these issues, it is advisable to have the texts of internal policies and regulations reviewed by French counsel in order to ascertain which parts of them may be applied to employees in France and the most effective legal manner to render them applicable to such employees. It is always better to examine this issue before any employees are hired so that such internal policies and regulations can be adapted to French law and attached to the French employment agreements.

Retaining Key Employees

When acquiring a company in France, it may be important to assure that key employees remain with the company. The contractual documents for the acquisition can provide for the preclosing condition of such employees being employed by the acquired company at the time of closing. If the key employees are also shareholders, the purchase agreement can and often does provide for payment to the selling shareholder/employee being made over a period of time to ensure that the selling shareholder/employee does not leave the company before the agreed period expires.

Although it is somewhat unusual to grant special benefits to retain key employees, this sometimes occurs when incoming management want key employees to stay for a set period of time and then leave the company, in which case the parties concerned usually arrange to enter into a negotiated termination agreement. However, such negotiated termination agreements pose a number of problems, the most important of which is that employees who leave their job voluntarily are not eligible for unemployment benefits. Sometimes, the employee must be dismissed and then if the dismissal is contested by the employee, the parties can negotiate and conclude a settlement agreement. However, as discussed earlier, if the provisions of the Agreement concerning negotiated amicable termination of employment agreements are enacted as law, these difficulties will to a large extent be eliminated.

SECTION III

My client wishes to sell its existing facility. What restrictions do we need to consider?

See Section II.

SECTION IV

My client wishes to replace its senior manager(s). What restrictions do we need to consider?

The laws and regulations applicable to the dismissal of senior managers are no different from those applicable to all other employees. Senior managers may be replaced only if the new management has a real and serious cause to dismiss and replace each individual concerned. If such real and serious cause exists and can be proved, then the senior managers may be dismissed, but the dismissal procedures must be followed and the dismissal indemnities and all other payments due to such persons must be paid.

However, it is rare that real and serious cause(s) will justify a total change in management after an acquisition. Usually, the reason is that the new shareholder or parent company wants to install its own management. This reason alone, absent any proof of misconduct on the part of the current managers, will not justify the dismissal and replacement of senior managers. However, senior managers are often open to discussions concerning a negotiated departure. The pitfalls of such agreements were discussed previously.

One way to accomplish a change in senior management would be for the new managers/shareholders to completely reorganize the company, making the jobs currently held by the senior managers redundant. However, such a plan would have to be presented and approved by the works council, which is likely to reject it if it is apparent that the sole motive for the plan is to justify the replacement of certain of the senior managers.

SECTION V

What prohibitions exist against discrimination on the basis of age, race, gender, disability, pregnancy, and other factors? What are the rights of employees, applicants, or former employees who believe that they have been discriminated against?

The French law No. 2002-73, of January 17, 2002, which incorporated several European Directives issued in 1978, 2000, and 2002, prohibits discrimination on the basis of union membership, age, gender, race, religion, nationality, ethnic origin, family situation, health, sexual orientation, physical appearance, disability, moral or political opinions, family name, or pregnancy.

Discrimination on the basis of union membership is punishable by fine and/or imprisonment of up to €3,750 for a first offense and up to €7,500 and one year of imprisonment for repeated offenses (Article L-412-2 of the Labor Code).

Discrimination of any type on the basis of pregnancy is prohibited by Article L-122-25 of the Labor Code, and the Labor Courts can and will award appropriate damages for violations. Such discrimination is also punishable under the penal code by a fine of a maximum of €1,500 and up to €3,000 in the case of repeated violations.

In addition, discrimination in hiring or dismissing on the basis of gender, race, religion, ethnic origin, nationality, family situation, age, handicapped status, morals, or health situation usually results in damages, three years' imprisonment, and a fine of up to €45,000 (Article 225-2 of the Penal Code).

Thus, a provision that prohibited the hiring of children of employees was held to be discriminatory and a violation of Article 225-2 of the Penal Code because it was discrimination on the basis of family situation.

The Labor Courts are competent to hear discrimination disputes and will award damages if an employee was dismissed due to discrimination or was otherwise treated in a discriminatory manner. As in other cases of unlawful dismissal, the Labor Courts can and sometimes do order the reinstatement of the wronged employee, but the employee does not have to accept the reinstatement.

Discrimination against employees who have been the subject of, or refused to be the subject of, or were witnesses to, or were whistle-blowers concerning sexual or moral harassment are sanctioned by the same Article of the Penal Code Section and Articles L 122-46 and L 122-49 of the Labor Code.

SECTION VI

On the Horizon: What key labor and employment law developments should an employer doing business in France anticipate occurring in the coming years?

As indicated in the beginning of this chapter, the Agreement entered into by the majority of the labor unions in January 2008 will be presented to the French

Parliament after this book is published. When the Parliament considers the provisions of the Agreement, it will most likely modify certain provisions and will certainly determine the details of the provisions through legislation and decrees.

It is anticipated that further changes will be made to the Labor Code during the remaining four years of the term of the current president, which may include further reductions of the work week and the encouragement of more harmonious negotiations between labor representatives, unions, and employers.

CHAPTER 6

LABOR AND EMPLOYMENT LAW IN GERMANY

THOMAS MÜLLER-BONANNI

SECTION I

My client wishes to establish a manufacturing facility in Germany and will need to hire a workforce. What are the key legal issues involved?

German Labor and Employment Laws: Whom Do They Apply To?

Germany's labor and employment laws apply to all employees. Whether or not a person qualifies as employee is a question of fact and does not depend on the signing of a written contract of employment.

The crucial test is whether the person in question (1) works for another person or legal entity (2) for remuneration and (3) subject to the other person's or legal entity's instructions as to the time, place, and content of the services that are to be provided. Based on this test, the vast majority of persons who are employees from a commonsense point of view also qualify as employees from a legal point of view. By contrast, independent consultants (*Berater*), commercial agents (*Handelsvertreter*), and board members (*Geschäftsführer, Vorstände*) are considered to be self-employed and do therefore not enjoy the protection of Germany's mandatory labor and employment laws.

Employment Contracts: Who Receives Them and What Must They Include?

There is no legal duty to provide employees with a written contract of employment. However, under the Act on the Evidencing of Employment Conditions (*Nachweisgesetz*) implementing European Council Directive 91/533/EEC, all employees are entitled to a written statement of the main terms and conditions of employment within one month of the start date of their employment. Most employers discharge their corresponding obligation in a formal contract of employment that provides the following information:

- Name and address of employer and employee
- Start date
- If fixed-term contract, term of employment
- Place of work
- Brief description of the services that are to be provided
- Rate and dates of remuneration
- Hours of work
- Holidays
- Notice periods
- Reference to the applicable collective bargaining agreements (*Tarifverträge*) and works agreements (*Betriebsvereinbarungen*), if any.

Where the employer is bound by collective bargaining agreements or works agreements it is possible simply to refer to those agreements instead of listing the aforementioned terms and conditions of employment (provided that the relevant collective bargaining agreement or works agreement covers these issues). Employment contracts for blue-collar workers will typically make use of this option and therefore tend to be rather short, whereas employment contracts for white-collar employees will normally be more detailed and include additional provisions (e.g., on bonuses, intellectual property, confidentiality, and restrictive covenants).

Staff handbooks are relatively uncommon in Germany since most issues that are typically dealt with in staff handbooks are subject to codetermination of the works council (*Betriebsrat*) and are therefore dealt with in works agreements (*Betriebsvereinbarungen*) (for more details, see "Works Councils").

Protection Against Termination

Employees who have been employed for more than six months enjoy protection against termination under the Unfair Dismissal Act (*Kündigungsschutzgesetz*), provided that the relevant establishment (i.e., the shop or work site, as opposed to the legal entity) employs more than 10 employees on a regular basis. Under the Unfair Dismissal Act, the employer cannot terminate the employment contract by way of notice unless there exists at least one of the three statutorily defined reasons for termination: breach of contract, incapacity, and redundancy. If the employer's notice lacks the necessary justification under the Unfair Dismissal Act it is void and will therefore not terminate the employment contract. It is thus not possible to employ staff "at will" in Germany (but see "Hiring Managerial Employees").

Fixed-Term Contracts

In order to avoid the inflexibilities of the Unfair Dismissal Act many companies employ newly hired staff on the basis of fixed-term employment contracts before signing an employment contract for an indefinite period of time. Fixed-term employment contracts can be entered into for a maximum term of up to two years without any justification being required. It is also possible to sign a fixed-term employment contract for a shorter period of time (e.g., six months) and to extend the term of the contract up to three times within the maximum term of two years. Fixed-term contracts for more than two years can be entered into if there are objective reasons justifying the term (e.g., a project), although such reasons are often difficult to prove in practice.

Hiring Managerial Employees

Board Members

Most of Germany's labor and employment laws (in particular, the Unfair Dismissal Act) do not apply to management board members (*Geschäftsführer, Vorstände*) although corporate law may provide them with a certain level of protection depending on the type of company in which they are a board member.

The appointment of a *Geschäftsführer*—a member of the management board of a limited liability company (*Gesellschaft mit beschränkter Haftung*, or *GmbH*)— can be revoked by the company's shareholders at any time without any justification being required. The board member's employment contract, by contrast, is distinct and separate from his board membership and can be terminated only in accordance with the contractually agreed upon terms and conditions. Typically, a notice period of six to 12 months will have been agreed upon so that the company must continue paying the *Geschäftsführer* during that period of time. The concept of payment in lieu of notice is unknown in German employment law but the company may send the *Geschäftsführer* on "garden leave" once his appointment to the board has been revoked.

In contrast, objective reasons are required to revoke the appointment of a *Vorstand*—a member of the management board of a large limited liability company (*Aktiengesellschaft*, or *AG*)—prior to the expiration of his or her term. Even where there are sufficient reasons to revoke the board membership of the *Vorstand*, however, this does not automatically allow the company to terminate the *Vorstand's* employment contract. Rather, as board members of an *Aktiengesellschaft* are normally employed on the basis of a fixed-term contract (with a maximum term of five years), their employment cannot be terminated prematurely unless they are in breach of contractual duties. In practice it is therefore common to agree on a voluntary resignation of the *Vorstand* and a payout of the contractually agreed upon remuneration for the remaining portion of the contract term in one lump sum (potentially reduced by interests and other earnings that the *Vorstand* may have during that period of time).

Other Managerial Employees

All other managerial employees enjoy basically the same protection and benefits as regular staff with three important exceptions. First, the works council (*Betriebsrat*) is not in charge of so-called *leitende Angestellte* (typically the senior management immediately below board level). Second, labor unions do not normally negotiate wages for senior and midlevel management (although the unions do sometimes negotiate other terms and conditions of employment). Third, managers who have the power to either hire or dismiss staff without having to seek third-party consent can be terminated "at will" (although they are entitled to a statutory severance payment if terminated without objective reasons within the meaning of the Unfair Dismissal Act; see "Statutory Restrictions on Dismissal Without Cause" in Section IV). In practice, however, this hiring and firing power is rarely granted, so managerial employees normally enjoy the same protection against termination under the Unfair Dismissal Act as regular staff.

Wages and Benefits

General

Wages and benefits vary considerably among industries and depending on whether or not the company is subject to a collective bargaining agreement (*Tarifvertrag*), as discussed later. However, some terms and conditions can be said to be standard across the economy.

Hours

Most industries work between 35 and 40 hours per week. Senior management normally work longer in accordance with business needs.

Wages

There is currently no minimum wage in Germany although there is a political debate on whether to introduce one.

In some industries (such as the construction industry), collective bargaining agreements have been declared binding on all companies of the given industry (whereas, normally, collective bargaining agreements apply only to companies who join the relevant employers' association), thereby establishing de facto a minimum wage. Regular staff will typically receive overtime pay in excess of the basic hourly pay rate whereas middle and senior management will normally not receive overtime pay.

Vacation

The Federal Vacation Act (*Bundesurlaubsgesetz*) provides for a minimum of 24 days of paid leave of absence per year based on a six-day work week (20 days based on a five-day work week). In most industries 28 to 30 days paid leave of absence per year based on a five-day week are common. Those days are in addition to public holidays, the number of which varies between states.

Other Benefits

Medical and unemployment insurance are covered by compulsory state plans, the cost of which are shared on an equal basis between the employer and the employee. Company plans are therefore uncommon.

There is also a compulsory state pension plan, which works along the same principles. Since the benefits under this plan are largely perceived to be insufficient, however, many companies offer additional, employer-sponsored plans.

The overall cost of these state plans comes to approximately 40 percent of the employee's gross salary (to be shared equally between the employer and the employee). However, contributions to the plans are due on salaries only up to certain threshold figures (€63,600 for the state pension and unemployment plan and €43,200 for the state medical and care plan in 2008). Employees who earn more than this will pay contributions only until the threshold is reached. Also, employees who earn in excess of the threshold figure for the state medical and care plan can choose to leave those plans.

Labor Unions

German labor unions negotiate collective bargaining agreements on wages, hours, and other terms and conditions of employment. They do not involve themselves in operational questions such as the hiring or dismissal of staff, the beginning and the end of daily working hours, and the like, which are the responsibility of the works council (*Betriebsrat*).

Collective bargaining agreements (*Tarifverträge*) are normally negotiated at industry level between an employer's association and the appropriate labor union. This is because most unions have organized themselves along industry lines. For example, there are labor unions for the metal industry (*IG Metall*), the services industry (*ver.di*), and the mining, chemicals, and energy industry (*IGBCE*). Collective bargaining agreements made between an individual employer and a trade union are possible but less common.

In accordance with the organizational structure of labor unions, collective bargaining agreements are normally made for all employees of a given establishment (the shop or work site). For example, in an establishment that belongs to the metal industry, the collective bargaining agreements signed with the metalworkers' union will also apply to the sales staff who, considered on a stand-alone basis, would belong to the services industry.

Labor unions do not have to "organize" a company in order to sign collective bargaining agreements on behalf of the company's staff. They are able to sign collective bargaining agreements for all companies within their industry sector as a matter of law. However, a collective bargaining agreement will become binding on the employer and the employee only if the employer is a member of the employers' association that signed the collective bargaining agreement (or if the employer itself signed the collective bargaining agreement) and the employee is a member of the relevant labor union. In practice, however, companies that are bound by a collective bargaining agreement normally pay all employees in accordance with the relevant agreement regardless of whether they are union members in order to avoid incentives to join the labor union. For some industries (such as the construction industry), collective bargaining agreements have been declared binding by the government on all companies of the given industry (i.e., they apply irrespective of whether the company is a member of the relevant employers' association).

Labor unions have a number of auxiliary capabilities, such as the right to initiate works council elections or to advise and support the members of the works council. Also, in companies that are subject to the codetermination laws (*Mitbestimmungsgesetze*), a certain fraction of the employee seats on the company's supervisory board are reserved for union members.

Works Councils

A works council (*Betriebsrat*) can be elected in every establishment (the shop or site, as opposed to the legal entity) that has at least five employees. The works council is distinct from the labor union in that, among other things, its members must belong to the staff of the relevant establishment (although many works council members are also labor union members).

Where a company (i.e., the legal entity) consists of more than one establishment, the works councils of the various establishments can choose to establish a company works council (*Gesamtbetriebsrat*). Within a group of affiliated companies, a group works council (*Konzernbetriebsrat*) can be established at the level of the ultimate (German) parent company if certain conditions are met. The rationale of having a council at each level is to establish employee representation bodies at every level at which decisions with a potential impact on the interests of the workforce are taken.

Company works councils and group works councils have the same rights and duties as "regular" works councils, but have authority in matters that cannot be dealt with at the next lowest level of employee representation. For example, if the employer intends to introduce a company-wide, uniform shift model (as opposed to a shift model at the level of one establishment only) this will come within the province of the company works council (and not the various local works councils). It is important to note, though, that where the company works council or the group works council is responsible for a given matter, it will represent the employees of all establishments/group companies irrespective of whether each employee is represented by a local works council.

Works councils have a wide variety of rights ranging from information to consultation and codetermination. Where the works council has a codetermination right, the employer cannot take the relevant measure without the works council's consent. This applies, for example, to ordering overtime work. If the works council and the employer cannot reach an agreement, either side may call for the creation of a mediation board (*Einigungsstelle*) consisting of an equal number of employees' and employer's representatives and a neutral chairman (typically a labor judge). The mediation board will then decide the matter with binding effect for both the employer and the works council.

In a number of areas the works council does not have a codetermination right within the strict meaning of the word, but ignoring the works council's rights will nevertheless have grave consequences. Most importantly, the works council must be heard and provided with certain information before notice of dismissal is given to employees who come within its purview. Failure to hear the works council or incomplete information will make the notice letter void. Also, the works council must be heard and provided with certain information before new employees are hired. Noncompliance with that procedure entitles the works council to seek a court injunction against the employment of the relevant employees.

Dealing with a works council that uses its full range of powers can be time-consuming and costly. However, most companies that have works councils do not experience major difficulties in their day-to-day operations.

SECTION II

My client is acquiring an existing business in Germany. How do I assess the existing workforce and consider changes?

Share Deals Versus Asset Deals

Share Deals

Share transactions (i.e., the sale and purchase of the shares of the target company) have no impact on the existing employment contracts. In particular, the change in share ownership as such does not entitle the company to terminate the existing employment contracts. Just like prior to the transaction, the termination of employment contracts is possible only in accordance with the rules of the Unfair Dismissal Act, as discussed in the previous section. Nor does a change in share ownership trigger any protective rights for the benefit of the affected workforce. The employing company remains subject to the same protective labor and employment laws and continues enjoying the same legal flexibilities as it did prior to the share transfer.

Share transactions may affect certain claims or rights of employees that are contingent on the employer company belonging to a particular group of affiliated companies. For example, the employees of the target company may lose share options that have been issued by the parent company, and bonus plans that relate to group-wide performance targets may have to be adjusted.

Asset Deals

In the event of an asset deal (i.e., a sale and purchase of some or all of the assets of the employer company), the existing employment contracts will transfer to the purchaser if the asset transfer satisfies the criteria of a transfer or partial transfer of undertaking within the meaning of Acquired Rights Directive 2001/23/EC and Section 613(a) of the German Civil Code, which implements the Acquired Rights Directive in Germany. If the sale of assets does not satisfy the criteria of a (partial) transfer of undertaking, the existing employment contracts will stay behind with the seller.

Whether or not a transfer of assets qualifies as a (partial) transfer of undertaking will be determined by the German courts on the basis of seven criteria: the type of undertaking or business concerned, whether tangible assets are transferred, the value of intangible assets at the time of transfer, whether the majority of employees are taken over by the new employer, whether customers are transferred, the degree of similarity between activities carried on before and after the alleged transfer, and the period, if any, during which those activities are suspended. This test will not be applied in a checklist-like manner. Instead, if one or more criteria are lacking, other criteria may compensate. Ultimately, the courts will look at all facts of the case at hand. This may make it sometimes difficult to predict whether a particular transaction qualifies as a transfer of undertaking. However, some general principles may serve as guidelines.

In an asset-based business (e.g., manufacturing) a (partial) transfer of undertakings will not occur unless the principal assets that are necessary to run the business (or a part of it) are transferred. Therefore, the sale of a single piece of equipment will normally not trigger a transfer of undertaking.

By contrast, in labor-based businesses (e.g., cleaning services), a (partial) transfer of undertaking may occur where the buyer offers employment to a significant part (in terms of number and qualification) of the seller's staff. For example, if the buyer of a cleaning business were to offer employment to 80 percent of the seller's staff, it is likely that a transfer of undertaking would be triggered and thus the buyer would also be obliged to take over the remaining 20 percent of the seller's staff—even if the buyer does not take over any significant assets.

The outsourcing of activities that are being completed in-house do not normally constitute a transfer of undertakings if neither assets nor staff are being transferred to the service provider.

In the event that an asset transfer qualifies as a transfer of undertakings, the employment contracts of all employees pertaining to the relevant entity will transfer to the buyer by operation of law with all rights and duties. In particular, the buyer will have to recognize the transferring employees' lengths of services spent with the seller and will have to pay the same salaries as the seller. However, the seller and the buyer may alter the transferring employees' terms and conditions of employment or even terminate staff in accordance with the generally applicable labor and employment laws. Section 613(a) of the Civil Code contains only very few limitations in this respect. The most important are the following:

- A transfer of undertaking as such is not a valid reason for the termination of employment (but the seller or the buyer may make staff redundant in the context of a transfer of undertaking).

- Detrimental amendments to the transferring employees' terms and conditions of employment (e.g., a salary decrease) require objective reasons (e.g., if without the salary decrease employees would have to be dismissed), even if the employees consent. (Different rules apply where alterations of the transferring employees' terms and conditions of employment are agreed with the labor union or the works council.)

- In the course of a (partial) transfer of undertaking the buyer will also become liable to pay the company pension (if any) of the transferring staff (but not of pensioners and employees who left the company with a vested pension right prior to the transfer), including past service obligations. This will have to be taken into account when determining the purchase price for the transferring assets.

Making Changes to Key Managerial Positions

Board Members

A share transaction has no effect on either board membership or the underlying employment contracts of the existing board members. Termination of board membership and the existing employment contracts by the buyer follows the rules set out in "Hiring Managerial Employees" in Section I.

The same is basically true for asset transactions, although in this case, termination of the board membership and the employment contracts of the existing board members will be the responsibility of the seller. This is because Section 613(a) of the Civil Code does not apply to board members, which means that they will not transfer to the buyer but rather will remain employed with the seller company.

Strategically it is advisable for the buyer (in both share transactions and asset transactions) to seek agreement on the future role of the existing board members at an early stage of the transaction so as to avoid potential conflicts of interests. Where the buyer does not want to retain one or more board members it is customary to allow them to resign "voluntarily" rather than to revoke their board membership and give notice of termination for their employment contracts.

Due diligence should have determined whether there are change-of-control clauses in place that entitle board members to special payments or early resignation from their position.

Other Managerial Employees

Section 613(a) of the Civil Code does apply to all managerial employees below board level; thus, upon an asset transaction that qualifies as a transfer of undertakings, their employment contract will transfer to the buyer. A share transaction leaves the employment contracts of managerial employees below board level unaffected since the employer company remains the same. In either case (share transactions and asset transactions), termination of employment follows the rules set out in "Hiring Managerial Employees" in Section I. This means, in particular, that termination of employment is lawful only when it is in line with the rules of the Unfair Dismissal Act. A change to the existing management structure that makes one or more managerial employees redundant may provide such objective reasons. By contrast, a change in ownership as such is not an objective reason that allows the buyer to terminate managerial employees.

Carrying Out a Workforce Reduction

Unfair Dismissal Act

Under the Unfair Dismissal Act (*Kündigungsschutzgesetz*) the employer cannot terminate an employee unless at least one of the statutorily defined reasons for termination exists. Redundancy is a statutorily recognized reason for termination, and the employer is free to decide on the size of its workforce. There is also no obligation on the employer to demonstrate economic difficulties before making staff redundant.

On the other hand, where part of the workforce is redundant, the employer cannot simply terminate the redundant employees but must make a selection among comparable employees on the basis of "social criteria" (age, seniority, family status, and disabilities). Employees are comparable in this sense if (1) they are on the same level of hierarchy, (2) the employment contract of the redundant employee allows the employer to transfer the redundant employee to the less-protected-employee's position, and (3) the redundant employee is qualified for the other employee's position. For example, where redundant employee A is 45 years of age, has been with the company for 20 years, is married, has two minor children, and is comparable to employee B who is 30 years of age, has been with the company for five years, and is single with no children, the employer cannot terminate employee A but only employee B. There is some flexibility in the selection process, allowing the employer to preserve the current age structure of the workforce and to retain employees with key qualifications. Moreover, the selection process does not have to be observed when signing termination agreements with employees (but only where the employer gives notice of termination).

The above principles apply to both share transactions and asset transactions.

Works Council Involvement

The works council must be informed and consulted with before each employee termination. Failure to comply with this procedure will render the notice letter void. However, a works council's objection to a particular dismissal does not affect the validity of the notice letter. The obligation to inform and consult with the works council is purely procedural.

Prior to a mass dismissal (defined in Section III) the employer will have to negotiate a compromise of interests (*Interessenausgleich*) and a social plan (*Sozialplan*) with the works council. The compromise of interests will contain an agreement with the works council on the number of employees who are to be dismissed, the process, and the timing. The social plan will provide severance payments and other measures, as appropriate, to the affected employees. Severance payments are in addition to the applicable notice period (normally four weeks to seven months depending on the employee's seniority) and will typically be calculated on the basis of the following formula:

$$\text{age} \times \text{seniority} \times \text{gross monthly salary} \div x = \text{severance payment}$$

where x is subject to negotiations with the works council and may be staggered for different groups of employees (e.g., for different age groups to take account of their risk of unemployment).

Strictly speaking, the employer must only *try* to reach an agreement with the works council on a compromise of interests (but is not required to actually sign such agreement) prior to giving notice of dismissal. However, the negotiation process is relatively formalized and may take several months (there is no time limit). Where the redundant staff cannot be employed in a meaningful manner during the negotiations with the works council, this may be a considerable cost factor. Disobeying the negotiation requirement may sometimes be a valid strategy as it does not render the dismissals void but only gives rise to a right for the affected employees to sue for a severance award. Such an award will be fixed by the labor courts and may amount to up to 12 months' or even 18 months' pay depending on the employee's age and company seniority (see "Statutory Severance Pay Requirements" in Section IV). It is therefore normally preferable to offer adequate severance packages in the negotiations with the works council on a social plan so as to induce the works council to sign a compromise of interests quickly.

Reorganizing the Workforce

Employment contracts will normally be flexible enough to allow the employer to implement small changes of the job location (e.g., within the same city) or job responsibilities (e.g., exchanging one or two of several of the employee's responsibilities for other responsibilities). More radical changes (e.g., a relocation to a different part of the country; an exchange of all of the employee's job responsibilities for other responsibilities) will often require the employer to give notice of termination while simultaneously offering continued employment with altered terms and conditions of employment (*Änderungskündigung*). This type of dismissal must be justified under the Unfair Dismissal Act, and so is not used very frequently.

Depending on how significantly the current organizational structures are to be changed, a reorganization of the workforce may trigger an obligation to negotiate a compromise of interests (*Interessenausgleich*) and a social plan (*Sozialplan*) with the works council. For example, if the employer intends to switch from a horizontal organizational structure to a vertical structure it will have to negotiate with the works council an agreement on if, when, and how this change is to be implemented (compromise of interests) and an agreement on how any adverse effects employees may suffer because of the change will be mitigated (social plan). Most of the procedural considerations outlined under "Statutory Severance Pay Requirements" in connection with mass dismissals apply.

The above principles apply to both share transactions and asset transactions.

Changing the Wage and Benefits Structure

Due diligence should have determined to what extent wages and benefits are flexible. Typical ways to make wages and benefits flexible are the granting of benefits on a voluntary or a revocable basis. Where a benefit has been granted on a voluntary basis (e.g., Christmas bonuses) the employer is free to decide anew every year whether or not to pay the benefit. Where a benefit has been granted on a revocable basis, the employer is basically under an obligation to pay that benefit but may stop doing so in future years provided that (1) there are objective reasons (e.g., economic difficulties of the company), and (2) the employer exercises its discretion in an equitable manner. Another way of making benefits flexible is to grant them for a fixed period of time only (bonus plans and stock option plans are often introduced for one or several years only and followed by new plans once the old plan has expired). The courts are reluctant to accept arrangements that make more than 24 percent of the employee's overall compensation package subject to unilateral changes by the employer.

Where employees have a contractual right to a certain benefit, an employer who wishes to dispense with the benefit must give notice of termination and, at the same time, offer continued employment at altered terms and conditions (*Änderungskündigung*). Given that this type of notice must satisfy the criteria of the Unfair Dismissal Act and can be challenged in court, this route of action is often impractical. In no event does the buyer's interest in harmonizing terms and conditions of employment following a transfer of undertaking justify such dismissals. Notice of termination (combined with an offer of continued employment at altered terms and conditions) aimed at reducing the employee's base salary (as opposed to fringe benefits) would be possible only in a near insolvency situation.

Certain benefits that have been granted on the basis of a works agreement (*Betriebsvereinbarung*) made with the works council may be altered (even to the employees' detriment) by way of a new works agreement. This is an instrument that is used frequently following a transfer of undertakings for purposes of harmonizing terms and conditions of employment.

Special rules apply to occupational pension plans. Broadly speaking, the claims of pensioners—employees who have left the company with a vested right to a company pension—and the accrued rights of active employees (past-benefit obligations) can be reduced only in quite extreme situations (e.g., to avoid insolvency), whereas future earnings can be reduced or even stopped from growing depending on the reasons for such alteration. These rules apply also to agreements made with the works council.

The above principles apply to both share transactions and asset transactions.

Consulting with Labor Unions or Works Councils

Share Transactions

Local works councils have no information or consultation rights with respect to share transactions, as their codetermination rights are directed against the employer company and the sale of the shares of the employer company takes place at shareholder level. It is best practice, though, to inform the works council in advance of a change in share ownership. Normally, this information will be provided shortly before the sale and purchase agreement on the employer company's shares is signed. Where there is an economic committee (*Wirtschaftsausschuss*) (a special employee representation body in charge of economic affairs that can be established in companies with more than 100 employees), there is a legal duty to inform that committee of changes in the share ownership of the employer company. Arguably, this information can be provided after the signing of the sale and purchase agreement but, again, it is best practice to do so shortly before signing.

There is no obligation to make available to employee representatives a copy of the sale and purchase agreement.

Where there is a European Works Council (*Europäischer Betriebsrat*), there may be an obligation to inform and consult with the council depending on the agreement that established it.

Asset Transactions

Regarding asset transactions, a distinction must be made between the sale of the entirety of an establishment (*Betrieb*) (i.e., the shop or work site) and parts of an establishment. Upon a sale of an establishment in its entirety the economic committee (and, if there is no economic committee, arguably the works council) must be informed and consulted with in good time prior to the sale, but the employer company does not need the economic committee's or the works council's consent to sign or complete the transaction. By contrast, where only part of an establishment is sold, there will normally be an obligation to negotiate a compromise of interests (*Interessenausgleich*) and a social plan (*Sozialplan*) with the works council. It must emphasized, though, that the works council's codetermination right does not relate to the transaction as such (i.e., the sale and purchase of assets) but to the organizational separation of the sold part of the business from the rest of the business. The transaction therefore can be completed even if negotiations with the works council are still pending. However, as long as the negotiations are pending, the buyer will have to coordinate all decisions that come within the responsibility of the works council (such as hirings, dismissals, and overtime) with the seller, and the works council will remain responsible for the sold part of the business also. Completion of the negotiation process with the works council is therefore often made a condition precedent to the consummation of the transaction.

Additionally, Section 613(a) of the Civil Code obliges the seller and the buyer to inform the transferring employees in advance of a (partial) transfer of undertaking of (1) the time of the transfer, (2) the reasons for the transfer, (3) the legal, economic, and social consequences of the transfer, and (4) any measures that the buyer intends to take with respect to the transferring workforce. This information must be provided in writing to every transferring employee.

Labor Unions

Labor unions have no information or consultation rights on either share transactions or asset transactions. However, labor unions have recently involved themselves more frequently in corporate transactions. In particular, where potential buyers were thought to plan major restructurings, labor unions have organized demonstrations or even strikes.

SECTION III

My client wishes to sell its existing facility. What restrictions do we need to consider?

Assessing Employment Contracts

The key issues the buyer will normally look at in its due diligence exercise are the following:

- The number of employees, in particular whether there are "hidden" employment contracts (freelancers or agency workers who are in reality employees of the seller company).

- The size of the seller's pension obligations. In particular, the buyer will review whether there is an underfunding of the seller's pension obligations. This is not only an issue in share transactions but also in asset transactions as, under Section 613(a) of the Civil Code, the buyer will assume liability for all pension obligations vis-à-vis the transferring employees by operation of law (but not for pensioners and employees who have left the company with a vested pension right prior to the transfer of undertakings).

- Restructuring obstacles such as an agreement with the works council that rules out dismissals on grounds of redundancies for a certain period of time (such agreements can sometimes be found where the company has recently undergone a restructuring).

- Change-of-control clauses in the management's employment contracts that entitle the management to certain payments or give them a right to terminate their employment early.

- Any liability relating to the time prior to the transfer (e.g., unpaid wages or social security, liability from illegal discrimination).

In the sale and purchase agreement, the seller will normally have to warrant that only a certain number of employees will transfer to the buyer and will have to indemnify the buyer against the costs of additional transferred employees. It is also customary that the seller indemnifies the buyer against liabilities relating to the time up until the transfer of undertakings (unless the buyer accepts disclosure in the due diligence exercise as sufficient). Whether or not the seller will be able to resist a purchase price reduction because of an existing underfunding of its occupational pension plans will depend on the circumstances of the case. Sellers should bear in mind in this context that, where pension obligations are totally unfunded (as is customary in Germany), the company's German balance sheet will not show the actual size of the company's liability but, because of tax law, only lower figures. The buyer will therefore often insist that an actuary calculates the company's full liability under U.S. generally accepted accounting principles or international financial reporting standards.

Consulting with the Government

Labor and employment law does not establish obligations to consult with government in the context of corporate transactions. There is an obligation, though, to notify the labor authorities in advance of a mass dismissal under the European Mass Dismissal Directive 75/194/EC and Section 17 of the Unfair Dismissal Act, which implements the Mass Dismissal Directive in Germany. A mass dismissal will occur where, within a period of 30 calendar days:

- In establishments (i.e., the shop or work site, as opposed to the legal entity) with more than 20 but fewer than 60 employees, more than five employees are dismissed;
- In establishments with at least 60 but fewer than 500 employees, 10 percent of the workforce or more than 25 employees (whichever is less) are dismissed;
- In establishments with at least 500 employees, at least 30 employees are dismissed.

Consulting with Labor Unions or Works Councils

The information and consultation requirements mirror those applicable to the acquisition of an existing business (see "Consulting with Labor Unions or Works Councils" in Section II).

Negotiating with the Purchaser: Special Labor Issues

Where a transaction triggers codetermination rights of the works council, it is important to coordinate the negotiations with the works council and with the buyer. The buyer will often make the closing of the sale conditional on the completion of negotiations with the works council.

In addition, the seller will have to negotiate with the buyer various warranties and indemnifications in the sale and purchase agreement, as outlined in this section.

❸ SECTION IV

My client wants to replace its senior manager(s). What restrictions do we need to consider?

Employment Contracts

The cost of terminating members of the senior management depend on whether they are board members or "regular" employees.

Board members do not enjoy protection against termination under the Unfair Dismissal Act. The cost of terminating their employment will therefore depend on the contractually agreed upon terms. Board members of a *Gesellschaft mit beschränkter Haftung (GmbH)*, that is, a limited liability company, will normally have a notice period of six to 12 months, during which the company must continue paying the board member. Board members of an *Aktiengesellschaft (AG)*, that is, a large limited liability company, are typically employed on the basis of fixed-term contracts with a maximum term of five years. In a separation scenario the company will often agree with the board member on "voluntary" resignation and pay out the remainder of the contract term. It is important to note that board membership is distinct from the underlying employment contract. In a *GmbH*, board membership can be revoked at any time without any justification being required, whereas in an *AG* a revocation of the board membership requires objective reasons.

Managerial employees below board level do enjoy protection against termination under the Unfair Dismissal Act. Notice of dismissal is therefore unlawful (and void) unless the employer company can demonstrate the existence of at least one of the statutorily defined objective reasons for termination. It is possible, though, to sign a termination agreement provided that the employee consents. Normal severance packages agreed upon in termination agreements range between 0.5 to 1.0 monthly remunerations (including all benefits) for every year of employment. Those payments are in addition to the applicable notice period.

See also discussions in Section I on employment contracts and hiring managerial employees.

Statutory Severance Pay Requirements

Employees

German law does not provide statutory severance payments. Within the scope of application of the Unfair Dismissal Act, notice of dismissal is either lawful, in which event the employer's notice letter will terminate the employment contract without any obligation on the employer to make a severance payment, or unlawful and therefore void, in which event the employment contract will continue.

There are only two exceptions to this rule: (1) social plans (*Sozialpläne*) negotiated with the works council and (2) certain situations in unfair dismissal litigation. More specifically, where the employer's notice is lacking the necessary justification under the Unfair Dismissal Act (and is therefore void) but there are objective reasons not to continue the employment contract, the court may dissolve the employment contract and order the employer to make a severance payment. Such severance payments are generally capped at 12 monthly remunerations (including all benefits). If the employee is at least 50 years of age and has been with the company for at least 15 years, severance payments are capped at 15 monthly remunerations (including all benefits); where the employee is at least 55 years of age and has been with the company for at least 20 years, a cap of 18 monthly salaries (including all benefits) applies. It is important to emphasize that the courts rarely make use of their power to dissolve an employment contract as the Unfair Dismissal Act is aimed primarily at continued employment.

Yet other rules apply to managerial employees who have the power to hire or dismiss staff without having to seek third-party consent (a power that is rarely granted in practice). If the employer company requests that the court dissolve the employment contract of such an employee, the court must grant the employer's motion irrespective of whether there are objective reasons for termination and order a severance payment to be made (within the aforementioned financial limits).

Board Members

Board members do not fall within the scope of application of the Unfair Dismissal Act and are therefore not entitled to statutory severance payments. Exceptions to this rule apply only where a board member is also an employee of the company (a situation that may arise in some circumstances).

Statutory Restrictions on Dismissal Without Cause

Outside the scope of application of the Unfair Dismissal Act, the employer does not need objective reasons to terminate an employment contract. By contrast, within the scope of application of the Act, the employer cannot terminate the employment contract unless at least one of the statutorily defined reasons for termination exists (described in Section I). It is not possible to terminate an employment contract in breach of the Unfair Dismissal Act. Where the employer's notice is lacking the necessary justification under the Act, it is void and will therefore not terminate the employment contract.

SECTION V

What prohibitions exist against discrimination on the basis of age, race, gender, disability, pregnancy, and other factors? What are the rights of employees, applicants, or former employees who believe that they have been discriminated against?

General Principle of Equal Treatment

Under the general principle of equal treatment the employer must not treat employees in similar situations differently without a justifying reason. For example, absent justifying reasons, it is unlawful to set up a company pension plan for the benefit of white-collar employees but not for blue-collar workers. Violations of the general principle of equal treatment will entitle those employees who have been discriminated against to the same benefits as have been granted to all other employees. In the aforementioned example, blue-collar workers would be also entitled to a company pension in accordance with the plan established for white-collar employees unless the employer can demonstrate objective reasons for the exclusion of blue-collar workers from the company pension plan. A violation of the general principle of equal treatment will not normally entitle the employee to damages, though.

Antidiscrimination Act

In 2006 a comprehensive Antidiscrimination Act (*Allgemeines Gleichbehandlungsgesetz*) was passed. The Act prohibits discrimination on grounds of race, ethnic origin, gender, religion, beliefs, disability, age, and sexual orientation. It covers direct as well as indirect discrimination (i.e., situations where a certain measure is neutral on its face but has an adverse effect on a protected group). The Act also prohibits retaliation and allows affirmative action. From a U.S. perspective it is noteworthy that, unlike the Age Discrimination in Employment Act (ADEA), Germany's Antidiscrimination Act prohibits any discrimination on grounds of age not only against older employees in comparison with younger employees but also against younger employees in comparison with older employees. Also, unlike under the ADEA, protection against discrimination on grounds of age is independent of the employee's age (i.e., there is no minimum age).

The Antidiscrimination Act covers employees, job applicants, and, particularly with regard to access to employment and career progression, board members (*Geschäftsführer, Vorstände*) also.

The rules on the justification of discriminations are relatively complex and vary depending on the "prohibited" criterion. As a rule of thumb, discriminations on the grounds of a prohibited criterion will be allowed only where the criterion is a bona fide occupational requirement.

Employees who want to bring a claim under the Antidiscrimination Act will normally have to demonstrate only a prima facie case of discrimination. The burden of proof will then shift to the employer, who will have to rebut the presumption of unlawful discrimination.

Employees who have suffered unlawful discrimination will be entitled to financial and moral damages. Moral damages, which compensate for suffering, mental anguish, besmirched reputation, and the like, are normally uncapped. However, moral damages for job applicants are capped at three months' pay (on the basis of the salary that they would have received in the vacant position), except that they are uncapped for the best-qualified applicant who, absent unlawful discrimination, would have received the position. It is noteworthy that the Antidiscrimination Act does not provide a right to be reinstated or a right to promotion. Applicants who were not hired and employees who were not promoted because of discrimination are limited to financial and moral damages.

The government has established an Antidiscrimination Agency (*Antidiskriminierungsstelle des Bundes*). The Agency provides legal and certain other forms of assistance to persons who believe that they have been unlawfully discriminated against. However, the Agency does not have investigatory powers or even the power to impose sanctions on employers.

❽ SECTION VI

On the Horizon: What key labor and employment law developments should an employer doing business in Germany anticipate occurring in the coming years?

In an attempt to deregulate the German labor market a broad range of changes, notably in the area of the protection against unfair dismissal and with regard to the social welfare system, have been implemented over the last couple of years. Recently, however, labor market reforms have slowed down.

There is currently a debate on whether to introduce a general minimum wage. To date, minimum wages exist only in selected industries (see "Wages and Benefits" in Section I).

CHAPTER 7

LABOR AND EMPLOYMENT LAW IN GREECE

IOANNA KYRIAZI
EFFIE MITSOPOULOU

SECTION I

My client wishes to establish a manufacturing facility in Greece and will need to hire a workforce. What are the key legal issues involved?

Employment Contracts: Who Receives Them and What Must They Include?

Employment Status and Distinction of Employees

Greek labor law distinguishes employees as blue-collar or white-collar according to the nature of the work performed.[1] The practical role of the distinction concerns mainly (1) severance payments, (2) the payment of salary (daily wage or monthly), and (3) compensation under Article 5 of Law 435/1976 due to retirement.

Mandatory Requirements

Labor contracts may be divided into (1) independent services contracts, (2) contracts for the hiring of work, or (3) employment agreements. Labor law governs only employment agreements that have the distinctive feature of the personal, legal, and financial dependency of the employee to the employer. Hence, it is not applicable to self-employed individuals providing services.

Basic Requirements

The basic requirements for a binding employment agreement are provided in Article 185 of the Civil Code, which states: "A person proposing the conclusion of contract is bound thereby for the whole period during which it can be accepted by the other person." When the offeree communicates acceptance to the offeror, the contract is executed.[2]

Form of the Employment Contract

The employment agreement must be in writing. However, even an oral agreement is binding upon the employer, who may be subject to sanctions for not observing the relevant legal requirements.[3] The parties are free to determine the content of their agreement, with the exception of specific requirements of law (for example, maximum hours of work per week, vacation days, and minimum legal severance).

Notice of any employment agreement must be provided, within eight days, to the pertinent labor authority. Special regulations concern the employment of particular categories of people, as 3 percent to 4 percent of the workforce of companies employing more than 50 people must be comprised of persons with special needs (people with disabilities, families with many children, war victims, etc.).

The right of foreign nationals to work in Greece is in general recognized and protected by relevant constitutional provisions, although the right of employment is subject to various restrictions, the most important of which is the reciprocity requirement. Reciprocity is not required for European Union nationals. EU countries have opened their job markets among each other, whereas non-EU countries regulate various employment issues (e.g., pensions) on the basis of mutual agreements, which include relevant reciprocity clauses.

The terms of employment are derived from the written employment agreement and from implied terms. Implied terms concern the public order and terms established by collective agreements.

In any case, it is recommended that the employment agreement be sufficiently precise to permit the contracting parties to understand its provisions clearly and the courts to find a solution if a dispute arises between the contracting parties.

Required Information

By virtue of Presidential Decree 156/1994, implementing Directive 91/533/EEC, the employer must provide the employees with the following minimum information:

- Full particulars of the contracting parties;
- The agreed place of work and the address of the employer or the firm's headquarters;
- The employee's post or specialization, rank, category of employment, and scope of work (job description);
- The date on which the employment contract or relationship starts (started), and its duration if fixed-term;
- Vacation policies;
- Notice of termination and severance pay obligations;
- Any and all amounts due to the employee for basic salary and bonuses, and the time and manner in which these will become due;
- Normal daily and weekly working hours; and

- Reference to the applicable collective labor agreement, which determines the minimum payment and work conditions of the employee.

Employees must be informed on the above by delivery of a written employment agreement (1) within two months of the actual starting date of employment if the agreement is for an indefinite term; (2) within 15 days for part-time employment; and (3) within five days for fixed-term employment.

A fine can be imposed on any employer infringing the provisions of Presidential Decree 156/1994.

In addition to the above explicit terms, the following implicit (compulsory) terms are applied in an employment relationship:

- The employer must abide by the maximum legal working hours per day and per week (discussed under "Wages and Benefits").
- The employee may not work on Sundays or on public holidays and is entitled to an annual vacation (discussed under "Wages and Benefits").
- The employee is entitled to take a leave of absence under certain circumstances (e.g., maternity leave, sick leave, marital leave, educational leave).
- The dismissal of an employee must be in writing, and severance pay is based on length of service (see table in Section IV).
- The employer must follow all applicable provisions regarding collective agreements (e.g., maximum working hours, minimum remuneration).

Fixed-Term and Part-Time Employment

The crucial distinction between indefinite-term and fixed-term employment contracts arises in cases of dismissals and severance payments. As opposed to an indefinite-term agreement, a fixed-term contract ends with no severance payment due when the contractual term expires or when the contractual work agreed upon is completed. However, the employer must abide by certain regulations to maintain the agreement as fixed. Article 671 of the Greek Civil Code provides that a fixed-term contract shall be deemed renewed for an indefinite period if, upon the expiration of its term, the employee continues to work without the employer's opposition. Article 8 of Law 2112/1920 prohibits employers from entering into successive fixed-term contracts with employees by, for example, dismissing and subsequently reemploying them when there is no justifiable reason. Presidential Decree 180/2004, which protects employees subject to fixed-term contracts, provides that if the fixed-term contract is for a period longer than one year or if the same employer and the same employee enter into more than two fixed-term contracts within a period of two years, the employment relationship is considered to be of indefinite term with all the consequences provided by law, including payment of compensation in case of termination.

Another category provided under Greek labor law is that of part-time employees. According to Law 1892/1990, as supplemented by Law 2874/2000, part-time work is contractually or informally defined work for an indefinite period of time, daily or weekly, of fewer hours than normal legal working hours. Part-time employees are entitled to full insurance coverage (when they work more than four hours per day), vacation, and bonuses.

Confidentiality and Noncompetition Clauses

Employment agreements usually include confidentiality and noncompetition clauses. Employees have a duty to keep confidential any information related to the employer and its business that is considered to be of a confidential nature. Moreover, employees are obligated to abstain from competitive practices during the duration of their employment and, very often, for a reasonable period of time after the termination of the employment agreement, if specific conditions are met. In such a case, compensation for the employee's compliance is provided in the relevant clause.

Hiring Managerial Employees

Greek labor law does not contain special provisions for managers and executives. Case law has regulated their special status.

Managers are in a dependent labor relationship, so labor law covers their dismissal and compensation. However, while they are considered to be salaried employees, they are exempt from certain provisions of labor legislation such as maximum hours and night or Sunday work; they also lack the right to vacation and are criminally liable for the company's breaches of the law.

Executives are defined as those who possess certain specific powers and responsibilities such as representing the employer, hiring and dismissing employees, and influencing the company or division's financial results. An executive receives a considerably higher salary than managers or other employees, but is not entitled to any overtime pay or vacation.

Changes to the Terms and Provisions

The employer is obligated to inform the employees or their union leaders, or both, on the following matters before any decisions are implemented:

- Changes in the legal status of the company;
- Transfers, expansions, or limitations of the company's operations;
- Introduction of new technology;
- Changes in the structure of the personnel (restructuring);
- Annual planning of investments in health and security measures;
- Planning of overtime work;
- General trends of the company's economic field that may affect the employees; and
- Financial statements of the undertaking and any related details.

The dissemination of such information must take place regularly (at least once a year) and every time that the works council requires, within 20 days of the council's request.

Wages and Benefits

Working Time

The legal working time is 40 hours per week, except for specific categories of employees including bank employees, electricians, builders, and underage employees, who are employed for fewer hours. The employer and employee can agree that the employee will be employed for fewer working hours but remunerated for 40 hours. After the 40 legal working hours per week, the first five hours (hours 41 to 45) are considered as overwork and are remunerated by an increase of 25 percent over the hourly wage. The next three hours after overwork (hours 46 to 48) are considered overtime, for which permission must be granted by the appropriate labor authority. If permission is granted, then the realized overtime is remunerated 50 percent over the hourly wage (up to 120 hours annually per employee) or at 75 percent over the hourly wage (in case of more than 120 hours annually per employee).

Any overtime for which the legal procedure has not been followed is considered special overtime and must be remunerated at twice the regular hourly rate.

Rest Breaks

Employees must not be scheduled to work on Sundays or on public holidays. If one does work on Sunday or on a public holiday, he or she must be compensated by a 75 percent increase over the hourly wage, and the employer must grant a compensatory day off.

Vacation

According to Law 3302/2004, employees are entitled, in the first year of their employment, to 20 days of paid vacation and proportional vacation allowance. After two years of employment, the employees are entitled to 21 days of paid vacation. During the first and second year of employment, the employees can take their vacation either proportionally to the time they have worked (two days per month), or cumulatively in December during the particular year.

After three years of employment, employees are entitled to 22 days of vacation, increasing to 25 days after 10 years of employment with the same employer or after 12 years of employment irrespective of the employer.

Labor Unions and Works Councils

Employees in businesses employing more than 20 people have the right to vote and establish a works council for their representation.

Works councils have three to seven members who are elected by the employees during a general assembly convocation. Works councils have an advisory role contributing to the improvement of working conditions and the development of the company. Hence, they make joint decisions with the employer on the following:

- Drafting of the regulations of the company;
- Health and security regulations;

- Planning holidays;
- Relocation of employees disabled by work accidents to appropriate posts; and
- Planning and managing cultural, entertainment, and social events.

Even though the existence of works councils is not common practice in Greece, the EU Directive 94/45/EC on the establishment of European Works Councils has been implemented into Greek law by Presidential Decree 40/1997. According to that Decree, the European Works Council may be created on the initiative of the central management of the undertaking or on the initiative of at least 100 employees or their representatives. Where no initiative is taken, there is no obligation to create a European Works Council.

The European Works Council representatives are elected by the trade unions, by works councils, or by the employees in a direct election.[4] According to Greek law, European Works Council representatives are covered by the same specific protections that Greek union members enjoy; for example, protection against dismissal during their term and for one year following the end of their term, and special paid leaves of absence up to 15 days per year in order to fulfill such duties as participation in meetings of the European Works Council. They are also entitled to two hours' leave per week in order to inform the employees of Council-related issues.

Presidential Decree 40/1997 does not refer directly to the term of the office of European Works Council representatives, but provides that the elections of the Greek representatives should take place according to Greek law (Laws 1767/1988 and 1264/1982), which regulates the election of local unions and provide that the elections take place every two years. Greek law does not provide for any legal consequences in the case of non-reelection of the representatives in question.

SECTION II

My client is acquiring an existing business in Greece. How do I assess the existing workforce and consider changes?

Share Deals Versus Asset Deals

Share Deals

In case of a shares purchase, there is no change in the identity of the employer (which continues to be the same company). Consequently, the rules of transfer of undertakings do not apply in the specific case. All rights, duties, and liabilities owed to, or by, the employees continue to be owed to, or by, that company, and the buyer therefore inherits all those rights, duties, and liabilities by virtue of being the new owner of the company. There is only an obligation to provide general information to the employee representatives either before or after such change. The employee representatives have no involvement in the business transaction.

Asset Deals

According to Acquired Rights Directive 2001/23/EC and Presidential Decree 178/2002, which implements the Acquired Rights Directive in Greece, an asset deal is considered a transfer of undertakings if there is a transfer of an economic entity that retains its identity, meaning an organized grouping of resources that has the objective of pursuing an economic activity, whether or not that activity is central or ancillary.

In such a case, according to Presidential Decree 178/2002, the new employer takes over all rights and obligations of the existing employment agreements at the date of the realization of the transfer (e.g., indefinite-term contracts, fixed-term contracts, part-time contracts, employment agreements of enterprises of temporary occupation, and contracts of lending of services of employees), without any need for new agreements.

The same rules apply for the employees as well, as they are bound to accept the change of the employer. If the employee decides not to continue the working relationship with the new employer, then, according to Greek law, said refusal constitutes a voluntary resignation (not a dismissal) with no severance payment due to the employee.

Carrying Out a Workforce Reduction

During a transfer, both the original and the new employers may dismiss employees for reorganization reasons. This is not, however, a solution for "getting rid" of employees during the transfer, since Greek legislation and case law examine meticulously the condition of each reorganization procedure, the correct application of the legal criteria that determine who will be dismissed first (employees with less seniority and fewer family obligations go first), and the necessity of the dismissals. Since employees have the right to contest dismissals, employers should be very cautious when dismissing employees under the claim of "reorganization."

Statutory Protection

The main protected rights of employees in case of transfer are remuneration status (salary and benefits), internal working regulation status (positioning in the job hierarchy, promotions, reassignments, and disciplinary measures), termination rights (early retirement right, severance packages), recognition of previous employment, recognition of all "internal practices" of the previous employer, and any existing company policies. The vendor and the purchaser remain jointly and severally liable for all claims arising out of the employment relationship up to the date of the transfer.[5]

The purchaser must preserve the terms and conditions stipulated in the applicable collective labor agreement of the vendor's enterprise. There are, however, situations where, after the transfer, the employees find themselves working for a different enterprise's sector, and one that belongs to a different collective agreement. For example, accountants working in a petrol company, under the collective labor agreement of petroleum companies, could be transferred to an auditing company that belongs to the collective agreement of enterprises providing services. In such a case, the collective labor agreement would no longer be applicable, but the purchaser must preserve its terms and conditions, and so all provided benefits would be evaluated and added to the total remuneration of the transferred employees. The same applies in cases where, along with the collective agreement, affiliation with a specific social security fund changes as well. In this latter case, the employees cannot hold on to their previous social security fund. Therefore, they will be covered by the new one.

Regarding employer pension plans, the purchaser has three options:

1. To continue the pension contract under the same terms and conditions;
2. To amend the existing pension plan, in which case the new employer should enter into negotiations with the employee's representatives to reach an agreement on the changes; or
3. To choose not to continue the plan, in which case it will be terminated and liquidated, and employees will receive what they are entitled to at the date of liquidation. In this case, neither the vendor (if it has fulfilled its obligations) nor the purchaser will be liable regarding the terminated pension schemes.

Special Considerations

In the event of a transfer, both employers may dismiss employees due to reorganization reasons. In such case, the employer should apply certain criteria established by law in order to choose the employees to be dismissed.

The most important criteria, according to case law, are the employee's job performance, seniority, age, family responsibilities, financial situation, and possibility of finding a new job. The employee's health and that of his or her relatives are other elements to be considered. The employer is obliged to make inquiry concerning these issues, but the employee may refuse to give such information to the employer.

The primary criterion is the performance of the employee. Terminating the employment agreement of an employee whose performance has been judged as inefficient will not be considered wrongful termination. The remaining criteria are applied when deciding the termination between two employees whose performance is equivalent. Such application must be based on a general, overall appreciation of all the criteria, without discriminating in favor of a particular one. However, certain court decisions provide a relative priority to the criterion of seniority.

In selecting employees to be dismissed, the interests of the company cannot be ignored. This interest imposes keeping in the company the employees with the best performance. However, performance must not be the only element to be taken into consideration, to the detriment of social criteria. If the difference in social criteria between two employees is great, the difference in performance must be even greater in order to retain the employee with superior performance.

In cases of transfer, the new employer can evaluate the personnel by the above criteria, taking into consideration the financial and other structural needs of the company (such as economies of scale and use of new technology). When, for example, a legitimate prerequisite for maintaining a position in the company after a transfer is fluency in English or computer skills, the employer has sufficient grounds to terminate an employment agreement. However, the employer must show either that it gave the dismissed employee the opportunity to train for such new needs, or that no alternative position exists for the dismissed employee.

It is prudent to obtain legal advice before selecting employees to be dismissed.

Layoffs

Collective terminations, or layoffs, are subject to strict conditions and prerequisites, and must follow specific procedures. Terminations are considered collective if a company with a workforce of 20 to 200 employees dismisses more than four employees within a month or if a company with more than 200 employees dismisses 2 percent to 3 percent of its workforce or more than 30 employees. In the case of such layoffs, the employer must consult with the representatives of the employees as well as with the Ministry of Labor and Employment, and must propose solutions to minimize the impact of the dismissals.

The employer must inform the employees' representatives of its intention to enact a layoff and provide its reasons, as well as other requisite information. It should thereafter proceed to consultations and negotiations, which should not last less than 20 days. Should the employer and the employees' representatives not reach agreement, the consultation can be extended for 20 more days by decision of the Minister of Labor and Employment. Where an agreement is not reached, it is for the Minister of Labor to accept or reject the demand for a layoff within 10 days. If again a decision is not made, then the employer may proceed to dismiss employees either within the limits of the agreement reached between the employer and the employees' representatives during the consultation process or, in the absence of any such agreement, only within certain thresholds.

In some cases, dismissals are not allowed at all due to particular circumstances (e.g., maternal leave, military service, war victims or veterans, and trade union officers).

If the employer does not respect the provisions of the law on layoffs, then the dismissals are null. In these cases, the employer will have to pay compensation to the employees for the period they were out of work and for any damages caused to the employees due to the dismissals.

In all cases of valid layoffs, the employer must apply the provisions concerning the termination of employment contracts, such as notification in writing and payment of severance.

Making Changes to Key Managerial Positions

In case of transfer of undertakings, all existing employment relationships are transferred to the new employer, without any distinction as to whether they are managerial or nonmanagerial positions.

Changing the Wage and Benefits Structure

In case of a transfer, the purchaser must respect the terms and conditions of the employment agreements in force at the time of the transfer. No detrimental modification can take place without employees' written consent. The new employer and the employees may agree on eventual changes.

Depending on the nature of each benefit and whether the previous employer has reserved its right to amend or revoke such benefit, the new employer may proceed with an amendment of the employee's benefits.

During a transfer, there are cases where the employees of the previous employer receive higher remuneration packages than the existing personnel of the new employer. Case law has made clear that in such cases, the new employer may not decrease the package of the transferred personnel, but it does not have to increase the package of the existing personnel.

Special provisions exist for pension plans. The new employer has the right to either continue the insurance contract under the same terms and conditions, amend it, or even terminate it.

There exist divergent opinions as to whether the employer may amend or terminate health and welfare programs, such as life and medical insurance programs.

Consulting with Labor Unions or Works Councils

Share Transactions

No specific statutory information or consultation requirements apply to a share sale. However, for reasons of good faith, it is advisable to inform the employees about the new shareowner.

Asset Transactions

According to Article 8 of Presidential Decree 178/2002, there is no specific time schedule regarding the process to be followed for notifying employees of a transfer, but the employee's representatives must be informed "on time, before the realization of the transfer." In practice, a period of 20 days is considered reasonable for the conclusion of the information process. Here, "employees' representatives" refers to the works council, not the company union. However, in practice, no issue usually occurs if the union instead of the works council is informed.

The employees' representatives must be informed as to the date of the planned transfer, the reasons for such transaction, the impact on the employees (legal, financial and social), and the measures for protection of the employees.

If the original or new employers intend to take measures that will amend the status of employees, the employees' representatives must be consulted in order to reach an agreement. The results of the consultation are drafted in minutes, which can either be an agreement or the final position of the two parties involved (employees and employers). However, the employers—under the condition of nonabuse of rights—may choose not to follow the position of the employee's representatives.

If the employer breaches the information and consultation process, Greek law provides for a fine, which can vary between US $212 and US $12,698 per violation. There is no specific statutory reference to other legal consequences, such as invalidity of dismissals, if the consultation procedure is not followed. However, such a risk cannot be excluded.

SECTION III

My client wishes to sell its existing facility. What restrictions do we need to consider?

Assessing Employment Contracts

The key issues the buyer will normally focus on are the following:

- The total number of employees of the seller company.
- Pension arrangements and liabilities.
- The existence of any bonus or retention bonus plans.
- The existence of any change-of-control provisions in connection with stock, benefits, or compensation, golden-parachute agreements, or any similar type of arrangement in which officers, directors, or employees participate.
- The existence of any other material liability regarding the employees (e.g., unpaid wages, pension obligations).

Consulting with the Government

There is no obligation to consult with the government in case of a transfer, except where layoffs take place, in which case the employer must consult with the Ministry of Labor and Employment (see "Layoffs" in Section II).

Consulting with Labor Unions or Works Councils

The information and consultation procedure is the same as the one applicable in case of an acquisition of an existing business (see "Consulting with Labor Unions or Works Councils" in Section II).

SECTION IV

My client wishes to replace its senior manager(s). What restrictions do we need to consider?

Employment Contracts

The law does not distinguish between the termination of senior managers and ordinary employees. In practice, however, individual employment agreements of top executives provide for a notice period of six months or more, so that if they are terminated without warning (which is the usual practice), these executives will be entitled to additional compensation equal to salaries and fringe benefits for the notice period.

Statutory Severance Pay Requirements

Statutory severance pay provisions are the same for all employees either in managerial or nonmanagerial positions.

The law dictates the amount of severance payment the employer must pay when it dismisses an employee. Severance payment is calculated based on the monthly base salary of the employee at the date of termination, multiplied by 14 (so as to take into account the Christmas bonus of one month's salary, the Easter bonus of half a month's salary, and the annual vacation bonus of half a month's salary), and divided by 12, in order to average it on a monthly basis.

This average salary is increased by all the fringe benefits the employee receives on a regular basis, such as car allowance or value of car, housing allowance, mobile telephone, insurance coverage, commissions (if the commission plan or variable pay plan forms part of the employee's individual agreement or is covered by a collective agreement), bonuses (if paid on a regular basis and on a predetermined percentage), and so on. The average of the last two months' fringe benefits is considered in calculating the amount that must be added to the base salary in determining the severance due.

If the employee receives an annual bonus, the average of the last two or even three years is considered, divided by 12 to calculate a monthly average. This applies only to bonuses that are not discretionary or revocable by the employer, as expressly agreed in the employment agreement.

Once the average monthly salary is calculated, the severance payment is determined by length of service, as follows:

Period of Employment	Severance Payment
2 months to 1 year	1 month
More than 1 year	2 months
4 years to 6 years	3 months
6 years to 8 years	4 months
8 years to 10 years	5 months
10 years	6 months
Each additional year	1 additional month
28 years	24 months

As provided by Law 2112/1920, an employer that terminates a contract without prior notice to the employee must pay the whole amount of the severance. If proper prior notice is given, the employer must pay only half of the calculated amount. The severance payment is subject to a cap, prescribed by Law 3198/1955, which varies depending on whether the employer belongs to the private or the public sector.

Paying the correct amount of severance in case of termination is extremely important because the employee has the right to file a lawsuit contesting the validity of the termination and requesting the court to declare it abusive and invalid. If the lawsuit is accepted by the court, then the employee is considered to have been employed by the company retroactively to the date of termination, and salaries due are owed to the employee (offset by severance paid).

In all cases, the termination must be in writing, the legal severance has to be paid at the time of termination, and the employer has to notify the labor authority of the dismissal of the employee. If the severance is not paid at the moment the written form of termination is delivered or served to the dismissed employee, the termination is void. If the employer does not inform the labor authority, a fine may be imposed.

Statutory Restrictions on Dismissal Without Cause

The termination of the employment agreement is also null and void if a court determines that the dismissal was wrongful. The employee has three months after the date of termination to contest the validity of the termination before the court.

In case of a wrongful or illegal termination, the employee should continue to offer his or her work to the employer. If the employer refuses to accept it, then the employer may be obliged to pay salaries due for the whole period. In addition, in case of a null termination, an employee may also ask for compensation for suffering or mental anguish.

SECTION V

What prohibitions exist against discrimination on the basis of age, race, gender, disability, pregnancy, and other factors? What are the rights of employees, applicants, or former employees who believe that they have been discriminated against?

The basic principle of equal treatment is regulated by the Greek Constitution and incorporated into Greek law according to the EU directives. In particular, Directives 2000/78/EC and 2000/43/EC have been recently implemented in Greece by Law 3304/2005.

Areas of Protection

By virtue of these legislative provisions, direct or indirect discrimination based on racial or ethnic origin, religion or belief, disability, age, or sexual orientation in the field of employment and occupation is not allowed. Direct discrimination occurs when a person is treated less favorably than another of the same or comparable employment status. Indirect discrimination occurs when a provision, practice, or criterion puts a person at a disadvantage as compared with other people of the same employment status. Indirect discrimination can be justified only by a legitimate purpose and where the means of achieving the purpose are appropriate and necessary.

Statutory Rules

The foregoing provisions apply to all persons, whether in the private or public sector, and apply to work access, all types of vocational training, vocational guidance, working conditions, involvement in workers' and employees' organizations, social protection, social advantages, education, and supply of goods and services that are available to the public.

Differentiation can be justified only if, due to the nature or the context of the particular working practice, it constitutes a basic and crucial working condition, if the aim is just and the condition appropriate.

An example is the principle of equality of Article 4, Paragraph 1 of the Constitution, according to which all Greeks are equal before the law, when the remuneration is fixed by law or by regulative provisions of Collective Labor Agreements. When the remuneration is given to the employee at the employer's free discretion or following an individual employment agreement, the principle of equal remuneration is derived from Article 288 of the Civil Code, which requires the employer to act according to good faith and morals and not to treat employees unequally.

When discrimination does not arise out of an employer's discretionary action, but results from a legislative provision or a Collective Labor Agreement that requires an employer to provide remuneration for specific conditions, then the employee who does not meet the prerequisites for receiving such remuneration is not entitled to claim the principle of equal treatment for equal work. For example, an unmarried, childless employee is not entitled to receive a marriage allowance or children's allowance.

Consequently, the principle of equal remuneration for equal work can take into account the character of the violation of the principle of equal treatment (when it refers to remunerations given voluntarily or due to company's policy) or the violation of the principle of equality, depending on whether the harmful discrimination arises out of a voluntary employer's act or out of a legislative provision.

Sanctions and Remedies

The violation of the principle of equal treatment renders the discriminatory treatment of an employee null and void, and the employee may claim the benefits associated with the application of said principle.

SECTION VI

On the Horizon: What key labor and employment law developments should an employer doing business in Greece anticipate occurring in the coming years?

In Greece, employment protection legislation ranks very high. It is widely felt that Greece's labor market is strictly regulated. New regulations concerning paid annual leave are anticipated. These will allow the employer to split the annual leave days of the employees of the company into more than two parts, without the prior approval of the Labor Inspection Authority, after their third year of service to the company.

NOTES

1. Supreme Court Decision 591, EED 53 (1994), p. 339.
2. Greek Civil Code, art. 192.
3. Presidential Decree 154/1996.
4. Act 1264/1982, art. 12; Act 1767/1988, art. 4.
5. Presidential Decree 178/2002, art. 4, para. 1.

CHAPTER 8

LABOR AND EMPLOYMENT LAW IN HUNGARY

TAMÁS RIESZ

SECTION I

My client wishes to establish a manufacturing facility in Hungary and will need to hire a workforce. What are the key issues involved?

Employment Contracts: Who Receives Them and What Must They Include?

Mandatory Requirements

The employment relationship is a contractual relationship between the employer and employee under an employment contract for the performance of a specific work under determined circumstances with reporting obligations. As a general rule, the employer must inform employees (nonexecutive and senior executive employees), even during the recruitment process, of any circumstances that may be important with respect to the performance of rights and obligations under the employment relationship. The employer is also obliged to inform the employee of any legal remedy available for the employee in case of any measures taken by the employer during the employment relationship.

Form of the Employment Contract

According to the Labor Code (Act XXII of 1992), the employment contract must be in writing. If the contract is not in writing, its validity may be challenged only by the employee within 30 days of the start of the employment relationship. The employer is bound by the agreement whether the contract is made orally or in writing.

List of Required Information

Under Hungarian labor law, the employment contract must include (1) the basic wage or salary; (2) the employee's position and work-related duties; and (3) the employee's place of work. In addition, the employment contract must set out the names of the parties and the parties' particulars (e.g., registered address, company registration number, employee's social security number) that are relevant to the employment relationship.

Furthermore the employer must at least verbally communicate to the employee the following issues at the time of entering into the employment contract. A further written notice regarding these issues must be provided to the employee no later than 30 days from the signing of the employment contract.

These issues are:

1. The relevant work order (detailed terms and conditions of work);
2. The elements of the pay other than the basic wage (overtime pay, reimbursements, bonuses, premiums, commissions, and other incentives);
3. The date of payment of the wages;
4. The date of commencement of work by the employee;
5. The method of calculating the amount of paid annual leave and the rules on taking such leave;
6. The rules for determining the termination notice period for the employer and the employee;
7. Whether the employee's employment relationship is governed by a collective agreement; and
8. Description of the labor union having representation of the employer and the works council (central works councils, works council representative), if any.

Except for items (4), (7), and (8), information may be provided by reference to provisions of law or a collective agreement.

Language

The Labor Code and Act IV of 1991 on job assistance and unemployment benefits do not contain provisions regarding the language of the employment contract. Naturally, in the case of expatriate employees, it is expedient (but not compulsory) to translate the employment contract to both the employer's and the employee's language. The labor, tax, and other authorities, during a supervisory procedure, usually ask for the employment contract drafted in Hungarian.

Changes to the Terms and Provisions

The employer and the employee may modify the employment contract only by mutual consent (with the exception of salary increase, but not decrease). Unlawful modification may result in the invalidity of such modification and compensation for damages. Collective agreements may not modify the contract to the disadvantage of the employee even if it is applicable to the employee. The employer may change the scope of the employee's work for a temporary period of time. However, the term of the change may not exceed 44 days in a year, and the salary of the employee must be changed accordingly to the scope of work and it must be at least equal to the former average salary of the employee.

Fixed-Term Employment

If the employment contract does not specify the term of the contract, it will be deemed to be indefinite. Where the parties intend to enter into a contract for a fixed term, they must expressly provide for this in the contract. The fixed-term employment contract has certain criteria, stipulated in the Labor Code, that differ from the indefinite-term employment contract. A fixed term of employment may not exceed an aggregate of five years. For this calculation, the terms of repeated definite-term employment agreements with the same employer must be aggregated if a subsequent fixed-term employment agreement is entered into within six months of the date of the prior agreement. The above rule is not applicable to employees in an executive position.

When an employee works at least one day longer than the fixed period set out in the contract with the knowledge of an immediate supervisor, the employment will automatically convert to an indefinite-term employment relationship. However, fixed-term employment contracts with a duration of 30 days or less are, in such a case, merely extended by the same definite period as originally agreed by the contracting parties.

Where a fixed-term employment contract is renewed or extended between the same parties without any rightful interest on the part of the employer and it is against the rightful interests of the employee, the employment is deemed to be established for an indefinite term.

Probation Period

The parties usually stipulate a probation period, with a maximum duration of three months, during which either party may terminate the employment contract with immediate effect and without having to give a reason for the termination. The agreed period of the probation may not be extended, even if it was originally entered into for less than the maximum probation period of three months.

Wages and Benefits

Minimum Wage Requirements

Salary may be determined based on time worked or performance, or both.

The personal basic wage, which employees must receive for the time they were employed by the employer even if the latter could not provide them with work, must be based on time worked. The parties are free to agree on the wage, but it may not be less than the minimum wage determined by law. In 2007, the personal basic wage of a full-time employee could not be less than HUF 62,500 (approximately €232) a month. Supplementary remuneration must be paid to the employee in certain cases, such as overtime, night work, or shift work. Other supplementary remuneration, in addition to that set out in the Labor Code, may be provided for in the individual employment contract.

Special Benefits Requirements

Working Time

The average working time is eight hours per day, 40 hours per week. An employment contract may specify a shorter working time. If the duty of the employee is of a stand-by nature or the employee is a close relative of the employer or an owner of the company (with more than 25 percent of the voting rights), an employment contract may specify a longer working time. Such working time may not exceed 12 hours per day and 60 hours per week. The aggregate duration of the time spent at work may not exceed 48 hours a week.

Overtime

As a rule, an employee may be ordered to work overtime only under special circumstances and with valid justification; however, certain classes of employees are exempt from overtime, such as (1) pregnant women, from the time their pregnancy is confirmed until the child reaches 12 months; (2) men raising children alone until the child reaches 12 months; and (3) employees who are employed in positions that are hazardous or damaging to their health as determined by law.

Overtime work may not exceed 200 hours per year or, if a collective agreement so provides, 300 hours per year. The restrictions on overtime work do not apply where the work is necessitated by accident, force majeure, or the need to avoid major damage, except for the exempt employee classes described above. In addition to receiving their usual pay for working overtime, employees are also entitled to supplementary remuneration amounting to 50 percent of their average pay for the time spent working overtime during hours different from the working time schedule or in excess of the working timeframe. The parties are free to increase, but not to decrease, the consideration for the overtime.

As consideration for working on their day off or on a public holiday, employees must receive their ordinary pay for work performed and either (1) supplementary remuneration of at least 50 percent of the ordinary pay plus a compensatory day off; or (2) if no compensatory day off is provided, supplementary remuneration of at least 100 percent of the ordinary pay for each day of work; or (3) for working on a public holiday, a further fee.

In addition to the regular 50 and 100 percent overtime payments, the following additional payments must be made: (1) For overtime work performed at night (normally two consecutive hours between 10 PM and 6 AM), the employee must receive a 15 percent shift differential; (2) for shift work (where the employees perform the same work with regular shifts) performed in the afternoon, the employee must receive a 15 percent shift differential and, for the same at night, a 30 percent shift differential.

Night Work

Employees carrying out night work are entitled to a shift differential of 15 percent. There is further additional remuneration for employees carrying out night work under special working time arrangements (e.g., night shifts, continuous working time arrangements).

Holidays and Vacations

An employment contract may specify for holidays and vacations more favorable to the employee than the Labor Code provides. Otherwise, the provisions of the Labor Code must be applied. A vacation allowance consists of basic and supplementary vacation. The basic paid vacation is a minimum of 20 days within one calendar year, which increases progressively with the age of the employee to a maximum of 30 days per year at the age of 45. Supplementary vacation may be offered based on the employee's circumstances (e.g., if the employee is pregnant, has young children, is disabled, or is a minor). Sick leave is up to 15 days' paid leave. Pregnant employees are entitled to 24 weeks' maternity leave. Such leave shall be scheduled so as to commence four weeks prior to the expected time of birth if possible. Men are entitled to five days' paternity leave. There are several other statutory leave benefits available in particular situations. In certain circumstances, at the request of the employee, the employer must provide unpaid leave to employees to enable them (1) to look after their child until the child's third birthday; (2) to look after their child until the child's 10th birthday provided that they receive a child-care allowance from a government assistance program for disabled children; and (3) to take care of a sick child under age 12.

Labor Unions

The primary functions of the labor union (*Szakszervezet*) are to promote and protect the employees' interests related to their employment relationship. The labor union performs different activities and it is granted different allowances.

One of the labor union's tasks is to receive and provide information, which means that the labor union informs the employees about their rights and obligations with regard to the work relationship. Moreover, the employer has to consult with the union about issues that may affect the business and social interests of the employees, such as rules on work conditions. The labor union's power to object is essential: The union has the right to file an objection to any unlawful arrangement or omission of the employer that may adversely affect the employees. Further, it is one of the fundamental rights of the labor union to enter into a collective agreement.

Union representatives are accorded work time allowance to conduct union business, and many rules in the Labor Code protect representatives from suffering job-related drawbacks due to their union activities.

Collective Agreements

A collective agreement (*Kollektív Szerződés*) may be entered into between, on the one hand, an employer, an organization representing the employer's interest, or several employers, and, on the other hand, a labor union or several labor unions; but it is not mandatory to have a collective agreement. Collective agreements facilitate the implementation of rules that are different from the Labor Code. However, these rules must be favorable to the employees.

Works Councils

Mandatory Requirements

According to the rules of the Labor Code, if the number of employees exceeds 50 persons at a workplace, a works council (*Üzemi Tanács*) must be elected. The number of council members shall be between three and 13 depending on the number of the employees. An employees' representative (*Üzemi Megbízott*) shall be elected at a workplace with at least 16 but no more than 50 employees. The employees' representative has the same rights and obligations as the works council. The works council is established to protect the employees' social and economic interests and to maintain peace in labor relations.

Functions and Frequency

All employees are entitled to participate in the election of the works council's members. The members are elected for three-year terms. The Labor Code provides detailed rules regarding the nominating of the members and the elections.

Employers must consult the works council prior to adopting a decision in connection with plans or actions affecting a large group of employees, and basically any matters concerning the employees' essential interests, including (1) plans for actions affecting a large group of employees (reorganization, transformation, privatization, modernization); (2) proposals for setting up a personnel records system, the set of data to be recorded, plans for the contents of the data sheet, and staff policy plans; (3) plans connected with the employees' training, proposals for job assistance, subsidies for the betterment of employment conditions, and drafts of plans for early retirement; (4) plans for actions pertaining to the occupational rehabilitation of persons whose capacity to work has reduced; (5) plans for annual vacation schedules; (6) the introduction of new work organization methods and performance requirements; (7) plans for internal regulations affecting the employees' substantive interests; and (8) tenders announced by the employer offering financial reward or recognition of exemplary performance. Furthermore, the employer has to notify the works councils at least every six months regarding the fundamental issues affecting the employer's economic situation, the plans for major decisions pertaining to a significant modification of the employer's scope of activities, investment projects, trends in wages and salaries, and the like. The Labor Code contains provisions related to the labor law protection and work time allowances of the members of the works council and the employees' representatives.

● SECTION II

My client is acquiring an existing business in Hungary. How do I assess the existing workforce and consider changes?

Share Deals Versus Asset Deals

The asset deal (i.e., business transfer or legal succession of the employer) is defined as the transfer of a segregated group of the employer's business or assets (e.g., factory, branch, or place of work) according to an agreement including, but not limited to, a sale and purchase, a swap or a lease agreement, or an entry into a business organization by way of a contribution in kind, for the purposes of continued operation. In a share deal, however, a change in ownership or control of a company does not qualify as legal succession of the employer, and thus the employer—the owned or controlled company—remains the same.

From a labor law point of view, therefore, asset deals require much more consideration., Employees' rights under the legal succession of their employer are safeguarded by several provisions of the Labor Code. Upon the business transfer, all rights and obligations of the transferor pass, at the time of the legal succession, to the transferee.

Carrying Out a Workforce Reduction

Statutory Protection

In all termination cases, the termination notice must be made in writing and the employee's attention must be drawn to the possible remedies available (e.g., initiating conciliation proceedings or bringing proceedings before a court of law). In addition, in the case of ordinary or extraordinary termination, the notice must be supported by reasons for the termination.

If the employer fails to provide the employee with a termination notice containing all of the required elements, the termination of the employment will be considered invalid and may expose the employer to labor law liability for invalid termination, civil law liability for damages payable to the employee for all losses suffered, and a penalty imposed by the Labor Authority.

Under Hungarian law, an employment relationship may be terminated (1) by mutual consent; (2) by ordinary termination; (3) by extraordinary termination; or (4) with immediate effect during any probation period (detailed in Section I.). Layoffs have special rules, which will be detailed on page 141.

Procedural Requirements

Probationary Period
During the probation period (which can be a maximum of three months) of an indefinite-term contract, either party may terminate the employment relationship with immediate effect without the requirement to support the termination with reasons.

Ordinary Termination
According to the Labor Code, an ordinary termination is one that is related to the employee's abilities, work-related conduct, or the employer's operations. Legal

succession of the employer cannot in itself be the reason for the termination of an indefinite-term employment contract by way of ordinary termination.

Should the employer terminate the employment relationship due to the employee's work-related conduct, abilities, or performance, the employee must be given the opportunity to defend such claims except in situations where it is evident that such defense would be fruitless.

Extraordinary Termination

Either the employer or the employee may terminate the employment relationship by extraordinary termination, that is, without a notice period, if the other party intentionally commits a material breach of essential duties arising out of the employment relationship, is grossly negligent, or otherwise demonstrates conduct that would make the continuation of the employment relationship impossible. Before delivering written notice of the extraordinary termination to the employee, the employer must inform the employee of the reasons for the extraordinary termination and allow the employee to defend his or her case, except when this could not reasonably be expected of the employer.

If a labor court of law holds that the employer terminated the employment relationship illegally, the employee may request the court to order his or her reinstatement to the original work position. The court may refuse this request if the employer shows that it cannot be expected to implement the reinstatement. However, reinstatement will be ordered if the termination breaches certain provisions, such as the prohibition of discrimination or the protection of elected labor union representatives.

If the employee does not request reinstatement, or if the court does not order reinstatement as a result of an application by the employer, the employee is entitled to a sum equal to his or her average pay of between two and 12 months. The size of the sum payable depends on the facts of the case, particularly the gravity of the illegal measure taken by the employer and its consequences.

If the employee is not reinstated, the employment relationship terminates when the court's decree establishing the illegal nature of the termination becomes effective. If the employment relationship has been terminated illegally, the employee is entitled to lost wages, other benefits, and further damages. If the employment has not been terminated by ordinary notice, the employee is entitled to a sum equal to the average pay for the period of exemption from work and a severance payment in addition to the sums mentioned above.

Severance Pay

The employee is entitled to a severance payment after a minimum of three years of service if the employment relationship has been terminated by ordinary termination by the employer, by extraordinary termination by the employee, or due to the cessation of the employer without a legal successor. However, an employee who qualifies as a pensioner on the date of termination is not entitled to severance pay. The amount of severance pay depends on the period of employment, ranging from one month's salary up to six months' salary.

An additional severance payment amounting to three months' salary must be made if the employee's employment relationship was terminated by ordinary termination by the employer within five years of the employee reaching retirement age, or if the termination was due to the cessation of the employer without a legal successor.

Layoffs

Dismissals by an employer for reasons relating to its operation must be considered as layoffs if the terminations are intended to take place over a period of 30 days and affect at least:

- 10 employees, if the employer employs more than 20 and fewer than 100 employees; or
- 10 percent of the employees, if the employer employs 100 or more but fewer than 300 employees; or
- 30 employees, if the employer employs 300 employees or more.

The calculation should be based on the average number of employees employed during the six months immediately preceding the decision to terminate (or over a shorter period if the employer recently commenced its activities).

The above conditions must be determined at each branch or place of operation, but if two or more branches or places of operation are located in the same county, the number of affected employees in the county must be aggregated. The employer must follow specific procedural rules in case of layoffs.

Fixed-Term Agreements

Fixed-term employment agreements may not be terminated by ordinary termination; instead, the employer may terminate such employment by paying the employee the salary due for the remainder of the term, to a maximum of one year's salary.

Changing the Wage and Benefits Structure

The Hungarian labor courts have ruled that in the case of legal succession (i.e., the asset deal) of the employer, the employment relationship of an employee established with the old employer continues with the new employer on the same terms and conditions, without any need to enter into a new employment contract, unless both the new employer and the employee wish to modify its terms. Naturally this rule shall be applied to the wage and benefits structure also, which is one of the elements of the employment contract. In addition, for the purposes of calculating the termination notice period and the amount of severance pay, the periods spent with the old and the new employer must be aggregated.

The transferor and the transferee have joint and several liability for the fulfillment of obligations undertaken by the transferor prior to the legal succession, if an employee raises a claim within one year of the legal succession. Moreover, the transferor is liable as surety for payments due on termination of employment to employees, provided that the transferor, or its related entities, has more than half of the voting rights in the decision-making body of the transferee, and that the employment relationship was terminated by the transferee within one year of the succession by (1) ordinary termination based on a reason in connection with the operation of the employer (in the case of an indefinite term employment) or (2) termination with a payment to the employee of the average salary for one year or, if the remaining term of the definite period is less than one year, for the remaining term (in the case of fixed-term employment).

Consulting with Labor Unions or Works Councils

Procedural Requirements

At least 15 days prior to the date of the legal succession, the transferor and the transferee must notify the labor union(s) or, if no labor union exists at the employer's undertaking, the works councils or the employees' representative(s) of (1) the planned date of the legal succession; (2) the reasons for the legal succession; and (3) the legal, business, and social consequences of the legal succession, and must initiate consultations with the labor union(s) about all envisaged measures.

At least 15 days before making a decision on layoffs, the employer must initiate a consultation process with the works councils or, in the absence of a works council, with a committee established from the members of the labor union(s) represented at the employer and from the employees' representatives. The employer must conduct this consultation until a decision has been made or an agreement reached.

At least seven days prior to the consultation, the employer must inform both the employees' representatives and the Labor Authority in writing of (1) the reasons for the intended layoff; (2) the number of employees affected, divided into categories of profession; and (3) the number of employees employed six months prior to the decision of layoff.

In the course of the consultation, the employer must inform the employees' representatives in writing and in due time on (1) the proposed duration and timing of the layoff; (2) the criteria for choosing which employees will be affected; and (3) the terms and conditions and the method for determining the amount of allowances given upon the termination of the employment relationship, if they differ from those set out by law and in the collective agreement.

The consultation must consider (1) possible ways to avoid the layoff; (2) the criteria for the layoff; (3) possible ways to alleviate the consequences of the layoff; and (4) possible ways to reduce the number of employees affected. If the employer and the employees' representatives reach an agreement in the course of the consultation, the agreement must be put in writing and sent to the Labor Authority.

If, after consultation, the employer decides to implement the layoff, the decision must set out the number of employees affected by the layoff, divided into categories of profession/occupation, and the commencement, closing date, and timing of the implementation of the layoff. The timing must be based on 30-day periods.

Sanctions and Remedies

If the employer does not comply with information and consultation requirements, the labor union may file an objection with a court. The labor court may find that the consultation procedure has been lacking and order the employer to take the appropriate measures. Where there has been a failure to inform or consult with the works councils, any action taken by the employer in contravention of these requirements (e.g., a decision to proceed with a transaction) is deemed invalid.

Consulting with the Government

Procedural Requirements

The employees affected by the layoff and the Labor Authority must be notified in writing of the decision relating to the layoff at least 30 days before the termination notice is given to the employees. At this point the employer must also inform the Labor Authority of: (1) the employees' personal information (name, birthplace, date of birth, social security number, and mother's maiden name); (2) their latest position; (3) their qualifications; and (4) the average salary of each employee affected by the intended dismissal.

This information must be provided even where the consultation of the employer with the employees' representatives results in a lower number of affected employees than initially envisaged, provided that at least five employees are terminated by ordinary termination in connection with the operation of the employer (and not the behavior of the employees).

Sanctions and Remedies

Breach of the obligation to inform the Labor Authority and the affected employees will result in the invalidity of the termination(s) or agreement to terminate. If the employer does not comply with the consultation procedure, the works council or the labor union has the right to apply to a court of law for a declaration of such invalidity.

⊕ SECTION III

My client wishes to sell its existing facility. What restrictions do we need to consider?

Assessing Employment Contracts

Because selling an existing facility (e.g., asset transfer) is classified as legal succession of the employer, such a business transfer may not affect the employees adversely. Terms and conditions of the employment contracts cannot be amended adversely with respect to the employees. If the new employer intends to reduce the workforce, it is expedient to examine the provisions of the employees' contract and also the collective agreement (if any) regarding the termination period, the severance payment, and compensation, especially in connection with protected employees (members of works councils or the labor union, pregnant women, etc.).

The Labor Code provides special rules regarding employees in an executive position. It must be considered that the collective agreement is not applicable to executives. An executive may be hired under a fixed-term employment contract that may exceed the normal limit of five years. In case of termination of an executive's employment contract, the general prohibitions and termination notice do not apply, unless the employer wishes to provide grounds for terminating the employment relationship.

Consulting with the Government

The employer is obliged to consult and notify the Labor Authority. This obligation is essential: If the employer fails to fulfill it, any subsequent action (transfer, layoff) may be deemed invalid by the court.

Consulting with Labor Unions or Works Councils

See Section II.

Negotiating with the Purchaser: Special Labor Issues

Usually nonsolicitation, noncompete, and business-confidentiality–related issues arise in connection with executive-level employees. The first two issues need to be dealt with in the transfer documentation. The related issues will be important points for the purchaser to maintain smooth operation of the acquired entity/ assets. The third point should already be in the employment contracts of the key employees; therefore the only issue is to check that the required provisions are included in the employment contracts and that the relevant employees are aware of these regulations.

In addition, both parties should be aware of any ongoing and potential labor lawsuits. The seller has to consider this possibility because of its joint and several liability for obligations undertaken prior to the legal succession. Employment agreement provisions that most often give rise to lawsuits and thus merit special consideration are those related to the notice or termination period, severance payments, and the rules of ordinary or extraordinary termination.

SECTION IV

My client wishes to replace its senior manager(s). What restrictions do we need to consider?

Employment Contracts

Consideration as Employees

The rights and obligations of executive employees may be governed either by an employment contract or by the provisions of the Civil Code relating to personal service contracts.

Statutory Protection

Special provisions of the Labor Code apply to managers and executive employees. Executive employees are the head of the employer and his or her deputy.

In addition, the owner or the entity exercising the ownership rights may prescribe that employees filling positions of key importance for the employer's operations are to be deemed executive employees for the purpose of extraordinary termination, rules of exclusion, work schedule, and vacation. The employee concerned shall be notified of this condition when establishing the employment relationship.

Common Contractual Protections

Data Protection

Employers may disclose facts, data, and opinions concerning an employee to third persons only as specified by law or with the employee's consent.

Noncompetition

An executive officer may not accept an executive position in another company whose main business activity is similar to that of the employer, unless permitted by the articles of association of the employer affected or if the supreme body of the employer (e.g., general meeting of shareholders) has granted consent.

Confidentiality

Executive employees must treat all business secrets of the employer as strictly confidential.

Unless otherwise provided by law, upon request by the members (shareholders), executive employees shall provide information concerning the affairs of the employer and allow inspection of its books and documents. In the event of any executive officer's failure to comply with such request, the member concerned may request that the court of registry instruct the employer affected to provide the information in question or to provide for inspection.

Executive employees shall be liable to the employer in accordance with the general rules of civil law for damages caused by any infringement of the law or any breach of the memorandum of association, the resolutions of the employer's supreme body, or their management obligations.

In the event of any imminent threat of the employer's insolvency, the executive employees shall conduct the management of the employer giving priority to the company's creditors. In the event that noncompliance with this obligation is verified and if the employer is deemed to be insolvent, the executive employees affected may be subject to financial liability toward the company's creditors.

Procedural Requirements

Ordinary Termination

Dismissal of executive employees can be ordinary or extraordinary. Executive employees are less protected against dismissal because of their special responsibility and the special relationship between them and the owners of the company.

Collective agreements do not apply in the case of dismissal of an executive employee.

In the event of ordinary termination, employers are not obliged to justify the termination of the executive employee, and the general rules of termination notice period are not compulsory. However, if the employer decides to give reasons for the ordinary termination, the general rules relating to the required content of the reasoning apply.

Extraordinary Termination

Either the employer or the employee may terminate the employment relationship with extraordinary termination, that is, without a notice period, if the other party intentionally commits a material breach of essential duties arising out of the employment relationship, is grossly negligent, or otherwise demonstrates conduct that would make the continuation of the employment relationship impossible. Before delivering written notice of the extraordinary termination to the employee, the employer must inform the employee of the reasons for the extraordinary termination and allow the employee to defend his or her case, except when this could not reasonably be expected of the employer.

The right of extraordinary termination shall be exercised within a period of 15 days of gaining knowledge of the grounds therefore, but no more than three years after the occurrence of such grounds (this period is only one year for general employees), or in the event of a criminal offense up to the statute of limitations. If the right of extraordinary termination is exercised by a committee, the date of gaining knowledge shall be the date when the committee, acting as the body exercising the employer's rights, is informed regarding the grounds for the extraordinary dismissal.

The employer shall be entitled to terminate the employment relationship of an executive officer if a close relative of such officer has become a shareholder in a company that is engaged in the same or similar activities or is in regular business contact with the employer, or has established an employment relationship or other employment-related legal relationship with an employer engaged in such activities. Close relatives are spouses, common-law spouses, next of kin, spouse's next of kin, adopted persons, stepchildren, foster children, adoptive parents, stepparents, foster parents, and siblings.

Protected Groups

Other than the prohibitions against discrimination discussed in Section V, there are no special groups of executive employees protected and no special period when termination is prohibited.

Statutory Severance Pay Requirements

An executive employee shall be entitled to severance pay if the employment relationship is terminated by ordinary dismissal or in consequence of the dissolution of the employer without legal succession. An executive employee who qualifies as a pensioner shall not be entitled to receive severance pay.

If the employer terminates the employment relationship of an executive officer in the course of bankruptcy or liquidation proceedings, the employer must also pay the executive a maximum of six months' average wages. The additional average wages payable to executive employees shall become due upon the conclusion of the liquidation proceedings or upon the approval of the closing liquidation statement or the closing simplified balance sheet.

Statutory Restrictions on Dismissal Without Cause

If a labor court of law holds that the employer terminated the employment relationship illegally, the executive employee may request the court to order his or her reinstatement. The court may refuse this request if the employer shows that it cannot be expected to implement the reinstatement. However, reinstatement will be ordered if the termination breaches certain provisions, such as the prohibition of discrimination.

If the executive employee does not request reinstatement, or if the court does not order reinstatement as a result of an application by the employer, the executive employee is entitled to a sum equal to his or her average pay of between two and 12 months. The size of the sum payable depends on the facts of the case, particularly the gravity of the illegal measure taken by the employer and its consequences.

If the executive employee is not reinstated, the employment relationship terminates when the court's decree establishing the illegal nature of the termination becomes effective. If the employment relationship has been terminated illegally, the executive employee is entitled to lost wages, other benefits, and further damages. If the employment has not been terminated by ordinary notice, the executive employee is entitled to a sum equal to the average pay for the period of exemption from work and a severance payment in addition to the sums mentioned above.

On the basis of the special regulations of the Labor Code on dismissal of senior employees, the employer is not obliged to give reasons to its decision. Ordinary termination is possible without any cause; therefore, there are no applicable restrictions.

❸ SECTION V

What prohibitions exist against discrimination on the basis of age, race, gender, disability, pregnancy, and other factors? What are the rights of employees, applicants, or former employees who believe that they have been discriminated against?

Statutory Rules

Direct and indirect discrimination are defined in the same way as in the Racial Equality Directive (2000/43/EC), which has been implemented into Hungarian law together with the Employment Equality Directive (2000/78/EC) and Council Directive 2004/113/EC of December 13, 2004 on the principle of equal treatment between men and women in the access to and supply of goods and services.

Fundamental antidiscrimination measures of Hungarian law are set out in the Equal Treatment Act (Act CXXV of 2003). This piece of legislation has replaced the former antidiscrimination measures and terminology of the Labor Code by introducing the principle of "equal treatment" instead of a prohibition of "discrimination."

Both direct and indirect forms of discrimination are prohibited. Provisions that are not considered direct negative discrimination and apparently comply with the principle of equal treatment but put any protected persons or groups at a considerably larger disadvantage compared with other persons or groups in a similar situation are considered indirect discrimination.

Areas of Protection

The Equal Treatment Act applies to all employment relationships and related legal relationships and recognizes 20 discrimination categories: gender, race, color, ethnic origin, belonging to national or ethnic minority, mother language, disability, health conditions, religion, political or other kind of opinion, family status, parenthood or pregnancy, sexual orientation, gender identity, age, social origin, financial status, social circumstances or nature of employment relationship (e.g., part-time or definite term employment relationships), and membership of an organization representing employees' interests, plus any other status, attribute, or characteristic.

Equal treatment of employees can be enhanced by the adoption of an Equal Treatment Plan in the framework of collective labor relationships for the purposes of eliminating differences that exist between various employee groups.

The Hungarian Labor Code contains special regulations on nondiscrimination policies. These are as follows.

Employers shall not terminate an employment relationship by ordinary dismissal during the periods specified below:

- Incapacity to work because of illness, an accident at work or occupational disease (with some limitations on the length of the protected period);
- During sick leave for the purpose of caring for a sick child;
- During an unpaid leave of absence for nursing or caring for a close relative, including children;
- During pregnancy, for three months after giving birth, or during maternity leave.

With respect to the remuneration of employees for the same work or for work to which equal value is attributed, no discrimination shall be allowed on any grounds (principle of equal pay).

The principle of equal treatment shall be based on the nature of work, its quality and quantity, working conditions, vocational training, physical and intellectual efforts, experience, and responsibilities. The wages of employees—whether based on the nature or category of the work or on performance—shall be determined without any discrimination among the employees.

A woman, from the time her pregnancy is established until her child reaches one year of age, shall be temporarily placed in a position suitable for her condition from a medical standpoint and approved by the employee, or the working conditions in her existing position shall be modified as appropriate, on the basis of a medical report pertaining to employment. The wages of an employee temporarily transferred to a different position or employed under modified work conditions without being transferred shall not be less than her previous average earnings. If the employer is unable to provide a position as appropriate for her medical condition, the woman shall be relieved from work and shall receive the wages payable for idle time for such period of time.

Employers shall continue to employ employees whose capacity to work has been reduced in the course of employment, in due compliance with the provisions of separate legal regulations, in positions suitable for their condition.

Venue and Procedure

A lawsuit under civil or labor law because of a violation of the principle of equal treatment before the court can be initiated by the Public Prosecutor, the Equal Treatment Office, or the social and interest representation organization, if the violation was based on a characteristic that is an essential feature of the individual and affects a larger group of persons that cannot be determined accurately.

It is considered a particular violation of the principle of equal treatment if the employer inflicts direct or indirect negative discrimination upon an employee within the following areas:

- Access to employment, especially in public job advertisements, hiring, and the conditions of employment;
- Procedures undertaken before the establishment of the employment relationship;
- Training before or during employment;
- Working conditions;
- Benefits and wages;
- Membership or participation in employees' organizations;
- The promotion system;
- Enforcement of liability for damages or disciplinary liability;
- Termination of the employment relationship.

The principle of equal treatment is not violated if (1) the discrimination is proportional, is justified by the characteristic or nature of the work, and is based on all relevant and legitimate terms and conditions; or (2) the discrimination arises directly from a religious or other ideological conviction or national or ethnic origin that fundamentally determines the nature of the organization, and the discrimination is proportional and justified by the nature of the employment activity or the conditions of its pursuit.

The Labor Law Act provides that if a court determines that the employer has unlawfully terminated an employee's employment, the employee may request the court to order his or her reinstatement to the original work position. The court may refuse this request if the employer shows that it cannot be expected to implement the reinstatement. These provisions shall not be applied if the employer's action violates the principle of equal treatment or restriction of termination or the employer has terminated the employment relationship of an employee under labor law protection prescribed for elected trade union representatives in violation of the provisions of Labor Law Act.

If the employee does not request reinstatement or if upon the employer's request the court refuses to reinstate the employee, the court shall weigh all applicable circumstances—in particular the unlawful action and its consequences—and order the employer to pay no less than two and no more than 12 months' average earnings to the employee.

Burden of Proof

In procedures initiated because of a violation of the principle of equal treatment, the injured party or the party entitled to assert claims of public interest must prove that the injured person or group has suffered a disadvantage and that the injured party or group belongs to one of the protected groups. If this has been proven, the other party has the burden of proving either that it has observed or that it was not obliged to observe the principle of equal treatment.

Affirmative Action

Affirmative action is regarded as lawful if it aims to eliminate unequal opportunities of a specific social group and is performed

- On the basis of a governmental decree or a collective agreement and is effective for a definite period; or
- In accordance with the constitutional or operational rules of a political party.

However, no affirmative action can breach constitutional rights, provide unconditional advantage, or exclude consideration of individual aspects.

Sanctions and Remedies

The principal governmental authority in charge of equal treatment matters is the Equal Treatment Office, but certain other administrative organizations also have jurisdiction in this regard (e.g., the labor supervisory authority).

The Equal Treatment Office may take administrative action if no other legal proceedings have been initiated in connection with the matter concerned. Moreover, it is entitled to impose the following sanctions:

- To suspend the unlawful conduct;
- To prohibit the unlawful conduct;

- To publish its resolution on the respective unlawful conduct; or
- To impose a pecuniary fine.

🌐 SECTION VI

On the Horizon: What key labor and employment law developments should an employer doing business in Hungary anticipate occurring in the coming years?

The latest significant amendment to the Labor Law Act is Law LXXIII of 2007, which entered into force on July 1, 2007. The amendment affected mainly the issues of working time, collective bargaining, and the determination of working time in cycles.

The modification of the Labor Law Act was necessary because the Hungarian regulation of working time used to be contrary to the European Union legislation and to the jurisprudence of the European Court of Justice (ECJ). The definition of working time was dealt in the cases SIMAP (C-303/98), Jaeger (C-151/02), Dellas (C-14/04), and Vorel (C-437/05) of the ECJ. The European Court of Justice held that all time on duty must qualify as working time. The Hungarian legislation was contrary to these provisions, because the totality of time on duty was not credited as working time. The aim of the amendment was to create a lawful and flexible regulation that harmonizes with the European labor law provisions.

Hungarian labor law is determined by the EU regulations. The employer doing business in Hungary should expect both the further harmonization of national law with the European provisions and a further development of labor law in Europe as a whole.

The Commission of the European Communities produced a Green Paper (Brussels, 22.11.2006, COM [2006] 708 final) on modernizing labor law to meet the challenges of the 21st century.[1] The Green Paper reports that European labor markets face the challenge of combining greater flexibility with the need to maximize security for all. The drive for flexibility in the labor market has given rise to increasingly diverse contractual forms of employment, which can differ significantly from the standard contractual model in terms of the degree of employment and income security and the relative stability of the associated working and living conditions.

The Green Paper highlights the need for the adoption of employment legislation to promote flexibility combined with employment security and reduce labor market segmentation.

This Green Paper looks at the role that the labor law might play in advancing a "flexicurity" agenda in support of a labor market that is fairer, more responsive, and more inclusive, and that contributes to making Europe more competitive.

In the context of globalization, ongoing restructuring, and the move toward a knowledge-based economy, European labor markets need to be both more inclusive and more responsive to innovation and change. Potentially vulnerable workers need to have a ladder of opportunity so as to enable them to improve their mobility and achieve successful labor market transitions. Legal frameworks sustaining the standard employment relationship may not offer sufficient scope or the incentive to those on regular permanent contracts to explore opportunities for greater flexibility at work. If innovation and change are to be successfully managed, labor markets will need to address three main issues: flexibility, employment security, and segmentation.

NOTE

1.   Brussels, 22.11.2006, COM(2006) 708 final.

CHAPTER 9

LABOR AND EMPLOYMENT LAW IN IRELAND

KEVIN LANGFORD

SECTION I

My client wishes to establish a manufacturing facility in Ireland and will need to hire a workforce. What are the key issues involved?

Employment Contracts: Who Receives Them and What Must They Include?

Under the Terms of Employment (Information) Acts, 1994–2001, an employer is obliged to provide an employee within two months after the commencement of the employee's employment with a statement in writing containing the following particulars of the terms of the employee's employment:

- The full names of the employer and the employee;
- The address of the employer in Ireland or, where appropriate, the address of the principal place of the employer in Ireland or the registered office;
- The place of work or, where there is no fixed or main place of work, a statement specifying that the employee is required or permitted to work at various places;
- The title of the job or nature of the work for which the employee is employed;
- The date of commencement of the employee's contract of employment;
- In the case of a temporary contract of employment, the expected duration thereof or, if the contract of employment is for a fixed term, the date on which the contract expires;
- The rate or method of calculation of the employee's remuneration and the pay reference period for the purposes of the National Minimum Wage Act, 2000;
- That the employee may, under Section 23 of the National Minimum Wage Act, request from the employer a written statement of the employee's

average hourly rate of pay for any pay reference period as provided in that section;

- The length of the intervals between the times at which remuneration is paid, whether a week, a month, or any other interval;
- Any terms or conditions relating to hours of work (including overtime);
- Any terms or conditions relating to paid leave (other than paid sick leave);
- Any terms or conditions relating to incapacity for work due to sickness or injury and paid sick leave and pensions and pension plans;
- The period of notice that the employee is required to give and entitled to receive (whether by statute or under the terms of the employee's contract of employment) to terminate the contract of employment; and
- A reference to any collective agreements that directly affect the terms and conditions of the employee's employment.

Within 28 days after the employee enters into a contract of employment, the employer must provide the employee with a notice in writing setting out the procedures that the employer will observe before and for the purpose of dismissing the employee.

It should be noted that instead of giving each employee details in writing, the employer may refer an employee to other documents, for example, a pension-plan booklet or a collective agreement, provided that the employee has easy access to such documents.

If an employer does not provide a written statement of the terms of employment, an employee may complain to the Rights Commissioner, who will order that a written statement be provided or that the employer pay the employee compensation up to a maximum of four weeks' remuneration.

Implied Terms

Terms may be implied into a contract by

- Statute (including terms concerning unfair dismissal, redundancy [layoff], minimum notice, and health and safety);
- Custom and practice (including terms concerning sick pay or enhanced severance payments); and
- General principles of employment law (including terms concerning an employer's duty to act with reasonable care to the employee, the mutual obligation of trust and confidence, the employer's duty to apply procedural fairness in relation to disciplinary matters and dismissals, and the employee's duty of fidelity to the employer).

Probationary Period

The contract may include a probationary period and may allow for this period to be extended. The Unfair Dismissals Acts, 1977–2007, will not apply to the dismissal of an employee during probation or while undergoing training at the beginning of the employment provided that

- The contract of employment is in writing; and
- The duration of probation or training is one year or less and is specified in the contract.

This exclusion from the Acts will not apply if the dismissal results from union membership or activity, pregnancy-related matters, or entitlements under the maternity protection, parental leave, adoptive leave, and carer's leave legislation.

Changes to Contract of Employment

Under Irish contract law, changes to the terms of a contract of employment must be agreed by both the employer and employee. Neither side may unilaterally change the contract. In addition, under the Terms of Employment (Information) Acts, an employer must notify an employee in writing of the nature and date of the change no later than one month after the change takes affect.

Wages and Benefits

Wages

Under the National Minimum Wage Act, as of the date of publication, the minimum wage for experienced adult employees is an average of €8.65 per hour over a pay reference period not exceeding one calendar month. An "experienced adult employee" is one who has been employed for more than two years and is over the age of 18.

The following rates apply:

- Employees under 18: 70 percent of the national minimum wage;
- Employees over 18 and in their first year of employment: 80 percent of the national minimum wage; and
- Employees over 18 and in their second year of employment: 90 percent of the minimum wage.

Special rates apply to employees over 18 who are undergoing structured training or directed study that their employer has authorized or approved.

Hours

The Organisation of Working Time Act, 1997 (the "Working Time Act"), states the law concerning working hours. Employees are entitled to

- A break of at least 15 minutes every 4.5 hours;
- A break of at least 30 minutes every six hours (this may include the 15-minute break);
- A rest period of at least 11 consecutive hours in a 24-hour period; and

- A rest period of at least 24 hours in a seven-day period (this must usually be preceded by an 11-hour daily rest period).

These rules do not apply to employees engaged in shift work when they cannot use the rest period because of shift changeover.

The employer cannot permit employees to work, in any seven-day period, more than 48 hours averaged over a four-month reference period (or a reference period of up to 12 months in certain circumstances). In addition, the employer cannot permit a night worker to work an average of more than eight hours in any 24-hour period (for certain night workers, the eight-hour limit is absolute). Night workers are narrowly defined.

Employees who are required to work on a Sunday must receive extra pay or a compensatory day off, or both. This does not apply if Sunday working has already been taken into account in an employee's pay.

Overtime

There is no legal entitlement to overtime pay in Ireland. However, if an employee is working in a particular type of employment that is covered by a legally binding collective agreement, then such agreement may provide for overtime rates that are binding on the employer.

In practice, employers typically do pay employees extra (e.g., time and a half or double time) for overtime and for weekend or holiday work.

Vacation

Under the Working Time Act, an employee is entitled to paid vacation equal to the following:

- Four working weeks in a leave year in which the employee works at least 365 hours (unless the employee changes employment during the year);
- One-third of a working week for each month in the leave year in which the employee works at least 117 hours; or
- 8 percent of the hours the employee works in a leave year (but subject to a maximum of four working weeks).

Provided that more than one of the above is applicable, the employee is entitled to whichever of the periods of leave is the greater.

In addition, an employee is entitled to the benefit of nine public holidays in each leave year.

Leave

Maternity Leave

The Maternity Protection Acts, 1994 and 2004, provide for maternity leave of 26 weeks, during which the employee is not entitled to be paid by the employer but may avail herself of state maternity benefits. The employee is also entitled to take an additional 16 weeks of maternity leave, during which the employee is not entitled to be paid by the employer nor is the employee entitled to maternity benefits from the state.

Adoptive Leave

In accordance with the Adoptive Leave Acts, 1995 and 2005, adopting mothers and single adopting fathers are entitled to adoptive leave. The basic period of adoptive leave is 24 weeks, during which the employee is not entitled to be paid by the employer, but the state provides adoptive benefit. As with maternity leave, the employee may take additional leave of 16 weeks, during which the employee is not entitled to be paid by the employer nor is the employee entitled to state adoptive benefit. Many employers pay the difference between the adoptive benefit and full salary during the period of basic adoptive leave.

Parental Leave

The Parental Leave Acts, 1998 and 2006, provide for unpaid parental leave of up to 14 weeks, which may be taken in separate blocks of a minimum of six continuous weeks or on more favorable terms with the agreement of the employer. This leave is available where the child is less than eight years of age, or 16 years of age if the child has a disability.

Force Majeure Leave

The Parental Leave Acts also provide for "force majeure" leave for urgent family reasons relating to the illness or injury of a child or other close family member. The maximum leave entitlement is three days in any 12-month period and five days within a 36-month period. Force majeure leave is paid leave.

Carer's Leave

In accordance with the Carer's Leave Act, 2001, a person who has been employed for 12 continuous months is entitled to take temporary unpaid leave to look after a person in need of full-time care and attention. Employees may be entitled to carer's benefits from the state provided they satisfy the contribution conditions of Pay-Related Social Insurance (PRSI), Ireland's social security program.

Sick Pay

Employees are not generally entitled to paid time off in the event of illness or injury. However, they may be eligible to receive social welfare benefits from the Department of Social and Family Affairs, provided they satisfy the PRSI contribution conditions.

Typically, an employer provides sick pay for a limited period of time (sometimes on a progressively reduced basis). If an employer provides sick pay, the employment contract usually provides that the employer either tops the amount the employee receives from the Department of Social and Family Affairs, or pays the full salary and requires the employee to refund to the employer any social welfare benefit it receives.

Benefits

Generally speaking, the provision of employee benefits—sick pay, private health insurance, pension plan, and the like—is at the discretion of the employer. Certain collective agreements provide for mandatory provision of employee benefits.

For example, per collective agreement registered with the Labour Court, both employees and employers in the construction sector must contribute to an occupational pension plan.

Pensions

Employers and employees do not make direct pension contributions to the state. However, they are required to pay Pay-Related Social Insurance, which funds the state pension system. Depending on the amount of PRSI the employee has paid, he or she may be entitled to a noncontributory or a contributory pension. A State pension (contributory) is paid to a person who has made qualifying PRSI contributions, whereas a State pension (non-contributory) is paid to a person who does not qualify for a State pension (contributory) based on their social insurance record.

An employer is not required to provide access to a supplementary pension plan for its employees. However, an employer must provide access to a personal retirement savings account (PRSA) to an excluded employee (that is, if the employer does not offer access to a pension plan, or if it does but the employee is ineligible to join) within six months of starting employment. An employer is not required to pay contributions to a PRSA.

Where an employer sets up a supplementary pension plan, the employer's contributions are tax-deductible, subject to revenue limits. Employees' contributions are also tax-deductible, subject to thresholds that depend on the employees' age:

- Under 30: contributions of up to 15 percent of salary are tax-deductible.
- 30 to 39: 20 percent.
- 40 to 49: 24 percent.
- 50 to 55: 30 percent.
- 56 to 59: 35 percent.
- 60 and above: 40 percent.

There is an earnings cap on contributions at €254,000, adjusted annually.

Although there is no absolute limit on employer contributions, the maximum benefits granted are typically two-thirds of final remuneration, with a salary cap of €254,000 and a minimum amount of service.

Trade Unions and Collective Agreements

Trade union recognition is not compulsory in Ireland. Where an employer recognizes a trade union, it is common for a written collective agreement to govern the employment terms. Collective agreements may apply to a particular employer, or to all employers within a particular geographic region or industry (for example, the hotel and retail sector). There is a rebuttable presumption that collective agreements are not legally binding, except where registered with the Labour Court.

If a collective agreement has been registered with the Labour Court, it is known as a registered employment agreement (REA). The REA sets out the prescribed terms and conditions applicable to employees in specific areas, such as working hours, overtime, vacation, and pay scales. REAs are enforced under the

Industrial Relations Acts, 1946–2004. Fines may be imposed of up to €1,269.70 (and, in the case of a continuing offense, further fines of up to €253.94 for every day during which the offense is continued), for example, where an employer does not follow an order of the Labour Court to pay an employee a certain rate of pay.

Works Councils

The Transnational Information and Consultation of Employees Act, 1996, provides for the setting up of European Works Councils or the arrangements for the information and consultation of employees.

It applies to "community-scale undertakings," which are undertakings with at least 1,000 employees within the member states of the European Union and at least 150 employees in each of least two such member states. It also applies to "community-scale groups of undertakings," which means a group of undertakings with at least 1,000 employees within the EU member states, with at least one group undertaking of at least 150 employees in one EU member state, and at least one other group undertaking with at least 150 employees in another member state.

Essentially, the Act (which is based on an EU directive) provides for the setting up of employee information and consultation forums for EU companies over a certain size in order that employee representatives may be appointed for the purpose of receiving information from and consultation with management representatives.

Additionally, the Employees (Provision of Information and Consultation) Act, 2006, applies to "undertakings" in Ireland that employ more than 50 employees. The Act gives employees a right to information and consultation in certain circumstances. Essentially, the legislation provides for the setting up of an information and consultation arrangement, which is a forum consisting of management representatives on the one hand and employee representatives on the other hand.

Breaches of the Employees (Provision of Information and Consultation) Act may be punished by criminal proceedings as follows:

- Summary conviction: a fine not exceeding €3,000 or up to six months' imprisonment, or both.
- Conviction on indictment: a fine not exceeding €30,000 or imprisonment of up to three years, or both.

SECTION II

My client is acquiring an existing business in Ireland. How do I assess the existing workforce and consider changes?

Share Deals Versus Asset Deals

The differences between share deals and asset deals are summarized in the following table.

Share Purchase Agreement	Asset Purchase Agreement
All assets and liabilities transfer to purchaser	Purchaser has flexibility to choose assets and liabilities
Stamp duty (transfer tax) is levied at a rate of 1%	Stamp duty is leviable at rates up to 9% (although intellectual property may be exempt)
Tax losses transfer to purchaser, subject to various antiavoidance legislation	Difficult for purchaser to secure tax losses
Employees transfer automatically	May be some flexibility not to take employees but this is rendered difficult by European Communities (Protection of Employees on Transfer of Undertakings) Regulations, 2003 (SI 131/2003)
Consideration paid to vendor's shareholders	Consideration paid to target company that then has to pay it to the vendor's shareholders

The Transfer of Undertakings Regulations

The Transfer of Undertakings Regulations—formally, the European Communities (Protection of Employees on Transfer of Undertakings) Regulations, 2003 (SI 131/2003)—came into effect on April 11, 2003, and apply to any transfer of an undertaking, business, or part of a business from one employer to another employer as a result of a legal transfer (including the assignment or forfeiture of a lease). Under the regulations all employees, whether full-time or part-time, temporary or permanent, who are employed at the time of the transfer and who are wholly or mainly assigned to the part of the business being transferred are entitled to the same terms and conditions of employment as applied before the transfer of ownership. However, although pension benefits accrued before the sale of the company must be protected, pension plans do not have to be continued by the new owner.

Under the Regulations, if an employee is made redundant in an asset transaction and not reemployed by the purchaser he or she may be able to bring an action for unfair dismissal against, at the employee's option, the vendor or the purchaser. Thus, the purchaser should always obtain an indemnity from the vendor in relation to such matters.

Due Diligence

The purchaser should establish the employment arrangements between the target company and its employees. It will be necessary to gather information regarding the term of employment contracts, remuneration (including bonuses and reviews), and termination provisions.

If there are no employment contracts in place, the purchaser must draw up an employment contract with the goal of getting the seller to formalize the agreement at the outset.

The purchaser should also establish details of any employee or employer liability claims made against the company and, if necessary, obtain an indemnity in this respect.

The purchaser will also investigate what type of pension plan is in place and obtain a list of current pensioners, their age, and benefits payable. If it is a defined contribution plan, the purchaser should investigate whether all contributions have been paid and if any promises of a defined benefit have been made to any employees. If it is a defined benefit plan, the purchaser should establish if the plan is adequately funded, with the assistance of an actuary if necessary.

The following details should also be provided to the purchaser regarding each employee and director of the company:

- Name, age, and position;
- The date of commencement of employment with the company;
- Weekly or monthly salary;
- The date on which the employee was admitted to the pension plan.

Finally, the buyer should seek a warranty that focuses on the status of employees. Along with a list of employees and details of their benefits, including salary, the warranty should address the following:

- That no one is entitled to a significant period of notice;
- That there are no liabilities or claims pending for unfair dismissal or redundancy;
- That there are no trade disputes;
- That all employee safety legislation has been complied with; and
- That pension plans are in place for employees and that they are properly funded.

Carrying Out a Workforce Reduction

Dismissal of Employees

The primary piece of legislation regarding workforce reduction is the Unfair Dismissals Act. Generally speaking, an employee must have at least one year's continuous service to be covered by the Act. The exceptions include dismissal for trade union membership or activity, dismissal for pregnancy or related matters, the exercise of rights under the National Minimum Wage Act, and dismissal by reason of penalization under the Safety, Health and Welfare at Work Act, 2005.

The Unfair Dismissals Acts provide that a dismissal must be fair in all of its circumstances and the burden of proof is on the employer to establish that the dismissal was not unfair. Fair grounds for dismissal include capability, competence or qualifications of the employee, conduct, and redundancy.

Disciplinary and Grievance Procedures

If dismissal arises from an allegation of misconduct, it is necessary to afford an employee fair procedures and due process. In addition, the Labour Relations Commission requires that employers should have written grievance and disciplinary procedures and they should give employees copies of these at the start of their employment. Under the Unfair Dismissals Acts, employers are required to give the employee written notice of termination procedures within 28 days of entering the contract of employment.

Where dismissal is by reason of incompetence, poor performance, or misconduct (except gross misconduct), an employer is required to have given the employee warnings over a period of time, generally a verbal warning, then a first written warning, then a final written warning.

An employee is entitled to the greater of either the written notice period provided for in a contract of employment and the notice provided for in the Minimum Notice and Terms of Employment Acts, 1973–2005, as set forth in the following table:

Length of Service	Notice Entitlement
13 weeks–2 years	One week
2 years–5 years service	Two weeks
5 years–10 years	Four weeks
10 years–15 years	Six weeks
15 years and up	Eight weeks

Redundancy

The law applicable to redundancy is principally derived from the Redundancy Payments Acts, 1967–2007; the Protection of Employment Acts, 1977–2007; the Unfair Dismissals Acts; and common law.

The Redundancy Payments Acts provide for payment to be made to qualifying employees on being made redundant. The Protection of Employment Acts apply to collective redundancy situations. The Unfair Dismissals Acts and common law impose obligations regarding the process of carrying out redundancies.

The Redundancy Payments Acts define "redundancy" as follows:

An employee shall be taken to have been dismissed by reason of redundancy if, for one or more reasons not related to the employee concerned, the dismissal is attributable wholly or mainly to:

(a) the fact that the employer has ceased or intends to cease to carry on the business for the purpose of which the employee was employed by him, or has ceased or intends to cease, to carry on that business in the place where the employee was so employed;

(b) the fact that the requirements of that business for employees to carry out work of a particular kind in the place where he was so employed have ceased or diminished or are expected to cease or diminish;

(c) the fact that the employer has decided to carry on the business with fewer or no employees whether by requiring the work for which the employee has been employed (or had been doing before his dismissal) to be done by other employees or otherwise;

(d) the fact that the employer has decided that the work for which the employee had been employed (or had been doing before his dismissal) should, from

then on, be done in a different manner for which the employee is not sufficiently qualified or trained; or

(e)   the fact that the employer has decided that the work for which the employee
had been employed (or had been doing before his dismissal) should, from
then on, be done by a person who is also capable of doing other work for
which the employee is not sufficiently qualified or trained.

An employee shall not be taken to be dismissed by reason of redundancy if:

(a)   the dismissal is one of a number of dismissals that, together, constitute collective redundancies;

(b)   the dismissals concerned were effected on a compulsory basis;

(c)   the dismissed employees were, or are to be, replaced at the same location or
elsewhere in the State (except where the employer has an existing operation
with established terms and conditions) by:

    (i)   other persons who are, or are to be, directly employed by the employer;
or

    (ii)   other persons whose services are, or are to be, provided to that employer
in pursuance of other arrangements;

(d)   those other persons perform, or are to perform, essentially the same functions as the dismissed employees; and

(e)   the terms and conditions of employment of those other persons are, or are
to be, materially inferior to those of the dismissed employees.[1]

This excerpt from the definition of redundancy in the Redundancy Payments Acts
concerns situations where an employer makes employees redundant in an attempt
to replace them with lower-cost workers. Under the Protection of Employment
(Exceptional Collective Redundancies and Related Matters) Act, 2007, for a transitional period of three years beginning May 8, 2007, these dismissals may be
found by the Labour Court to be "exceptional collective redundancies." (There is
provision in the Act for extension of this three-year transitional period).

To be classified as exceptional collective redundancies, the proposal to create
collective redundancies may be referred by the employer or the employee representatives to the Redundancy Panel. The Redundancy Panel is composed of an
independent chairperson, and a member of each of the main employee and
employer bodies. Ultimately, the matter may be referred to the Labour Court for
an opinion as to whether the proposed collective redundancies are exceptional
collective redundancies.

Collective Redundancies

The Protection of Employment Acts define "collective redundancies" as dismissals
effected by an employer for one or more reasons not related to the individual
concerned where in any period of 30 consecutive days the number of such dismissals is

- At least five in an establishment normally employing more than 20 and
fewer than 50 employees;
- At least 10 in an establishment normally employing at least 50 but fewer
than 100 employees;

- At least 10 percent of the number of employees in an establishment normally employing at least 100 but fewer than 300 employees; and
- At least 30 in an establishment normally employing 300 or more employees.

The term "establishment" means an employer or a company or a subsidiary company or a company within a group of companies that may independently effect redundancies.

The Protection of Employment (Exceptional Collective Redundancies and Related Matters) Act came into full force on May 8, 2007. It establishes a Redundancy Panel, which aims to ensure that collective redundancies are genuine redundancies. The employer or the employee representatives may refer a proposal to create collective redundancies to the Redundancy Panel during the 30-day consultation period.

If the Redundancy Panel considers that a proposed collective redundancy is an exceptional redundancy, it may seek the opinion of the Labour Court. If the Labour Court concludes that the collective redundancy is exceptional, the Minister for Enterprise, Trade and Employment may refuse to pay the tax rebate that typically arises on redundancy, or pay a reduced rebate.

In addition, the Act has removed the upper age limit for entitlement to redundancy payments.

This depends on the reason for which the employer is dismissing the employee. In the event of dismissal by reason of redundancy, there are procedural requirements for dismissing an employee with at least two years of continuous service, which includes the issuing of a Form RP50 at least two weeks prior to the date of termination of employment.

Procedure

On redundancy, an employer must follow fair procedures and provide at least two weeks' notice, during which employees are entitled to reasonable paid time off to look for work and any outstanding vacation time or payment in lieu of vacation time.

When collective redundancies arise, employers must, at the earliest opportunity and at least 30 days before notice of the first dismissal is given, enter into consultations with employee representatives with a view to reaching agreement on whether there are any alternatives to the redundancies. Employers also must inform the Minister for Enterprise, Trade and Employment of the proposed redundancies in writing at least 30 days before notice of the first dismissal is given.

The employer must provide the following information in writing to the employee representatives during the 30-day consultation period:

- The reasons for the redundancy;
- The number and job descriptions of the employees affected;
- The number and job descriptions of employees usually employed;
- The period in which the redundancies will happen;
- The criteria for selecting employees for redundancy; and
- The method of calculating any redundancy payment.

Severance Payments

Under the Redundancy Payments Acts, if employees have been dismissed due to redundancy and have at least two years of continuous service, they are entitled to a tax-free statutory redundancy payment of two weeks' pay for each year of service plus an extra week's pay, with a ceiling on the week's pay of €600. The employer may claim a rebate of 60 percent of the statutory redundancy payment from the Irish Government.

In addition to statutory redundancy entitlements, employers in Ireland frequently pay enhanced (or "ex gratia") termination payments, depending on a number of factors, including the length of an employee's service, the industry or sector concerned, and common practice or precedent in the employment concerned or the industry concerned.

SECTION III

My client wishes to sell its existing facility. What restrictions do we need to consider?

Confidentiality and Data Protection

Employers in Ireland should be aware of the Data Protection Acts, 1988 and 2003, which implement EC data protection law. They provide rights to employees and impose obligations on employers.

Employees have the following rights in relation to their personal data:

- The right to be informed of the existence of such data;
- The right of access to their personal data;
- The right to object to the use of their personal data;
- The right to block certain uses of data; and
- Freedom from automated decision-making (for example, important decisions concerning an employee, such as the rating of work performance, cannot be made solely by computer or automated means unless the employee consents).

Employers have the following obligations:

- To fairly obtain and process personal data;
- To establish specific rules in relation to processing sensitive data;
- To take security measures over personal data;
- To keep data safe and secure and ensure that it is accurate and up-to-date;
- To ensure that data is adequate, relevant, and not excessive;
- To retain data no longer than is necessary for the specified purposes; and
- To provide any employee with a copy of his or her personal data file on request.

The Data Protection Acts also established the office of the Data Protection Commissioner who regulates data protection law in Ireland.

The seller of a company will generally have to disclose employee data during the due diligence process. Ideally, this eventuality should be foreseen in a company's data protection policy. The policy should provide that certain specific personal data may be disclosed in the context of acquisition discussions, given that secrecy is often a condition of negotiations. In any event, the disclosure of personal information should be subject to a confidentiality agreement to protect the privacy of the individuals concerned.

Adherence to Data Protection Acts requirements is vital in the due diligence process. Section 2A(1)(d) of the Data Protection Acts provides that nonsensitive personal data may be disclosed to prospective buyers if the disclosure is in the legitimate interests of the employer. Disclosure of sensitive data, such as individual employees' health data or union membership details, should be avoided. Section 2(D) of the Acts requires that data subjects be informed of disclosures of their personal data.

The Data Protection Commissioner has issued the following general guidelines that should be followed by sellers in these situations:

1. Ensure, wherever practicable, that information handed over to another organization in connection with a prospective acquisition or merger is anonymized. Disclosure of sickness records that will entail the processing of sensitive personal data must be avoided—only aggregate data relating to absence levels should be disclosed.

2. Only hand over personal information prior to the final merger or acquisition decision after securing formal assurances that:
   - It will be used solely for the evaluation of assets and liabilities;
   - It will be treated in confidence and will not be disclosed to other parties; and
   - It will be destroyed or returned after use.

3. Wherever practicable, before an acquisition or merger takes place, advise workers whether their employment records are to be disclosed to another organization. If the acquisition or merger proceeds, make sure that employees are aware of the extent to which their records are to be transferred to the new employer.

4. Ensure that, if you intend to disclose sensitive personal data, a sensitive personal data condition is satisfied. Generally, such disclosures should not be necessary in the context of due diligence exercises.

5. Where a merger or acquisition involves a transfer of information about an employee to a country outside the European Economic Area (EEA), ensure that there is a proper basis for making the transfer.

6. New employers should ensure that the records they hold as a result of a merger or acquisition are accurate and relevant and do not include excessive information. Within a few months of the merger or takeover, the new employers should review the records they have acquired (for example, by checking the accuracy of a sample of records with the workers concerned), and should make any necessary amendments. [2]

Warranties and Indemnities

Sellers should ensure that all employee-related issues are in order before providing a buyer with warranties and indemnities in respect of same.

SECTION IV

My client wishes to replace its senior manager(s). What restrictions do we need to consider?

The same principles of employment and contract law apply to senior managers of a company as they do to all other employees, including the requirement of fair procedures under the Unfair Dismissal Acts and the provisions of the Redundancy Payment Acts.

However, an area in which seniority is taken into account is that of notice periods required for terminating employment. At common law, in the absence of agreed notice an employer is obliged to give an employee "reasonable notice." The Irish High Court has held that "reasonable notice" is commensurate with an employee's seniority. In the case of Lyons v. MF Kent & Co (International) Ltd (in liquidation),[3] the High Court held that a senior accountant was entitled to a notice period of 12 months. The court took the following into account:

- The employee's status within a group of companies;
- His or her engagement in substantial work abroad;
- His or her very considerable responsibilities related to the size and nature of the contracts in which he or she was involved, and that the work took place in foreign countries;
- That he or she was a professionally qualified person; and
- That he or she was required to work abroad even though he or she was Irish and was based with his or her family in Ireland.

SECTION V

What prohibitions exist against discrimination on the basis of age, race, gender, disability, pregnancy, and other factors? What are the rights of employees, applicants, or former employees who believe that they have been discriminated against?

The Employment Equality Acts, 1998–2007, outlaw discriminatory practice in relation to the following:

- Access to employment
- Conditions of employment
- Training or experience for or in relation to employment
- Promotion
- Classification of posts

On any of the following grounds:

- Gender
- Marital status
- Family status
- Sexual orientation

- Religion
- Age
- Disability
- Race, color, nationality, or ethnic or national origins
- Membership of the traveling community (similar to gypsies or nomads in Continental Europe)

Both direct and indirect discrimination is prohibited. Direct discrimination is less favorable treatment on the basis of one of the nine grounds. Indirect discrimination arises when an apparently neutral provision puts a person of a particular characteristic or group at a particular disadvantage in employment, unless such provision can be objectively justified by a legitimate aim and the means of achieving that aim are appropriate and necessary.

Burden of Proof

With regard to direct discrimination, the burden of proof is on the claimant in the first instance to make out a prima facie case of discrimination. The burden is then on the employer to prove that the discrimination did not take place.

With regard to indirect discrimination, where an apparently neutral provision puts persons to whom a discriminatory ground applies at a particular disadvantage compared with other employees of the employer, the employer shall be treated as having discriminated against the complainant unless the provision is objectively justified by a legitimate aim and the means of achieving that aim are appropriate and necessary.

Redress

An employee or prospective employee who believes he or she has been discriminated against may make a complaint to the Equality Tribunal. This must be done within six months of the last act of the alleged discrimination (except in cases of equal pay), or 12 months in exceptional circumstances. Where an Equality Officer finds in favor of someone who has made a complaint, the officer must award redress. The following orders may be made:

- In equal pay claims, an order for equal pay and/or arrears for a period not exceeding three years before the date of the claim;
- In other cases, an order for equal treatment and compensation up to a maximum of two years pay, or €12,697 where the person is not an employee;
- An order that the complainant be reinstated in the same job or a similar job with the same employer with or without an order for compensation;
- An order that a named person or persons take a specific course of action.

Either side may appeal the Equality Officer's decision to the Labour Court within 42 days.

A person who believes he or she has been discriminated against on grounds of gender may apply directly to the Circuit Court for redress. The Circuit Court may order arrears of pay in respect of six years before the date of claim and compensation as it feels appropriate. However, while the Circuit Court may award higher compensation, the legal fees involved should always be borne in mind.

SECTION VI

On the Horizon: What key labor and employment law developments should an employer doing business in Ireland anticipate occurring in the coming years?

There exists a need for a major enhancement and expansion of the existing Labour Inspectorate with a view to increasing its effectiveness, particularly in light of the changing labor market in Ireland. Accordingly, the National Employment Rights Authority (NERA) was established under the social partnership agreement "Toward 2016."

On April 14th, 2008, the Minister for Labour Affairs announced the appointment of the NERA Advisory Board. The main functions of the Board are to advise NERA on:

- Issues relating to compliance with, and enforcement of, employment legislation, including the provision of information;
- Aspects of NERA's work program and strategy statement;
- Delivery of a high standard of customer service; and
- Proposals for research, surveys, and studies.

The number of Labour Inspectorates under this office will progressively increase as part of an initiative to increase the staffing resources of the Employment Rights Bodies generally. Inspectorates will be specially selected and trained and will be deployed on a regional basis.

There is also a need for improved recordkeeping in order to protect workers' employment rights. Accordingly, new legislation will be published as necessary, consistent with the EU Treaties, to provide that every employee must have an identifiable employer within the country who has legal responsibility for compliance with all aspects of the applicable employment rights legislation.

To support more effective inspections, it has been proposed to prescribe the form in which payroll and working time records must be kept by employers. Legislative powers will be introduced to provide for these statutory employment records, so as to be consistent with the existing record keeping requirements for employers in relation to, for example, taxation and social welfare.

It has been agreed that the unions and the employers will participate with the Revenue Commissioners, the Department of Social and Family Affairs, and the Department of Enterprise, Trade and Employment in setting out legal requirements for statutory employment records covering time records and pay slips.

The onus will be on the employer to maintain and produce up-to-date statutory records in accordance with legislation to be enacted. Failure to do so will be a criminal offense. Where redress proceedings in relation to nonpayment of statutory entitlements are being taken to the Rights Commissioners, Employment

Appeals Tribunal, Labour Court, or a court of law, the onus of producing evidence of payments made or deductions from pay and hours worked will rest with the employer. The penalty for nonmaintenance of statutory employment will be up to € 250,000.

🌐 NOTES

1. Redundancy Payments Acts, 1967 to 2007.
2. Data Protection Acts, 1988 and 2003.
3. [1996] ELR 103.

CHAPTER 10

Labor and Employment Law in Italy

MARCELLO GIUSTINIANI
VITTORIO POMARICI

🌐 SECTION I

My client wishes to establish a manufacturing facility in Italy and will need to hire a workforce. What are the key issues involved?

Employment Contracts: Who Receives Them and What Must They Include?

According to Article 2094 of the Italian Civil Code, a subordinate employee is an individual who undertakes to cooperate within an enterprise for remuneration by contributing intellectual or manual work as an employee and under the direction of the entrepreneur. Employees are generally divided into four categories: (1) blue-collar workers (*operai*); (2) white-collar workers (*impiegati*); (3) high ranking white-collar workers (*quadri*); and (4) executives (*dirigenti*).

The main characteristic of an employee is the element of "subordination." Employees carry out their work activity in favor of the employer in accordance with the employer's instructions and directions, and the employer exercises disciplinary and hierarchical powers over them. In contrast, self-employed persons (agents, consultants, etc.) perform their work activity autonomously, without being subject to any disciplinary or hierarchical power, and without schedule restrictions.

Consultancy agreements that are structured on a continuous and coordinated basis (*contratti di collaborazione coordinata e continuativa*) are the most common type of self-employment. Such consultancies are often used as an alternative to employment due to their higher flexibility (consultants do not enjoy the protection granted to employees) and lower cost (e.g., reduced social security contributions, no minimum wage requirements). In 2003, Italian legislation changed significantly when it set stricter requirements for entering into these types of contracts. In particular, all consultancy agreements (save for some limited exceptions) are now required to refer to one or more specific projects or work programs or phases thereof. These are determined by the principal and managed autonomously by the consultant, to achieve a result by coordinating with the principal's organization and regardless of the amount of time required to perform the job. The "specific projects or work programs or phases thereof" must be in writing in the agreement. Failure to comply with these requisites risks a reclassification of the consultancy agreement into an employment contract.

Form of the Employment Contract

Except for certain specific contracts (such as part-time, temporary, and apprenticeship employment contracts) or clauses (including probationary period clauses or noncompetition covenants), employment contracts do not necessarily have to be in writing.

At the time of hiring, the employer must provide the employee with a written statement containing the data that will be recorded in the company employee register (*libro matricola*)[1] and set out the main terms and conditions of the employment.

The employer must also provide the employee with the following information in writing (if not already in the employment contract) within 30 days of the hire date:

- Identity of the employer and the employee;
- Place of work (if the employee is to work in various locations, that must be so stated) and the employer's main address;
- Hiring date;
- Duration and type of contract (indefinite or fixed term);
- Duration of the period of probation, if any;
- Job title, level, and qualifications of the employee, or a short description of the duties;
- Initial salary and the time of payment;
- Number of vacation days or the method by which they are determined;
- Working hours;
- Length of termination notice.

Some of the above information can be provided by making reference to the applicable collective agreement.

Language

Italian law sets no mandatory requirements regarding the language of employment contracts. However, it is common practice to draft the employment contract in a language known by the employee; should the employment contract be drafted in a foreign language unknown to the employee, the latter could claim it to be invalid.

Fixed-Term Employment

The standard employment contract is for an indefinite term and full-time work. However, in certain cases and provided that certain conditions are satisfied, employees may be hired under a fixed-term and/or a part-time employment contract.

Fixed-term employment contracts may be entered into only for technical, production, organizational, or staff-replacement reasons, and the reason must be specified in writing in the employment contract. A fixed-term employment contract will be reclassified as indefinite if a reason is not given, if the reason given is not valid, or if the reason given is not the same as the activity actually carried out by the fixed-term employee. In addition, the national collective agreement may set further restrictions on the maximum number of fixed-term employees that can be hired.

Wages and Benefits

Minimum Wage Requirements

Italy does not have minimum wage legislation. The only restriction is set by Article 36 of the Italian Constitution, which states that employees are entitled to receive remuneration proportional to the quality and quantity of the work performed.

The minimum wage is set by the collective agreement that applies to the employment. If a collective agreement is not applied, the employer must pay the employee an adequate salary, which is usually based on the minimum wage granted to employees of the same category by the national collective agreement of the relevant sector of industry.

If a collective agreement is applied and the salary paid to the employee exceeds the minimum wage set by the collective agreement, the excess salary (the so-called *superminimo*) is subject to the "principle of absorption." Any salary increase set by the collective agreement is absorbed by the *superminimo*, unless the contrary is expressly stated in the collective or individual agreement or the employee's higher salary is paid in connection with specific merits or work performance.

The annual base salary is usually paid in 13 or 14 installments, one per month with the additional installments (known as *tredicesima* and *quattordicesima*) paid in December and July. The remuneration (or, more likely, a part of it) can also vary depending on the achievement of targets, provided that the total salary is not less than the minimum wage limits stated above.

Special Benefit Requirements

TFR

Employees are entitled by law to an allowance (the so-called *trattamento di fine rapporto*, TFR) equal to the total salary paid during employment divided by 13.5. Until June 30, 2007, the TFR had to be set aside by the employer every year and paid to the employees (revalued at the rate of 1.5 percent every single year, plus 0.75 percent for every point of increase of the cost of living index) as a lump sum in the event of termination of employment. As of July 1, 2007, each employee may choose whether the amount due as TFR is to continue to be accrued—by the employer or by the national social security authority, Istituto Nazionale di Previdenza Sociale (INPS), to which employers with more than 50 employees must contribute—and paid at termination of employment, or should be contributed to an integrative pension fund.

Sick Pay

Employees are entitled to leave of absence for illness or injury and to statutory job protection for a period of time (the so-called *periodo di comporto*) as set forth by the collective agreements. This means that they cannot be dismissed during their absence (except in the case of termination for cause), and if they are on notice of termination, the notice period is suspended until the expiry of a certain term, the length of which depends on the employee's level and seniority. In addition, blue- and white-collar employees are entitled to sick pay that is paid by the INPS, and is usually equal to a percentage of their normal salary. Most collective agreements specify that the employer must also contribute to sick pay so that the employee receives full remuneration. Executives do not receive sick pay from the INPS during their absence, but are entitled to full remuneration that is entirely borne by the employer under the national collective agreement.

Vacation

Employees are entitled to a minimum period of four weeks of paid vacation for each year of service (national collective agreements may provide for a longer period) that cannot be waived. In principle, vacation days cannot be replaced by monetary payment.

Pension

Italian law provides a significant state pension, for which social security contributions are paid at a rate of approximately 40 percent of the employee's remuneration (30 percent from the employer, 10 percent from the employees). Social security contributions are paid to the INPS.

Besides the mandatory state pension, voluntary pension funds are provided for by certain national collective agreements.

Labor Unions and Works Councils

The Italian Constitution provides a general principle of trade union freedom, meaning that employees have the right to form or join union associations and to carry out union activity either within or outside the workplace.

Confederations, which are national and provincial, are the most dominant labor organizations formed outside the workplace. They bring together all the associations organized by employees of different business fields. The confederations play a main role in bargaining with the government and the employers for the protection of labor rights and interests of their members.

The most important unions at company level are the Rappresentanza Sindacale Aziendale (RSA) and the Rappresentanza Sindacale Unitaria (RSU), which function as works councils.

RSAs are plant-level unions that, according to law, may be formed within every business unit with more than 15 employees, by employees enrolled in trade unions that signed the collective agreement applicable to that business unit. The law grants RSAs several rights, including the right to gather at the workplace, the right to conduct secret ballots among employees, and the right to collect contributions.

RSUs are plant-level union structures that are regulated by the National Multi-Industry Agreements (Accordi Interconfederali), for both the manufacturing (Agreement dated December 1, 1993) and commercial (Agreement dated July 27, 1994) sectors. These Agreements extended the legal rights that RSAs have to RSUs. The main difference between RSAs and RSUs is that the members of RSUs are elected by all employees of the company (and not only by those enrolled in trade unions that signed the collective agreement applicable to the business unit); as a consequence, RSUs (as opposed to RSAs) represent the entire workforce and can enter into company-level collective agreements.

RSAs and RSUs play an important role in bargaining with employers to guarantee employees their rights in the workplace. However, in many companies, this role may also be played by other, autonomous trade union associations that do not belong to the major confederations and are not incorporated in either the form of RSAs or RSUs (for example, the Comitati di Base, an independent union that often uses extreme forms of protest).

Collective Agreements

Employment relationships are governed by law, by the individual employment contract, and, normally, by the applicable national collective agreement.

A national collective agreement is an agreement that is entered into between a trade union organization and an employers' association and that outlines the main terms and conditions of employment to be applied to individual contracts. Each industry sector has its own national collective agreement. Further collective agreements at a lower level (such as company or plant collective agreements) may also be entered into.

Collective agreements are not statutes, but rather private contracts. They are solely binding on those (employers or employees) who (1) are members of the employers' association and of the trade unions that are a party to it, or (2) specifically provide in their individual employment contracts that the provisions of a collective agreement are applicable.

If a collective agreement applies, the provisions of the individual employment contract cannot be less favorable than those set out by the national collective agreement. However, under certain conditions, a collective agreement may be entirely or partially replaced by another collective agreement (national or local) that has less favorable provisions.

The law does not set any provisions regarding the procedure or scope and duration of collective agreements, which are freely determined by the parties.

❂ SECTION II

My client is acquiring an existing business in Italy. How do I assess the existing workforce and consider changes?

Share Deals Versus Asset Deals

Share Deals

Share transactions (i.e., sale and purchase of the shares of the target company) do not imply a change of identity of the employer and, therefore, do not have any impact on the existing employment contracts and the parties. Individual or collective dismissals following a share transaction as well as any change to the terms and conditions of employment continue to be governed by the ordinary rules.

Asset Deals

With reference to asset transactions (i.e., sale and purchase of part or all of the assets of a company), specific provisions govern the transfer of employment contracts only where the assets transferred qualify as a business or a part of it.

A transfer of business is defined by law as any transaction that, upon execution of a sale agreement or of a merger, results in the change of ownership of an organized economic activity. This definition is applicable regardless of whether the business is carried out on a profit-making basis and regardless of the kind of agreement or provision pursuant to which the transfer is executed, including by means of usufruct or lease contract. The subject of the transfer must be an organized economic activity or, in the case of a transfer of part of a business, a functional and autonomous part of an organized economic activity, which is identified as such by the seller and the purchaser at the moment of the transfer. This does not mean that the parties may arbitrarily gather completely different or heterogeneous groups of employees before the transaction in order to create a part of business ad hoc. The transferring part of the business must in any event be provided with functional autonomy; that is, it must be capable of autonomously carrying out an organized economical activity.

Transfer of Employment Contracts

Where a transfer of a business, or a part of a business, takes place, the employment contracts are preserved, automatically continuing on the same basis with the purchaser. The employees retain all the rights deriving from their individual employment contracts with the original employer (while the rights deriving from the collective agreement may change). Any employee whose terms and conditions of employment are substantially modified by the new employer in the three months following the transfer may resign from employment and be paid the compensation in lieu of notice that he or she would have been entitled to for dismissal.

The seller remains jointly liable with the purchaser for all claims that the transferred employees had at the time of the transfer, unless the employees release the original employer from the obligations deriving from the original employment relationship through specific procedures.

The transfer of a business does not qualify per se as a legitimate ground for the employee's dismissal.

Carrying Out a Workforce Reduction

Termination Procedures

A termination must be communicated in writing. Employees under a permanent employment contract may be lawfully terminated only for cause, without prior notice, or for a justifiable ("objective" or "subjective") reason, with prior notice.

"Cause" is a very serious infringement of the obligations relating to the performance of the job, or an external act, such as committing a crime, that jeopardizes the relationship of trust between the employer and the employee. An "objective" reason (i.e., redundancy)[2] is defined by law as a reason relating to the production activity, the organization of work, and the regular functioning of the business. In this case, the employer must show that the dismissed employee may not be transferred to other job positions of the same kind as formerly performed within the company. A "subjective" reason consists of a serious nonfulfillment of the employee's contractual obligations, but one that is not serious enough to result in a dismissal for cause.

Italian law requires an employer to display a disciplinary code in a place accessible to all employees, and that a specific procedure be followed each time the employer intends disciplining an employee (including *dirigenti*).

The steps of the procedure are as follows:

1. Unless the sanction merely consists of a verbal warning, the employer must send the employee a letter with a detailed description of the disciplinary charges.
2. The employee must submit a written or oral defense to the employer within five days of receipt of the disciplinary letter. During this five-day period, the employer may not impose sanctions against the employee, apart from a temporary release from duties (with full pay).
3. After receiving the employee's defense (or if the employee has not submitted any defense within five days), the employer may apply the proper sanction to the employee by written communication.

The sanction may be a written warning, a fine, work and pay suspension, or dismissal for subjective justifiable reasons or for cause.

Failure to comply with the above requisites renders a dismissal unlawful. Unlawfully dismissed employees (but not *dirigenti*; see Section IV) are granted two different types of protection, depending on the size of the employer's workforce:

- If the employer employs more than 15 employees within a business unit (or more than 60 within the Italian territory), the unfairly dismissed employee can choose between being reinstated in his or her previous job or being paid compensation of 15 months' salary, plus damages for loss of salary from the date of dismissal until the date of actual reinstatement, with a minimum threshold of five months' salary;
- Employers that do not fall under the size limits stated above may choose between rehiring the unfairly dismissed employee or, alternatively, paying the employee compensation in lieu of notice, if applicable, plus damages

ranging from 2.5 months of salary to 14 months of salary, depending on the employee's length of service.

The duration of the notice of termination is set by the collective agreement applied, and is based on the employee's seniority and level. During the period of notice, the employment continues as usual. If the parties agree (or, according to a more recent trend in case law, even without the consent of the employee), the employer may immediately terminate the employment by paying the employee the salary due for the remaining portion of the notice (including the average of bonuses paid during the last three years—or shorter period—of employment, if any). The payment in lieu of notice is subject to social security contributions at the same rate as the normal salary.

If the parties agree, they may terminate the employment by mutual consent. This is usually done by way of a compromise agreement, whereby the employee waives any rights deriving from the employment and its termination in exchange for the payment of a lump sum that under certain conditions is not subject to social security contributions and benefits from a more favorable tax treatment. In most cases, other provisions are also agreed upon (such as noncompetition covenants and joint press announcements). Italian law states that any waiver or settlement that concerns the statutory mandatory employment rights of the employee may be challenged by the employee within six months from the date of its execution (or the date of termination of employment, if later), unless the waiver or settlement is executed before certain authorities (Labor Office, trade unions association, or an employment court).

Layoffs

Layoffs are governed by specific rules that are applicable under the following circumstances:

- The company employs more than 15 employees;
- The dismissals are due to a reduction, transformation, or cessation of business or labor;
- The dismissals concern at least five employees employed within the same business unit or within the jurisdiction of a given province, and take place within a period of 120 days, where connected to the same reduction or transformation.

Where all the above requirements are met, the employer who intends to reduce the workforce must follow the following specific consultation procedure:

1. The company must give prior written notice to the works councils and to the trade unions of the relevant sector (if there are no works councils, notice must be given to the unions of the relevant sector belonging to the trade-union confederations with the largest number of representatives at a national level). The notice has to provide specific information, including the reasons for the redundancy, the number of employees

affected and the positions they hold, the timing of the layoff, and possible measures to ameliorate the social consequences of the layoff.

2.   Within seven days from the date of receipt of notice, if requested by the trade union representatives, the parties must meet to discuss the reasons for the layoff and possible alternatives.

3.   The procedure must be completed within 45 days from the beginning of negotiations (23 days if fewer than 10 employees are involved). The company must give written notice of the results of the negotiations to the competent Labor Office. If an agreement was not reached, the director of the Labor Office must summon all parties for a final round of negotiations that may not last for more than 30 days (15 if fewer than 10 employees are involved).

Whether or not the parties reach an agreement, the company is entitled to dismiss the redundant employees by giving them written notice. Furthermore, the company must provide the Labor Office, the Regional Commission of Employment, and the trade unions with a written list of the dismissed employees' names, addresses, status, seniority, age, dependent relatives, and a detailed description of the selection criteria applied. The selection of the employees to be laid off must be made according to the technical-productive and organizational needs of the company, pursuant to the criteria set forth by the law (i.e., (1) dependent relatives, (2) seniority, and (3) technical-productive and organizational needs so that employees with longer seniority or a higher number of dependent relatives are the last to be dismissed), to be applied in combination with each other or the different criteria agreed upon with trade-union representatives.

Failure to give written notice or to comply with the procedure or the selection criteria will result in an unlawful dismissal.

If the company has received funding from Cassa Integrazione Guadagni Straordinaria (CIGS), a wage supplementation fund, the same procedure must be followed even if only one dismissal is served at the end of the funding period. The CIGS is a government- and industry-funded program that aims to avoid permanent layoffs at financially troubled companies in certain industries by paying, for up to 48 months, part of the salaries of employees whose employment is temporarily suspended or reduced.

Provisions for layoffs and CIGS do not apply to executives (*dirigenti*).

Reorganizing the Workforce

Statutory Protection

As a general principle, the employees may not be assigned to duties inferior to those for which they were hired or have subsequently been assigned to. Any agreement to the contrary, even if with the consent of the affected employee, would be invalid. Where there is a change of duties, the employee assigned to higher duties has the right to the corresponding remuneration. In case of assignment of equivalent duties, the employee's base salary may not be reduced.

Breach of the above general principles may trigger the right of the affected employee to (1) obtain an injunction to be reassigned to his or her previous duties or the equivalent; (2) resign without notice for cause (constructive dismissal), alleging a serious breach of contract by the employer and, as a consequence, claiming the compensation in lieu of notice that would have been granted in the event of dismissal; or (3) according to certain court decisions, refuse to carry out the lesser duties assigned. In addition, the employee would be entitled to damages determined by the court as a portion of the salary for the period of demotion.

Employees may be permanently transferred from one business unit to another, provided that the transfer is based on technical, organizational, or production needs. An employee's unjustified refusal to a transfer would be a justifiable reason for dismissal. No limitation is set forth in case of a temporary transfer of the employee from one business unit to another or a temporary or permanent transfer within the same business unit.

Italian law sets forth certain exceptions to the above general principles that are based on health reasons or on company needs. The employer may assign employees duties of a lower level, with their consent, in case of (1) pregnancy, (2) disability caused by prior injury or sickness, (3) specific jobs exposing the employee's health to risk, and (4) redundancy procedures (where the demotion of the employee is the only alternative to dismissal). Except for change of duties due to redundancy, the employee lawfully assigned to lesser duties has the right to the same remuneration as previously earned.

Making Changes to Key Managerial Positions

Share Deals

On a share sale, the relationships of the target company's board members continue with the purchaser. The purchaser may terminate these relationships in compliance with the ordinary rules, although it is common practice for the seller to procure the resignation of the directors at closing under the sale and purchase agreement.

Change of share ownership should not have a direct impact on executives (*dirigenti*), as their employment continues unchanged with the same employer. Nevertheless, a minority trend in case law has extended to share deals the executive's right under an asset transaction to resign and receive severance pay.

Asset Deals

Where an asset transaction takes place, the relationships of the board members do not transfer automatically to the purchaser and they continue to hold their office within the seller.

Ordinary rules govern the purchaser's termination of executives' contracts. However, executives are granted an additional protection under certain national collective agreements: Should a transfer of business take place, they have the right to resign from employment within 180 days and to be paid a severance amount (usually equal to a portion of the compensation in lieu of notice provided for in the event of dismissal).

Changing the Wage and Benefits Structure

Upon a transfer of business, the purchaser must honor all economic and legal benefits granted by national, local, and company collective agreements entered into by the seller until their expiry, unless the purchaser already follows other collective agreements of the same level. Where this is the case, the original collective agreements are replaced by the corresponding agreements followed by the purchaser, even if the latter provides less favorable terms and conditions. Normally, the transition from one collective agreement to a less favorable one for the employees is regulated by a specific agreement entered into with the trade unions/ works councils.

As a general principle, even with their consent, the employees' salary may not be decreased. However, some components of remuneration, such as bonuses for particular kinds of work, may be reduced to a limited extent.

Consulting with Labor Unions or Works Councils

Share Deals

The law does not provide any specific consultation procedures in the case of share transactions; nevertheless, certain information duties may be required under the collective agreements.

Asset Deals

In the case of a transfer of business (or part of it), a specific consultation procedure need be followed only when more than 15 employees are employed by the seller (irrespective of the number of employees who are actually transferred):

1. At least 25 days before the sale and purchase agreement is executed (or, if earlier, before a binding agreement between the parties is reached), both the seller and the purchaser must inform the works councils and the trade unions that signed the collective agreements applied by the company regarding (1) the date or proposed date of the transfer; (2) the reasons for the transfer; and (3) the legal, economic, and social consequences for the employees and the related measures that the company intends to implement. If there are no works councils, notice must be given to the most representative of the general trade unions.
2. Within seven days after receipt of the above notice, the works councils and trade unions may request a meeting to discuss the transfer. The negotiations must begin within seven days from the receipt of the request. The consultation is considered complete 10 days after it begins, even if the parties have not reached any agreement on the transfer.

The above procedure only aims to inform works councils/trade unions of the actual consequences of the transfer on the employees and the business strategies of the purchaser. Once the seller and the purchaser supply the above information, the works councils/trade unions have no right to question the transfer.

Any breach of the consultation procedure could lead to an injunction to halt the effects of the transfer on the affected employees and an order to pay damages. A few decisions of the employment courts have also deemed the entire transfer as invalid or totally or partially ineffective.

🌐 SECTION III

My client wishes to sell its existing facility. What restrictions do we need to consider?

Assessing Employment Contracts

The main issues that the buyer needs to investigate in its due diligence activity are as follows:

- The number of employees, in particular whether there are "hidden" employees, such as freelance workers who might be reclassified as being under employment contracts or employees engaged under temporary employment contracts that might be deemed indefinite-term employment contracts;
- The national collective agreements and the company-level agreements that are applied;
- Any bonus or fringe benefits available to the employees, other than those set forth by law and under the national and company-level agreements;
- Any liability arising prior to the transfer pursuant to the applicable provisions of law and contract (i.e., unpaid remunerations or social security contributions);
- Details relating to key employees, including change-in-control clauses that give the executives the right to extra bonuses or to early termination of the employment;
- Reorganization obstacles, such as any agreement under which the employer is bound to refrain from terminating the employment for a given period of time (*patto di stabilità*), or that gives employees made redundant by the buyer the right to be rehired by the seller within a certain period of time following the transfer.

Consulting with Labor Unions or Works Councils

See "Consulting with Labor Unions or Works Councils" in Section II.

Negotiating with the Purchaser: Special Labor Issues

In an asset transaction, the seller normally guarantees the buyer that there are no other subordinated employment relationships other than the employees listed in the company's books and registers. Consequently, the seller usually must hold the buyer harmless and indemnified against any liabilities arising from freelance workers or temporary employees whose status is changed by a court's order. A crucial point in the determination of the indemnification is that additional employees would also be afforded strict protection against unfair dismissal. If the company meets certain size requirements (outlined in "Carrying Out a Workforce Reduction" in Section II), the employees would have the right to be reinstated in their job in case of unfair dismissal. As a consequence, an indemnification should also take into account any damages connected to additional employment contracts imposed on the buyer for an undetermined period of time.

Moreover, the seller normally warrants that there are no other forms of compensation or special conditions of employment or benefits, other than those provided by law, national collective agreements, and company-level agreements; the seller also indemnifies the buyer against any and all other liabilities existing at the time of the transfer (unless the buyer deems the disclosures in the due diligence exercise as sufficient).

⊕ SECTION IV

My client wishes to replace its senior manager(s). What restrictions do we need to consider?

Termination of Directors

The cost of terminating the relationship with senior managers depends on whether they are members of the board or simply employees without other appointments. In joint stock companies (*società per azioni*), members of the board of directors may be appointed for a maximum period of three years and have very little protection in case of termination. According to law, a director whose mandate is terminated without cause prior to its expiry is entitled to damages that are usually quantified as equal to the fees that he or she would have received from the date of early termination until the expiry date of the office (without prejudice to any possible mitigation of loss).

The company's shareholders' meeting, which must be called with prior notice (usually between 30 and 45 days), has the authority to decide the termination of directors. As a consequence, the shareholders' resolution is often preceded by a resolution of the board of directors (which may be convened with a much shorter notice) so as to immediately revoke the powers granted to the director that will be terminated at a later stage.

Double Status as Director and Employee

Most top managers are usually granted more restrictive protection under specific service agreements. In particular, CEOs normally have both the status of managing director (*amministratore delegato*), a member of the board with delegated powers, and of employee, with duties and title of general manager (*direttore generale*). This double status may cause some difficulties. On one hand, it could mean a partial saving of costs (as directors' fees are subject to reduced social security contributions), but on the other hand, it may result in the INPS or the involved individual claiming that the requisites necessary for one of the two relationships are nonexistent, with the consequence of reclassifying the relationship into the other.[3] The double status can also create uncertainties with regard to the termination of the two relationships, as they are governed by completely different rules.

To mitigate the above risk, the duties assigned to the individual as an employee must be clearly distinct from the activities attributable to the office held within the board of directors. Furthermore, the individual must not be granted powers of extraordinary management that are not compatible with the status of employee, and must be subject to the control, disciplinary and hierarchical power of the employer. Lastly, the relevant provisions in respect of termination of the two relationships must be harmonized by linking them so that the termination of one relationship would also cause the termination of the other. It is quite common to regulate these aspects under a single agreement covering both roles of employee and director.

Protection Against Termination of Executives

Specific rules contained in the law and in the national collective agreements govern the termination of employees who perform executive duties (*dirigenti*). Pursuant to Italian law, an executive employed under a permanent employment contract may be dismissed without notice for cause, or for no particular reason by giving prior notice. Stronger protection is granted by the national collective agreements, according to which the dismissal, if not for cause, must be grounded on acceptable reasons.

The combination of the rules governing the dismissal of executives both under Italian law and the national collective agreements yield three possible scenarios:

1. Dismissal for cause, without notice. See "Carrying Out a Workforce Reduction" in Section II.
2. Dismissal with prior notice for a reason acceptable under the applicable national collective agreement. The national collective agreements do not expressly state what reasons are acceptable; in general, the objective and subjective reasons provided with regard to nonexecutive employees (see "Carrying Out a Workforce Reduction" in Section II) may also qualify as legitimate grounds for the dismissal of an executive. However, according to the majority of the Italian court rulings, executives may be dismissed only provided that the decision is not arbitrary and is made in good faith.
3. Dismissal for no reason (unfair dismissal). In this case, the employer must pay the executive a supplementary compensation in addition to the notice period or the compensation in lieu thereof. The range of the supplementary compensation is set out in the national collective agreements, from a minimum that is equal to the notice or to the notice plus two months' salary to a maximum of 18–22 months' salary, and the precise award is determined by the courts. Furthermore, if the age of the dismissed executive is within a certain range (for example, between 46 and 56 years for executives of industrial companies or between 50 and

64 years for executives of commercial companies), the supplementary compensation is automatically increased (in the range of two to seven months' salary for executives of industrial companies and four to nine months' salary for executives of commercial companies).

SECTION V

What prohibitions exist against discrimination on the basis of age, race, gender, disability, pregnancy, and other factors? What are the rights of employees, applicants, or former employees who believe that they have been discriminated against?

Areas of Protection

Italian law expressly prohibits all kinds of discrimination based on sex, race, language, religion, political opinion, and personal and social conditions.[4] This principle of nondiscrimination represents a general limitation on the employer's powers, both at the moment of hiring of employees, and during the course of employment.

Statutory Rules

Italian employment laws set forth certain specific antidiscrimination provisions. In particular, employers are forbidden to carry out any of the following actions:

- Inquiries about the employee's political, religious, or trade union opinions, as well as about facts that do not concern the employee's professional skills, both before hiring employees and during the course of employment;
- Individual dismissals based on political or religious belief, union affiliation, or participation in trade union activities;
- All acts and agreements that in any way discriminate against an employee because of union affiliation or nonaffiliation, religious or political beliefs, race, language, gender, disability, age, or sexual preferences;
- Granting of uneven collective economic treatment based on union affiliation or nonaffiliation, religious or political beliefs, race, language, gender, disability, age, or sexual preferences;
- All direct or indirect discriminatory actions based on race, ethnic origins, religion, personal opinion, disability, age, or sexual preferences.[5]

Some exceptions to the nondiscrimination principle are admitted:

- Different treatment among employees is not considered discriminatory when the reason on which it is based is connected to an essential and crucial characteristic of the work activity;
- If religion or personal opinions are an essential requirement for the activities of religious organizations or other public or private organizations (the *imprese di tendenza*), different treatment of employees based on religion or personal opinions is not considered discriminatory.

Gender Discrimination

According to the Equal Opportunity Code,[6] discrimination, both direct and indirect,[7] against an employee based on gender is prohibited. This prohibition concerns (1) the moment of hiring; (2) the remuneration; and (3) the period of performance of the employment.

Molestation and sexual harassment are also considered discriminative on the grounds of gender[8] pursuant to the Equal Opportunity Code.

Exceptions to the prohibition of gender discrimination are admitted when gender is a decisive factor for the work activity; for example in the sectors of art, fashion, and entertainment, and in the case of particularly heavy work duties, as agreed with the trade unions or works councils.

The Equal Opportunity Code also expressly promotes affirmative action against discrimination, that is, initiatives aimed at removing obstacles that hinder equal opportunities for male and female workers.

Mandatory Hiring of Disabled Workers

Depending upon the number of employees, public and private employers are required to hire a minimum number of disabled personnel:

- One disabled employee, if the employer employs between 15 and 35 employees;
- Two disabled employees, if the employer employs between 36 and 50 employees; and
- 7 percent of the total number of the employees, if the employer employs more than 50 employees.

Maternity Rights

Female employees enjoy special protection during pregnancy and maternity. There is no minimum period of employment for the enjoyment of this protection.

Mandatory rules governing the period of compulsory leave of absence from work provide for a complete cessation of work during the period from two months prior to the expected date of birth until three months after it.[9] The mother may also optionally abstain from work for an additional period of six months during the infant's first three years, and (unpaid) during any periods of illness of the child until the child is three years old, and for a maximum of five working days each year if the child is between three and eight years of age.[10]

In addition, from the beginning of pregnancy until one year after the child's birth, the mother cannot be dismissed, except in cases of (1) serious misconduct resulting in a dismissal for cause; (2) termination of the employer's activity; (3) ending of the specific work for which the employee was hired or expiry of a fixed-term employment contract; or (4) negative outcome of the probationary period.

Sanctions and Remedies

Any employee who is discriminated against based on race, ethnic origins, religion, personal opinion, disability, age, or sexual preferences may obtain a court order that declares the discriminatory behavior unlawful and invalidates it. The discriminated employee can also sue the employer for damages.

The following acts or agreements are invalid:

- Discriminatory dismissal;[11]
- Dismissal[12] because of pregnancy or maternity;[13]
- Dismissal of a female employee in the period from the date of publication of her wedding until one year after the ceremony, and all contractual provisions pursuant to which marriage is a reason for terminating the employment contract.[14]

Moreover, certain administrative and criminal sanctions may be imposed on the employer in the case of violation of the rules against discrimination.

SECTION VI

On the Horizon: What key labor and employment law developments should an employer doing business in Italy anticipate occurring in the coming years?

The Ministry of Labor recently proposed a general amendment of the provisions of law that govern the labor market. These amendments are described in the Agreement (the *Protocollo*) reached with the national trade unions on July 23, 2007. The amendment proposed by the government focuses primarily on five areas: (1) the welfare system; (2) the social security cushions; (3) the labor market (in particular, increasing job offers and reducing the use of employment contracts that cause job insecurity); (4) competitiveness in terms of labor costs; and (5) disadvantaged workers (young persons and women). Among the amendments proposed, it is worth mentioning (1) the cancellation of social security contributions due for overtime work; (2) the cancellation of "job on call" employment contracts (a special type of employment contract under which employees are available to perform their activity on a discontinued or intermittent basis, in accordance with the employer's requests); (3) stricter controls on the correct use of contracts such as project-based consultancy contracts, apprenticeships, and "occasional" consultancy contracts; (4) further restrictions on the use of fixed-term employment contracts; and (5) an increase in the minimum state pension benefits.

NOTES

1. In the *libro matricola* (to be kept in original form, at the employer's head office), the employer must record certain information related to the employees, such as name, employee registration number, fiscal code, hiring and termination date, and job category.

2. A specific consultation procedure is required in the case of collective dismissals. See "Layoffs" in Section II.

3. Should the manager be classified as a self-employed director, INPS would annul the social security position connected to the employment and declare that the related social security contributions were wrongfully paid. Within the limit of the 10-year period provided for by the applicable statute of limitations the employer may, in theory, seek a refund of the paid-in contributions. Obviously, the employee would then lose the accrued social security seniority.

Should the manager be classified as an employee, the employer would be liable for any obligations relating to salaries or damages that the employee may claim with reference to all activities, including the remuneration for the position of director, with the consequent recalculation of all direct and indirect elements of salary and other payments (bonuses, severance pay, compensation for vacation days not taken, etc.). Further, all remuneration ever paid to the director would be reclassified as part of the employment salary, and the employer would be liable to INPS for back payment of social security contributions plus related sanctions.

4. "All citizens have equal social status and are equal before the law, without regard to their sex, race, language, religion, political opinions, and personal or social conditions. It is the duty of the Republic to remove all economic and social obstacles that, by limiting the freedom and equality of citizens, prevent full individual development and the participation of all workers in the political, economic, and social organization of the country." Italian Constitution art. 3.

5. According to the relevant legislation: (1) there is direct discrimination when an employee is treated, for one of the abovementioned reasons, in a different way compared with another employee who is in the same situation; and (2) there is indirect discrimination when an apparently neutral provision, rule, practice, act, agreement, or behavior may lead to a disadvantage for a person of a certain race, ethnic origin, religion, ideology, age, or sexual preference, or who has a disability.

6. Legislative Decree No. 198/2006 (*Codice delle pari opportunità tra uomo e donna, a norma dell'articolo 6 della legge 28 novembre 2005, n. 246*).

7. The Equal Opportunity Code states that (1) any act, agreement, or behavior that leads to discrimination of an employee based on the grounds of gender is considered direct discrimination; and (2) any apparently neutral provision, rule, practice, act, agreement, or behavior that may lead to a disadvantage for a person of a certain gender compared to a person of the other gender is considered indirect discrimination, except where the different treatment concerns an essential requirement of the work activity.

8. Molestation is defined as "undesired behavior on the grounds of gender" and sexual harassment as "undesired behavior with sexual connotations, expressed in a physical way, verbal or not verbal," both "having the aim or the effect of violating the employee's dignity and of creating an intimidating, hostile, degrading, humiliating, or offensive environment."

9. A father is entitled to paternity leave for the same period if the mother has died, is severely infirm, or has abandoned the child, or if the father has sole custody of the child.

10. During compulsory maternity leave, the woman is entitled to an indemnity of 80 percent of her remuneration, which is paid by the INPS. Collective agreements usually provide that the employer has to pay the employee the difference up to the full normal salary while on maternity leave. During optional maternity leave, the woman is entitled to an indemnity of 30 percent of her remuneration that is paid by the INPS (normally without any payment by the company of the difference up to the full normal salary).

11. In case of discriminatory dismissal, the stronger protection provided by the law against unlawful dismissal (i.e., reinstatement in the previous job) is applicable, regardless of the size of the company (see "Carrying Out a Workforce Reduction" in Section II).

12. Where the father was entitled to paternity leave and the dismissal was served within the first year following the child's birth, his dismissal is invalid.

13. A part of case law considers dismissal because of pregnancy or maternity discriminatory; see footnote 11. Where the mother (or the father, if he is entitled to paternity leave) resigns during the period between the beginning of pregnancy and one year after the child's birth, she is entitled to payment due in case of dismissal (in particular, payment of compensation in lieu of notice).

14. A part of case law considers this dismissal discriminatory; see note 11.

CHAPTER 11

LABOR AND EMPLOYMENT LAW
IN THE NETHERLANDS

ELS DE WIND
ANNEKE MEULENVELD

🌐 SECTION I

My client wishes to establish a manufacturing facility in the Netherlands and will need to hire a workforce. What are the key issues involved?

Employment Contracts: Who Receives Them and What Must They Include?

In the Dutch Civil Code an employment contract is legally defined as "a contract by which a party, the employee, commits himself or herself to perform work for another party, the employer, for a certain period of time in exchange for remuneration." This definition then leads to the following criteria for the establishment of an employment contract: (1) remuneration paid to an individual employee in return for (2) the personal performance of particular duties for an employer (3) under the supervision and direction of such employer. Both employee and employer have certain duties, most of which are set out in the Civil Code. As a general rule, the employer and the employee must act in good faith (as a good employer and a good employee) vis-à-vis each other.

Form

A written employment agreement is preferred as evidence of the terms of employment, though it does not have to be in writing or in any particular form. It can be agreed upon orally. The employer does have the obligation to provide the employee with certain specific information in writing, such as the date the employment starts, the name and domicile of both parties, the function of the employee, the place where the work is performed, whether the employment is for a limited period of time (and for how long) or for an indefinite period of time, the number of vacation days, the notice period (if applicable) for each of the parties, the salary, the pay-out date, and the usual daily or weekly working hours. Also, certain provisions, notably those regarding probation period and noncompete agreement, must be embodied in a written agreement signed by both parties, otherwise such provisions will be void.

Duration of Employment

An employment agreement may be for a fixed or indefinite term. A fixed-term contract may be either for a specific period of time or for the term of a particular project. If a fixed-term agreement is continued (tacitly or in writing) it will be deemed to be extended under the same terms and conditions and for the same period of time (subject to a maximum of one year), unless the agreement itself provides that it will continue for an indefinite period. Parties are free to enter into consecutive fixed-term agreements, under two restrictions.

1. The aggregate duration of the consecutive employment agreements— that is, the different links (*schakels*), each with intervals of no more than three months—may not exceed three years. If the aggregate duration is longer than three years, the last employment agreement in the chain will become an agreement for an indefinite period as of the day the three-year period has been reached.

2. A maximum of three consecutive employment agreements is allowed. If the number of consecutive links exceeds three (with intervals of no more than three months), the fourth employment agreement will be considered to be for an indefinite period. If, for instance, four employment agreements for six-month terms are entered into consecutively, the last of these is deemed an agreement of indefinite duration.

An employment agreement for three years or longer may be extended only once by another employment agreement for not more than three months, immediately following the three-year agreement. The extended fixed-term agreement then ends by operation of law.

If an employee enters into consecutive employment agreements, with interruptions not exceeding three months, with several employers who must reasonably be considered each other's successors in respect of the work performed, these employment agreements are considered links in the same chain. This situation will occur particularly where the employee started out doing temporary work for a company while being employed with a temp agency, and subsequently enters into a fixed-term agreement with that particular company. The contract for temporary employment is the first link in the chain, and the fixed-term employment agreement is the second. However, a temp worker could easily have had more than one relevant agreement with the temp agency. Consequently, when hiring a temporary employee first through a temp agency and subsequently as a regular employee, there is a very real risk that an employer automatically enters into an employment agreement for an indefinite time.

Part-Time and Full-Time Employees

A large number of Dutch employees work part-time. Full-timers under certain conditions have a right to work part-time. The employer can refuse to cut down on working hours only for serious business reasons. Part-timers have the same rights as full-timers and cannot be discriminated against on the basis of the number of hours they work.

Temporary Workers

Besides the employment contracts for a fixed and an indefinite term and for full-time and part-time, common forms of employment are employment through temp agencies (*uitzendburo's*) and hiring a person on the basis of a consultancy contract (with that person individually or its company). Many Dutch employers (initially) work with temporary employees (*uitzendkrachten*). Temporary workers are employed by the temp agency and not by the company hiring that person from the temp agency. Temp agencies have their own collective labor agreement (*collectieve arbeidsovereenkomst*), the rules of which apply to the employment agreements between the temp agency and the temporary worker. Temp agencies are prohibited from charging temp workers money (or any other consideration) for being given temp work. Temp agencies must inform temps in writing about the working conditions at the place of work in advance.

Parties may choose a consultancy agreement if it is not their intention to enter into an employment agreement. It is wise to check beforehand whether the risk exists that the consultancy agreement is considered an employment agreement by the tax authorities in which case the company contracting the consultancy services runs the risk to have to pay wage taxes on the consultancy fees.

Probation Period

The parties to an employment agreement may agree in writing on a probation period that should be of the same length for both the employer and employee. During the probation period either party may terminate the employment agreement immediately without any further obligation. A maximum probation period of one month may be agreed for a fixed-term employment contract of less than two years, or a fixed-term employment contract linked to a project or for the replacement of an employee (with no agreed termination date). A maximum probation period of two months may be agreed in a fixed-term employment contract of two years or longer and in an indefinite-term agreement.

The probation period is ironclad: When the rules regarding a probation period are not followed, the probation period is null and void. It cannot be extended, not even if the employee is sick and unable to work during the probation period. Generally a probation period can occur only once during employment and within consecutive employment agreements, except when the nature of the work performed considerably changes. If the employee has no knowledge or experience in performing the new job, the employer is entitled to a new probation period.

Noncompete Clauses

Noncompete clauses purporting to restrict the employee's freedom to choose employment elsewhere after the termination of the employment agreement are fairly common in the Netherlands. Such a provision will be valid and binding only if (1) the employee has reached the age of 18 and (2) the provision is agreed in writing and signed by both parties. A generally accepted term for a noncompete period is one year. It is strongly advisable to confirm or renew the noncompete period if and when an employee starts performing considerably different work, for example when the employee is promoted and will get more responsibilities. Without such renewal or confirmation, the noncompete restriction might ultimately be regarded by a court as having lapsed. A noncompete clause may be annulled or limited by a court if the court finds, while balancing the employer's interests in protecting trade secrets or sensitive information against the employee's interests in not being unreasonably restricted in accepting another job, that the interests of one or the other should prevail.

Confidentiality

Dutch law provides a general rule on confidentiality of the employer's business information and forbids a systematic solicitation of customers or relations of the employer by the employee. However, it is prudent and common to provide additional rules in the employment agreement.

Remuneration

The Dutch Civil Code contains a number of provisions as to the employer's duty to pay wages and the way this has to be done. The employer is obliged to pay wages at a specified time and place. Wages can be paid in currency or in kind and are paid monthly or every four weeks. The employer is obliged to provide the employee with an itemized pay slip at each time of payment of wages, which must show the deductions taken as well as the amount of statutory minimum wage to which the employee is entitled. There is a statutory minimum wage for employees aged 23 or over. In addition there is a statutory minimum wage for employees aged between 15 and 22, the level of which varies according to age. These minimum wages are indexed and may be adjusted twice a year, on January 1 and July 1.

Vacations and Vacation Allowance

A full-time employee (40 hours per week) is entitled to a minimum of 20 vacation days each year. It is fairly common to provide the employee with more than the statutory minimum; 25 is customary. In addition to vacation days, an employee is generally entitled to public holidays of which there are normally seven each year; no extra day is automatically given should a public holiday fall on a weekend. In the Netherlands, the following are generally observed public holidays: New Year's Day, Easter Monday, Queen's Day, Liberation Day, Ascension Day, Whit-Monday, and Christmas Day. Even though Dutch law considers these days national holidays, employers are not statutorily obliged to provide their employees with a day off. A growing percentage of Dutch companies give their employees Good Friday off. Liberation Day (May 5) is a national holiday, but many collective agreements specify that employees have that day off only every fifth year. Remembrance Day (May 4), however, is not a national holiday.

The employer is obliged to pay a statutory vacation allowance of 8 percent of the employee's salary, but only to that part of the salary which equals three times the minimum wage. It is possible to agree on an employee's salary inclusive of the vacation allowance if the employee earns more than three times the minimum wage, provided that this is agreed in writing.

Leave

The Work and Care Act—which to a large extent creates conditions for a better work-life balance of employees in the Netherlands—offers various opportunities for an employee to take a leave of absence, such as

- *Parental leave:* unpaid leave on a part-time basis to care for a child under the age of eight for a continuous period of up to six months;
- *Maternity leave:* 16 weeks of paid leave, starting six weeks before the expected due date and ending 10 weeks after; this benefit is paid by the General Unemployment Fund;
- *Paternity leave:* two days of paid leave for the partner of the woman who has given birth; and
- *Emergency leave:* paid short-term leave when the employee cannot work because of exceptional personal circumstances.

Pension Plans

Old age pension is provided by the state within the national social insurance plan. This ensures a socially acceptable minimum, and there is no statutory obligation for the employer to provide for an additional amount. However, compulsory pension funds exist in several sectors of industry, for example, in the construction industry. These compulsory pension funds provide for benefits in addition to the state social insurance plan.

Where no such sector funds exist, it is fairly common for individual employers to provide employees with an additional pension plan. Distribution of the insurance contribution for additional pension plans is a matter of negotiation between employee and employer.

Illness

When the employee is prevented from working due to illness, the employer is by law required to continue to pay 70 percent of the employee's salary (up to a certain maximum) for 104 weeks, and during the first 52 weeks at a level of at least the minimum wage. Contractual provisions providing for higher payments (for example, 70 percent of the last earned salary with no maximum, or even 100 percent of the last earned salary) are customary for the first year of illness. Dutch employers have usually insured themselves with private insurance companies against this risk.

After the first 104 weeks of illness, the payment of the employee during illness is insured under the Work and Income Act (WIA), the law on income related to capacity to work, and possible obligations of the employer are limited to making supplementary payments on top of the WIA benefits up to the agreed salary.

In general, dismissal during illness is not allowed unless the employee has been ill for two consecutive years. However, if the ill worker does not follow reasonable control prescriptions, is not cooperative in establishing a reintegration program, or refuses to perform "suitable work," the employer is not only entitled but should stop payment of wages. Suitable work is work the employee is able to perform and that the employee may be requested to perform taking into consideration any physical, psychological, and social circumstances.

Health and Safety

The employer is obliged to ensure the employee's safety in the workplace. The employer not complying with this obligation is liable to compensate damages incurred by the employee as a result of the negligence. Most issues of health and safety are dealt with in the Health and Safety at Work Act (*Arbeidsomstandigheden-wet*), providing for the employer's obligation to observe the health and safety standards as specified in the Act. Obviously, the standards will vary depending on the sector of industry. Compliance with the rules and regulations of the Health and Safety at Work Act is supervised by the Labor Inspection (*Arbeidsinspectie*), which has far-reaching powers, including the ability to order the temporary or permanent closure of a business.

Working Hours

Dutch law provides for maximum working hours for all employees. For example, the Working Hours Act (*Arbeidstijdenwet*) sets a maximum of 12 hours per shift and 60 hours per week for employees aged 18 years and older. No more than 768 hours may be worked within a period of 16 weeks, which is an average of 48 hours per week. No more than 220 hours may be worked within a period of four weeks, which results in an average of 55 hours per week. These statutory provisions are often improved by collective labor agreements. In most cases, they provide for an average working week of 36 to 40 hours. The Working Hours Act also contains provisions on overtime, night work, Sunday work, and rest periods.

Foreign Employees

On the basis of the Foreign Labor Act (*Wet arbeid vreemdelingen*), a work permit is required for workers from a non-European Union (EU) country. The permit is issued by the Dutch Labor Office, known as the Center for Work and Income (CWI), and has to be requested by the employer. As a rule, an employer will receive such a permit only if it can be proved that no EU workers are available for the job. A work permit is granted for the maximum duration of three years. In practice, more than 50 percent of the permits are granted for only six months. Workers from outside the EU who have worked legally in the Netherlands for at least three years as well as persons admitted on humanitarian grounds no longer need a work permit.

The application for a work permit by the employer will be dealt with by the authorities only once the foreigner has applied for an authorization for temporary residence (*machtiging tot voorlopig verblijf*, MVV) before coming to the Netherlands. Foreigners from a number of countries (including the United States of America, Canada, New Zealand, and Australia) are not required to have an MVV. However, these foreigners need to have filed an application for a residence permit prior to their employer's application for a work permit.

A residence permit is required to stay in the Netherlands longer than three months. Generally, the holder of a residence permit is under the same obligations as Dutch nationals (for instance, taxes, social security contributions, and customs duties). Residence permits are usually issued for periods of six months to one year. After five years of main residence in the Netherlands, performing work on a regular basis and gaining sufficient income, a foreigner qualifies for a permanent residence permit (*verblijfssvergunning*).

Termination of Employment

Fixed-Term Agreements

Agreements for a fixed period of time or for the duration of a project automatically end after the fixed period has lapsed or the project has been finalized. No CWI dismissal permit or court approval will be necessary and notice is only necessary if agreed. Also, the statutory dismissal prohibitions do not apply.

Indefinite-Term Agreements

Agreements for an indefinite term end automatically with the death of the employee. Sometimes it has been agreed that the agreement automatically ends at the occurrence of a certain event. Indefinite contracts previously ended automatically when the worker reached the statutory retirement age of 65. However, compulsory retirement is being challenged lately as age discriminatory. Therefore, it is advisable to insert a provision in the employment agreement stating the agreement will end automatically when the employee reaches the age of 65.

There are various ways to terminate an indefinite-term employment agreement.

Dismissal with Labor Office Permit

The employer wishing to terminate an indefinite-term employment agreement or a fixed-term employment agreement with a prior notice clause, or one that requires notice for another reason, must first obtain a permit from the Labor Office before serving the notice of termination, stating the reason(s) for the intended termination. The purpose of this procedure is to put the Labor Office in a position to prevent unreasonable or socially unjustifiable dismissals. Employees do not need the approval of the Labor Office to give notice.

The Labor Office approval procedure will usually take about two months, provided that the reasons for termination are clear. If the reason is difficult to substantiate, the Labor Office may not consent. There is no appeal from the decision of the Labor Office. However, if the Labor Office denies approval, the employer could bring an action in court to dissolve the contract.

Even if a contract is terminated with Labor Office consent and with due observance of the applicable notice period, the employee may still take the employer to court and contest the dismissal on the grounds that such dismissal was "obviously unreasonable," and may claim compensation.

Notice Periods

Once permission is granted, the employment may be terminated, observing the applicable notice period. The term of notice to be observed by the employer is one month for the first five years of service, which term is extended by one month, with a maximum of four, for each subsequent five years of service. These terms may be extended further by written agreement and may be reduced by collective labor agreement. The term of notice to be observed by the employee is one month, but the parties may deviate from this rule in writing. If they agree on another notice period, the term of notice to be observed by the employer must be at least double the term of notice to be observed by the employee, which may not exceed six months (and therefore the notice period for the employer may not exceed 12 months). Notice is usually given at the end of a calendar month.

To compensate for the time involved in the dismissal procedure, the employer may reduce the term of notice by one month, provided that at least one month remains. Any applicable collective labor agreement should be checked for deviating rules. The reduction of one month does not apply if the parties choose to settle their dispute with mutual consent (e.g., without asking the court of Labor Office to formally decide on the termination).

Prohibited Dismissals

Under certain circumstances, employment agreements may not be terminated via the Labor Office (CWI) procedure. The employer would need to go to court. Termination would be null and void during (1) the first two years of illness; (2) the period during which the employee is pregnant (including the period up to and including the 16th week after childbirth); (3) military (or alternative compulsory) service; and (4) membership in a works council, European Works Council, or labor union.

The employer may, however, request the court at any time to terminate the employment agreement of such employees. Also, the prohibited dismissals (except the one on maternity protection) do not apply in case of a total close-down of the company.

Dismissal Without Labor Office Permit

Termination of an agreement without the approval of the Labor Office is null and void, except under the following circumstances.

- *The termination is by mutual consent.* It is very common for an employer and an employee to mutually settle their employment conflict. This may be done instead of going to court or the Labor Office, simultaneously with or prior to either such procedure (if one of the parties insists on getting the agreement confirmed by the court or the Labor Office). The outcome of the settlement is determined by the expected outcome of the court or Labor Office procedure, the amount of compensation based on the Court Formula, transactional costs, and management time. It is advisable that a termination by mutual consent is confirmed in a written agreement. If disputed, the employer must produce clear evidence of the mutual consent.

- *The termination is for urgent reasons (summary dismissal).* Urgent reasons (*dringende redenen*) for dismissing an employee are those acts or circumstances that result in a situation where the employer could not reasonably be expected to continue the employment agreement any longer. The summary dismissal should take place immediately upon or shortly after the occurrence of such a situation, and all the reasons justifying the dismissal must be communicated to the employee, preferably in a letter sent immediately by registered mail to the employee. The Civil Code gives a list of examples as to when the employer may be justified in taking such a course of action, such as theft. Courts tend to be reluctant to accept such summary dismissals.

- *The court terminates the employment agreement.* The employer may at any time request the court to have the agreement terminated immediately or in the near future for certain important reasons. The court may award "reasonable compensation" to the employee at the expense of the employer (or to the employer, which hardly ever occurs) and such awards may amount to substantial sums.

- *The termination occurs during the trial period.* As mentioned in Section I, during a trial period either party may terminate the agreement without notice or reason, with immediate effect and no further obligations on either party.

- *The termination is of a member of the company board.* A member of the board of directors of the company who is also an employee of that same company may be dismissed at will, but certain procedural rules apply.

Layoff

The aim of the Collective Dismissal Act (*Wet melding collectief ontslag*) is to protect employees in the case where a group of at least 20 employees is involved. Notice of an intention to dismiss such a group (or any members thereof) must be provided to the Labor Office. The notification should include the reasons for the layoff, whether or not the works council has been consulted, the criteria used to determine which employees will be laid off, and the calculation method for severance pay.

In case of a layoff, relevant trade unions need to be notified. Relevant trade unions are those unions that have members employed by the company and that are actively involved in the company's affairs or the affairs of the sector of industry as far as employment and social policy are concerned. As a practical matter, this means that where a collective labor agreement applies to the company's affairs, the contracting trade unions would be deemed to be interested. If no collective labor agreement applies, such an interest would be dependent on actual involvement of the unions in the day-to-day affairs of the company over recent years. This may be evidenced by involvement in the institution or election of a works council. However, individual representation for members would also qualify. In rare cases, it may be determined that there are no interested unions. In that case, only the Labor Office is to be notified.

In most cases of layoff, a request for advice needs to be addressed to the company works council or another employee representation body (if there is one). After notification, the company may choose to follow the individual termination procedures with the labor office, to ask the court to terminate the employment agreements (although some courts would refer the company to the Labor Office once it finds out that a layoff is involved), or to settle each termination case with the employee involved.

Termination Compensation

The "Court Formula"

The court may order the employer to pay to the employee a "reasonable compensation." There are no statutory rules with respect to the amount of compensation to be paid in case of termination of the agreement. However, the courts have made recommendations as to how the amount of compensation should be determined in case of termination by the court.

The recommendations provide—briefly—that the compensation to be awarded will be determined by the following formula:

$$A \times B \times C$$

where

$$A = \text{number of years of service}$$
$$B = \text{employee's earnings}$$
$$C = \text{the court's correction factor}$$

For determining the number of years of service, the total duration of the individual's employment is rounded-off to the nearest full year; any period of six months and one day deemed to be a whole year. If the employee is under 41 years of age, the years of service are multiplied by 1. If the employee is aged between 41 and 50, the years of service completed since the age of 41 are multiplied by 1.5. Years of service completed after age 50 are multiplied by 2. These factors are applied cumulatively.

The measure of calculating earnings are the employee's gross monthly wages or salary, plus agreed fixed-pay components such as vacation allowance, end-of-year payment, regular overtime pay, and regular shift-work allowance.

If the application for an order terminating the employment contract is based on "neutral grounds," the correction factor will be 1; the grounds for termination are deemed "neutral" when neither the employer nor the employee is to blame for them; for example, the employee is made redundant as the result of a reorganization (in which the rules of seniority have been observed) and there are no exceptional financial circumstances. However, there may be circumstances that justify an adjustment—upward or downward—of the correction factor. The court may even apply a correction factor of zero if in its opinion the circumstances of the case do not justify any compensation at all, for example, serious dereliction of duty or misconduct by the employee.

The amount of compensation—save any damages for emotional suffering (which are rarely awarded)—will be limited to the expected loss of earnings until the employee reaches pensionable age.

Supplementary Payments

Less commonly used, the supplementary payments approach is taken in the case of reorganizations for economic reasons, leading to mass layoffs. It provides that the unemployment benefit is supplemented up to a certain percentage of the employee's last earned salary, for a certain period of time. The length of the period depends on age and years of service. The compensation due based on this plan is sometimes paid as a lump sum. Currently, most agreements call for payment of severance as per the court formula discussed previously.

Collective Labor Relations

Labor Unions

There are a couple hundred labor unions in the Netherlands, each with a few hundred to half a million members. However, union membership is low in the Netherlands, being one of the least unionized countries of the EU. Traditionally, most unions consider themselves as representing the interests of all workers and not just the interests of their members.

Employers' federations exist in most sectors of the Dutch economy. The organization rate among Dutch employers is high. Organized employers are assumed to employ approximately 90 percent of all workers in the private sector of the Dutch economy.

The general freedom of association enshrined in the Constitution also extends to employers' and employees' associations. The Netherlands has signed a number of international documents recognizing labor union rights, such as the European Social Charter. An individual worker or employer has the freedom to join an association of his or her choice. An association is not required to accept an applicant as a member.

Collective Labor Agreements

A collective labor agreement is an agreement between one or more labor unions on the one hand and one or more employers' associations or a particular company on the other. In the Netherlands, it is usual for employers' associations and labor unions in each of the existing sectors of industry to enter into a collective labor agreement for and on behalf of their members. The collective labor agreement is binding only upon the members of the parties to the agreement unless the agreement is declared "generally binding" (*algemeen verbindend*) by the Minister of Social

Affairs, in which case it applies to every employment agreement in a particular sector of industry (e.g., to every employment agreement in the construction industry).

Collective labor agreements normally deal with a wide variety of issues, such as wages, wage structures, pensions, vacations, working hours, and overtime pay. Any provision in an individual employment agreement that restricts the rights of the employee under an applicable collective labor agreement is null and void. In such cases the collective labor agreement provision prevails. In case provisions of an individual employment contract conflict with the applicable collective labor agreement, both the employee and the labor unions who are a party to the collective labor agreement may bring a claim before a Dutch court.

Strikes

There are very few strikes in the Netherlands. However, the limited number of strikes goes hand in hand with a relatively high number of court cases relating to strikes. Strikes are not regulated by legislation. The court rules whether or not a strike is allowed. A strike is lawful if used as a last resort, if it is not in conflict in any way with applicable law or the applicable collective labor agreement, and if its aim is proportionate to the means used.

Employee Representation

The Works Council
Under the Dutch Works Council Act, a business that employs 50 or more employees must have a works council. Less far-reaching participation structures are provided for smaller businesses with between 10 and 50 employees. Small companies with fewer than 10 employees may have a voluntary works council or another type of voluntary representation body. If the management of a company does install a works council when required, every interested party may ask the court to order the installation of a works council. There is no administrative or criminal law penalty for not instituting a works council.

The works council is an independent body elected by the employees from their midst. It has its own bylaws. The works council may appoint committees and call in experts; it may use certain facilities of the company (such as conference rooms, copying machines, and telephones) and holds its meetings as much as possible during working hours, as determined in consultation with the company. Works council members may interrupt their work for internal consultation, training, and education. Works council members have a certain obligation of secrecy. They enjoy job protection, meaning that they may be dismissed on proper grounds but only by court order.

Employees' Representative Body
A business that regularly employs at least 10 but fewer than 50 workers may be obligated to establish a so-called employees' representative body (*personeelsvertegenwoordiging*). An employees' representative body may be established upon the request of a majority of the workers or it may be installed voluntarily by the employer.

Such a body has comparable but much more limited powers than the works council. According to the Works Council Act, some of the provisions applicable to a works council are also applicable to the employees' representation body.

Employees' Consultation Meeting

An enterprise with 10 to 50 employees but neither a works council nor an employees' representative body must permit an employees' consultation meeting (*personeelsvergadering*) with the entrepreneur at least twice a year to discuss matters regarding the company. The entrepreneur is further required to hold such a meeting upon the request of at least 25 percent of the employees.

Powers of the Works Council

The management of the company has consultation meetings with the works council at least six times a year. At two of those meetings, the general course of business and management of the company has to be discussed. The works council has a right to advise on certain reorganizational matters and a right of approval as to certain changes in secondary benefits, all described in the Works Council Act. It also has a right of initiative and a right to gain information under certain circumstances.

When the management has to seek the works council's advice, such advice must be requested in writing and at such a time that will allow the works council to have a significant impact on the decision that is to be taken. When the advice is sought, the works council is to be furnished with the grounds for the decision, the expected consequences for the employees, and the measures proposed in response. The works council's advice may be positive, negative, neutral, or conditional. If the advice goes against the intended decision and the employer nevertheless takes the decision, the decision may not be implemented during a period of one month from the day the works council was informed of the decision or could have reasonably know about the decision. The works council has a right to appeal to a special Division of the Court of Appeal in Amsterdam. The ground for appeal may be the breach of procedures by the management or on the basis that "no reasonable employer would have taken the decision under the circumstances." In most of the cases won by the works council, the appeal was lodged for reason of breach of procedure.

The works council's approval is required for certain decisions regarding the implementation, amendment, or withdrawal of certain benefit plans, failing which approval the decision is null and void. The company may then ask the court to allow it to take the decision after all. The works council, on its turn, may ask the court to state that a certain decision is null and void because it would have required its prior approval.

Joint Works Councils, Group Works Councils, Central Works Councils

In larger groups of companies, a group works council or central works council may be established and may have to be established at the request of a certain number of employees if this is conducive to the application of the rules of the Works Council Act. A joint works council may or has to be established for the same reason in the case of two or more businesses where 50 or more persons are employed. A central works council or a group works council may or has to be established for the same reason. Both the central works council and the group works council deal only with matters that are of common interest for all or the majority of the businesses for which they are established.

European Works Council

A European directive provides for the obligation of the member states to enact legislation providing for the institution of works councils for community scale undertakings for the purpose of improving the right to information and to consultation of the employees. In the Netherlands, the directive is implemented in the European Works Councils Act (*Wet op de Europese ondernemingsraden*). The obligation to set up a European Works Council within a group arises if a group employs at least 1,000 employees and if at least two group-companies in different EU member states employ at least 150 employees. The Act provides for creating a European Works Council or, alternatively, for instituting "a system of information and consultation of workers." The rights of a European Works Council are not only far less extensive than those of a local Dutch works council, they are different in nature as well.

SECTION II

My client is acquiring an existing business in the Netherlands. How do I assess the existing workforce and consider changes?

Share Deals Versus Asset Deals

If all or part of the shares in a company are sold, the company will have a new shareholder. The employees will remain employed with the company. The employees do not necessarily notice the change of shareholders in their daily work. On the other hand, if all or part of the assets of a company are sold, in many cases the employees transfer along with the assets to the buyer's company.

The transfer of undertaking rules stemming from Acquired Rights Directive 2001/23/EC are implemented in Articles 7:662 *et seq.* of the Dutch Civil Code. If a transfer of all assets of a company falls within the scope of these transfer of undertaking rules, employees will generally transfer to the buyer. If only part of the assets of the company are being sold, employees who can be said to work in that part of the company will transfer to the buyer. The employees transferring to the buyer on the basis of the transfer of undertaking rules become automatically employed with the buyer on the same terms and conditions as were applicable before the transfer. All rights and obligations of the seller transfer to the buyer. The seller and buyer will be jointly and severally liable for one year after the transfer for all claims arising out of the employment relation before the transfer date. Whether a specific transaction constitutes a transfer of undertaking depends on the circumstances of the case. The main criterion is whether or not the company or part of the company sold retains its identity after the transfer.

In both share transactions and asset transactions, there are various requirements as to employee involvement. Notwithstanding the fact that the parties to such deals often impose mutual confidentiality obligations, the works council should be informed of the plans and be given the opportunity to render advice early enough in the process to be able to influence the transaction. The members of the works council are under a duty to keep the information they obtain confidential. Also, depending on the applicable collective labor agreement, both seller and buyer may be obliged to consult with the unions. Finally, notice of a share or asset deal will under certain circumstances have to be provided to a special merger committee on the basis of the rules of the Dutch Merger Code. The merger committee supervises the observance of the Merger Code and consists of representatives of employers, employees, and independent members.

Carrying out a Workforce Reduction

If the buyer of a business wants to carry out a workforce reduction or another type of reorganization, it should first consider that in a transfer of undertaking as referred to above, the transfer itself may not be the reason for the dismissals. The company wanting to start dismissal procedures will need a so-called ETO reason: a reason of an economic, technical, or organizational nature. If a workforce reduction may indeed be carried out, the new owner is bound to the regular dismissal restrictions under Dutch law. Dismissal rules applicable to the choice of the employees to be laid off, such as seniority considerations, must be applied to the joint group of employees: those who have always been employed in the company of the new owner and those who were transferred from the company that was taken over.

Dismissals may generally be based on economic reasons or restructuring. However, businesses in less dire straits may also limit or reorganize their work force. Strategic reasons are generally acceptable, but the more sound the company, the more difficult it is to obtain the necessary approvals. For example, the mere fact of a merger of two businesses is (without any other arguments) in general not sufficient to reduce staff significantly.

Changing the Wage and Benefits Structure

The changing of employment terms and conditions is not thoroughly regulated under Dutch law. Most of the situations must be judged according to the general principles of law, for example on the principle of good employership and good employeeship. It can be concluded that the employer may unilaterally amend employment terms and conditions if these concern the mere organization of work. However, the employer may be limited, for instance, by individual and collective labor agreements, by the works council, by the trade unions, and by customs and practices.

With regard to the most crucial aspects of employment, primarily wages and working times, the power of the employer to unilaterally amend is narrow. Whereas employees have a specific right to have their working times changed (based on the Working Time Adjustment Act; *Wet aanpassing arbeidsduur*) provided that there is no serious objection on the grounds of company interests, the employer is statutorily prohibited from unilaterally reducing the working time below 48 hours a week with corresponding reduction of salary. Employees may challenge a unilateral change in working conditions, invoking the general principle of good employership. Even if the contract of employment or an applicable company rule empowers the employer to amend the working conditions set out in the employment contract, the employer may invoke such a provision only if it has such an important interest in the amendment that—according to standards of reasonableness and fairness—the interests of the employee must give way.

A transfer of undertaking is not in itself sufficient reason to amend working conditions. This is important because often the new employer wishes to harmonize the employment terms and conditions of the "new" and "old" employees. Pension plans form an exemption to this rule. Furthermore, the transfer of undertaking itself may not be the reason for dismissal of employees who are to be or have been transferred, though they may be dismissed for ETO reasons—within the limits of the stringent Dutch law on dismissals, as discussed previously. Employees transferring to the new employer carry over their full seniority with regard to the notice period and severance pay, which the new employer will have to respect in case of dismissal.

The transfer of undertaking rules do not apply if a business or part of a business is taken over from a bankrupt company. The acquiring company may choose which employees to keep and under what terms and conditions. Attempts to abuse this rule by employers who purposefully had their company declared bankrupt and sold the business without transfer of undertaking strings attached have been punished by the court.

Consulting with Labor Unions, Works Councils, and the Government

Pursuant to the Works Council Act, an employer is required to give the works council an opportunity to render advice on any intended decision that may have important consequences for the company as a whole, such as intended decisions on the transfer of control of the company or a part thereof, a substantial reduction of business, the closing of the company or a substantial part thereof, and a substantial change in the organization of the company (Article 25 of the Works Council Act). The advice should be asked early enough in the decision-making process that the works council can influence the decision. The works council is obliged to treat the received information as confidential.

An employer is not required to inform any other employee representatives before it decides to transfer its employees, unless an applicable collective labor agreement (a sector collective labor agreement or a company collective labor agreement) states otherwise.

There is no Dutch state authority that needs to be consulted in case of a reorganization or transfer of undertaking. However, the Dutch Merger Code (*SER Fusiegedragsregels 2000*), established by the Dutch Social and Economic Council

(*Sociaal Economische Raad*), applies if the asset or share deal results in a transfer of control of an undertaking in the broad sense defined therein. The code includes rules of conduct designed to protect the interests of employees in the event of a merger. The Merger Code does not constitute legislation. In case of breach of the Merger Code, a public reprimand may follow, which is generally feared by most companies.

An employer needs to comply with the Merger Code if one of the companies involved in a merger or acquisition employs 50 persons or more in the Netherlands or forms part of a group of companies that as a whole employs 50 persons or more in the Netherlands. Pursuant to the Merger Code, notice of the intention to merge should be provided to the merger committee, and relevant trade unions must be informed of the intended sale. This needs to be done if and when the expectation is justified that parties will reach agreement on the basic terms of the agreement.

Furthermore, an intended acquisition of the shares in the company may be subject to notification under the European Merger Regulation or the Dutch Competition Act, which both contain a system of preliminary merger control. Whether a transaction is subject to such notification depends on whether the transaction may be qualified as a concentration within the meaning of the respective laws and whether specific turnover thresholds in the preceding calendar year are met.

If the Merger Code is applicable, the employee representatives concerned must be notified when the negotiations reach a stage that justifies the expectation that an agreement can be reached. The employee representatives must be informed in writing of the reasons for the transfer and its legal, social, and economic consequences, as well as when the works council has been or will be informed. Notice of the intended transfer has to be given to a special merger committee.

Finally, an employer is not obliged to consult the individual employees before deciding to, for example, transfer them to another company. However, the general duty of care requires that the employer inform the individual employees of such a decision.

SECTION III

My client wishes to sell its existing facility. What restrictions do we need to consider?

See Section II.

SECTION IV

My client wishes to replace its senior manager(s). What restrictions do we need to consider?

In the Netherlands, termination of the relationship with a managing director who has been formally appointed to the board of directors (*statutair bestuurder*) is covered by aspects of corporate law and employment law. Employees not belonging to this category and having the title of manager because they function at a management level are considered regular employees in this respect.

Corporate Law Aspects

Under Dutch law, the general meeting of shareholders of a private company with limited liability (*Besloten Vennootschap*) may remove a managing director from office at any time. However, the managing director has an advisory vote in all shareholders' meetings—even when his or her own dismissal is at stake—and must be given the opportunity to offer a defense against the shareholders' allegations in this meeting. Failure to meet this formal requirement may result in a court annulment of the dismissal decision.

A shareholders' meeting must generally be convened with 15 days' notice. However, the director may be heard with respect to the dismissal in an informal meeting rather than an official shareholders' meeting, provided the director has been given sufficient time to prepare for the meeting. There is no hard-and-fast rule setting how much time constitutes "sufficient time." The safe approach would be to allow 15 days' notice, as with the shareholders' meeting.

Even if the above requirements are met, the shareholders' decision to dismiss the managing director may still be nullified if the director was not previously cautioned that his or her position was at stake (for instance, as a result of poor performance). Preferably, such warnings take place in writing.

The articles of association of the company may contain further requirements that need to be observed in order for the shareholders' decision to be valid.

Pursuant to the Works Council Act, the company's works council (if any) must in principle be consulted prior to the dismissal of a managing director. The works council does not have a veto as to the dismissal. The works council may be obliged to maintain confidentiality.

The shareholders' decision to dismiss the director may be combined with or preceded by a decision to suspend the director. Such decision would in principle be subject to the same procedural requirements as those for the shareholders' decision to dismiss the director.

If the company has a supervisory board, the rules applying to the dismissal of a director may be different. It is wise to check the law in this respect and the articles of association of the company involved.

Employment Law Aspects

Generally—but not always—a managing director will also have an employment relationship with the company. Below it is assumed that this is indeed the case. It should be noted that the removal of the director automatically includes termination as an employee unless specifically agreed otherwise.

The absence of dismissal protection is the only aspect of Dutch employment law in which the director is distinguished from any other employee. In other words, a director benefits from all the rights the law provides to employees, except for the dismissal permit requirement typical for Dutch employment law.

Just as with a regular employee, a managing director may not be dismissed for being ill. This statutory protection from dismissal is effective for a maximum of two years. On the one hand, from a corporate law point of view, this protection in principle does not limit the right to dismiss the managing director by shareholders' decision. On the other hand, from an employment law point of view, the contractual position of the managing director as an employee of the company would still continue to exist in case of such corporate dismissal.

When giving notice of termination, the statutory or contractual (if any) notice period must be observed. Assuming the applicable notice period is observed, the question of whether severance payment is due depends on whether a court would deem the dismissal "obviously unreasonable." The director could sue the company in this regard within six months after the last day of employment. The court would examine, among other things, the grounds for dismissal and the compensation offered to the director. Payment in lieu of notice is very unusual in the Netherlands. Not only would dismissal without observing the contractual notice period (even with payment in lieu thereof) increase the potential liability on account of unreasonable dismissal, the company might not be able to enforce a noncompetition period, if any.

All provisions and risks regarding notice—including those related to the notice period, protection during illness, and liability for severance—may be avoided if the company, instead of dismissing the managing director, requests the court to terminate the employment agreement. However, the court could then immediately award the director compensation.

The managing director may also request the court to terminate the employment agreement, even after notice of termination has been given. The aim would be to get immediate agreement on the monetary component of the dismissal.

As with ordinary employees, the company may summarily dismiss the director, but only if and when the grounds for termination are so serious that immediate termination without severance is warranted. Fraud is a typical example. Summary dismissals are seldom upheld when challenged in court.

Amicable Settlement

It is possible to terminate the employment agreement with a managing director by mutual consent. In general, in order to convince the director to agree to an amicable settlement, sufficient compensation would have to be offered. There are no statutory rules with respect to the amount of compensation due in case of dismissal of a managing director. In practice, the rules of thumb for regular employees serve as a basis for calculating the termination compensation of managing directors. However, when the compensation package of a director includes a fairly large benefits package, these rules may not be adequate. Besides purely financial compensation, other aspects may constitute an important element of an amicable settlement. Managing directors are usually particularly interested in how the separation is communicated, internally as well as externally. Internal as well as external communication regarding the director's departure are almost always a matter of particular concern.

While an amicable approach is not always appropriate, where the grounds for dismissal are neutral or difficult to substantiate, it may be preferable to agree on the terms and conditions of termination of the employment agreement amicably.

SECTION V

What prohibitions exist against discrimination on the basis of age, race, gender, disability, pregnancy, and other factors? What are the rights of employees, applicants, or former employees who believe that they have been discriminated against?

In the Netherlands, there are many different sets of equal treatment and non-discrimination rules, part of which stem from European Law. Article 1 of the Dutch Constitution states that all persons residing in the Netherlands must be treated equally in equal cases. Equal treatment and nondiscrimination are also laid down in the Dutch Civil Code and the Equal Treatment Act. An employer should take preventive actions against discrimination, which includes equal treatment on the basis of age, race, gender, religion, belief, political conviction, nationality, sexual orientation, marital status, disability or chronic disease, and type of contract (temporary or permanent, full-time or part-time). Over the last few years, court cases involving equal treatment and nondiscrimination have primarily concerned age discrimination and equal treatment of men and women in regard to salary and pension payments. An employee experiencing perceived unequal treatment may ask the Equal Treatment Commission to launch an investigation.

SECTION VI

On the Horizon: What key labor and employment law developments should an employer doing business in the Netherlands anticipate occurring in the coming years?

Over the last few years, on many occasions the government has proposed changes in the Dutch rules on termination of employment. The current dual system of procedures—the Labor Office and the courts—is seen as too protective of the employees. Employee representative bodies and the unions have been opposed to these proposed changes, and the dual system still exists. In the fall of 2007, the Dutch government yet again proposed changes in the laws relating to labor contracts, specifically those on termination of employment. These proposals are part of a wider approach to increase labor participation by giving employers more flexibility in hiring and dismissing employees. The proposed changes include a mutual obligation of employer and employee to properly and constantly train the employee, more flexible rules relating to dismissal, a statutory maximum on dismissal compensation, and better protection of employees working under fixed-term contracts. Employers would be allowed to deduct training costs from the dismissal compensation they would have to pay to the employee, for up to a quarter of a month's salary per year of service.

In the current system, termination is possible only through the courts or the Labor Office. The new plan would allow employers to terminate employment contracts without prior approval of the court or Labor Office, provided they have proper reasons to do so. The obligation would exist generally to pay compensation to the employee who is being terminated. In case of dismissals pertaining to business economics, the obligation to pay the statutory compensation would in principle not exist, provided the dismissal has been approved by the Labor Office. In cases of layoff, it would still be possible for the employer to negotiate with the employees on the rules of compensation. The 2007 plans provide a maximum dismissal compensation of a one year's income, capped at €75,000. For older or more senior employees, the maximum is set at €100,000.

CHAPTER 12

LABOR AND EMPLOYMENT LAW IN NORWAY

TROND STANG

SECTION I

My client wishes to establish a manufacturing facility in Norway and will need to hire a workforce. What are the key issues involved?

Employment Contracts: Who Receives Them and What Must They Include?

Mandatory Requirements

The relationship between the employer and the employee is mainly governed by the Norwegian Working Environment Act (WEA) (*Arbeidsmiljøloven*). The WEA is, as a starting point, applicable for all enterprises that employ employees. An employee is defined as "anyone who performs work in the service of another." An employer is defined as "anyone who has engaged an employee to perform work in his or her service."

Whether the employee is an employee in the meaning of the WEA or is an independent contractor depends on a specific assessment, where the following elements are of importance: (1) whether the person is obligated to place his or her personal working capacity at disposal; (2) whether the employer may supervise the work and give instructions; (3) whether the parties have agreed on a period of notice and periodic compensation; (4) whether the employer bears the risk for the work result; (5) whether the person may hire/engage others and if he or she is responsible for paying them; (6) whether the employer shall place premises and equipment at the worker's disposal; (7) whether the attachment between the parties is of a steady character; and (8) whether the person is free to work for others.

Form of the Employment Contract

The WEA requires that a written employment contract is entered into between all employers and employees. It is the duty of the employer to draft the employment contract. However, also an oral contract will be binding for both the

211

employer and the employee, but the exact content of the "contract" may be difficult to prove.

Required Information

The employment contract must contain information about matters that are of vital importance in the employment relationship. As a minimum, the employment contract must include the following:

1. The identity of the parties.
2. The place of work. If there is no fixed or main place of work, the employment contract must state that the employee is employed at various locations and provide the registered place of business or, where appropriate, the home address of the employer.
3. A description of the work or the employee's title, post, or category of work.
4. The date of commencement of the employment.
5. If the employment is temporary, its expected duration.
6. Where appropriate, provisions relating to a probation period of employment.
7. The employee's right to vacation and vacation pay and the provisions concerning the fixing of dates for vacations.
8. The period of notice applicable to the employee and the employer.
9. The pay applicable or agreed on commencement of the employment; any supplements and other remuneration not included in the pay, such as pension payments and allowances for meals and accommodation; method of payment; and payment intervals for salary payments.
10. Duration and disposition of the agreed daily and weekly working hours.
11. Length of breaks.
12. Agreement concerning a special working-hour arrangement.
13. Information concerning any collective agreements regulating the employment relationship. If an agreement has been concluded by parties outside the enterprise, the contract of employment must identify the parties to the collective agreement.

The information in items 7 through 11 may be given in the form of a reference to the acts, regulations, or collective agreements governing these matters.

Language

The WEA does not require that the employment contract be written in Norwegian, but such requirement may follow from collective agreements.

Timing Issues

The employment contract must be available as soon as possible and no later than one month after the commencement of the employment relationship if it has a duration of more than one month. If the employment relationship has a duration of less than one month, the employment contract must be available immediately.

Changes to the Terms and Provisions

Changes to the terms of the employment relationship must be included in the written employment contract as soon as possible and no later than one month after the changes came into force.

Fixed-Term Employment

In general, employees are hired on a permanent basis. However, a fixed-term contract may be agreed upon (1) when warranted by the nature of the work, and the work differs from that which is ordinarily performed in the enterprise; (2) for work as a temporary replacement for another person or persons; (3) for work as a trainee; (4) for participants in labor market schemes (temporary employment measures to provide work experience to those who have trouble getting into the labor market) under the auspices of or in cooperation with the Labor and Welfare Service; and (5) for athletes, trainers, referees, and other leaders within organized sports. Further, the managing director may always be appointed for a fixed-term. If the employee works under successive fixed-term contracts for the same employer, the employment relationship may turn into an indefinite-term contract depending on the circumstances. After a period of four years, it turns into an indefinite-term contract,[1] with a few exceptions.

Probation Period

Even if the employee will be hired on a permanent basis, the parties may agree on a probation period of up to six months. During the probation period, the employee may be dismissed on the grounds of lack of suitability for the work, or lack of proficiency or reliability. After the probation period or if a probation period has not been agreed upon, the employer may terminate the employment relationship only if the dismissal is objectively justified by circumstances connected with the enterprise, the employer, or the employee. However, by written agreement in advance, the managing director may waive his or her protection against dismissal in exchange for payment of compensation after termination of the employment relationship.

Wages and Benefits

Minimum Wage Requirements

There is no minimum wage by law in Norway. However, for some lines of business collective agreements have been given general validity. Further, many employees are bound by collective agreements, and are therefore entitled to the minimum wage as stated in the applicable collective agreement.

Wages and benefits vary considerably among industries, lines of business, and enterprises. Wages and benefits also vary depending on whether a collective agreement is applicable and depending on the position of the employee. However, some benefits are required by law, as described below.

Special Benefit Requirements

Working Hours

The WEA establishes 40 hours per week as a starting point. However, the normal working hours in Norway are 37.5 per week for ordinary daytime work, and down to 33.6 hours per week for different kinds of shift work. This implies that the normal working time each day is eight hours, minus a 30-minute lunch break. As a starting point, all employees are protected by the WEA's provisions regarding working time. However, employees who have a leadership position or an autonomous position (such as a traveling salesperson) are exempted from these provisions, and may therefore work more hours.

Overtime

Employees who do not have a leadership or autonomous position are entitled to overtime pay of at least 40 percent above the normal hourly wage. Thus, if the employee has an hourly rate of NOK 150 (US $25), the overtime pay shall amount to at least NOK 210 (US $35) per hour.

Vacations

The employees' right to vacation and vacation pay is regulated by the Norwegian Vacation Act (*Ferieloven*). The employee is entitled to 25 days of vacation each year. The 25 days include Saturdays, so the vacation is equal to four weeks and one day. However, many collective agreements entitle the employees to five full weeks of vacation. Many employees are also given this right in their individual employment contract.

The employee is entitled to vacation pay amounting to 10.2 percent of the total pay that the employee received the year before. If a collective agreement entitles the employee to five full weeks of vacation, the vacation pay will amount to 12 percent of the total pay that the employee received the previous year. Vacation pay of 12 percent is also common if the employee is given the right to five full weeks of vacation in the individual employment contract.

Other Benefits

With a few exceptions, all enterprises must have a pension plan for their employees. The pension plan may be a defined benefit pension plan or a defined contribution pension plan. Minimum requirements are stated in the Norwegian Mandatory Occupational Pension Act (*Lov om obligatorisk tjenestepensjon*). Most traditional industries/lines of business have better pension plans for their employees than the law requires. Traditionally, defined benefit pension plans with a benefit level of 62 to 66 percent of the wage at the time of retirement have been most common. However, a not insignificant transition to defined contribution pension plans with various input levels has taken place recently. The employer must contribute a minimum of 2 percent of the salary.

All enterprises must guarantee occupational injury insurance for their employees. Further, it is not unusual for enterprises to provide group life insurance, health insurance, travel insurance, and similar benefits for their employees; however, this is not mandatory.

In addition, many enterprises give extra benefits such as newspaper subscriptions, mobile phones, and company cars, depending on the employee's position.

Labor Unions

Labor unions are normally structured with one nationwide umbrella organization on the top, with suborganizations for lines of business or occupational groups, which in turn have local suborganizations in the form of work councils in the individual enterprise. The organization on the employer side is structured correspondingly, with an umbrella organization on the top and with suborganizations for each line of business and with the individual enterprise as a member of the relevant suborganization. The principle of freedom to organize prevails for both employees and employers.

Collective Agreements

In traditional lines of business the percentage of organized employees has been relatively high, and wages and other terms have largely been regulated by collective agreements. In newer lines of business, such as the information technology sector and consultancy and counseling services, collective agreements are not as common.

To establish a collective agreement at an individual enterprise, one or more employees in the enterprise must first organize themselves in a labor union for the relevant line of business or occupational group. This labor union may then put forth a demand for a collective agreement, either to the employer organization for that line of business or, if the enterprise is not organized, directly to the enterprise. There are no legal requirements as to how many or what percentage of the employees must be organized before a demand for a collective agreement may be put forward. However, some basic agreements entered into between the nationwide umbrella organizations on the employer's and the employee's sides contain provisions regarding this.

A separate labor dispute act states the procedures in the case of disputes regarding collective agreements demands, which must be followed before a strike may be implemented. Provisions regarding boycott are found in a separate law, and other organized employees' right to implement sympathy actions is normally regulated in their collective agreement. Collective agreements are usually valid for two years at the time, with the right to wage adjustment in the year between.

Works Councils

Once a collective agreement has been established, the employees will normally have the right to elect shop stewards and, depending on the number of organized employees, to establish a works council. The shop stewards have extensive rights with regard to frequent, relevant information about operational and staffing matters, and also to discussions about matters that affect the employees before a decision is made. Failure to discuss such matters with the shop stewards may subject the employer to sanctions. Collective agreements also normally have provisions regarding the establishment of cooperation committee for shop stewards within the group.

Provisions in the basic agreement between the umbrella organizations Norwegian Confederation of Trade Unions (*Landsorganisasjonen i Norge*) and Confederation of Norwegian Business and Industry (*Næringslivets Hovedorganisasjon*) address the establishment of a European Works Council. The obligation to set up a European Works Council arises if a Norwegian enterprise employs at least 1,000 employees within the European Economic Area and at least 150 employees in each of two different European Union member states other than the United Kingdom.

SECTION II

My client is acquiring an existing business in Norway. How do I assess the existing workforce and consider changes?

Share Deals Versus Asset Deals

As a member of the European Economic Area, Norway has implemented Council Directives 77/187/EEC and 98/50/EC concerning transfers of undertakings by the 2005 Working Environment Act (WEA) (*Arbeidsmiljøloven*), Chapter 16. WEA Section 16-1 states that the "transfer of undertakings" regulations apply on a "transfer of an undertaking or part of an undertaking to another employer." The same section defines a "transfer" under these regulations as a "transfer of an autonomous unit that retains its identity after the transfer."

The main condition is that the transfer to another employer implies a change of the legal or physical person that owns the business. A mere purchase of shares, which does not change the employer's legal person, will not be assessed as a transfer of business.

According to case law, three conditions must be fulfilled in order to be a transfer of an autonomous unit: (1) the transfer relates to an economic entity, (2) the activity of this entity is transferred, and (3) the economic entity retains its identity following the transaction in question. With respect to the last condition (identity is retained), this must be assessed in view of the specific interpretation factors:

- Type of undertaking or business;
- Whether tangible assets such as buildings and movable property are transferred;
- The value of intangible assets at the time of transfer;
- Whether the majority of employees are taken over by the new employer;
- Whether the customers are transferred;

- The degree of similarity between the activities carried out before and after the transfer; and
- The period, if any, for which those activities were suspended.

The transfer has to be a result of transfer of ownership. However, it is not necessary that there be a direct contractual relationship between the former and the new owner. The European Court of Justice, the European Free Trade Association Court, and Norwegian courts have all held that third-party relationships can also be regarded as a transfer of business according to the WEA; for example, in a situation in which a service contract is terminated and a new contract for similar work is entered into with a second entity.

WEA Chapter 16 delineates the rights of employees and corresponding obligations for the employer in the event of transfer of ownership of undertakings. According to WEA Section 16-5 (1), the former and new employers must, as early as possible, provide information concerning the transfer and discuss it with the employees' elected representatives. The procedures relate to the employees' representatives; where there are no employees' representatives, the information must be given directly to all the employees.

Carrying Out a Workforce Reduction

As a general rule, the dismissal of an employee must be objectively justified by the circumstances connected with the enterprise, the employer, or the employee. "Circumstances connected with the enterprise" may be workforce reductions, curtailed operations, or closing down. "Circumstances connected with the employee" may be substantial lack of effort or qualifications, breach of the duty of obedience, lack of loyalty, absenteeism, and other kinds of improper behavior. In very severe cases, circumstances related to the employee may also give grounds for dismissal without notice.

The law states that an employee may not be dismissed on the grounds that the employer wishes to employ a better qualified person—"simple replacement." Thus, in order for a workforce reduction to be justifiable, the company's situation in itself must give justifiable reason for dismissal. Dismissal is not objectively justified if the employer has other suitable work to offer the employee in the enterprise. Further, when deciding if dismissal on these grounds is warranted, the needs of the enterprise must be weighed against the inconveniences a dismissal will involve for the individual employee.

Layoffs

The WEA defines a layoff as a notice of dismissal given to at least 10 employees within a period of 30 days, without being warranted by reasons related to the individual employee.

An employer who is considering a layoff must consult with the employees' representatives before making any final decisions. The purpose of such negotiations is to avoid the layoff or to reduce the total number of dismissals. Before the consultations, the employer must notify the representatives in writing regarding the grounds for the workforce reduction, the number of affected employees, and the period of time during which the layoff may be effected.

The employer is also obligated to meet with each employee being considered for dismissal to explain the reason for the possible termination, how the layoff selection criteria apply to the employee, and the possibility of finding other employment within the enterprise. The employee must be given the opportunity to present his or her view on the matter, and to inform the employer of personal or social circumstances that should be taken into consideration before a decision is made.

The criteria for choosing which employees to dismiss in the event of workforce reductions are normally the employee's competence and experience related to the relevant position(s), seniority, and personal or social considerations.

Procedural Requirements

The process of workforce reduction usually consists of the following main points:

- Description of the "new organization" and its accompanying positions;
- Initial evaluation of employee competence;
- Evaluation of the selection criteria such as competence, seniority, and social circumstances;
- Placement of the workers in the new organization;
- Exploration of other appropriate positions in the business for the redundant workers;
- Dismissal procedure of the redundant workers.

Period of Notice

Unless otherwise agreed in writing or stipulated in a collective agreement, the employer must give one month's notice of termination, counting from the first day of the following month, if the employee has less than five years' seniority. The notice period is increased to two months after five years of consecutive employment, to three months after 10 years, and to a maximum six months for employees over 60 years of age and with more than 10 years of seniority. During a probation period the notice is a minimum of 14 days, and often agreed in the contract to be one month.

Notice of dismissal must be given in writing[2] and must disclose the employee's right to demand negotiations and institute legal proceeding; the right to remain in his or her position during negotiations with the employer and during possible ensuing legal procedures; the employee's preferential claim to new employment in the company, if applicable; and the time limits applicable for demanding negotiations or instituting legal proceedings as well as for claiming the right to remain in the position. Information about the employer and the appropriate defendant in case of legal proceedings must also appear in the notice of dismissal. The notice must be delivered to the employee in person or sent by registered mail to the address given by the employee.

The WEA has detailed and strict provisions regarding the form, delivery, and content of notices given by the employer. If the notice does not fulfill these requirements, there are no time limits for instituting legal proceedings, but if the employee institutes legal proceedings within four months, the notice will automatically be regarded as invalid.

Severance Pay

Norwegian legislation has no procedures or requirements for severance payments to employees. Some of the main collective agreements have some regulations regarding severance payments for older employees, but as a main rule, the dismissed employees are only entitled to their salary during the period of notice. Norwegian law has no social protection rules that bind an employer economically or otherwise. Unemployment is the responsibility of the public social security system.

However, settlements or exit packages to avoid disputes are becoming more and more common. Such packages may include several months' salary plus outplacement services. The employer must pay payroll tax on the severance payment at the same rate as on ordinary salary.

Statutory Protections

Employees who have been dismissed due to work reductions have a preferential claim to new employment in the same enterprise for a period of 12 months from the end of the notice period. This preference shall also apply to temporary engaged employees (those who fulfill the requirements in Section I, "Fixed-Term Employment"), but not to employees engaged as temporary replacements (those who work for someone else for a certain period, as a substitute).

Dismissed employees have the right to remain in their positions, and hence the right to their regular salary, until the expiration of the notice period. In the event of a dispute concerning the lawfulness of a dismissal, the employee is, as a general rule, entitled to remain in his or her post while the case is pending and until a final and enforceable judgment supports the notice or dismissal. The employee may also claim compensation for damages and tort, in addition to or instead of demanding that the dismissal be ruled invalid. The compensation for damages and tort will be of such amount as the court deems reasonable in view of the financial loss, circumstances relating to the employer and the employee, and other facts of the case.

In certain situations, the employee has special protection against dismissal. These situations include absence due to accident or sickness, pregnancy and parental leave, and leave of absence due to military service. This special protection does not provide an employee with a general protection against dismissal. However, if an employee who is dismissed when he or she is in such a situation institutes legal proceedings claiming that the situation is the actual ground for the termination, the employer must prove that this is not the case.

Reorganizing the Workforce

Every employer has the right, known as the "management prerogative," to make certain decisions without consulting its employees. In Norwegian law this prerogative presents a fundamental starting point in every employment contract. There are, however, certain limits as to what the employer may do without the employees' consent. Actions may not be brought if they present unreasonable consequences for the employees.

A general principle of objectivity must also be interpreted into the management prerogative as a limitation to its scope. In addition, the management prerogative is also limited by relevant legal provisions and provisions in individual or collective agreements that are applicable to the employment relationship. It is generally assumed that an employer may not unilaterally regulate the scope of work in such a way that the basic character of the working conditions, taken as a whole, is substantially different from what the contract of employment assigns. However, if the employer has valid and weighty grounds for reorganizing, this speaks in favor of changes being made in the employer's organization and in the employees' work tasks.

For all changes exceeding the limits of the management prerogative, the employer must have fair and valid grounds. If so, the employer may freely offer an employee a new role in the new organization.

Changing the Wage and Benefits Structure

Norwegian case law shows that pay reductions do not normally fall within "management prerogative." It may be assumed that as a rule this will be the case in all incidents of pay reduction. If the company has legitimate reasons for wishing to reduce the employees' pay, it must consider whether it can offer some sort of compensation to the employees and still meet its own needs. Therefore, the limits of the prerogative may be different, but the main point is still that the management must stay within certain reasonable boundaries.

Consulting with Labor Unions or Works Councils

Consultations with the employees' representatives are required for all reorganizational matters.

Consulting with the Government

The employer must send a written notification on the foreseen redundancies to the Employment Service Division, a part of the Labor Directorate, which is placed under the responsibility of the Department of Employment. Notice on grounds of redundancy may not take effect earlier than 30 days after the Employment Service Division has been notified. If it is required in order to secure an agreement between the employer and the employees' representatives, the Employment Service Division may prolong the 30-day period by up to 30 additional days.

SECTION III

My client wishes to sell its existing facility. What restrictions do we need to consider?

Assessing Employment Contracts

Prior to an acquisition, a potential purchaser will normally wish to do a due diligence report of all aspects relating to the seller's business that may affect the price of the undertaking. Accordingly the seller should also do a due diligence report of its own business to uncover circumstances that the purchaser may see as a price-reducing factor. By doing such a due diligence report, the seller will have the opportunity to smarten up the business to be able to obtain a better price. Thus, before entering negotiations, both the buyer and the seller should pay special attention to the following employment-related topics:

- *Severance pay.* Norwegian law has no provisions regarding severance pay, but individual employment contracts may contain clauses giving rights to it.
- *Noncompetition clauses.* It may be of great importance to have valid noncompetition clauses in the contracts of key employees. However, the extensive use of these clauses can easily invalidate them.
- *Intellectual property rights.* Clauses pertaining to the protection of intellectual property rights are particularly important for some businesses, particularly technology enterprises.
- *Bonuses.* Bonus clauses can often create problems for a new employer who wishes to change the bonus system.
- *Pension.* The employer's pension plans must be in accordance with the minimum mandatory requirements of the act regarding mandatory occupational pension. Further, it is important that the plans not be underfunded.
- *Insurance.* The employer is required by law to establish occupational injury insurance. If such insurance is not established for all of the employees, it is also important to check if there have been any occupational injuries, as the employer may be economically responsible for any loss that would have been covered by insurance.
- *Hired labor and consultants.* The use of hired labor (someone not employed by the company for which he works, but usually employed by another company) and consultants should be checked to see whether it is in line with labor and tax law. However, this is difficult to uncover through due diligence, because it depends on thorough research of the actual situation.

- *Labor conflicts.* The record of labor conflicts should be checked to ensure that no important cases are pending.

The buyer will normally do both a legal and a financial due diligence report. Only the legal due diligence is relevant for this analysis. Some of the subjects of the financial due diligence report may, however, also be relevant to a legal due diligence report, depending on what kind of due diligence report, focus, and level of detail the buyer requires. Questions as to the number of employees, the scope of the seller's pension and insurance obligations, and accrued wages, vacation pay, and payroll taxes are of importance for the liquidity in the seller's undertaking, but normally these topics do not address any legal problems. The seller should rather focus on demonstrating a sufficient level of safety for the purchaser, as for example ensuring that the company has agreements with all employees pertaining to protection of intellectual property rights. To fix such agreements with the employees may not incur any costs for the seller, but it may affect the purchase price or even the buyer's interest in the company.

Consulting with the Government

According to the Norwegian Working Environment Act (WEA) there is no obligation to "consult" with the government. However, the Public Employment Service must be notified if notice of dismissal is given to at least 10 employees within a period of 30 days, without being warranted by reasons relating to the individual employee.[3] The legal provision regarding notice to the Public Employment Service applies to the seller only if the layoff takes place while the seller is the employer of the employees. After the transfer of the employees, the purchaser will be responsible for satisfying all WEA requirements in connection with eventual layoffs. The notification must include information regarding (1) the grounds for the layoff, (2) the number of employees to be laid off, (3) the categories of workers to which they belong, (4) the number of employees normally employed, (5) the categories of employees normally employed, (6) the period during which such layoffs may be effected, (7) the selection criteria for the employees to be laid off, and (8) the criteria for calculation of extraordinary severance pay, if applicable.[4] Projected layoffs may not come into effect earlier than 30 days after the Public Employment Service has been notified.[5] The Public Employment Service may extend the period of notice pursuant to the Labor Market Act.[6]

Consulting with Labor Unions and Works Councils

In the event of an asset sale, the seller is obligated to consult with the trade unions if the seller arranges layoffs prior to the sale of the business. Normally, collective agreements contain provisions specifying the consultation procedures.

Council Directives 77/187/EEC and 98/50/EC concerning transfers of undertakings were implemented in Norway by WEA Chapter 16. Thus, WEA Chapter 16 regards the rights of employees and the corresponding obligations for the employer in the event of transfer of ownership of undertakings. For the purposes of WEA, a transfer means the transfer of an autonomous unit that retains its identity after the transfer.[7]

If WEA Chapter 16 does not apply, other provisions in the WEA may cause an obligation for the seller regarding collective consultations. WEA Section 15-2 is applicable when notice of dismissal is given to at least 10 employees within a period of 30 days, without being warranted by reasons related to the individual employee. An employer contemplating collective redundancies must "at the earliest opportunity enter into consultations with the employees' elected representatives." The employer is obliged to give the employees' elected representatives all relevant information and notification regarding certain subjects.[8]

A new Chapter 8 in WEA includes provisions regarding information and consultations in several defined situations in undertakings that regularly employ at least 50 employees, and for undertakings that are not bound by collective agreements.

The Norwegian legislation has no provisions on economic remuneration paid to the employees for noncompliance with the obligation to consultation in connection with layoffs or transfers of undertaking. However, noncompliance may have an effect on the court's judgment of whether each specific dismissal is warranted or valid.

SECTION IV

My client wishes to replace its senior manager(s). What restrictions do we need to consider?

In Norway board members are not considered to be employees. However, the managing director/chief executive officer (CEO), the financial director/chief financial officer (CFO), and other managers are considered employees, and as such enjoy as a general rule the same protection under the WEA as any other employee. (See "Carrying Out a Workforce Reduction" in Section II for employee termination procedures.) One exception is that the WEA allows the company and its topmost leader, usually the CEO, to agree that the leader relinquishes the right to employment protection in accordance with the WEA in exchange for compensation on termination of employment.[9] This agreement is generally written into the employment contract.

Termination agreements to avoid dismissal and legal proceedings are especially common for managerial employees. It is usual in Norway that the parties to a termination agreement agree to keep the contents of the agreement confidential. It is also usual to include a nondisparagement clause in the termination agreement, or to agree on the contents of a press release.

SECTION V

What prohibitions exist against discrimination on the basis of age, race, gender, disability, pregnancy, and other factors? What are the rights of employees, applicants, or former employees who believe that they have been discriminated against?

Areas of Protection

In Norway, there are three acts protecting workers and applicants from work-related discrimination: the Norwegian Working Environment Act 2005 (WEA) (*Arbeidsmiljøloven*), the Anti-Discrimination Act 2005 (ADA) (*Diskrimineringsloven*), and the Gender Equality Act 1978 (GEA) (*Likestillingsloven*).

Chapter 13 of the WEA prohibits direct and indirect discrimination based on political views, union membership, sexual orientation, disability, or age. The prohibition applies to all aspects of the employment relationship, including advertising of posts, appointment, relocation, promotion, training and further education financed by the employer, pay, working conditions, and termination of the employment relationship. The WEA equally protects permanently employed, temporarily employed, part-time employed, and self-employed persons and contract workers.

Section 4 of the ADA prohibits direct and indirect discrimination on the basis of ethnic or national origin, descent, color, language, religion, and belief. The GEA prohibits such discrimination based on gender (including detrimental treatment of women because of pregnancy or birth). The scope of these acts covers all areas of society, including employment relationships. The GEA mentions in particular that no discrimination may occur in connection with recruitment, promotion, dismissal, and layoff of employees, that women and men must receive equal payment for work of equal value, and that women and men must be put on equal footing when it comes to training, retraining, and leave.

The three acts state that the employer, in the advertisement of a job vacancy or otherwise, may not demand or presuppose that applicants should have a particular sex, or demand information concerning the applicants' sexual orientation, union membership, or political, religious, or cultural views, unless there is an obvious just reason for it.

If an employee or applicant submits information that gives reason to believe that discrimination has taken place in violation of one of the three acts, the employer must substantiate that such discrimination has not occurred.

Sanctions and Remedies

Anyone who has been discriminated against in contravention of one of the three acts may claim an equitable compensation before a court without regard to the employer's fault. The employee or applicant may claim compensation for pecuniary loss suffered as a result of the discrimination pursuant to general principles of tort law. As a rule, this means that the employer must have been negligent.

Provisions in wage agreements, contracts of employment, company regulations, and bylaws that contravene with WEA Chapter 13 are considered void.

🌐 SECTION VI

On the Horizon: What key labor and employment law developments should an employer doing business in Norway anticipate occurring in the coming years?

The Norwegian Working Environment Act (1977) has recently been replaced by a new act with the same name, which passed the legislature in June 2005 and was amended in December the same year, due to a change of government in Norway. The new act was a result of a comprehensive work laid down from 2001 to 2004 by a committee of members from the main organizations both on the employer and the employee side, as well as other relevant groups. The Act entered into force on January 1, 2006. No other substantial changes are expected in the coming years. If there is a new change of government after the election of autumn 2009, some areas of the law could, however, be liberalized.

🌐 NOTES

1. *See* Norwegian Working Environment Act 2005 (*Arbeidsmiljøloven*) [hereinafter WEA] § 14-9 (5).

2. *See* WEA § 15-4.

3. *See* WEA § 15-2(3).

4. *See* WEA § 15-2(3) para. 2; *cf.* § 15-2(3) para. 1.

5. *See* WEA § 15-2(5).

6. *See* Labor Market Act 2004 § 8, para. 3.

7. *See* Norwegian Working Environment Act 2005 [hereinafter WEA] (*Arbeidsmiljøloven*) § 16-1 para. 1.

8. *See* WEA § 15-2(3) para. 1.

9. *See* WEA § 15-16.

CHAPTER 13

LABOR AND EMPLOYMENT LAW IN POLAND

ALEKSANDRA MINKOWICZ-FLANEK

SECTION I

My client wishes to establish a manufacturing facility in Poland and will need to hire a workforce. What are the key issues involved?

Employment Contracts: Who Receives Them and What Must They Include?

Mandatory Requirements

An employment contract is made between an employer and an employee obliging the employee to perform work of a defined type for the benefit of the employer, under the employer's supervision, and in the time and place indicated by the employer. If all these conditions are met, the parties are not allowed to make any type of contract other than an employment contract. The employment contract is the basic form of employment under Polish law.

The parties are free to decide the terms of the employment contract provided that they are not less favorable than those in the Labor Code and other sources of employment law. For example, provisions on minimum paid leave may not be disregarded. If the parties do not agree on specific terms, the corresponding provisions in the Labor Code generally apply.

Form of the Employment Contract

A verbal employment contract is valid. However, the employer must provide written confirmation of the type of contract and its terms to the employee on the date of starting employment at the latest; otherwise, the employer may be liable to pay a fine to the State Treasury.

Required Information

The following terms should be set out in an employment contract:

- Date on which the employment begins
- Type of work
- Location where work is to be performed
- The remuneration corresponding to the type of work
- Working hours or days

Additionally, within seven days following the commencement of work, an employer must inform the employee in writing about the following:

- Restrictions on working hours
- Intervals at which remuneration is paid
- Vacation entitlement
- Notice period

If there are no internal regulations concerning the organization of work at the workplace, the employer must inform the employee about the following:

- Night time work (during any 8-hour period between 9 p.m. and 7 a.m.)
- Time and place of salary payment
- Applicability of a collective agreement
- Method of confirming the arrival and presence at work, as well as the method of justifying absence at work

The employers may request only the following information from the employees:

- Name
- Parents' names
- Home address
- Qualifications
- Employment history
- Details required for the employee to benefit from particular statutory rights (for example, the right to receive social benefits)
- Personal ID number
- Other data that is required under certain statutory provisions

Language

The employment contract must be drafted in Polish.

Timing Issues

An employment contract must be made on the day of work commencement at the latest. The aforementioned additional written information on terms and conditions of employment is to be delivered within the following seven days.

Changes to the Terms and Provisions

An employment contract may be amended at any time by mutual consent of the parties. The employer may also offer the employee new terms and conditions related to his or her position or work hours, thus terminating by notice the relevant provisions of the existing contract. Such an "amending termination" must be made in writing. The employee must be instructed that by the halfway stage of the termination notice period he or she may accept or refuse the new conditions. Upon acceptance of the new terms, the employment contract is binding in its amended shape after the lapse of the statutory notice period. Rejection of the offer by the employee leads to definitive termination of the contract after the same period.

Fixed-Term Employment

A fixed-term employment contract is generally admissible under Polish law. However, the law limits the number of consecutive fixed-term contracts. If the same parties had already concluded two fixed-term contracts, and the time gap between them did not exceed one month, a further fixed-term contract shall be treated, in its legal consequences, as an indefinite-term employment contract. Exceeding the term by an annex is deemed as making a new contract for the purposes of this regulation.

Moreover, fixed-term contracts may not be terminated by notice unless the contract is made for a period longer than six months and it includes a termination clause providing for a two-week notice period.

Wages and Benefits

Minimum Wage Requirements

The minimum wage is adjusted annually. In 2008, the minimum gross monthly wage for all employees was PLN 1,126 (about US $536).

Special Benefit Requirements

Employment in Poland is highly regulated and almost all benefits are specified by law. Collective agreements or internal regulations applicable at particular employers may improve the conditions but may not impose less favorable terms than those regulated by generally applicable laws.

Pension

The pension system is regulated by law in detail as an element of social security. Pension and disability pension contributions are calculated and remitted by the employers. They are financed partially from the employees' salaries by deductions. Private pension insurance is not mandatory.

Sick Pay

Sick pay is also an element of the social security system. In the case of illness or injury, employees have the right to sick leave, which is granted on the basis of a medical certificate. During sick leave, employees generally receive 80 percent of their standard pay. However, if the illness occurs during pregnancy or the injury is caused by an accident on the way to work, employees receive 100 percent. The employer is responsible for sick pay up to the first 33 days of illness or injury. From this point onward, the Social Security Office makes the sickness payments. However, sick pay is not available for more than 182 days (270 days in the case of tuberculosis).

Vacations

All employees are entitled to annual paid vacation of 20 or 26 days in each calendar year. The vacation entitlement depends on how long the individual has been in employment or taken part in other qualifying activities (recognition is given for various educational attainments; for example, completion of college is equivalent to eight years' work).

Labor Unions

Establishment and Recognition Requirements

Labor unions are independent, voluntary, and self-governing organizations that are established to represent and defend the rights and professional interests of the employees.

The right to establish a labor union is vested in all kinds of employees, members of farmer production cooperatives, and persons employed on the basis of agency agreements, if they are not employers themselves.

A labor union is created on the basis of a resolution adopted by at least 10 persons entitled to create the union. The founders adopt the charter and elect an establishing committee composed of three to seven persons. The union is subject to mandatory registration at the National Court Register and upon registration obtains full legality.

Labor unions are not obliged to notify an employer about their establishment, but they may not execute their rights against the employer until they are recognized. The rights are executed by a so-called workplace trade unions organization, that is, an organization of at least 10 employees. This organization is authorized to represent its members in individual cases such as dismissal, but represents all the employees (including nonunionized) in collective cases (e.g., remuneration plan regulations).

To benefit from its rights, the trade union workplace organization is required also to inform the employer on a quarterly basis about the number of members to confirm that the level indicated by law is met.

Exclusive Bargaining

Collective agreements are negotiated and agreed between the employers and labor unions. No other form of employee representation is authorized to bargain.

Collective Agreements

Duty to Bargain

A party eligible to make a collective agreement may not refuse to negotiate an agreement with another eligible party This duty to bargain applies if (1) there is no collective agreement in force; (2) a collective agreement exists but one of the parties wants to amend it due to a material change in the financial situation of the employer or because it is detrimental to the employees' situation; or (3) the existing collective agreement is set to expire in 60 days.

Each of the parties is legally required to bargain in good faith and with due regard for the fair interests of the other party.

Form Requirements

A collective agreement is made in writing, for a defined or undefined period of time. It is subject to registration with the Minister of Labor (if the collective agreement applies to more than one workplace) within three months of the filing of an application by one of the parties or with the District Labor Inspector (if the collective agreement applies to one workplace only) within one month of the filing.

Mechanisms of Dispute Resolution

According to law, the provisions of a collective agreement are interpreted in mutual consultation by its parties. Disputes are resolved by the Labor Court.

Changes and Termination

Changes are introduced by the parties to the collective agreement in the form of "additional protocols."

The collective agreement terminates either (1) by mutual consent of the parties, (2) after the lapse of the term for which it was made, or (3) after the lapse of the termination notice period (the notice period is three months unless the parties decided otherwise). Termination must be made in writing.

Works Councils

Mandatory Requirements

The Act on Informing and Consulting Employees 2006 (*Ustawa o informowaniu pracowników i przeprowadzaniu z nimi konsultacji*) implements Directive 2002/14/EC establishing a general framework for informing and consulting employees in the European Community. The Act applies to employers of more than 50 people and regulates conditions for informing and consulting employees as well as rules of works council election.

Functions and Frequency

The employer must inform and/or consult the works council about (1) the employer's activities and financial position, and any expected changes relating to these; (2) the structure and probable development of employment, and measures planned to maintain the current level of employment; and (3) any decisions likely to lead to substantial changes in work organization or contractual relations.

The employer provides the works council with the aforementioned information in case of planned actions or upon the written request of the works council. The parties may set in writing the rules and procedures for information delivery.

National and Regional Groups

Works councils are established at the local level in a given workplace. European Works Councils are established in corporations that meet the requirements for size, locations within the European Union, and number of employees. These bodies are authorized to be consulted on European level and do not discuss strictly local issues.

Relation to Labor Unions

The works councils are made up of delegates elected by "representative" trade unions that exist in a particular workplace, or by the employees if there is no representative trade union in a particular workplace (a representative trade union is defined in the Labor Code). Therefore in many cases the works council's composition mirrors the trade union operating in the given workplace.

In addition, certain regulations require an employer to inform and consult with the employees or their representatives, which means in practice the trade unions. These regulations concern, in particular, the transfer of an enterprise (in whole or in part) to a new employer or planned layoffs. Consultations of this type must be held in addition to providing information to the works council.

The members of works councils are legally required to keep corporate secrets confidential. In particularly justified cases, the employer may refuse to make available certain information whose disclosure could, according to objective criteria, seriously disrupt the company's activity or expose it to damage.

SECTION II

My client is acquiring an existing business in Poland. How do I assess the existing workforce and consider changes?

Share Deals Versus Asset Deals

For purposes of this section, a "share deal" is defined as a transaction where the shares in a commercial company are purchased. An "asset deal" means the purchase of particular assets, an organized part of an enterprise, or the enterprise itself.

Due Diligence Requirements and Considerations

Employment due diligence in the case of the share deal should be focused on the potential liabilities of the employer toward employees arising from individual contracts as well as from internal remuneration regulations and collective agreements constituting the source of labor law. It is crucial to verify the contracts of the management board and executives and their termination conditions. Because there is no change of the employer in a share deal, no notification procedure is required.

Asset deals in the majority of cases result in transfer of the workplace or a part thereof, which results in a direct and automatic change of the employer. Therefore it is important to investigate during a due diligence process which employees are linked with the business or assets subject to the transfer and, therefore, will be taken over by the buyer. Their individual employment terms and conditions should be taken into consideration and compared with those applicable at the new employer's workplace to prepare for the transfer and assess the costs of unification.

Statutory Regulations Concerning Transfer of Business

In Poland, business transfers are regulated by provisions of the Labor Code and the Trade Unions Act. If a business is transferred (in whole or part) to another employer, that employer becomes by virtue of law a party to the existing employment relations. Thirty days before the transfer, each of the employers is required by law to inform its employees about the planned date of the transfer, its reasons, and consequences for the employees. If there are trade unions operating in the workplace they are informed instead of the individual employees. In any case, the works council should be informed, if one exists.

A business transfer (in whole or part) to another employer may not in itself constitute grounds for dismissal. Nevertheless, each transferred employee is entitled to terminate his or her contract with seven days' notice during the two-month period following the transfer.

The new and the previous employer remain jointly and severally liable for employment-related claims raised before the transfer date.

During the year following the transfer, the new employer must retain the existing collective agreement for the employees who were transferred. After this period, the employer may offer new payment terms and harmonize them with those of its original employees. If the new terms are less favorable and the employees reject them, their contracts terminate after the notice period ends. The employer may offer better terms and conditions of employment at any time. In cases where there is no collective agreement, the new terms and conditions can be offered immediately after the transfer.

Carrying Out a Workforce Reduction

Statutory Protection

Statutory notice period depends on the type of employment contract and the length of employment. The notice periods are as follows.

Indefinite-Term Employment Contract

Length of Employment	Required Notice Period
Less than 6 months	2 weeks
6 months to 3 years	1 month
More than 3 years	3 months

Fixed-Term Employment Contract

Length of Contract	Required Notice Period
6 months or less	Termination not possible
More than 6 months	2 weeks if the contract includes a termination clause

Contract for the Substitution of Another Employee

Length of Contract	Required Notice Period
Any	3 working days

Probation Employment Contract

Length of Probation Period	Required Notice Period
2 weeks or less	3 working days
More than 2 weeks but less than 3 months	1 week
3 months (the maximum allowed)	2 weeks

A notice period is fully remunerable. In addition, if the only reason for termination is attributable to the employer (such as elimination of a given position or reorganization of the workplace), the dismissed employee is entitled to severance pay of up to three months' salary, capped at 15 times the minimal statutory monthly wage (in 2008, the monthly minimal statutory wage was PLN 1,126, approximately US $536).

Procedural Requirements

Employees must be given written notice of dismissal that includes information on their right to appeal to the Labor Court within seven days (termination with notice) or 14 days (termination without notice). If an indefinite-term contract is being terminated, the employer must provide a valid reason. Unless the reason stated is true and accurate, the dismissal may be ineffective.

Consultation procedures apply only to employees who belong to trade unions or were taken under a union's protection upon their individual request. In these circumstances, the employer must inform the trade unions representing the affected employees about its intention to terminate particular employment contracts and specify the reason for the terminations. A trade union can present written reservations within five days (if the termination was with notice) or three days (if the termination was without notice) if it believes that the dismissal is unjustified. However, the trade union's opinion is not binding and the employer has full discretion to give notice of dismissal after receiving the trade union's reply. An exception to this rule applies to pregnant women and certain trade union members. If such employees are to be dismissed, the trade union's consent is required.

Protected Groups

An employer must not give notice of dismissal in particular to:

- Employees who will retire in less than four years
- Employees on vacation or sick leave
- Pregnant employees, or those on maternity, paternity, adoption, or parental leave
- Trade union representatives
- Members of the works council
- Members of a European Works Council
- Other protected employees specified in various detailed regulations

An unlawfully dismissed employee may demand reinstatement or compensation. Usually the compensation does not exceed remuneration for a termination notice period. In cases regarding protected employees, the reinstatement may be combined with payment of remuneration for the whole period of unemployment.

Reorganizing the Workforce

See "Carrying Out a Workforce Reduction," previously. In addition it should be noted that the employer reorganizing the workforce is entitled to deliver to the employees a so-called "amending termination letter." This is an offer of new terms and conditions of employment combined with the termination of the currently binding conditions. If an employee accepts this offer, the contract remains binding with the new terms in place of the previous ones. If the offer is rejected, the contract terminates definitively after the lapse of regular notice period.

These rules apply if the changes are to the detriment of the employee. If the changes are beneficial for the employee, the new terms apply automatically.

Consulting with Labor Unions or Works Councils

Procedural Requirements

Wages and benefits are regulated by collective agreements or remuneration regulations. If there are trade unions in the company, the wording of the remuneration regulations and any amendment thereto must be negotiated with them. If there is no trade union, the remuneration regulations are developed by the employer and announced in the manner adopted in the given workplace. They become fully effective after 14 days following their announcement.

Only trade unions may negotiate collective agreements with the employer. Any amendment to a collective agreement must be approved by the parties and is made in the form of a so-called "additional protocol." Collective agreements that are applicable to one employer must be registered with the District Labor Inspection. Agreements that are applicable to more than one employer, in practice usually to the whole industry sector (for example, the power sector), must be registered with the Ministry of Labor.

Termination of a Collective Agreement

In case of a transfer of the business, the new employer is required to follow, at a minimum, the provisions of the previously binding collective agreement for one year following the transfer date. The new employer may, however, apply better conditions than those provided by the collective agreement in question. After one year, the employer may change the previously binding conditions but must do it through "amending termination" (see "Reorganizing the Workforce," previously).

A collective agreement may be terminated either (1) by the mutual consent of the parties; (2) upon the lapse of its term; or (3) upon the lapse of the termination notice period. Termination notice must be made in writing. The notice period is three months, unless the parties to the collective agreement decided otherwise and expressed it in the collective agreement.

If it is justified by the financial situation of the employer, the parties (the employer and the employees' representatives, in particular trade unions) may agree to suspend the collective agreement in whole or in part. The maximum term of suspension is three years. This agreement has to be reported to the District Labor Inspector.

Consulting with the Government

Consulting with the government is not required other than the registration of collective agreements as discussed in "Consulting with Labor Unions or Works Councils," previously.

❸ SECTION III

My client wishes to sell its existing facility. What restrictions do we need to consider?

Assessing Employment Contracts

The potential buyer usually assesses employment contracts during the due diligence process in order to determine the cost of employment and the legal consequences of potential reorganization of the workforce after acquisition.

Consulting with the Government

Selling of the facility or a transfer of business does not require consultation with any governmental organization with regard to its intent or to the process itself.

Consulting with Labor Unions or Works Councils

See related discussions in Section II.

Negotiating with the Purchaser: Special Labor Issues

Use of Warranties in Transfer Agreements

A contract concerning the sale of a facility usually contains a number of employment-related representations and warranties, including (1) compliance with labor laws; (2) compliance with social security and personal income tax advance payments; (3) lack of layoffs or the reasons thereto during a defined period preceding the transfer; (4) lack of side agreements guaranteeing some employees additional benefits not disclosed in their contracts.

Means for Retaining Key Employees

Because transfer of the facility will trigger automatic transfer of the employees to the buyer, a seller who wishes to retain valuable employees should offer them jobs that are not related to the transferred facility before the date of the transfer.

The means for retaining key employees depend on the character of a given workplace and vary from one facility to another. Bonuses are used rather often, especially to maintain good quality performance during the transition period. Recently, there have been retention plans that provide for significant severance in case of termination of the employment contract for reasons not attributable to the employee.

Other Special Labor Issues

In a transfer of business, the previous and the new employer are jointly and severally liable for any employment-related claims that arose before the transfer. Thus the seller and the purchaser should negotiate the share of responsibility and contractual indemnification in case of potential claims.

SECTION IV

My client wishes to replace its senior manager(s). What restrictions do we need to consider?

Employment Contracts

Statutory Protection

Under Polish law, the position of the employee does not affect the procedure adopted in case of dismissal. An employer planning a termination should consider in particular the following issues:

- Type of employment contract
- Cause for dismissal
- Length of termination notice period
- Trade union membership or protection
- Existence of a noncompetition agreement binding after the termination of employment contract
- Extraordinary contractual clauses ("golden parachutes")

The period of notice depends on the type of employment contract and the length of employment. See the table in Section II.

Common Contractual Protections

Many senior managers' employment contracts provide for termination notice periods longer than those regulated by statutory provisions. A six-month notice period is common, with some as long as 12 months.

A decision to offer a senior manager such a long termination notice period should be carefully considered by the employer. That is because, in accordance with one of the basic rules governing employment law in Poland, the provisions of an employment contract may not be less beneficial to the employee than the provisions of the statutory regulations. Therefore, a senior manager who decides to terminate the employment contract could argue that the termination notice period applicable in this case should be the shorter statutory period. The manager could argue that the longer termination notice period applies only if the employer initiates the dismissal.

Procedural Requirements

The employer who wants to terminate the employment contract with notice must observe the statutory procedure. The termination notice must be made in writing, describe precisely the reason for termination (the cause), and explain the employee's right to appeal against the termination to the Labor Court. If no cause is given or the employer gives a false or inaccurate cause, the termination may be questioned before the Labor Court.

Three groups of causes to be used by the employer are distinguishable:

1. Causes not attributable to the employee, such as liquidation of the employer, change of its business profile, liquidation of the position, or change of organizational structure;
2. Reasons attributable to the employee of a general nature such as unsatisfactory performance of professional duties, loss of confidence, lack of improvement, or breach of internal regulations;
3. Reasons attributable to the employee that justify termination of employment without notice.

Reasons included in group (3) are enumerated by the Labor Code. The most common reason is the grave violation of the employee's basic duties. Such a violation must be committed intentionally or because of gross negligence. As this is an exceptional method of employment contract termination, it should be used with particular due diligence.

Before delivery of the termination notice to the employee, the employer is legally required to consult with the trade union representing the given employee (whether because the employee is a member of the trade union or has asked for its protection). The trade union may express its opinion within five days (in the case of termination with notice) or three days (in the case of termination without notice). This opinion is not binding on the employer, unless it refers to the planned termination of contract of a trade union representative, or the immediate termination of contract of a pregnant employee. In such cases, the union could effectively block the employer's action.

If the senior manager is also a board member, the termination of the employment contract must be properly signed on behalf of the employer. Pursuant to the law in this situation, the company may be effectively represented by its supervisory board (a relevant resolution is required) or by an attorney-in-fact appointed by way of a resolution adapted at a meeting of the shareholders. After the manager is dismissed from his or her board position, the employment contract may be terminated by the remaining board members in accordance with general rules of company representation.

Protected Groups

Polish employment law provides for particular protection against the termination of an employment contract for many types of employees. The most common examples are the following:

- Employees who will retire in less than four years;
- Employees on vacation or sick leave;
- Pregnant employees, or those on maternity, paternity, adoption, or parental leave;
- Trade union representatives;
- Members of the works council; and
- Members of a European Works Council.

The employer is not allowed to terminate a protected person's employment contract with notice. It is legal, however, to terminate a contract without notice, if there is sufficient cause to do so.

Sanctions and Remedies

The employee may appeal against the termination of an employment contract to the Labor Court. The appeal should be filed with the court within seven days (in case of termination with notice) or 14 days (in case of termination without notice). The employee may require reinstatement or compensation for unfair dismissal. The court may ignore the claim for reinstatement if the reinstatement would be impossible or unjustified, and instead award compensation. However, in the case of the unlawful dismissal of a pregnant woman or an employee who has less than four years to retirement, a claim for reinstatement must be accepted, if it is justified. Pregnant women, parents on maternity leave, employees who have less than four years to retirement, and trade union representatives who were reinstated to work are entitled to receive remuneration for the whole period of unemployment. Other groups of employees are entitled to receive salaries for a maximum of two months.

The compensation for unfair dismissal must not be lower than the remuneration for the termination notice period. This is an additional argument against setting longer termination periods in employment contracts.

In case of the unfair termination of a fixed-term contract the employee may claim compensation only. The compensation is limited to three months' remuneration.

Statutory Severance Pay Requirements

Statutory Rules

Employees dismissed for reasons not attributable to themselves are entitled to severance pay in addition to the remuneration for work and for the given termination period. This severance payment is paid by employers employing more than 20 persons (smaller employers are not required to do so). The payment is calculated as follows:

- One month's salary if the employee has been employed by the employer for less than two years;
- Two months' salary if the employee has been employed by the employer for two to eight years;
- Three months' salary if the employee has been employed by the employer for more than eight years.

Total severance pay may not exceed 15 times the minimum salary as provided for by the generally binding regulations (the minimum monthly salary in 2008 was PLN 1,126 gross; about US $536).

Noncompete and Confidentiality Agreements

Noncompete periods and confidentiality agreements are commonly used tools strengthening the links between the employer and the employee.

Two types of noncompete periods are provided by law: the agreement binding during the term of employment and the one binding for a fixed time after the termination of employment. Both must be made in writing to be valid. The noncompete period binding during employment may be made with any kind of employee and does not require the employer to pay any compensation for the observance of the noncompete period by the employee. By contrast, a noncompete agreement covering the period after termination of employment is limited by additional formal requirements: (1) the agreement must be made for a defined period of time; (2) the employee must have had access to particularly important information during the employment; and (3) the employee must be compensated for observing the compete activity ban. The lower limit of such compensation is 25 percent of the employee's ending salary level.

Generally, binding provisions of law provide that the employee is not allowed to disclose the business secrets of the employer during the period of three years following termination of employment, unless the contract provides otherwise. Employers whose business secrets are disclosed illegally may claim compensation. It is very often difficult, however, to prove the damage suffered; therefore, it is advisable to negotiate a confidentiality agreement with the employee and to specify the liability for a breach of the obligation. A confidentiality agreement is very often included in a noncompete agreement, but may be made independently as well. No special formal requirements exist in that respect.

The issuance of a reference by the employer to the employee is not obligatory under Polish labor law. It is, however, legal to offer an employee an reference to support the employee's job seeking in the future. The facts of employment, in particular the position, length of employment at the given employer, number of vacation days utilized, and length of sick leave, are included in the employment certificate that must be issued by the employer promptly after the employment is terminated. The certificate may not refer to the quality of performance nor to any opinion about the employee.

SECTION V

What prohibitions exist against discrimination on the basis of age, race, gender, disability, pregnancy, and other factors? What are the rights of employees, applicants, or former employees who believe that they have been discriminated against?

Areas of Protection

The Labor Code prohibits any direct or indirect discrimination in any type of employment (full-time, part-time, fixed term, or indefinite term), particularly that relating to gender, sexual orientation, age, disability, race, nationality or ethic origin, religion or beliefs, political preferences, and trade union membership.

Employees must receive equal treatment in relation to their (1) terms of employment, (2) promotion, (3) access to professional training, and (4) rights on dismissal.

The Labor Code also prohibits harassment, which is defined as behavior that is aimed at or results in humiliating employees or violating their dignity. Harassment under the Labor Code constitutes a form of discrimination and is penalized accordingly.

The Labor Code specifically defines prohibited sexual harassment. This is any unwelcome behavior of a sexual character or behavior related to an employee's gender, which has the aim of or results in the humiliation or abasement of an employee.

Statutory Rules

An employer, or the people acting on its behalf, that does not observe the equal treatment principle or that encourages others to breach it is guilty of discrimination. Equal treatment is one of the employer's basic duties. Though the Labor Code provides a list of bases for discrimination, the employer must not discriminate against the employee in general, for any reason, even if it is not listed in the Code (for example, on the basis of the employee's weight).

Burden of Proof

The burden of proof that the measures adopted by the employer are not discriminatory but based on objective criteria rests on the employer. The employee is required, however, to deliver the evidence of the facts that he or she claims took place and that they are of a discriminatory character.

An employee may not be terminated for raising a discrimination claim.

Legal Effect of Nondiscrimination Policies

One of the employer's duties is to prevent discrimination as well as to make the employees familiar with the wording of legal regulations concerning equal treatment in employment. The employer must distribute this wording in the workplace in the manner adopted by the given employer. The legal requirement could be fulfilled by the issuance of nondiscrimination policies.

Each employer employing more than 20 employees is required to regulate the rules concerning the organization and order at work that constitute the source of employment law (which has a normative character). The nondiscrimination policies could be attached to the rules as their appendices and, therefore, become the part of internal law binding the employer and all its employees.

Venue and Procedure

Nondiscrimination employment claims are heard by labor courts constituting separate divisions of the common state courts. They could also be settled by the arbitration court if the parties to the conflict so decide. It is not, however, legal to agree on arbitration before the claim is raised by the employee.

In discrimination cases, the labor courts follow a procedure aimed at supporting employees as the weaker party, and the trial, as a rule, is less formal than trials held in accordance with general civil proceedings. If the parties settle their claim before the court issues its final ruling, the settlement may not be to the detriment of the employee. The court is entitled to overturn an unfair settlement.

Sanctions and Remedies

An employee who has experienced discrimination is entitled to monetary compensation of at least the minimum monthly pay (in 2008 it was PLN 1,126; approximately US $536). There is no legal limit to the amount of damages that the court may award, but the general rule is that the compensation may not exceed the damage suffered. In practice the compensation may not be the source of the employee's wealth and it is deemed to redress the employee's damage rather than to punish the employer.

The termination of an employment contract in violation of the nondiscrimination regulations may be challenged before the labor court. The employee is entitled to claim reinstatement or compensation (usually limited to three months' salary).

SECTION VI

On the Horizon: What key labor and employment law developments should an employer doing business in Poland anticipate occurring in the coming years?

Parliament and the government are currently discussing the following issues:

- *The extension of a temporary work period.* It is likely that the maximum length of temporary work performance at one employer by a temporary worker will be extended from 12 months to 18 months.

- *Amendments to the Labor Code.* For example, employers will be paying for only 14 days of sick leave, not 33 days (as it is presently). An extension on the length of maternity leave is also being considered.

- *Remuneration for the work of CEOs in State Treasury companies.* Changes in these executives' salaries may depend on two elements: (1) their basic salary and the maximum amount of the six-month average remuneration in their sector of companies, and (2) a motivating element, dependant on the financial situation of company, generated profits, and executed investments. Currently, CEO salaries do not contain the second motivational component.

CHAPTER 14

LABOR AND EMPLOYMENT LAW IN PORTUGAL

CÉSAR SÁ ESTEVES
MARIA DE LANCASTRE VALENTE

SECTION I

My client wishes to establish a manufacturing facility in Portugal and will need to hire a workforce. What are the key issues involved?

As a preliminary note, the information set out below applies to employees only.

In some cases, it is not easy to qualify the relationship between the beneficiary of the activity and its provider. This is common in cases where, although the agreement executed between the parties is nominally qualified as a provision of services, materially, the terms and conditions under which the activity is provided lead to its qualification as an employment contract.

Pursuant to the Labor Code, it is presumed the parties entered into an employment contract when the provider is under the dependence and is integrated in the organizational structure of the beneficiary and performs his or her activity under the orders, direction, and supervision of the beneficiary, subject to the payment of remuneration.

Given the difficulty in determining the nature of the contractual relationship, Portuguese jurisprudence also takes into consideration the following:

- If the activity is performed in offices of the beneficiary of the activity, or at a place controlled by the latter;
- If the provider is remunerated based on the time spent on the performance of the activity, or is under the economic dependence of the beneficiary;
- If the beneficiary of the activity supplied the work instruments;
- If the provider is subject to a work schedule, or to the control by the beneficiary of his or her attendance; or
- If the provider performs his or her activity exclusively for the beneficiary.

Employment Contracts: Who Receives Them and What Must They Include?

As a general rule, the law does not require that an employment contract be governed by a written document; however, it is advisable that the main terms and conditions of the employee's activity be specified in writing. This corresponds to the best practice; in fact, the normal outcome of a negotiation process between an employer and any candidate to whom it wishes to offer employment will most likely result in the execution of a written agreement between the parties.

The Labor Code, as an exception to the general rule, expressly provides that the following types of employment contract must be subject to execution in writing:

- Promissory employment contracts;
- Contracts for subordinated telecommuting;
- Term employment contracts;
- Employment contracts with foreign employees;
- Employment contracts under a commission of services regime (see Section IV);
- Employment contracts with multiple employers;
- Part-time employment contracts;
- Early retirement contracts; and
- Contracts for the temporary assignment of employees.

Duty of Information

Although, as mentioned, the validity of an employment contract does not depend on its execution in writing, the employer is nonetheless bound by a duty of information toward the employee in relation to the following:

1. Employer's identification—if the employer is a corporation, the existence of a group company relationship;
2. Place of work, as well as registered office or address of employer;
3. Employee's category and summary of its content;
4. Date of execution of the contract and date on which it will become effective;
5. Anticipated duration of the contract, in the event it is subject to a term;
6. Vacation period duration, or if such is not possible, the criteria for its determination;
7. Notice periods to be given by employer and employee for termination of employment, or if such is not possible, the criteria for their determination;
8. Remuneration amount and periodicity;
9. Daily and weekly normal working time periods, specifying those periods that are defined in average terms; and
10. Applicable collective bargaining agreement, if any.

The information foreseen in (6), (7), (8), and (9) may be replaced by a reference to the applicable legal provision, to the applicable collective bargaining agreement, or to a company policy.

Such information must be provided in writing, in a single document or several documents, and signed by the employer. When the information is provided in more than one document, one of the documents must indicate that which is identified in (1), (2), (3), (4), (8), and (9). The duty of information is considered fulfilled whenever this information is included in an employment contract subject to the written form or whenever a promissory employment contract is executed.

Language

There is no mandatory legal provision that states that the employment contracts must be executed in Portuguese.

However, it is highly advisable that any documentation executed in a foreign language relating to employee terms and conditions be simultaneously translated into Portuguese, based on the general principle of law that imposes, as a prior requirement for the validity of any declaration, that the issuer of such declaration fully understands its content.

To that effect, in order to ensure that the employees validly agree to any form of contractual proposal, term and condition, or amendment, such proposal, term and condition, or amendment should be set out in writing in the employees' native language. This will avoid any issues arising in the future about the interpretation and/or comprehension of the terms and conditions set out in the contract, especially considering that local law will, in principle, apply, and that in the case of any court dispute, the relevant documentation would have to be translated into Portuguese.

If the parties have preference for the execution of the employment contract in another language, a bilingual document should be prepared and signed, in which case it should be expressly stated that if any discrepancies regarding interpretation arise in the future, the Portuguese version would prevail.

Fixed-Term Employment Contracts

Although technically employers may make use of fixed-term employment contracts only in exceptional circumstances, market reality contradicts this statement. It is, therefore, common for an employer to resort to fixed-term employment contracts when hiring new employees.

In accordance with the requirements set out in the Labor Code, the validity of a fixed-term employment contract requires that the terms and conditions of employment be set out in writing, and that a justification for the limited duration of the contract be expressly set out in the contract. Its main characteristic, therefore, lies in the need for a material justification.

The justifications may have as their origin any of the following: (1) a temporary need of the company (an exceptional increase in the company's activity, temporary replacement of an absent employee, seasonal activity, etc.); (2) the start-up of a new activity or the incorporation or start-up of a company or establishment; or (3) the hiring of employees looking for their first job (as defined by law) or long-term unemployed employees (as defined by law).

If no written contract is signed, or if the justification is not defined or is invalid, the employee will be deemed to have an employment contract for an unlimited term.

In general, fixed-term contracts may not exceed three years, including renewals, or may not be renewed more than twice.

However, once the three-year period has elapsed or once the maximum number of renewals has occurred, the contract may be renewed for a further minimum of one year and a maximum of three years, provided the justification that originated the limited duration still exists and, as such, remains valid.

The duration of a fixed-term employment contract is limited to 18 months in the case of employees looking for their first job, or two years in the case of the start-up of a new activity, the incorporation or start-up of a company or establishment, or in relation to long-term unemployed employees (as defined by law).

Probationary Periods

Employment contracts, irrespective of their duration, may include probationary periods. In the case of standard permanent employment contracts, the maximum probationary periods permitted by law vary in accordance with the employee's position or seniority in the company, as follows:

- 240 days for managerial and other senior positions;
- 180 days for positions of a complex technical nature, with a high level of responsibility, or that require special qualifications, as well as for duties entailing a high level of trust; and
- 90 days for the majority of employees.

In relation to fixed-term employees, the maximum probationary periods vary in accordance with the duration of the contract, as follows:

- 30 days for contracts with a duration equal to or greater than six months; and
- 15 days for contracts with a duration of less than six months.

The probationary periods may be reduced upon agreement by the parties and by the applicable collective bargaining agreement. The parties may also agree on the exclusion of the probationary period.

Employers will typically make use of the existence of probationary periods, and it is common practice to include them in employment contracts.

During the probationary period, either party is free to terminate employment without prior notice and without the need for just cause, and with no entitlement to compensation, unless otherwise agreed in writing by the parties. However, in the event that the probationary period has lasted more than 60 days, the employer must give a notice of at least seven days prior to the termination date.

Changes to Terms and Conditions of Employment

The terms and conditions that govern the employment relationship between employer and employee normally result from an agreement between the parties. Therefore, any changes to existing and agreed terms and conditions may take place, provided the employee gives his or her consent thereto. In the event that the terms and conditions were laid down in writing, it is advisable that the new terms and conditions also be in writing.

Sometimes the parties are not allowed to freely amend or remove certain terms and conditions, despite their agreement. For example, this is the case regarding remuneration whereby any changes in breach of the principle of nonreduction of remuneration will be deemed void, irrespective of employee consent.

Generally, whenever the terms and conditions do not result from an agreement but from a unilateral decision of the employer based on the law, unilateral amendments to such terms and conditions may be carried out irrespective of employee consent. In this case the employer is bound by a duty of information to inform the employee in writing of the changes in the 30 days following the date on which they become effective.

Wages and Benefits

Aside from the minimum statutory monthly salary, published annually by the government and standing at €426 for the year 2008, employees are not entitled to any special benefits under an employment contract. The parties may, however, contractually agree on the existence of benefits and the terms and conditions under which such benefits will be granted.

Collective bargaining agreements may include the entitlement of specific benefits, as well as a minimum salary reference higher than the minimum statutory salary. Such minimum salary reference is based on the employees' professional category and job level.

The employee is entitled to 14 remuneration payments per calendar year: (1) 11 monthly remuneration payments corresponding to the number of months of work effectively performed; (2) vacation pay, corresponding to that which he or she would receive if working; (3) a vacation bonus, corresponding to the employee's base salary and any other amounts paid to the employee as a result of the duties he or she performs (e.g., remuneration due to the employee as a result of night shift work); and (4) a Christmas bonus, which corresponds to the employee's base salary.

All employees must be covered by workers' compensation insurance, in accordance with the applicable standard policy ruled by law.

Other terms and conditions such as vacations and leave are ruled in accordance with the provisions set out in the Labor Code and, where applicable, the respective social security legislation. These other terms do not qualify as "benefits" as such, because their existence does not depend on their inclusion as a term and condition of employment in the employment contract itself but rather results automatically from the law.

Working Hours

In general, an employee may not exceed the maximum daily and weekly working time periods, which are set by the Labor Code at eight and 40 hours respectively.

Other working time regimes may, nevertheless, be agreed to, such as an exemption from normal working hours agreement under which the employee is not subject to the referred maximum limits or an adaptability regime pursuant to which the employee's normal work period is defined in average terms based on a specific time frame.

Alternative working time periods may also be set out in collective bargaining agreements.

Vacation Entitlement and Accrual

Employees are entitled to a minimum of 22 working days of vacation per calendar year. This right falls due on January 1 and relates to work performed in the previous year. The employee is also entitled to national public holidays (13) and the municipal holidays of his or her workplace.

The number of days of vacation to which the employee is entitled will be increased if the employee had no or few justified absences in the previous year. In this way, these 22 working days of vacation are increased up to a maximum 25 days to reward employees for good attendance when (1) the employee had no unjustified absences and (2) the employee had only justified absences (e.g., due to sickness) in the following amounts:

- A maximum of one day or two half days of justified absence entitles the employee to an extra three days of vacation;
- A maximum two days or four half days of justified absence entitles the employee to an extra two days of vacation; and
- A maximum three days or six half days of justified absence entitles the employee to one extra day of vacation.

Therefore, the number of days of vacation to which the employee is entitled varies according to (1) the existence or otherwise of unjustified or justified absences; and (2) the number of absences.

In the year that the employment contract is agreed, the employee becomes entitled to vacation only after six months of the contract are completed. The vacation entitlement is calculated on the basis of two days for each month up to a limit of 20 days.

In the event that the calendar year changes before vacation entitlement falls due, or before the employee has taken the vacation days, he or she may do so until June 30 of the subsequent year.

However, the sum of the vacations acquired but not taken in the first year of employment and the vacations acquired in the second year of employment may not exceed 30 working days.

In relation to contracts with a duration of less than six months, the employee is entitled to two days of vacation for each completed month of the contract.

Employment-Related Taxes and Contributions

Under an employment contract, the employer is obliged to withhold a variable percentage of the employee's remuneration as withholding income tax. Such percentage varies depending on the employee's marital status (if the employee is married or equivalent, and if so, if his or her spouse or partner also receives a regular income) and number of dependents.

Further, pursuant to the social security regime applicable to employees, the employer is also obliged to pay a contribution currently equal to 23.75 percent of the employee's remuneration; the employee must equally pay a contribution currently equivalent to 11 percent of his or her remuneration, which is deducted by the employer.

Collective Agreements

Depending on the employer's business sector, a collective agreement may exist. Collective agreements are negotiated and agreed upon by the trade unions at different levels: (1) at a company level (i.e., with a single employer); or (2) at a collective level (i.e., with various companies operating in the same sector or with employer associations).

As a general principle, collective labor agreements are only enforced in relation to employees who are affiliated in a trade union directly or indirectly bound by it, and in relation to the employers who negotiated such a collective labor agreement and/or who are affiliated in an employer's association that negotiated it.

However, the government, through a so-called extension regulation (*regulamento de extensão*) may render collective agreements mandatory and binding for all companies operating in a specific sector.

Works Councils

The existence of works councils (*comissões de trabalhadores*) is not mandatory. Local works councils may intervene in company decisions and management by means of a prior consultation right or a mere information right.

SECTION II

My client is acquiring an existing business in Portugal. How do I assess the existing workforce and consider changes?

Share Deals Versus Asset Deals

Share Deals

Share deals do not affect employment relationships and do not require any consultation or information process. However, if employee benefits are transferred to a different group company—for example, global bonus plans, stock options, or share option plans—a share deal may lead to the need to change employee terms and conditions in that respect.

Asset Deals

Due diligence work will, under an asset deal where a client is the purchaser, normally involve the identification and quantification of the seller's workforce; that is, the assessment of all personnel that perform duties for the seller, be it under an employment contract, a provision of services agreement between the seller and a third company, temporary work, and so on. This is particularly significant given the nature of the activity performed by the provider and his or her formal characterization, as opposed to his or her potential material characterization as an employee.

The analysis of fixed-term employment contracts is also important since a particular hiring, if deemed invalid, may determine that the employee will be bound to the seller, and consequently the purchaser, under a permanent contract, which will, in the future, limit the purchaser's ability to terminate employment.

Other due diligence guidelines involve the assessment of the sellers' observation of its labor obligations, such as payment and registration of overtime, the working hours regime in force by the seller, payment of social security contributions, and so on.

In the event of the sale and purchase of a part or all of the assets of the employer company, the existing employment contracts will transfer automatically to the purchaser/transferee, provided the criteria currently set out in Articles 318 to 321 and 555 of the Labor Code, which implements (albeit with several particularities) the European Acquired Rights Directive into local law, are fulfilled.

Criteria for the Transfer

Pursuant to the Labor Code, in the event of the transfer, by any means or form, of ownership of an undertaking or business, or part of an undertaking or business, that constitutes an economic unit, the transferee is assigned the legal position of employer in the employment contracts of the respective employees, as well as the responsibility for payment of any fine arising from labor offenses.

In this way, the transfer of employees will operate automatically (i.e., employee consent is not required, provided all other formalities are complied with, such as the observance by the transferor and transferee of a duty of information toward the employee representatives or the employees themselves) whenever (1) a transfer of ownership of an undertaking or business, either partial or total, occurs, (2) provided that such undertaking or business is considered an economic unit (i.e., an organized group of resources with the objective of pursuing an economic activity, whether or not such activity is central or ancillary, as defined by law).

The main concept, therefore, to bear in mind is that of economic unit. In other words, provided that the undertaking or business, be it total or partial, constitutes an economic unit in itself, the employees dedicated to such economic unit will automatically be transferred to the transferee.

Portuguese law does not include any rule in relation to those situations in which the employee is only partially dedicated to the economic unit to be transferred. However, it has been understood that only the employees who are mainly dedicated to the transferred business (i.e., dedicate more than 50 percent of their working time thereto) are subject to the automatic transfer.

In brief, Portuguese law requires as the main criterion for an automatic transfer of employees the existence of an economic unit. However, in the definition of economic unit, the criterion of "autonomy" and the existence of a set of tangible and/or intangible assets are also included.

In the event that no real transfer of an economic unit exists, the main risk is that an automatic transfer of the affected employees will not apply and, therefore, they may refuse to perform work for the transferee and remain working for the transferor. If under an invalid transfer of undertaking or business an employee suffers damages as a result thereof, compensation may be claimed from the transferor.

The transferor will be jointly and severally liable for one year after the transfer for all labor claims arising before the transfer date. Such joint liability also applies to fines applied by the Ministry of Employment as a result of the inobservance of labor obligations by the transferor.

The transferee may, however, limit its liability by notifying the employees that they are entitled to claim eventual credits (unpaid amounts due to the employee by the transferor at the transfer date) within a period of three months, after which such credits will not be transferred to the transferee.

Information and Consultation Formalities and Requirements

(a) Labor law states that the transferor and transferee must inform the affected employees' representatives—local works councils (*comissões de trabalhadores*), interunion committees, trade union committees, and trade union representatives—or, in their absence, the employees themselves, of (1) the date of and reasons for the transfer; (2) the legal, economic, and social consequences arising there from; and (3) the projected measures to be taken in relation to such employees (if any).

(b) The date of and reasons for the transfer must be provided "in good time": (1) in writing; (2) before the transfer occurs; and (3) at least 10 days prior to the consultation referred in (c) below.

(c) The transferee and transferor must, together, consult the representative of the affected employees prior to the transfer date, with a view to reach an agreement on the measures referred to in (a)(3) above (if applicable), without prejudice to the legal and contractual provisions applicable to the measures that are the subject of agreement.

The noncompliance of the requirements referred in (a) and (b) above may determine the application of a fine by the Portuguese Work Inspectorate, depending on the company's turnover and the degree of fault.

Refusal by Employees to the Transfer

In case the transfer occurs in full compliance with the criteria set out in the Labor Code, the employees may not validly refuse the transfer and the performance of work for the transferee who will acquire the position of employer.

If the employees do refuse the transfer and or refuse to perform work for the transferee, they will be acting in breach of contract and may therefore be subject to a disciplinary proceeding with a view to their dismissal.

On the other hand, if the transfer is not valid, the affected employees may lawfully refuse it and also refuse the performance of work for the transferee. In this case, if the transferor persists in sustaining the existence of the transfer and does not hand work over to the employees, the employees may terminate their employment contracts with just cause and claim compensation under the terms set out under the Labor Code.

Impact of the Transfer on Employee Rights and Benefits

In principle, the transferee will remain subject to the rights and obligations of the transferor as a result of the employment contracts in force prior to the transfer date. Any change to the employment contracts posttransfer will depend on the employees' individual consent.

Moreover, planned changes to the terms and conditions of the transferred employees must always be subject to the agreement mentioned in (c) previously (if applicable).

Employees Not Affected by the Transfer

The regime set out above regarding the transfer of an undertaking or a business does not apply in relation to employment contracts with employees who have, in the meantime, been transferred by their employing entity to another undertaking or part of the business, or an undertaking that was not "absorbed" by the transfer and that constitutes a separate economic unit of the employer.

Therefore, in order for the remaining employees not to be affected by the business transfer, they will have to be validly transferred by the employer, prior to the business transfer date, to another company or undertaking, or part of a company or undertaking, that constitutes a separate economic unit from the object of the business transfer.

Carrying Out a Workforce Reduction

Termination of Employment—Basic Principle

The basic principle that should be borne in mind when an employer is considering reducing its workforce is that the employer may not unilaterally terminate employment without just cause.

Just cause may be objective or subjective, depending on the motivation of the termination. It is considered objective when the dismissal is originated by a reason not attributable to the employee (i.e., due to market, technological, or structural reasons, as defined by law). Termination of employment will, under this scenario, occur under a layoff, a dismissal due to the termination of the employee's job position procedure, or a dismissal due to the employee's inadaptability procedure, as expressly required in the Labor Code.

Subjective just cause, on the other hand, has as its origin a breach by the employee of his or her legal or contractual obligations, which, in light of its gravity and consequences, renders the maintenance of the employment relationship practically impossible. The Labor Code provides a series of examples as to what may be considered subjective just cause and guidelines as to how it should be assessed (taking into account the degree of damage caused to the employer, the nature of the relationship between the parties or between the employee and his or her coworkers, etc.).

Notice and Other Procedural Requirements

In addition to the material need for just cause, the employer must also observe a complex procedure that, in the case of subjective just cause, involves the existence of a disciplinary proceeding and the issuance of a decision by the company as to the sanction that is to be enforced, in this case, the employee's dismissal.

As regards objective just cause, the Labor Code also includes several procedures, which involve a complex set of notification and negotiation formalities in which the employer, the employees, the employees' representative bodies, and government entities all play active roles.

In certain cases, such as a layoff or a termination of an employee's job position, payment in lieu of notice is possible under the terms set out in the Labor Code for each regime and provided all other requirements, material and procedural, are also complied with.

The procedure requirements vary, therefore, in accordance with the type of dismissal and are mandatory.

Government agencies may be required to intervene in certain termination procedures.

This regime does not apply to cases such as the unilateral termination by the employer of fixed-term employment contracts or employment contracts under a commission of services regime, where it is possible to terminate without cause, within the established limits and requirements provided for by law.

Employee representatives and pregnant and nursing employees enjoy special protection rights regarding termination of employment.

Severance

The unilateral termination of an employment contract by the employer entitles the employee to the right to severance pay in the following situations:

- At the expiry of a fixed-term contract, the employee is entitled to severance pay equal to three days of base remuneration (plus seniority subsidy, that is, amounts due to the employee as a result of the applicable collective labor agreement, based on his or her length of service in the company or in a particular position, if applicable) for each month of duration of the contract if the contract has lasted six months or less, and two days for each month if the contract was for more than six months. A fraction of a month is calculated on a pro rata basis.

- For layoff, termination of an employee's job position, or termination due to inadaptability of the employee, the employee is entitled to severance pay equal to one month's base salary (plus seniority subsidy, if applicable) for each complete year of service and to a minimum of three months' pay. A fraction of a month is calculated on a pro rata basis.

In the event the termination is considered void by a court ruling, the employee may be rewarded for pecuniary and moral damages and will, unless he or she opts for compensation, be reinstated.

Compensation in lieu of reinstatement is set by the court and ranges between 15 and 45 days of base remuneration, plus seniority subsidy, if applicable, for each complete year or fraction of year of service, which may not be lower than three months' base remuneration plus seniority subsidy, if applicable.

In some cases (when the employer is able to demonstrate that the employee's reinstatement will seriously compromise its business activity and provided the employee performs duties under a directorship position or is employed by a company up to a maximum of 10 employees), the employer may oppose reinstatement. If the court rules in favor of such opposition, the employee will be awarded a compensation amount between 30 and 60 days of base remuneration, plus seniority subsidy, if applicable, per each year or fraction of a year of service, but not less than six months' base remuneration plus seniority subsidy, if applicable.

The employee will further be entitled to the amounts he or she stopped receiving as of the date of termination until the final court ruling, less any amounts received as a result of the termination that the employee would not be entitled to had the dismissal not occurred. Also, any unemployment benefits the employee received during such period will also be deducted and returned to the social security authorities.

Reorganizing the Workforce

Other organizational changes that do not involve termination of employment, such as permanent changes in the employees' job position or duties, will, in principle, require employee consent, since they affect terms and conditions of employment that resulted from agreement between the parties. In some cases, they may require the intervention of the Work Inspectorate.

Functional mobility, within the established legal limits, may also be considered for the purposes of workforce reorganization, in which case employee consent will not be necessary, provided, among other aspects, the change is temporary. In this case, the employee will be entitled to at least the same remuneration he or she was receiving prior to the change in his or her job functions. The employer must also notify the employee in writing with indication of the reason for the change as well as of its estimated duration. No specific notice period is required by law; however, the employer is bound by a general duty of good faith and should therefore ensure that the employee is notified within a reasonable period of time prior to the change taking effect.

Employees may also be subject to a temporary or permanent geographical transfer, provided the transfer does not cause the employee serious difficulty. As is the case with unilateral changes to job positions, the employer is required to notify the employee of the transfer in writing (1) 30 days prior to it taking effect, in the case of a permanent transfer; and (2) eight days when the transfer is temporary and which, in principle, may not exceed six months.

In this respect, individual analysis of the employment contracts is also important, since the parties may have agreed on a specific mobility regime, which will therefore prevail.

Changing the Wage and Benefits Structure

According to the Labor Code, remuneration shall include any amount to which the employee is legally or contractually entitled under his or her employment relationship, or by virtue of existing company internal policies or practices, as a result of work performed (i.e., the employees' base remuneration and all amounts paid regularly and periodically, directly or indirectly, in money or in kind).

Furthermore, the Labor Code foresees a principle of nonreduction of the employee's remuneration whereby the employer, irrespective of employee consent, may not reduce the employee's remuneration, unless under specific circumstances.

To that effect, the characterization of a certain amount in money or in kind is significant in the sense that the employee may try to demonstrate that all payments or benefits made either in money or in kind form part of his or her global remuneration, namely in those cases where the employee suffers a global reduction of his or her remuneration (in breach of the previously mentioned principle) as a result of the unilateral replacement or removal of a particular benefit by the company.

The characterization of a certain amount as remuneration is also significant as a result of legal protection of an employee's credits. These credits are graded more favorably when compared to other debts of the employer.

Therefore, remuneration constitutes a term and condition of employment and, as such, any changes thereto will, in principle, require employee consent.

If the employer, however, is able to demonstrate that a particular remuneration item is granted unilaterally and does not result from the law or from a collective bargaining agreement, it may be replaced or removed, provided the employee's global remuneration amount is not reduced. Such a decision should be communicated unilaterally to the employee, in compliance with the employer's duty of information to the employee. Likewise, if the employer is able to demonstrate that a certain benefit is granted on a discretionary basis, and that its award does not entitle the employee to create any expectation as to its payment in the future, then any changes related to its award, namely its removal, may be unilaterally decided by the employer. It should be noted that this evaluation should be made on a case-by-case basis and is not risk-free since the employee may argue its qualification as a remuneration item.

Consulting with Labor Unions or Works Councils

Local works councils (when they exist) must be notified and consulted so as to issue a nonbinding formal opinion regarding any management decisions that relate, inter alia, to (1) the change of basic criteria regarding professional classification; (2) the change of the company or undertaking's place of business activity, measures that will result in a substantial decrease of the company's or undertaking's number of employees or the substantial worsening of the latter's working conditions, as well as any decisions that will most likely affect the company's workforce, work organization, or employment contracts; and (3) the closing of undertakings or production lines.

Local works councils must also be informed of the decision to terminate employment under a layoff or termination of a job position, be permitted to negotiate with the company, and be notified of the company's formal decision. The negotiation process aims at reaching an agreement on the dimension and the effects of the measures to be taken, as well as the enforcement of other measures to reduce the number of employees to be dismissed (suspension or reduction of the activity, professional reconversion and reclassification, early retirement and preretirement). The negotiation will also involve defining the severance amounts to be paid to each employee.

Failure to comply with the legal procedural rules regarding the intervention of the local works council in a unilateral termination scenario will render the dismissal void.

⊕ SECTION III

My client wishes to sell its existing facility. What restrictions do we need to consider?

Employment contracts do not normally contain any provisions that cover the possibility of the facility being sold.

In the event of an asset transfer, for example, assuming the relevant criteria foreseen in the Labor Code are complied with, namely that the assets fall within the concept of an economic unit, the existing employment contracts will automatically transfer from the seller to the purchaser. In this case, the consultation procedures discussed in Section II under "Information and Consultation Formalities and Requirements" will have to be observed.

If the employer wishes to retain key employees it should ensure that such employees do not primarily perform duties within the scope of the economic unit that will transfer to the purchaser. Such may be achieved by a permanent change of the employee's job position prior to the transfer, in which case the most likely option would be to agree upon the change with the employee in writing as an addendum to his or her employment contract. In any event, the retention will depend on individual negotiation. Moreover, the seller, the purchaser, and the employee may agree that the latter remain working for the seller.

If the selling employer is bound by a collective bargaining agreement, such collective bargaining agreement will apply in relation to the purchaser until the term of its enforceability and for a minimum 12 months' period as of the transfer date, unless another collective labor instrument becomes applicable in the meantime.

SECTION IV

My client wishes to replace its senior manager(s). What restrictions do we need to consider?

Portuguese labor law does not differentiate between types of employees for termination purposes. Save for the exceptions provided for by law, all employees, irrespective of their duties and position, benefit from the same statutory and contractual protection regarding termination of employment. Therefore, the general principle of prohibition of termination without just cause applies, in principle, to all employees.

The only exceptions relate to (1) those employees who are hired under a fixed-term employment contract (which is not common in the case of a senior manager), and who will be subject to a termination regime that differs based on the temporary nature of the justification that serves as a basis for its valid execution; and also (2) those employees who are hired to perform their duties under an employment contract under a commission of services regime.

Commission of Services Regime

According to the Labor Code board or equivalent positions, directorship positions that report to the board of directors, as well as the directors' secretarial personnel, and any other positions noted in collective bargaining agreements whose nature also presupposes a special fiduciary relationship may be performed under a commission of services regime.

In this way, the commission of services regime is specifically oriented toward the performance of duties of a fiduciary nature, namely board or directorship positions, as may be the case of a senior manager.

Unlike the standard employment contract, the employment contract under a commission of services regime must be in writing. In the case of an employee who is hired after the beginning of his or her contractual relationship under a commission of services regime, the contract must indicate (1) the identity of the parties; (2) the position or duties that the employee will perform, with express reference to their execution under a commission of services regime; and (3) the activity the employee will perform once the commission of services has ended (if no reference is made in this respect, the termination of the commission of services presupposes the termination of the employment contract), if applicable.

In the event that the commission of services is not agreed in writing or in the event that the indication in (2) above is not made, the contract is understood as not being subject to the referred regime.

Unilateral Termination

Termination of an employment contract under a commission of services regime is subject to a more flexible regime. In this case, termination may occur unilaterally at any time, irrespective of just cause. The employer must, nonetheless, notify the employee of its decision in writing at least 30 or 60 days prior to termination, depending on whether the commission of services has lasted up to two years or more than two years.

Termination of employment contracts under a commission of services regime is, therefore, much more flexible than termination under standard employment contracts. Such flexibility is justified by the special trust that characterizes the position and duties performed by the employee in question.

Upon termination of the commission of services, assuming that the employee is not bound by any previous employment relationship with the employer, the employee is entitled to compensation equal to one month's base remuneration for each complete year of service, with a fraction of a year being calculated on a pro rata basis, although the parties are free to increase such amount contractually.

If the commission of services is terminated by reason of dismissal through fault of the employee (subjective just cause), no such compensation is due.

Therefore, a company that is considering replacing a senior manager should first confirm if the manager was hired under a standard employment contract or an employment contract under a commission of services agreement. In the first case, standard rules on individual termination will apply and, unless the company has any valid reason to dismiss the employee (either objective, through a unilateral dismissal by termination of the employee's job position, or subjective), the only alternative will be to negotiate the employee's exit under a mutual agreement scenario.

If, on the other hand, the employee was hired under a commission of services regime, termination may operate unilaterally in the terms referred above, that is, the employer is not required to justify its decision to terminate the contract, provided it complies with the referred notice period and pays the employee the agreed compensation.

Termination by Mutual Agreement

Employer and employee are free to terminate the employment contract by mutual agreement at any time by means of a written agreement, which must indicate the date of its execution as well as its effective date. Although not mandatory, it is common to pay the employee compensation in order to persuade him or her to accept termination. The employee may revoke the termination up to seven days following the date of its execution by communicating this decision to the employer in writing along with repayment of the compensation paid by the employer. This revocation is not possible if the parties' signatures were notarized.

The amount of termination compensation is freely negotiable between the parties, but usually employers do not begin a negotiation with an offer lower than one month's pay per each year of service (or fraction thereof).

Amounts paid as compensation for termination of an employment agreement are exempt from social security contributions and are also exempt from income tax up to the following limit:

$$Y \times 1.5 \times Z$$

where

Y = Average monthly remuneration received in the 12 months prior to termination

Z = Years, or fraction thereof, of work

In other words, the tax authorities treat compensation payments calculated as 1.5 times the monthly average remuneration per year of service, times the employee's number of years of service, or fraction thereof, as exempt from income tax. Therefore, it is very common to consider a compensation payment based on this tax reference.

The Labor Code requires that in the case of dismissal by the employer without just cause, the employee may choose to receive compensation as an alternative to his or her reinstatement in the company, which varies between 15 to 45 days' base remuneration for each complete year of service, or fraction thereof. This maximum variation amount coincides approximately with the tax criterion set out above.

The Labor Code also foresees that the employer may oppose reinstatement when, for example, the employee in question is a member of the company's board of directors or holds a directorship position, in which case, should the court recognize such opposition, the compensation amount shall be calculated between 30 and 60 days' base remuneration for each complete year of service or fraction thereof.

Therefore, this legal provision may also be taken as a reference for negotiation of the termination of employment contracts by mutual agreement, in the cases of senior executives (members of the company's board of directors or employees who hold directorship positions in the company).

Termination of an Employee Who Is Also a Board Member

It may occur that the senior manager in question has both an employment contract and a board member position in a private limited liability company (*sociedade por quotas*). It has been understood by Portuguese doctrine and jurisprudence that such a combination is possible in relation to this type of company in those cases where the employee is appointed director (i.e., board member) but continues to perform his or her activity under the employer's direct supervision and instructions.

Such a dual role is not possible in public limited liability companies (*sociedades anónimas*), as a provision in the Portuguese Commercial Companies Code (PCCC) (*Código das Sociedades Comerciais*) expressly states that during the period for which they have been appointed, directors may not perform, whether temporarily or permanently, any duties for the company or for a company that is related thereto (in the terms set out in the PCCC) under an employment contract or a provision of services agreement. When an employee is appointed a board member of a public limited liability company, his or her employment contract will be suspended or terminate automatically, depending on whether its duration has lasted more or less than one year, respectively.

Board members either are appointed in the bylaws of the company or are elected by the company's general assembly, in compliance with the electoral procedures and formalities set out in the PCCC.

SECTION V

What prohibitions exist against discrimination on the basis of age, race, gender, disability, pregnancy, and other factors? What are the rights of employees who believe that they have been discriminated against?

Discrimination

The Labor Code contains various provisions that govern the principles of and rights to equality at work and nondiscrimination. It clearly states that the employer may not discriminate, directly or indirectly, based on, inter alia, parentage, age, sex, sexual orientation, marital status, family situation, genetic heritage, reduced work capacity, disability, chronic disease, nationality, ethnic origin, religion, political or ideological convictions, or union affiliation.

These provisions are further regulated in the law that enacts the Labor Code (Law No. 35/2004, of June 22, the so-called Regulation of the Labor Code), which, among other aspects, defines the types of situations and circumstances in which a particular act may be deemed discriminatory.

The candidate or employee who alleges discrimination must show evidence of the discrimination and indicate the employee or employees in relation to whom he or she considers him or herself discriminated against. It is then the employer's duty to prove that the differences in the employee's hiring or working conditions are not a form of discrimination as listed above.

Harassment

The Labor Code defines harassment as any undesirable behavior relating to any factors of discrimination as described previously that occur while applying for a job position or in the workplace itself, during time at work or professional training, with the intent or result of affecting the person's dignity or creating an intimidating, hostile, degrading, humiliating, or destabilizing atmosphere, in particular, regarding any undesirable behavior of a sexual nature, whether verbal, nonverbal, or physical.

Without prejudice to the employer being subject to an administrative proceeding that may result in its having to pay a fine, any discriminatory act that causes the candidate or employee moral or pecuniary damages entitles the latter to seek compensation, in the terms set out in the Portuguese Civil Code regarding civil liability.

🌐 SECTION VI

On the Horizon: What key labor and employment law developments should an employer doing business in Portugal anticipate occurring in the coming years?

Discussions at a national level among the government, employers' confederations, and trade union confederations are currently underway regarding the reform of employment and labor relations in Portugal, the result of which will bring changes to the current Labor Code.

The main topics under discussion relate to:

- *Employment contracts:* inter alia, changes to their legal characterization, the adoption of government incentives for the hiring of employees under permanent employment contracts through the reduction of social security contributions, the limitation of the maximum duration of fixed-term contracts to three years (thereby abolishing the current exceptional renewal following the maximum three-year period), the increase of probationary periods, and the increase of social security contributions regarding fixed-term employment contracts;

- *Flexibility regarding working time organization and maternity and paternity leave:* inter alia, the creation of new adaptability regimes and specific working schedules that concentrate working hours on certain days followed by greater rest periods, and an increase in remunerated parental leave;

- *Collective bargaining:* inter alia, the creation of simpler negotiation methods, an increase in matters that may be governed through collective labor instruments, better articulation between collective labor instruments and the law, and a promotion of means to incentive collective bargaining;

- *Termination of employment:* inter alia, the simplification of procedures for termination of employment, while maintaining the general principle of prohibition of dismissal without just cause; and

- *Compliance:* inter alia, the reinforcement of human resources for the supervision of compliance of the law regarding working conditions and reinforcement of penalties associated to their breach.

It is not envisaged that this reform and subsequent changes to the Labor Code will take effect before 2009.

CHAPTER 15

LABOR AND EMPLOYMENT LAW IN SLOVAKIA

TOMÁŠ RYBÁR
BRANISLAV HAZUCHA

SECTION I

My client wishes to establish a manufacturing facility in Slovakia and will need to hire a workforce. What are the key issues involved?

Employment Contracts: Who Receives Them and What Must They Include?

The main characteristic of an employment relationship (*pracovný pomer*) is the personal, material, and financial dependence of the employee on the employer. The employee is thus an individual who performs dependent work for the employer pursuant to the latter's instructions, using the latter's facilities and instruments, and for a wage or other type of remuneration.

Mandatory Requirements

There are two ways to hire an employee. Some workers are hired upon special works agreements (*dohody o prácach vykonávaných mimo pracovného pomeru*). This way of hiring workers is more an exception than the rule, since it heavily depends upon the amount of work (up to 350 hours per year or up to 10 hours a week) or workers (e.g., students, trainees). The majority of employees are hired upon an employment contract (*pracovná zmluva*).

Form of the Employment Contract

The employer is obliged to provide the employee with a written copy of the employment contract. The failure to conclude the employment contract in writing does not, however, cause its invalidity.

List of Required Information

The Labor Code (Act No. 311/2001 Coll., as amended) imposes upon an employer the obligation to inform employees of the conditions applicable to employment. This is done through an employment contract. The contract is thus required to contain the following essential terms expressly agreed between the employer and employee, and formulated in an exact and clear way:

- The type of work for which the employee was hired;
- Brief description of the type of work;
- The location of the work;
- The date when the employee is to commence working for the employer; and
- Wage conditions, unless agreed in the applicable collective agreement (*kolektívna zmluva*) concluded between the employer and the labor union (*odborová organizácia*).

In addition to these substantial requirements, the employment contract must also contain other working conditions, particularly concerning payment terms, working hours, paid vacation, and notice period. It is, however, sufficient to make a reference to the relevant provisions of the collective agreement or provisions of the Labor Code. Other conditions in the interest of the contracting parties, in particular the conditions concerning additional material benefits, may be agreed in the employment contract (e.g., if the work location is abroad). If the written version of the employment contract does not contain these additional conditions, the employer is obliged within one month from the commencement of the employment to provide the employee with a written declaration containing them. Some employers, in particular in big enterprises, use employee's handbooks, containing excerpts from collective agreements and other important bylaws adopted by the employer.

Language

Pursuant to the State Language Act (Act No. 270/1995 Coll., as amended), the employer is required to issue all written legal documents under employment or other similar relationship in the state language, Slovak. In practice, foreign investors often use bilingual documents especially in case of employment contracts concluded with higher-level managers. Employment contracts with ordinary workers are usually simple forms drafted in Slovak.

Changes to Terms and Provisions

How employment terms and provisions are changed depends on whether they were adopted contractually (in an employment contract or collective agreement), or unilaterally by the employer's decision (in internal bylaws). The former may be altered only upon a mutual written agreement between the contracting parties, that is, the employer on one side and the employees or their representatives (if the change may be affected via a collective agreement) on the other. The latter may be changed either unilaterally by the employer, or after consultations with, or with an approval given by, the employees' representatives (e.g., a labor union or works council—*zamestnanecká rada*), depending on the type of document. These changes, especially those adopted unilaterally by the employer, may not contravene the contractually agreed conditions or the provisions of the Labor Code and other applicable legal regulations.

Fixed-Term Employment

The Labor Code limits the probation period (*skúšobná doba*) to a maximum of three months and sets strict conditions against unfair dismissal (e.g., dismissal only upon statutory causes, notice period, severance pay).

In order to circumvent these restrictions, some employers prefer to hire certain employees for a fixed term. To avoid the abuse of these practices, the fixed-term employment is strictly regulated. An employer may agree with an employee on a fixed term only up to three years. This term must be expressly stated in the written employment contract, otherwise it is invalid. The fixed-term employment may be extended or concluded again (within six months after the termination of a previous fixed-term employment) only once within those three years. There are statutory exemptions when this time restriction does not apply. They depend on a particular type of work (e.g., a substitution of another employee, seasonal work) or employees (e.g., top-level managers, scientists, artists, employees hired by an employer with a maximum of 20 employees).

Wages and Benefits

An employer is obliged to provide an employee with a wage for performed work. The contractual freedom in relation to wage conditions is limited by certain exceptions, such as minimum wage, minimum wage entitlement for a set work difficulty level, and nondiscrimination requirements. The latter requires the equality of the wages for same or similar work as to complexity, responsibility, difficulty, working conditions, and achievement of the same efficiency and results. The minimum wage entitlement for a set work difficulty level applies in case no collective agreement was agreed and is calculated based on the minimum wage increased by indexes set for difficulty levels.

Minimum Wage Requirements

The minimum wage requirements are set up by the Minimum Wage Act (Act No. 90/1996 Coll., as amended). The exact amount of minimum wage is determined by an implementing regulation adopted by the government usually as of October 1 each year and is based on the increase in the average wage in the national economy. These requirements concern the employees in employment and similar labor relationships (e.g., members of a cooperative). If the wage of an employee is below the minimum wage requirement, the employer is required to pay the employee an additional payment. As of 2008, the minimum wage is SKK 46.6 (approximately US $2.42) on an hourly basis or SKK 8,100 (approximately US $423) on a monthly basis.

Special Benefit Requirements

In addition to wages, the employees may also obtain other payments such as wage compensations (e.g., for unjust termination, unspent paid vacation, etc.), severance pay, discharge benefits, travel reimbursements, contributions from the social fund, or compensation for on-call work. The conditions on wages and other benefits either stem directly from the Labor Code or may be agreed in the collective agreement.

Paid Leave

An employee is entitled to (1) paid vacation; (2) supplementary paid vacation; (3) maternity and parental leave; and (4) sick leave or leave for certain personal reasons (e.g., to care for a sick relative). The basic paid vacation is at least four weeks per year. It is extended by another week depending upon the collective agreement, the seniority of the employee (an employee working for more than 15 years since the age of 18) and the type of work (e.g., mining, health-endangering working conditions). In certain industries, paid vacations are extended by one week in a collective agreement, and therefore employees are usually entitled to five or six weeks of paid vacation, depending upon the seniority of the employee. In addition, collective agreements often provide one additional week for recuperation, visiting a doctor, or arranging other personal issues. Finally, there are 15 days of public holidays per year.

Labor Unions

Establishment and Recognition Requirements

A labor union may be established by at least three persons, where at least one of them is more than 18 years old. A labor union is established on the day following the delivery of application for its registration to the Ministry of Interior (*Ministerstvo vnútra Slovenskej republiky*). The application is required to be accompanied by two copies of the articles of association (*stanovy*) containing the necessary organizational provisions (e.g., the name of labor union, the place of its seat, goals of its activities, its bodies and the method of their establishment, and the determination of bodies and persons entitled to act on its behalf). In order to commence its activities, the labor union is required to inform the employer on its commencement therein. It is also obliged to submit to the employer the names of the members of its body (*odborový orgán*) who are entitled to communicate and negotiate with the employer. The employer has the statutory obligation to allow the activities of labor unions at the working place. Restrictions apply for termination of employment in case of employees' representatives. In addition, the representatives are entitled to paid leave for performance of trade union activities.

Role of Employees' Representatives

One of the fundamental principles of the Labor Code is that employees or their representatives have the right to obtain information on the employer's economic and financial situation and on the expected development of the employer's activities in a comprehensible manner and within a reasonable time frame. The employer may refuse to provide information that could harm the employer or may require that the information is regarded as confidential. The employees have the right to express their opinion on the provided information and submit their proposals with regard to the employer's plans that may influence their status. In addition, in order to ensure just and satisfactory working conditions, the employees may participate in the employer's decision making concerning their economic and social interests, either directly or by means of competent trade unions, works councils, or works trustees (*zamestnanecký dôverník*), which closely cooperate. The employees' representatives exercise their powers in relation to the employer by (1) joint decision making; (2) negotiations; (3) the right to information; and (4) inspection activities. For more details on the relationship between trade unions on one side, and works councils or works trustees on the other, see "Works Councils, Relation to Labor Unions" later in this section.

Collective Agreements

The collective agreements are to be concluded in writing. Depending upon the contracting parties, there are two types of collective agreements: enterprise collective agreement (*podniková kolektívna zmluva*) and collective agreement of higher instance (*kolektívna zmluva vyššieho stupňa*). The former is concluded between the employer and the enterprise labor union. The latter is usually agreed for a particular industry between an association of employers and an association of labor unions in the industry. It normally binds the members of the particular industry association; however, the Ministry of Labor, Social Affairs, and Family (*Ministerstvo práce, sociálnych vecí a rodiny Slovenskej republiky*) may decide that it applies to a particular industry notwithstanding membership in the respective industry association. The collective agreements are usually renegotiated each year.

Duty to Bargain

The parties are obliged to start negotiating a new collective agreement at least 60 days before the expiry of the concluded one. Any contracting party may submit to the other a written proposal of collective agreement. The proposal's addressee is to respond within 30 days unless agreed otherwise. The written response must address the issues that have not been accepted. Both parties are required to continue in negotiation and to provide the necessary assistance to each other.

Dispute Resolution

If the parties do not reach an agreement on the conclusion of a collective agreement, they may agree to appoint a mediator (*sprostredkovateľ*). If there is no agreement within 60 days of submitting the written proposal of collective agreement, any negotiating party may request the Ministry of Labor, Social Affairs, and Family to appoint a mediator. The mediator is to prepare a written report within 15 days of his or her appointment. This report is to contain the proposal on the dispute settlement. If the solution is not found within 30 days from the mediator's appointment, the mediation (*konanie pred sprostredkovateľ'om*) is considered terminated. The parties may then initiate arbitration (*konanie pred rozhodcom*) or strike (*štrajk v spore o uzavretie kolektívnej zmluvy*). The time frame in case of arbitration is similar to mediation. The arbitral award may be challenged before a court within 15 days from its delivery.

Works Councils

Mandatory Requirements

A works council may be established at an employer who employs at least 50 employees. In case of an employer who employs fewer than 50 but at least five employees, employees may elect a works trustee, who is vested with the rights and obligations of a works council. The works trustee and members of the works council are elected for a four-year term.

Relation to Labor Unions

The employees have the right to collective bargaining only through the relevant trade unions. If both a trade union and a works council operate at the same employer, the trade union body has the collective bargaining, joint decision making, and control and information rights. The works council has the right to negotiate and inform. They have the right of joint decision making (in the form of an agreement concluded with an employer or a prior consent given to the measures taken by an employer) only when the working or employment conditions where their participation is required by law are not regulated by a collective agreement.

National and Regional Groups

The employers or members of groups operating in the territory of several European Union (EU) member states are obliged to provide their employees with supranational information and negotiation concerning the employees' interests. In order to do so, a European Works Council is to be established, or a procedure for informing employees and negotiation is to be agreed with the aim to provide the employees with necessary information and to negotiate with them. The obligation to provide supranational information and negotiation under the Slovak Labor Code applies to the following:

- The employers and groups of employers operating in the territory of EU member states with their registered seat in the Slovak Republic;
- The organizational units of employers or groups of employers operating in the territory of member states with their registered seat in the Slovak Republic; and
- The representatives of an employer or a group of employers operating in the territory of the member states with their registered seat in the Slovak Republic.

SECTION II

My client is acquiring an existing business in Slovakia. How do I assess the existing work-force and consider changes?

Share Deals Versus Asset Deals

The difference between share deals and asset deals is in the extent to which the individual deal has legal consequences for the employment relationships on the side of the vendor. In share transfers, the deal has no legal consequences to the position of the acquired company in the employment relationships with its employees. The purchaser merely acquires the shares of a company that is in the position of the employer toward the affected employees. The change of control over the employer has therefore no direct legal consequences to the employment relationships. In the case of an asset deal, the employer's position is transferred to another subject. Accordingly, although no change in the business activities occurs, the person who acts as the employer in the affected employment relationships alters. Subject to fulfillment of statutory conditions as specified below, the person to whom the business is transferred enters into already established employment relationships as the employer and acquires all the rights and obligations accrued from them.

Due Diligence Requirements and Considerations

In the case of a share deal, the shares of a company are acquired. The due diligence exercise should therefore also focus on the position of the members of the board of directors (*predstavenstvo*) in case of a joint stock company or the executive directors (*konatelia*) in case of a limited liability company (altogether hereinafter "board-level managers") (for more details, see Section IV). In this regard, it should be noted that in performance of this function, board-level managers are not deemed employees under the Labor Code and the contractual freedom of parties under the Commercial Code (Act No. 513/1991 Coll., as amended) is not as limited as in case of the employment contracts. Although the protection against unfair dismissal under the Labor Code does not apply to them, the corporate documents (e.g., articles of association) or the agreement under which they were appointed may contain special provisions on profit participation or payment in case of their recalling. In practice, the board-level managers are quite often insiders. In such a case, they perform other functions as managers who are employed by the company under an employment contract. The due diligence exercise should therefore also examine to what extent the provisions on dismissal and severance pay may apply to board-level managers.

Another issue concerns the involvement of employees' representatives in the deal. In case of a share deal, the law does not require negotiations or consultations with the employees or their representatives unless the shares are admitted to trading on a regulated securities market organized by a stock exchange. Both the target company and the bidder are then required to inform their respective employees or their representatives on the content of a takeover bid.

In case of asset deals, the key issue is to identify the number and structure of affected employees and other issues related to them (see "Assessing Employment Contracts" in Section III). In practice, the problem is to achieve the disclosure of all necessary information by the seller, since much of this information relates not only to the affected employees but also to the seller's entire workforce.

Statutory Regulations Concerning Transfer of Business

Under the Labor Code, a business transfer is understood as a transfer of an organizational unit that is capable of independent activities regardless of their character (i.e., main or supplementary activities). If a business, part of a business, or a business activity is transferred to another employer, the rights and obligations arising from labor law relations toward the transferred employees, including collective employment relations (e.g., the rights and duties under a collective agreement), pass to the transferee employer.

In such a case, the Labor Code imposes information and consultation duties upon the employee. No later than one month prior to the transfer of rights and obligations arising from labor law relations, an employer is obliged to inform, in writing, the employees' representatives (or the concerned employees) of (1) the actual or proposed date of transfer, (2) its reasons, (3) labor law, economic, and social implications for the employees, and (4) the planned measures affecting the employees. With a view to achieving consensus, an employer is obliged to discuss measures affecting the employees with the employees' representatives no later than one month prior to their implementation. These obligations also apply to the transferee employer. Noncompliance with these information and consultation duties does not affect the transfer.

After the transfer, the new employer is obliged to adhere to the collective agreement as agreed upon by the preceding employer until its expiry. In addition, the legal position and function of employees' representatives is retained until the termination of their function period unless agreed otherwise. It should be noted that the transfer per se constitutes no cause for the termination of any employment relationship under the Labor Code.

Carrying Out a Workforce Reduction

In case of workforce reduction, two possible ways of employment termination are applicable: by an agreement or a notice. If an employee and an employer agree on the termination of the employment in writing, the employment terminates upon the agreed day. The agreement is to stipulate the cause for the employment termination if so requested by the employee or if the termination takes place due to organizational changes.

Period of Notice

An employment relationship may be terminated by giving a two-month notice. If the notice is given to an employee who has worked for the employer for at least five years, its period is at least three months. Notice must be given in writing and delivered to the other party. An employer may give notice to an employee only for causes expressly stipulated in the Labor Code (e.g., the employee's redundancy or health conditions, or partial or complete winding-up or relocation of the employer's business). The cause of dismissal must be expressly mentioned in the notice in terms of facts so that it may not be confused with a different cause. The failure to satisfy any of the abovementioned requirements by the employer causes the invalidity of notice. Notice period commences on the first day of the calendar month following the delivery of notice, and terminates upon expiry of the final day of the respective calendar month.

Statutory Severance Pay Requirements

An employer is required to provide an employee with severance pay if the employment relationship is terminated for certain causes (e.g., the employee's redundancy or health conditions, or partial or complete winding-up or relocation of the employer's business) except in the case where an employee is transferred to another employer because of organizational changes or implementation of rationalization measures. Upon the employment termination, an employee is entitled to severance pay of a minimum of two average monthly earnings. An employee who has worked for the employer for more than five years is entitled to severance pay of a minimum of three average monthly earnings. If it is the employee's first termination of employment after reaching pension age, the employee is entitled to a discharge benefit of a minimum of one month's average earnings.

Layoff

If an employer or its branch terminates employment with at least 20 employees over a period of 90 days either by a notice or an agreement for certain statutory causes (partial or complete winding-up or relocation of an employer's business, or the employees' redundancy), the special provisions on layoff (*hromadné prepúšt'anie*) in the Labor Code set up the requirements on consultations with the employees' representatives and the supervisory authority. There are certain statutory exemptions from this regime (e.g., bankruptcy, fixed-term employment, crew members of vessels flying the flag of the Slovak Republic).

If an employer violates the obligations to negotiate with the employees' representatives and to provide them with all necessary information, an employee who is subject to the termination of an employment under a layoff is entitled to wage compensation of a minimum of two months' average earnings.

Protected Groups

The Labor Code guarantees a higher level of protection against the dismissal of certain groups of workers (e.g., pregnant workers, workers on a maternity or sick leave, disabled workers). For the termination of employment in case of employee representatives, see "Establishment and Recognition Requirements" in Section I.

Sanctions

If the termination of employment is invalid, the employee may claim before a court its invalidity within a period of two months from the day when the employment was supposed to terminate. As to the actual termination of an invalidly terminated employment, the key aspect is whether the employee insists on remaining in employment with the employer. If so, the employment continues, unless a court finds that the employer may not be justly required to continue employing the plaintiff. In addition, the employee is entitled to damages (wage compensation for the period when he or she was not able to work for the employer). If the employee does not insist on continuing the employment, the employment terminates on the date that would apply if the termination was valid. In case of an invalid immediate termination or invalid termination in probation period, the employee is also entitled to wage compensation for the two-month notice period.

Reorganizing the Workforce

In exceptional circumstances (e.g., pregnancy, health conditions) an employee may be moved to another place or type of work than was agreed in the employment contract. Accordingly, the workplace and the type of work is often defined in the employment contract sufficiently broadly to allow certain flexibility for an employer in cases of reorganizing the workforce. If reorganization is not possible within the scope of employment contracts, the employer and employees must agree to change the contracts. If an employee does not agree with the change and thus becomes redundant for an employer, it is statutory cause for dismissal.

Reassignment (*dočasné pridelenie*) of employees to another employer also requires the employee's consent. In such a case, special contracts need to be concluded outlining the terms of the reassignment (one with the employee and another between the concerned employers). An employer may reassign employees only for actual operational reasons. For a commercial reassignment, a license for a temporary employment agency (*agentúra dočasného zamestnávania*) is required.

Changing the Wage and Benefits Structure

The wage conditions are the obligatory content of employment contracts. They may not, therefore, be changed unilaterally. In case of ordinary workers, the employment contracts often refer to collective agreements as to the wage conditions. The change of wage conditions may then be agreed individually (by an amendment to an employment contract) or collectively (by an amendment to a collective agreement or a conclusion of a new one). As to managers, the wage conditions are usually individually agreed in their employment contracts and partially depend on the achieved results. In such a case, the employer has certain flexibility when the company does not perform well and needs to be reorganized.

Additional benefit structures for ordinary workers are usually agreed in a collective agreement. Conversely, the benefit structures for managers are partially agreed in a collective agreement and partially in the individual employment contracts. Accordingly, their changes depend upon the way in which the benefit structure was agreed (see "Changes to Terms and Provisions" in Section I).

Consulting with Labor Unions or Works Councils

The employer is required to consult, in advance, with the employees' representatives on the following issues concerning reorganizing the workforce:

- The state, structure, and expected development of employment and planned measures, mainly if employment is threatened;
- The decisions that may lead to fundamental changes in the organization of labor or in contractual conditions; and
- Organizational changes that could be considered as the reduction or termination of the employer's business, merger, splitting, or change to the legal form of the employer (e.g., from a joint stock company to a limited liability company).

These consultations must be held in a comprehensible way and appropriate time, and with adequate content and the goal of achieving an agreement. The employer is therefore required to provide the employees' representatives with the necessary information, discussions, and documentation. He is also obliged, within his power, to take into account the opinions of employees' representatives.

As to dismissals of employees, it should be noted that the employees' representatives must be consulted in advance of any dismissal given by an employer. The failure of to do so causes the dismissal to be invalid. The employees' representatives are obliged to deal with this issue within 10 calendar days of the delivery of the employer's written request. If they fail to do so, the employer may dismiss the employee without actually consulting them. If there is no employees' representative active in the workplace, the duty described in this paragraph does not apply.

In case of layoff, the employer is obliged, at least one month prior to the implementation of dismissals due to layoff, to negotiate with the employees' representatives (or with the affected employees) measures to avoid or reduce it, such as the placement of employees at other workplaces of the employer. For this purpose, the employer is obliged to provide the employees' representatives with all necessary information and to inform them in writing, in particular as to (1) the causes of the layoff; (2) the number and structure of employees subject to the termination of employment; (3) the overall number and structure of employees employed; (4) the period over which the dismissal of affected employees will be implemented; and (5) the criteria for selection of employees to be terminated.

Consulting with the Government

At the same time that the employees' representatives are informed in writing in case of a layoff, the employer is required to submit a transcript of this written information to the supervisory authority, the respective Office of Labor, Social Affairs, and Family (*úrad práce, sociálnych vecí a rodiny*). After negotiations on the layoff with the employees' representatives, the written information on their outcome must also be submitted by the employer to the supervisory authority and the employees' representatives. One month after this written information is delivered, the employer may then proceed to terminate the employment of affected employees either by a notice or agreement for the abovementioned causes.

During this period, the supervisory authority will seek solutions to the problems raised by the planned layoff. In addition, the employer has to negotiate with the supervisory authority the measures enabling the prevention or reduction of the layoff, in particular: (1) the conditions for maintaining employment levels; (2) the possibility of employing discharged employees by other employers; and (3) the possibility of employing discharged employees in the case of their retraining.

SECTION III

My client wishes to sell its existing facility. What restrictions do we need to consider?

Assessing Employment Contracts

The key issues the buyer will normally look at in its due diligence exercise are, inter alia:

- The fulfillment of statutory requirements for the employment contracts and any special provisions agreed, in particular concerning benefits, vacation, and severance pay;
- The number and structure of employees, especially whether any workers who should be employed under the Labor Code have been hired as independent contractors;
- The agreements concluded with the board-level managers and the corporate documents regulating their position, rights, and obligations (e.g., recalling of board-level managers, benefits structure);
- The organization of employees' representatives and the content of collective agreements (e.g., employer's obligations, benefits structure);
- Any liability relating to the time prior to the transfer (e.g., unpaid wages or premiums under health insurance, social security or old age insurance, unsettled claims from work accidents).

Consulting with the Government

There is no statutory requirement to consult the sale of an existing facility with a regulatory or supervisory authority, unless there are special circumstances (e.g., the facility is in bankruptcy or was privatized, or is an industry subject to special takeover requirements). The above is without prejudice to the need to obtain a merger control clearance under antitrust law, if the notification thresholds are met.

Consulting with Labor Unions or Works Councils

The information and consultation requirements mirror those applicable on the acquisition of an existing business (see "Consulting with Labor Unions or Works Councils" in Section II).

Negotiating with the Purchaser: Special Labor Issues

The seller will have to negotiate, with the buyer, various warranties and indemnifications concerning the issues discovered by the due diligence process in the sale and purchase agreement, in particular as outlined above. The buyer will also likely require that the retaining of key personnel is secured, for example, via separate agreements with such employees or withholding of a certain portion of the purchase price. Furthermore, Slovak law does not permit postemployment noncompete obligations, and any restriction of competitive conduct provided for in an employment relationship may apply only during the employment term.

❂ SECTION IV

My client wishes to replace its senior manager(s). What restrictions do we need to consider?

Employment Contracts

As mentioned previously (see "Share Deals Versus Asset Deals" in Section II), there are two types of managers. The first group is composed of the board-level managers who are not employed under the Labor Code for the performance of their functions. They are, however, quite often inside directors. In such a case, they also perform other functions in the company under employment agreements. Thus, any protection provided by the Labor Code to employees against unfair dismissal applies to their work performed under the employment contract.

Other managers below the board level are hired by an employment contract. The Labor Code does not distinguish between ordinary workers and managers as to the protection against unfair dismissal (for more detail in this regard, see "Carrying out a Workforce Reduction" in Section II).

Statutory Severance Pay Requirements

As the board-level managers are not employees for the purposes of performance of their board-level functions, they are not entitled to any statutory severance pay. Whether they are entitled to any payment upon their recalling depends upon the corporate documents of the particular company or the agreement with the individual board-level manager. If they are inside directors, the general provisions on severance pay under the Labor Code apply.

The managers below the board level are employees. There are no separate provisions on severance pay. Accordingly, the general provisions on severance pay applicable to other employees apply to this type of managers (see "Statutory Severance Pay Requirements" in Section II). However, their employment contracts or the collective agreement may contain special terms or provisions on severance pay to senior managers.

Statutory Restrictions on Dismissal Without Cause

The board-level managers may be recalled for any reason or even without stating any cause by decision of the shareholders' general meeting, unless the articles of association or another applicable corporate document provide otherwise. If they are inside directors, they continue to hold the position for which they are hired under the employment contract. In order to dismiss them or any other managers below the board level, the strict provisions against unfair dismissal under the Labor Code apply (see "Carrying out a Workforce Reduction" in Section II).

🌐 SECTION V

What prohibitions exist against discrimination on the basis of age, race, gender, disability, pregnancy, and other factors? What are the rights of employees, applicants, or former employees who believe that they have been discriminated against?

Areas of Protection

One of the fundamental principles of the Labor Code is that natural persons are granted rights without any sort of direct or indirect discrimination on grounds such as sex, marital or family status, race, color, language, age, health, belief and religion, political or other opinion, trade union activity, national or social origin, association with a national minority or ethnic group, property, birth, or other status, unless law provides otherwise (e.g., affirmative action). The ban on discrimination also includes discrimination on grounds of (1) pregnancy or maternity and gender or sexual orientation; (2) relationship with a person of certain racial, national, or ethnic origin; (3) relationship with a person of a certain religion or belief, or discrimination against an atheist; (4) previous disability or discrimination against a person who, because of external symptoms, may appear to have a disability.

Under the Act on Equal Treatment in Certain Areas and on the Protection against Discrimination (Antidiscrimination Act) (Act No. 365/2004 Coll., as amended), the equal treatment principle applies to the rights of natural persons in relation to:

- Access to employment, occupation, and other gainful activities or functions, including recruitment requirements and selection criteria and modalities;
- Employment and conditions of work including remuneration, promotion, and dismissal;

- Access to vocational training, professional upgrading, and participation in active labor market policy programs including access to vocational guidance services; and
- Membership and activity in organizations associating employees, employers, or persons of certain occupations, including the benefits that these organizations provide to their members.

The refusal or omission of the employer to adopt appropriate measures to enable a person with a disability to have access to employment, to work of a certain type, to promotion or other advancements, or to training is also deemed to constitute indirect discrimination based on disability unless the adoption of such measures would impose a disproportionate burden on the employer. To determine whether the measures give rise to a disproportionate burden, the following aspects are to be taken into account: (1) benefits to the disabled person; (2) the employer's financial resources; and (3) alternative solutions. The Antidiscrimination Act provides a list of circumstances of unequal treatment that are not considered discriminatory but rather objectively justified differences of treatment.

Limits of Protection and Affirmative Action

As mentioned above, any discrimination, whether positive or negative, is prohibited unless law provides otherwise. The ban against discrimination does therefore not apply to cases where discrimination stems from actual reasons based on preconditions or requirements for performance and nature of specific work. Furthermore, the objectively justified differences of treatment on grounds of sex are not deemed to constitute discrimination where (1) they consist in the fixing of different retirement ages for men and women, or (2) their purpose is the protection of pregnancy or motherhood.

Affirmative action is also possible and under certain circumstances required by law when it is necessary due to the employee's health conditions or other specific conditions, for instance, pregnancy, taking care of a child, disability, or in the case of young workers. In relation to disabled employees, the employer is to provide them with suitable working conditions, to execute their training and preparation for work, and give special attention to increasing their qualifications. The employer must employ disabled citizens in numbers corresponding to at least 3.2 percent of the total number of employees hired by the employer who work in Slovakia. This requirement applies if the employer employs at least 20 employees and if a sufficient number of disabled citizens are registered as job-seekers with the supervisory authority.

Remedies

Any person who considers that his or her rights, legitimate interests protected by law, or freedoms were violated due to a breach of the equal treatment principle is allowed to pursue a claim before the courts. The plaintiff may, in particular, seek that the person violating the equal treatment principle is ordered to refrain from such conduct and, where possible, to rectify the illegal situation or to provide adequate satisfaction. When the plaintiff submits to the court evidence reasonably supporting the claim that the equal treatment principle was breached, the defendant has the duty to prove that the violation of equal treatment principle did not occur. The victim has the right to ask for legal assistance and representation by the Slovak National Center for Human Rights (*Slovenské národné stredisko pre l'udské práva*), a specialized governmental agency.

In cases where the victim's dignity, social status, and social functioning have been significantly impaired by the employer's misconduct, the victim may also seek nonpecuniary damages. In determination of their amount, the court is to take into account the extent of such damage and all other circumstances in the case.

In the case of disabled employees, the employer failing to meet the statutory quotas of employing disabled citizens is obliged, by March 31 of the following calendar year at the latest, to transfer to the supervisory authority's account a levy for each shortfall equivalent to the currently applicable three-month minimum wage.

✪ SECTION VI

On the Horizon: What key labor and employment law developments should an employer doing business in Slovakia anticipate occurring in the coming years?

As of September 1, 2007, and January 1, 2008, the provisions of labor and employment law were amended in order to increase the level of the employee's protection. No further increase of regulation is currently anticipated. The new rule allowing the Ministry of Labor, Social Affairs, and Family to decide that a collective agreement of higher instance applies to the whole particular industry is currently being challenged before the Constitutional Court of the Slovak Republic (*Ústavný súd Slovenskej Republiky*). If this provision is found unconstitutional, it will become ineffective and unenforceable.

In addition, the Slovak labor and employment law is significantly influenced by EU legislation. At the time of writing this chapter, all adopted EU directives were implemented in the Slovak law. The detailed analysis of their implementation goes, however, beyond the scope of this chapter.

CHAPTER 16

LABOR AND EMPLOYMENT LAW
IN SPAIN

VICENTE CALLE

Preliminary remark: In Spain, the rights and obligations pertaining to employment relations are governed by

1. The legal provisions and regulations of the State.
2. Collective bargaining agreements, which may be specific for a certain industrial or professional sector or apply to a certain company, and which rank after the legal provisions and regulations of the State.
3. The will of the parties expressed in the employment contract, provided that its purpose is lawful and that no conditions are stipulated that are less favorable or contravene the aforementioned legal provisions and collective bargaining agreements.
4. Local and professional custom and usage.

SECTION I

My client wishes to establish a manufacturing facility in Spain and will need to hire a workforce. What are the key issues involved?

Employment Contracts: Who Receives Them and What Must They Include?

An employment contract is an agreement between the employer and the worker whereby the latter undertakes to render certain services for the employer and under the employer's direction in return for remuneration.

Formalization and Characteristics of the Labor Contract

Capacity to Contract

- Persons of legal age (18 years).
- Persons under 18 years who are legally emancipated.

- Persons over 16 years and under 18 years:
  - If they live independently with the express or implied consent of their parents or guardians.
  - If they have the authorization of the parents or of those who have them in their charge.
- Foreigners, in accordance with the legislation applicable to them.

Form of the Contract

Labor contracts are valid whether oral or in writing. They must be recorded in writing when so required by statute or specific regulation. This applies in particular to work experience and trainee contracts; part-time, indefinite-term contracts for seasonal work; contracts for partial replacement of semiretired workers; domestic labor contracts; contracts for a specific project or service; and insertion contracts, as well as those of workers hired in Spain to serve Spanish companies abroad.

Contracts for a fixed period of time that exceeds four weeks must also be in writing. If this requirement is not observed, the contract will be presumed to be entered into for an indefinite period and on a full-time basis, in the absence of proof to the contrary.

Either of the parties may demand that the contract be entered into in writing, even throughout the course of employment.

Term of the Contract

The labor contract may be for an indefinite period or for a fixed term, where legally possible.

Trial Period

The establishment of such a period is optional. If agreed, it must be in writing in the contract. The length varies depending on the category of employees, but in any case the maximum is six months.

Workers' Information

When the labor relation with the worker exceeds four weeks, the employer must provide the latter, in writing, with the essential elements of the labor contract and the principal conditions of performance of the labor obligation, within two months from the date of commencement of employment.

The following aspects must be included:

- The identity of the parties to the labor contract.
- The date of commencement of the labor relation and, in the case of a temporary labor relation, the foreseeable term.
- The company's registered office or, where relevant, the address of the employer and the workplace where the worker habitually renders services. If the worker habitually renders services at different workplaces or in mobile or itinerant workplaces, these circumstances must be stated.

- The category or the occupational group of the job held by the worker or the characterization or brief description of such job, in terms that allow the specific content of the work to be ascertained with sufficient accuracy.
- The initial basic salary and additional salary payments, as well as the intervals at which they are to be paid.
- The duration and distribution of the ordinary working day.
- The duration of the vacation and, where relevant, how vacation is determined.
- The prior notice periods that, where relevant, must be observed by the employer and the worker in the event of termination of the contract. If it is not possible to provide this information at the time of supply of the information, the means by which such prior notice periods are to be determined.
- The collective labor agreement applicable to the labor relation.

Right of the Workers' Legal Representatives to Information Regarding Contracts

A basic copy of the contracts, which must be executed in writing (except for contracts governing senior management special relations, of which notification is sufficient), must be supplied within 10 days to the workers' legal representatives, who will sign it for the purpose of proof that it has been supplied. They must also be notified within the same period of extensions of such contracts, as well as notices of termination.

A basic copy of the contract is one that excludes personal data of the employee (e.g., domicile, ID number).

Part-Time Contracts

The labor contract will be deemed to be entered into on a part-time basis where the provision of services is agreed for a number of hours per day, per week, per month, or per year that is less than the working hours of a comparable full-time worker. "Comparable full-time worker" means a full-time worker of the same company and workplace and with the same type of labor contract who performs the same or a similar job. If there is no comparable full-time worker in the company, the full-time working hours provided in the applicable collective labor agreement, or in the absence thereof, the statutory maximum working hours, shall be deemed to be the full-time working hours.

Hiring of Executives

Definition

Executives are defined as personnel who exercise powers belonging to the legal ownership of the company, relating to its general objectives, independently and with full responsibility.

They are considered to be employees but of a special kind, as their position is between the board of directors and the rest of the company.

Persons who purely and simply hold the position of member of the board are not considered senior executives.

Basic Characteristics

- This labor relationship is based on the mutual trust of the parties, who adapt the exercise of their rights and obligations to the requirement of good faith.
- It is governed by what is agreed by the parties and the legislation in this respect.
- Any matters not governed by the legislation applicable to it or by an agreement between the parties shall be governed by the provisions of civil or mercantile legislation and its general principles.
- The contract is executed in writing, in duplicate. A trial period may be agreed that may not in any event exceed nine months, if the contract term is indefinite.
- In the absence of a written agreement, the labor relation will be defined by the duties the worker carries out.
- Where the senior executive has received specialized professional training at the company's expense for a certain period of time, it may be agreed that the employer is entitled to damages if the employee leaves the job before the term established.
- The senior executive may not enter into other contracts with other companies, in the absence of the employer's authorization or a written agreement to the contrary.
- The term of the noncompetition agreement after the termination of the contract may not exceed two years, and is valid only if the following requirements are met:
  - The employer has an effective industrial or commercial interest in it.
  - Adequate compensation is paid to the senior executive.
- Notification of these contracts must be made to the workers' legal representatives.
- The contract may be terminated at the request of either of the parties, in which case three months' advance notice must be given. If the termination occurs due to the employer's withdrawal from the contract, the worker will be entitled to the indemnity agreed in the contract. In the absence of an agreement, the indemnity will be equal to seven days' pay per year of service, up to a limit of six months' pay.
- If the dismissal is declared unjustified, the amounts agreed in the contract will be observed. In the absence of such agreement the indemnity will be 20 days' pay per year of service up to a maximum of 12 months' pay.
- The remuneration of these personnel enjoys the salary guarantees established by the Wage Guarantee Fund and the rules on the settlement and

payment of salaries established apply to it. The amount equivalent to the national minimum wage may not be attached.

Wages and Benefits

The salary is the total compensation received by workers, in cash or in kind, for the professional provision of their labor services, whether reflecting actual work, irrespective of the form of remuneration, in cash or in kind, or the rest periods that may be taken into account as work.

The structure of the salary is established by collective bargaining or by the individual contract and must include the basic salary and additional salary payments.

The salary taken altogether and calculated overall, that is, with all its complements, may in no case be lower than that provided in the reference collective bargaining agreements applicable to the company (for example, the metal agreement for the Madrid Community) though it can be improved by the employer by means of different mechanisms: higher fixed salary, variable salary depending on targets, salary in kind (company car, restaurant vouchers), improved benefits (private health insurance), and so on.

Collective Agreements

Collective bargaining agreements have the binding force of law and establish a minimum, which the employee may not waive.

Under interprofessional agreements or collective bargaining agreements, the most representative trade unions and employer associations at the national or autonomous community levels may establish the structure for collective negotiation, as well as the procedure for the settlement of dispute in events of conflict between collective agreements of different scopes of application.

In this respect, collective bargaining agreements are binding on all employers and workers included within their scope of application, for their entire term of effectiveness, in important aspects such as working time, shift work, remuneration system, working system and yield, paid and unpaid leaves of absence, vacations, and so on. Thus, they may be changed only by reaching agreement with the workers' legal representative, or failing this, with the workers affected—but the conditions established by a bargaining agreement may never be worsened.

In practical effect, collective agreements are actually "laws" that govern the day-to-day contractual affairs in the provision of professional services between workers and employers.

In general terms, there is always an applicable collective agreement. Which one will apply depends on the company's activity and its territorial scope (e.g., a metal industry in Madrid will have to apply precisely the existing collective agreement for the metal industry in Madrid, unless the company decides to negotiate a collective agreement at company level).

Labor Unions

Labor unions have constitutional recognition under the Spanish Constitution (Article 28.1). They are essential to the functioning and understanding of Spanish labor law.

Labor unions seek to defend and improve the working conditions of its members or, to use the common expression, the collective promotion of workers.

The unions' basic and most important function may be defined as compensating for the power of the employer by producing, in agreement with it, a set of legal-labor provisions in the form of collective bargaining agreements, which is therefore a legislative power.

Union presence in companies consists of the Workers' Committees, elected by and from company's employees, and the union sections, which are officers designated by the union from the company's employees.

The capacities of these union bodies in the company could be classified as (1) negotiating authorities, (2) information and/or consultation authorities, (3) surveillance and control authorities, and (4) other authorities and powers.

The great importance of the trade unions in Spanish labor law should be stressed as they act as valid and legitimate counterpart to the employer in the adoption by the employers of all manner of measures of employment or affecting the contractual relation that always exists between the employer and the worker, such as

- Massive layoffs (redundancy procedures);
- Negotiation of collective bargaining agreements, both those applicable at the company level and those of a business or professional sector scope;
- Temporary and/or final postings of workforces;
- Strikes and temporary suspensions of employment contracts (lockouts); and
- Any other measure that may materially affect the contractual relations existing within the performance or provision of professional services by the employer.

Works Councils

Mandatory Requirements

The Workers' Committee is the body representing the group of workers in the company or workplace, for the defense of their interests. It can be organized in each work center with 50 or more workers. Workplaces having from 10 to 50 workers will instead be represented by a certain number of workers' representatives.

Although usually this body is responsible for one workplace, the organization and operation of an inter-workplace Workers' Committee is possible, but only when it is agreed by a collective agreement, with a maximum of 13 members who must be designated from among the members of such workplace committees.

The number of members of the Workers' Committee is established according to the number of workers of the workplace in question, and may have from five members (workplaces having from 50 to 100 workers) to 75 members (for workplaces having more than 1,000 workers).

The workers who become members of the Workers' Committee are elected through trade union elections, which may be promoted by the most representative trade unions, by those having at least 10 percent of the representatives in the company, or by a majority of the workers of the workplace in question. In any of the above events, the promoters of the elections shall inform the company and the public office attached to the labor authorities of their intention to hold the elections at least one month in advance of the commencement of the process.

Functions and Frequency

Once the Workers' Committee has been organized or the personnel representatives have been elected, the members of the committee or the representatives, as appropriate, hold office for four years, and remain in office until new elections are promoted and held.

The main duties and powers of the Workers' Committee are as follows:

- To receive quarterly information on the general evolution of the economic sector of the company and of the evolution of the situation of the company;
- To receive the basic copy of the agreements that must be remitted to it, and of their extensions and notices for their termination, within 10 days after they are made;
- To know the balance sheet, the statement of income, the notes to the financial statements, and, if appropriate, any other documents made known to the shareholders of the company, on the same terms and conditions as they are made known to the shareholders;
- To issue a report prior to the implementation by the employer of its decisions on matters such as reorganizations of payroll and complete or partial removals, reductions of working time and total or partial relocation of the facilities, company professional training plans, implementation or review of work control and organization systems, time studies, implementation of premium or incentive systems and assessment of posts of work;
- To issue a report if a merger, consolidation, or change of the legal status of the company implies a reduction in the volume of employment;
- To know the forms of written employment contract that are used in the company, and of the documents used for the termination of contracts;
- To be informed of any penalties imposed for gross infringements;
- To know, on a quarterly basis at least, the statistics on the absenteeism ratio and its causes, industrial accidents and occupational disease and their consequences, the industrial accident ratios, the regular or special reports on the labor environment and the prevention mechanisms used;
- To monitor compliance with the labor, social security, and employment provisions in force, taking any appropriate legal action;
- To cooperate with management in the implementation of such measures as may maintain and increase productivity, in compliance with the collective bargaining agreements; and

- To inform its constituents of the above matters where these have or may have consequences on the employment relationships.

Note also that Article 68 of the Worker's Statute grants a series of safeguards to workers who are workers' representatives, specifically: (1) to initiate an adversary proceeding in the case of penalties for serious or gross infringements; (2) priority to remain in the company or workplace over the rest of the workers in events of suspension or termination on technological or economic grounds; (3) not to be dismissed or penalized for their acts in the discharge of their representative duties; and (4) to be granted a certain number of paid monthly hours to discharge their representative duties.

Once the Workers' Committee has been organized, it will act with absolute independence from the trade unions to which its members are parties. Nevertheless, it is customary practice for the Committee to receive advice from the trade unions, which may even play active roles in certain situations such as layoffs.

SECTION II

My client is acquiring an existing business in Spain. How do I assess the existing workforce and consider changes?

Initial Assessments

It will first of all be necessary to assess the situation of the managers of the company, specifically the special contractual conditions tying them to the company, for the purpose of being able to assess their change of conditions or even termination of their contracts with the company (these aspects will be dealt with in further detail later).

Second, and prior to transfer of companies, it will be necessary to analyze the type of conditions, both collective and individual, governing in the Spanish company, so as to be able to determine the impact (fixed and variable costs) which that operation implicitly entails.

In this regard, it is a good idea to analyze (1) the collective bargaining agreement that is the object of application in the Spanish company (if it is a company agreement, or a sector agreement at the state level, or even if there are various sector agreements at the provincial or autonomous community level due to the fact that the company has plants or offices in various regions); (2) the existence of collective specific agreements for certain matters that would improve the conditions of the agreement regarding topics as important as salaries, working hours, working day, vacations, and so on (both with a particular group of workers and with all the employees of the company); and (3) the existence of special contractual conditions with certain workers, agreed on an individual basis, that would affect questions as important as salary, working hours and day, and so on.

Having assessed all these questions, one may find a duplication of jobs as a result of the existence of synergies of the market/sector where the company operates (as a consequence of the transfer). Or, it may appear that the company could substantially alter the work conditions of the employees of the Spanish company, with the aim of improving its competitive situation on the Spanish market by means of a better reorganization of its resources. In that case, there exist different procedures existing in Spanish labor legislation to carry out those changes.

Share Deals Versus Asset Deals

Under Spanish law, the mere acquisition of shares in a company does not imply a transfer of undertaking for labor purposes, mainly because the person in the position of the employer remains unchanged. In other words, even if the shareholders or owners change, the company does not change its legal status. Thus, the acquisition of shares does not in itself imply a change of employer and does not have direct consequences on the employment relationships.

However, where the company itself is acquired, including the entire business and the activity (for example, a merger), the legal transaction implies a change in the person of the employer, which necessarily has consequences on the employment relationships.

In this second case, legislation establishes that the change of owner of a company, workplace, or independent production unit will not in itself terminate the employment relationship and that the new employer will be subrogated to the former employer in its previous labor and social security rights and obligations, including pension undertakings, on the terms of specifically applicable legislation and, in general, such supplementary employee welfare obligations as may have been acquired by the transferor (Article 4 of the Spanish Workers' Statute).

For labor purposes, a transfer of undertaking is any transfer over an economic entity that maintains its identity, meaning a set of organized means to carry out an economic, essential, or ancillary activity.

In the event of a transfer of undertaking, both the transferor and the transferee should inform the workers' legal representatives affected by the change, in writing, of the following facts:

- Intended date of transfer;
- Reasons for the transfer;
- Legal, economic, and social consequences of the transfer for the workers; and
- Measures it intends to implement in respect of the workers.

Such information shall be made available sufficiently in advance of the date of the transfer to enable the workers to negotiate or establish the labor conditions of the transfer. Although no specific term is established, 15 days will normally suffice. However, contesting the transfer (should the Workers' Committee so decide) will not stop or suspend the transaction.

In addition, the transfer should be reported to the social security office by filing Form TA-8, signed by both companies, the transferor and the transferee.

The following should be attached to Form TA-8:

- List of the names of all the workers who are transferred, including their tax and social security identification numbers;

- Description of the powers of the person signing the form as the representative of the transferor;
- Document evidencing the representative powers of the person acting on behalf of the workers' representatives (notice signed by the Workers' Committee);
- Description of the powers of the person signing the form as the representative of the transferee company, together with a certified photocopy of his or her National Identity Document; and
- Documents evidencing the commercial transaction from which the transfer of undertaking originates (business lease agreement).

In addition, the transferor must send an individual notice to each of the workers informing them that the system of the transfer of undertaking will apply and that the workers' rights and obligations will be maintained. It is also advisable to report the transfer of undertaking to the National Employment Institute where the contracts of the workers who will be transferred were registered.

Legislation establishes that, unless otherwise agreed, after the transfer of undertaking has been completed under a company agreement between the transferee and the workers' representatives, the employment relationships of the workers involved in the transfer will continue to be governed by the collective bargaining agreement applicable in the transferred company, workplace, or independent business unit. It will continue to apply until its expiry or until another, new collective bargaining agreement applicable to the transferred economic entity is effective.

The procedure established by legislation for transfers of undertaking are explained in more detail in Section III, referring to the transfer (sale) of the company.

Carrying Out a Workforce Reduction

The reduction of personnel should be arranged legally, by means of a collective dismissal or by individual elimination of the jobs sought to be reduced—even if it were as a group, as we will see. In any event, it is not a matter of free choice, as will be explained next.

The transfer, by itself, cannot constitute the basis for the dismissal; there must be economic, technical, organizational, or production reasons that could justify the transfer.

Collective layoff means the termination of labor contracts based on economic, technical, organizational, and production-related reasons, when in a period of 90 days, the termination affects at least

- 10 workers in companies that employ fewer than 100 workers.
- 30 workers in companies that employ 300 or more workers.
- 10 percent of the workers in companies that employ between 100 and 300 workers.

The above-mentioned reasons will be deemed to exist where the adoption of the proposed measures contributes, if economic reasons are considered, to overcoming the company's negative economic situation—or, if they are technical, organizational, or production-related reasons, to guaranteeing the future viability of the company and of employment in it through a more suitable organization of resources.

Termination by Elimination of the Job

The formal requirements that must be observed in a termination of a contract due to the elimination of the job are as follows:

- Written notification to the worker stating the reason for terminating his or her contract (economic, technical, organizational, or production-related);
- An indemnity to the worker of 20 days' salary per year of service, dividing pro rata by months the periods of time below one year, with a maximum of 12 months' salary; and
- Advance notice of 30 days, calculated from the delivery of the written notification until the actual termination of the labor contract. If this prior notice period is not observed, the employer will pay financial compensation, in full or pro rata to the period for which prior notice is not given. A copy of the prior written notice will be given to the workers' legal representatives.[1]

Collective Layoff Procedure

The essential characteristics of this procedure, provided in Article 51 of the current Workers' Statute and of Royal Decree 43/1996, of January 19, 1996, are as follows: The employer must negotiate the appropriateness of the terminations of the contracts and the terms applicable, with the workers' legal representatives (Workers' Committee, personnel delegates) or, if there are no representatives, with the workers themselves. In addition, the authorization of the competent labor authority must be obtained.

The minimum statutory indemnity is 20 days' salary per year of service, subject to a maximum of 12 months' salary. There is no maximum statutory indemnity, but rather the final amount will be the subject of negotiation between the employer and the workers' representatives.

Changing the Wage and Benefits Structure

Throughout the duration of the labor relation, circumstances may give rise to modifications in the terms of the contract relating to functional mobility, geographical mobility, or substantial modifications of the terms of employment.

Functional Mobility

Functional mobility refers to a job change within the same professional group, between different professional groups or professional categories, or a change of duties not agreed or included in the previous points.

Geographical Mobility

Geographical mobility is the transfer or posting of the worker to another workplace, in a different city, which involves a change of residence by the worker. A transfer occurs where the worker (who has not been specifically hired to render services in companies with mobile or itinerant workplaces) is allocated to a different workplace of the same company that requires changes of residence on a definitive basis, or when a posting exceeds 12 months in a period of three years.

Transfers must be for economic, technical, organizational, or production-related reasons. Companies may temporarily post their workers for these reasons, or due to hiring relating to the business activity, to other workplaces that require residence in a town other than that of their habitual residence, provided that this period is less than 12 months in the course of three years.

Substantial Modifications of the Terms of Employment

The management of the company, when there are proven economic, technical, organizational, or production-related reasons, may initiate a procedure to approve substantial modifications of the terms of employment. The measure must follow a collective or an individual procedure similar to that for the collective dismissal.

Modifications affecting the following subjects, inter alia, will be considered substantial modifications of the terms of employment:

- Working hours
- Timetable
- Shift-work system
- Remuneration systems
- System of work and output
- Duties, where they go beyond the limits of functional mobility

Economic, technical, organizational, or production-related reasons will be deemed to exist where the adoption of the proposed measures contributes to improving the company's situation through a better organization of its resources, to favoring its competitive position in the market, or to improving its response to demand.

Individual termination decisions are fundamentally tied to the terminations of job contracts, given that there exist many situations in which, both for reasons of confidence and due to the requirements of the absorbing company, the latter places its own people in certain jobs, with changes being carried out at all levels of the company.

Consulting with Labor Unions, Works Councils, and Government

The company's consulting or information obligations when carrying out the aforementioned modifications are as follows:

- In the case of functional mobility, no information need be provided to the workers' representatives or to any other body or entity.

- In the case of geographic mobility, three different events may exist:
  - ○ Temporary postings do not need to meet any information or consultation requirement;
  - ○ Individual postings require mere communication of the decision to the workers' representatives;
  - ○ Collective postings require a period of at least 15 days of consultations with the workers' representatives. The company may implement the decision even if no agreement is reached with the workers' representatives, although they may subsequently contest the decision.
- Material modification of the working conditions, on the terms explained in the above section, has the same legal treatment as a posting, so that the decision will merely have to be communicated to the workers' representatives, if the modification is individual, but a consultation period of at least 15 days will be required in the case of collective modifications.

No communication or consultation to any administrative or governmental body is required in any of the above events.

SECTION III

My client wishes to sell its existing facility. What restrictions do we need to consider?

Legal Regime of the Succession of Employer

In the light of labor law, any legal transaction that implies the transfer of business, tangible and intangible assets, and personnel of a company or part of it to another that will continue the transferred business is apt to be considered an event of "succession of employer" under Article 44 of the Workers' Statute.

If the transfer may be statutorily classified as an event falling within the scope of Article 44 of the Workers' Statute, a series of major legal labor consequences would arise, among which are the following:

- Enforceability of the transfer;
- Legal subrogation of the new employer to the rights and obligations of the transferred workers in effect at the date of transfer; and
- Joint and several liabilities for labor obligations.

Requirements to Apply the Subrogation Contemplated in Article 44 of the Workers' Statute

The statutory event requires two essential requirements to be met:

Subjective: Change of owner of the company, workplace, or independent production unit, from the former employer (assignor) to the new employer (assignee). The type of transaction used for the transfer is irrelevant (assignment, contribution of business or business unit, purchase and sale, etc.).

Objective: Actual delivery of the set of essential operating factors of the employer, permitting the continuation of the business activity. These factors should conform to the company as a whole, or to its workplace, or to an independent production unit of the company.

In addition to these two requirements, it will be necessary for the transaction not to be performed for fraudulent purposes to the detriment of the rights of the workers.

Article 44 authorizes three types of succession of employer:

1. Of the company as a whole.
2. Of a workplace.
3. Of an independent production unit (IPU).

The company and the workplace, as units to be transferred, in general give rise to no problems of interpretation to establish whether or not a succession of employer has occurred.

Nevertheless, the definition of the term "independent production unit" has given rise to major difficulties in those cases where the production unit in question is not clear, and to a certain extent is mingled with the business as a whole and the means and organization of the company are globally considered.

In principle, the IPU should comply with the definition given in Article 44 of the Workers' Statute of the term "employer" for the purposes of succession: "an economic entity that should maintain its identity, understood as a set of organized means to perform an essential or ancillary economic business."

Labor Effects and Consequences of the Succession of Employer

- *Enforceability of the transfer:* The effects of succession are imposed on all the parties in the transaction (assignor, assignee, and workers) by legal imperative. Consent from the worker is not required for the transfer.
- *Legal subrogation of the new employer to the rights and obligations in effect for the transferred workers at the date of the transfer:* The assignee is under the legal obligation to observe both the individual and the collective working conditions in effect in the assignor company for the transferred workers (length of service, professional category, salary, working hours, nonsalary accruals, working system, etc.).
- *Applicable collective bargaining agreement:* The collective agreement that applied in the company, workplace, or independent production unit transferred will continue to apply until it expires or a new one comes into force.
- *Situation of the workers' representatives after the succession:* The mandate of the legal representatives elected in the transferring company will be maintained only when the scope of their representation (the workers that elected them) is fully maintained. For example: transfer of the entire workplace or company. If only some of the workers are transferred and these are included in the workplace of an assignee that has its own representatives, the representatives transferred forfeit their status as such. If, as a

result of the succession, the assignee increases the number of workers but does not have the number of representatives as required by Article 66 of the Workers' Statute (which sets forth minimum numbers of representatives based on the number of workers), then the employees may propose that an election of representatives be held.

Formal Obligations of the Succession of Employer

Notification and Information to the Workers' Representatives

The assignor and the assignee should inform the legal representatives of their respective workers who are subject to the change of owner of the following circumstances:

- Intended date of transfer;
- Reasons for the transfer;
- Legal, economic, and social consequences of the transfer for the workers; and
- Forecast measures in respect of the workers.

Harmonizing Management Measures

The company (assignee and assignor) should decide whether or not to adopt management measures affecting the manner in which the workers were providing their work.

These measures may be of many different kinds (material changes, collective dismissals, etc.) and it must be established whether any changes are due to the transfer or otherwise, since Article 44.9 contemplates a specific consultations procedure for measures adopted due to the succession.

These criteria should be interpreted prudently and in accordance with the principle of good faith, taking into consideration in each event the protection sought by the provision and the reasonable connection with or independence from the change of employer.

Possible measures to be adopted due to the transfer:

- *Material changes of the working conditions:* Transfers, working hours, timetable, shift system, remuneration system, work system, yield, and duties, among others. The procedure information and consultation to implement these measures should comply with the specific formalities contemplated in Articles 40.2 and 41.4 of the Workers' Statute.
- *Other statutorily classified measures:* When provisions exist that are applicable to other measures (such as collective dismissals or suspensions of contract for economic causes) and these expressly contemplate an information and consultation procedure, this procedure should be adopted, despite the fact that Article 44.9 of the Workers' Statute has not provided this expressly.

- *Nonspecific measures:* Doubts may arise when employer decisions may affect the manner in which the work is provided and do not fall within the two above categories, such as adaptations of professional profiles, new engagements, application of guidelines to be followed with the clientele, uniformity, ethical codes, use of computer means, and nonmaterial amendments.

These decisions in ordinary circumstances could be made (1) by the employer alone (because of its management authority) on occasions without need for any formality, (2) by the employer with notification to the workers' representatives (for example, for plans to make new contracts; Article 64.1.1 of the Workers' Statute), and (3) by the employer after requesting a report from the Workers' Committee (for example, to establish professional training plans or to implement a work control system; Article 64.1.4 of the Workers' Statute).

Article 44 of the Workers' Statute, which seeks to increase the ordinary guarantees, attempts to reinforce the protection afforded to the workers affected by the subjective novation of employer. The executive powers of the employer are restricted or conditioned in this case, so that decisions that may be adopted at the employer's discretion in ordinary circumstances are subject to the participating procedure described previously.

SECTION IV

My client wishes to replace its senior manager(s). What restrictions do we need to consider?

One of the most particular features of the legislation governing senior management personnel is the wide margin of freedom allowed to the parties. Rights and obligations pertaining to the employment relation will be governed by the will of the parties, subject to the provisions of the Royal Decree.

The termination process demonstrates clearly these freedoms to self regulate. The Royal Decree for senior management personnel, unless agreed otherwise in the contract, places senior management in an inferior position as compared with ordinary workers. Unilateral termination of senior management without cause gives rise to an economic cost of seven days of salary per year worked, up to the maximum limit of six months of salary. In contrast, ordinary employees may receive 45 days per year worked, up to a maximum of 42 months of salary in the event of dismissal declared to be unfair, for objective or disciplinary causes.

As a result, when the legislation governing senior management personnel came into force, the majority trend was to include in employment contracts clauses stipulating a higher indemnification than that established by law. The term *blindado* ("golden parachute") applied to the commitment to pay a higher economic compensation in any event of unilateral termination by the employer (except for fair dismissal) or resignation by the executive for cause.

However, agreements containing golden parachute clauses, in Spanish business practice, establish indemnification not only higher than that of the Royal Decree but also higher than that established by the Workers' Statute for unfair dismissal.

One of the main issues that is discussed during negotiations to engage senior management personnel is regarding these clauses, not only in the event of unfair dismissal (exceeding 20 days of salary in cash per year of work) but also for unilateral termination by the employer, and resignation by the top executive for cause.

Statutory Severance Pay Requirements

In this section we analyze the formal dismissal procedure that must be adopted by the employer when dismissal is unjustified, that is, in which there is an obligation to pay indemnity to the worker as a result of the employer's unilateral termination.

When the dismissal is declared unjustified, the employer, within five days from the notification of the judgment declaring such lack of justification, may opt either to reinstate the worker, paying the salaries for the duration of the proceedings (the worker's salary for the days between the date of dismissal and the date of notification of the judgment), or to pay the following sums (which must be established in the judgment):

1. Indemnity of 45 days' salary per year of service, periods of less than one year being divided proportionally according to months, up to a maximum of 42 months' salary.

2. An amount equal to the sum of the salaries not received from the date of dismissal until notification of the judgment declaring it unjustified, or until the employee finds other employment, if such placement was prior to such judgment and the employer proves what was received, in order for it to be deducted from the salaries for the duration of the proceedings.

Statutory Restrictions on Dismissal Without Cause

In Spain, there is no employment at will. Hence, dismissals must be based on cause.

The absence or insufficiency of cause is considered as an unfair dismissal, with few exceptions related mainly to discrimination or pregnancy. In general, the effect of a dismissal without reason in Spain is that the employer must pay to the worker indemnity of 45 days' salary per year of service, subject to the limit of 42 months' salary.

Other formalities are necessary, since otherwise a dismissal could be classified as void, the reinstatement of the worker at the company being mandatory.

Thus, the dismissal must be put in writing to the worker, stating the facts justifying the dismissal and the date on which it will take effect.

Other formal requirements for the dismissal may be established by collective labor agreement.

A dismissal that is motivated by any of the causes of discrimination forbidden by the Constitution or by law, or that violates the fundamental rights and public liberties of the worker, will be void.

A dismissal will also be void in the following cases:

- That of workers during the period of suspension of the contract due to maternity, paternity, risk during pregnancy, adoption, or fostering, or that of workers who were notified on such a date that the prior notice period ends within such period.
- That of pregnant workers, from commencement of the pregnancy until commencement of maternity leave, and that of workers who have requested reduction of the working day for nursing infants or have requested leave of absence to care for children.
- That of female workers who are victims of domestic violence and have exercised their rights to change their working time, geographic mobility, or workplace, or to suspend the employment relationship.
- That of workers after being reinstated in their post of work on expiry of the periods of suspension of contract for maternity, adoption, fostering, or paternity leaves, provided that not more than nine months have elapsed from the date of birth or adoption of the child.

The terms of the previous paragraphs will apply unless the dismissal is declared to be justified by reasons not related to the pregnancy or to the exercise of the right to the leave.

If the dismissal is declared void, the worker will be immediately reinstated.

Following the provisions of the Workers' Statute, the labor contract may be terminated by decision of the employer, through a dismissal based on a serious and culpable breach of the worker. The following are considered breaches of contract:

- Repeated unjustified absenteeism or lack of punctuality;
- Insubordination or disobedience at work;
- Physical or verbal abuse of the employer, fellow employees, or family members who live with them;
- Breach of contractual good faith or abuse of trust in the performance of the work;
- Willful and continuous diminution in normal or agreed job productivity;
- Habitual drug or alcohol abuse that adversely affects job performance; and
- Harassment due to racial or ethnic origin, religion or convictions, disability, age, or sexual orientation of the employer or of persons who work in the company.

❸ SECTION V

What prohibitions exist against discrimination on the basis of age, race, gender, disability, pregnancy, and other factors? What are the rights of employees, applicants, or former employees who believe that they have been discriminated against?

Areas of Protection

Prohibited discrimination is defined as follows:

- Any distinction, exclusion, or preference based on race, color, gender, religion, political opinion, or national or social origin that has the effect of annulling or altering the equality of opportunities or of work, employment, and occupation;
- Any other distinction, exclusion, or preference having the effect of annulling or altering equality of opportunities or treatment in access to employment or occupation, along with any distinction that is not objectively justified by the employer, among groups or employees who perform the same professional duties within a company (for example, giving more vacations to one worker than to another who performs the same job with the same length of service and salary and contractual conditions).

Likewise, Article 17 of the Workers' Statute provides that "provisions or regulations, clauses of collective labor agreements, individual agreements, and unilateral decisions of the employer that contain unfavorable discrimination due to age or when they contain favorable or adverse discrimination in employment, as well as in remuneration, working hours, and all other terms of employment based on gender, origin, marital status, race, social status, religious or political ideas, membership or nonmembership of trade unions and adhesion to their agreements, kinship to other workers of the company, and language within the Spanish State shall be deemed to be void and without effect."

The antidiscriminatory rule applies both at the precontractual or employment stage and during the performance of the contract by the worker already employed. Thus, discrimination is unlawful

- Before the labor contract comes into existence; and
- During the course of the labor relation once employed, using the terminology of Article 42(c) of the Workers' Statute.

Both times are clearly defined in Article 3 of European Directive No. 2000/78, referring on the one hand to "conditions for access to employment, including selection criteria and recruitment conditions," and on the other hand to "employment and working conditions, including dismissals and pay." The discrimination may have its source in provisions of regulations, clauses of collective labor agreements, individual agreements, and employer's decisions.

Sanctions and Remedies

If the worker provides evidence to the competent labor court of the existence of discriminatory conduct by the employer, the remedies against such discriminatory act would consist of

- The declaration of nullity of the discriminatory decision and the discontinuance of any practice of this kind;

- Indemnity for the damage caused, in accordance essentially with the rules of precontractual liability; and
- The restoration of the situation at the time prior to the occurrence of such discrimination.

SECTION VI

On the Horizon: What key labor and employment law developments should an employer doing business in Spain anticipate occurring in the coming years?

In general the following could be mentioned:

- Greater flexibility in the Spanish system of collective bargaining, which provides greater discretion for the parties when negotiating the rules under which the obligations and rights both of the worker and of the employer, will be developed.
- The establishment in labor law of full specific legislation regarding cases of mobbing or psychological harassment, in order to avoid the deprival of both workers and employers of the right to defend themselves.

Finally, we provide the address of various Web pages that deal with the regulation of labor law in Spain and that may be of great assistance to any lawyer specializing in labor matters in any other country:

- http://www.westlaw.es
- http://www.aranzadi.es

We also draw attention to the following handbooks:

- Alfredo Montoya Melgar, *Manual del Derecho del Trabajo*
- Manuel Alonso Olea and María Emilia Casas Baamonde, *Manual del Derecho del Trabajo.*
- *Guía Laboral y de Asuntos Sociales,* published annually by the Ministry for Labor and Social Affairs.

NOTE

1. The majority of case law considers that when the Workers' Statute refers to the prior written notice, in reality it is referring to the written notice of termination itself, since the prior notice is a period that may or may not exist as it may be replaced by payment of the relevant salaries. In the end, the purpose of the rule is simply to allow control by the workers' representatives of the number and reasons for terminations performed for those reasons, which is possible only by being aware of the content of the written notice of termination itself.

An employer's breach of this requirement would involve the declaration of the termination as unjustified, and not as void.

CHAPTER 17

LABOR AND EMPLOYMENT LAW IN SWEDEN

OLLE JANSSON

Preliminary remarks: Sweden's long-standing tradition of strong labor unions dates to the beginning of the last century. Two nationwide agreements between employers and unions were entered into. The employers accepted employee unionism and unions accepted employer prerogatives. Collective bargaining and regulation of employment conditions through collective agreements were recognized. The right to resort to industrial action was accepted and a negotiating system was laid down to solve legal disputes and differences in interpretation of collective agreements. In order to reduce industrial conflicts without intervention by the legislators, the parties took responsibility for defining illegal strike actions. Even more important than the formal responsibilities of the parties was their willingness to cooperate and discuss different solutions to problems. The parties recognized that they shared a common responsibility toward society and assumed responsibility for the undisturbed functionality of the labor market. The employers accepted the union's control of the supply side of the employment force in return for a strong commitment not to resort to industrial action. This marked the coming of age of the Swedish model for industrial relations. Through this agreement the government remained passive and legislation was avoided within the area of employment agreements and collective employment law.

A civil order with no state interference was thus created and is still lasting in many respects, forming the foundation of the Swedish (Nordic) model. Sweden followed suit from Denmark, where a couple of years earlier the social parties agreed on a negotiation order and identified employers' rights.

For decades there was very little development in the legislation.

The legislators' passivity was broken in the 1970s. This change in attitude may be seen in an international perspective. Employees and unions throughout many parts of the world demanded influence on their employers. This was coupled with a growing recognition of the need to protect older workers because this group had difficulties securing employment and thereby income.

Once dismissed, this group tended to stay unemployed for longer periods than younger workers in the same situation. Some feared the development of a two-tier market—especially in the expectation of structural changes—where age would be the dividing factor. The government initiated a number of reforms. The Employment Protection Act for certain employees (older employees) in 1971 was followed by the Employment Protection Act (for all employees) in 1974. A system of compensation for damages was extended rather than introducing severance payments. The 1976 Act on Codetermination at Work is another example of the new regime. Even though employment law nowadays is regulated, there still are many areas not yet subjected to legislation and where the labor market parties have the ability to conclude agreements. Sweden's position in implementing EU directives quite often is to favor labor market solutions rather than resorting to legislation. The current state of affairs is a combination of rules laid down in the legislation and civil law provisions agreed in collective agreements.

✪ SECTION I

My client wishes to establish a manufacturing facility in Sweden and will need to hire a workforce. What are the key issues involved?

Employment Contracts: Who Receives Them and What Must They Include?

Sweden lacks a specific definition of "employee." There is a quite extensive test laid down in case law. The criteria may vary since the assessment is made in light of the general objectives of the individual law at hand. It is further an analysis based on fact. Written contracts and labeling of the relationship is irrelevant. Important features are the following:

- Only natural persons may be employees.
- The acceptance of working for someone has to be voluntary.
- The employee shall perform the work for someone else.
- The employee is subject to instructions and control.
- The employer provides facilities, machines, and tools needed.
- Salary is paid and costs reimbursed.
- The employee may not work for others.
- The party performing work is socially and financially comparable to an employee.

Directors of the board elected by the shareholders are not considered to be employees and thus are not protected by the Employment Protection Act and do not benefit from other employment laws. The same would normally apply to union representatives on the board of directors.

Labor and employment laws apply in general to all employees (as defined previously). However, the following are excluded from the application of the Employment Protection Act and the statutory protection against dismissal:

- Employees whose duties and conditions of employment are such that they may be deemed to occupy a managerial or comparable position (business leaders);
- Employees who are members of the employer's family;
- Employees employed for work in the employer's household; and
- Employees who are employed for work with special employment support, in sheltered employment, or in development employment.

All other managers and other employees are protected by the Employment Protection Act.

Who is deemed to be a business leader depends on the size of the business and the position of the leader. A managing director (in a company limited by shares) will always be regarded as a business leader. In smaller business only the leader is exempted. In midsize companies the exemption is to be applied to the managing director, his or her deputy, and perhaps some employees with specific independent responsibilities. In larger companies the exemption is applicable not only to the managing director but also to division heads.

The contents of employment contracts are, to a great extent, derived from the collective agreements applicable to the particular employer/employee relationship. However, there are still many details that have to be formalized, for example, type of employment. The main rule is that employment is until further notice (i.e., permanent). Limited periods of employment, deputyship, and seasonal work are also common. Employment for a limited period (fixed-term) may also be admissible. Fixed-term contracts may not—unless provided for in the contract—be terminated prior to the expiry of the fixed term unless there is a gross breach of contract.

An employment contract may be oral or in writing. Not later than one month after the commencement of work the employer shall inform the employee, in writing, of the terms and conditions applicable to the employment. The information shall contain:

- Name and addresses of the employer and employee, the commencement date of the employment, and the workplace;
- The employee's duties, occupational designation, or title;
- Whether the employment is for a fixed or indefinite term or whether it is probationary, and
  - With respect to indefinite-term employment, the periods of notice applicable;
  - With respect to fixed-term employment, the final date of employment or the conditions governing its termination and the form of limited employment the employee has;
  - With respect to probationary employment, the length of the probationary period;
- The starting rate of pay, other wage benefits, and the intervals at which payment is to be made;
- The length of the employee's paid annual leave and the length of the employee's normal working day or working week; and
- The collective bargaining agreement applicable, where relevant.

Protection Against Termination

Swedish law contains strong protection against termination in non-reorganization situations. Notice of termination may be given by the employer in two different situations: for personal reasons or because of shortage of work.

Notice of termination by the employer must be based on objective grounds. A termination may be based on either (1) circumstances relating to the employee personally or (2) shortage of work. The two categories are technically separated by the qualification that what is not personal is subsumed under the concept "shortage of work." Objective grounds for notice of termination do not exist where it is reasonable to require the employer to provide other work in its business for the employee. Notice based on circumstances relating to the employee personally must not be based solely on circumstances that were known to the employer for more than two months before notice.

The employer must also follow certain rules on priority when giving notice due to shortage of work. Employees with longer employment shall have priority for continued employment over employees with shorter employment. At a workplace with 10 or fewer employees, the employer may exclude two employees from the list of priority, provided the employer considers them to be of significant importance to the company's further business. The employer's selection of key employees and terminations following this selection may not be tried in court. However, selections and terminations violating any legislation preventing discrimination may be brought to trial. When it is only possible to offer an employee continued work after reassignment to a different position, priority for continued employment shall be given to the employee who has satisfactory qualifications for the remaining job.

An employee who has been terminated because of shortage of work has a right to reinstatement. This right also applies to an employee who has been employed for a fixed term. The right is exercisable from the time of notice of termination until nine months from the date that the employment ended.

Termination of Indefinite-Term Employment: Notice Period

The minimum period of notice for the employer as well as the employee is one month. The employee is entitled to notice of termination of employment of

- Two months, if the aggregate length of the employment with the employer is at least two but less than four years;
- Three months, if the aggregate length of the employment is at least four but less than six years;
- Four months, if the aggregate length of the employment is at least six but less than eight years;
- Five months, if the aggregate length of the employment is at least eight but less than 10 years; or
- Six months, if the aggregate length of the employment is at least 10 years.

An employee is obliged to work and is entitled to retain pay and other employment benefits during the period of notice. Notice periods may vary to the employee's benefit in collective agreements.

Wages and Benefits

Hours

The Working Hours Act is semicompulsory, which means that it may be replaced wholly or partly by collective agreements, as is the case for the majority of private companies. Full-time employment may be a maximum of 40 hours per week. In many agreements the working hours are shorter. For part-time workers, the working hours are regulated in the employment contract. Overtime is limited to 48 hours over a four-week period and no more than 200 hours per year. If more overtime work is needed, the employer must negotiate with the trade union. The Working Hours Act applies to all employees, except for those in managerial positions.

Wages

There are no minimum wages regulated by Swedish law. Wage issues are the responsibility of the labor market parties. Some collective agreements include rules on minimum wages. These rules are usually applied to blue-collar workers.

Vacation

The Annual Leave Act covers all employees. A person employed on August 31 at the latest in an annual leave year (April 1 to March 31) is entitled to five weeks (25 working days) of annual leave that very year, counted in full days. If the employment starts after August 31, the employee is entitled to five days of leave the first year of employment. The employee is also entitled to annual vacation pay. The vacation pay is calculated as 12 percent of the salary paid out during the relevant year. Broadly speaking, salary for work performed is paid for 11 months and vacation pay for a bit more than one month; that is, vacation pay does not come on top of the employee's 12 monthly payments per year. The Annual Leave Act is semicompulsory; it may entirely or partially be replaced by vacation regulations in collective agreement, which is the case in the majority of workplaces.

Freedom of Association

Employees and employers enjoy full freedom of association, and may be members of a collective union. The employee may work to establish a union, belong to such an organization, make use of the membership, and work for the organization. Any violation against an employee's freedom of association is also cause for payment of damages. Employees are thus protected against any kind of discrimination on the basis of union membership.

Labor Unions

Collective Agreements

As a practical matter, the opportunity to conclude collective agreements at the request of the unions will often depend on the size of the business and the relevant industry established. If the establishment is made as a start-up rather than an acquisition it is less likely that a collective agreement will surface.

Unique to Swedish law is a system with semicompulsory provisions (sometimes also labeled as quasi-optional). Semicompulsory provisions may be replaced only by collective agreements, not with agreements in general. Whether or not a provision is semicompulsory is either stated in the law or found in the preparatory works. Some 80 percent of the Swedish working force is unionized and more than 90 percent of Swedish workplaces are under collective bargaining agreements. This fact, together with the inherent nature of semicompulsory provisions, affords the collective agreements a statutory standing and vast reach and coverage within their application field. The belief is that the labor market parties are in a better position to adjust provisions to demands of individual trade or workplaces than the government is. The conclusion is that the stability of the labor market is best ensured through agreements between the labor market parties.

The collective agreement automatically binds the members of the trade union and the employer that is a member of the employer's organization concluding the agreement. A person who is not a member of the trade union usually has no formal rights under the collective agreements and does not receive damages in the event of breach of the collective agreement. However, the employer shall apply the same rules to everyone.

Obligation to Negotiate

The Codetermination Act orders that all important decisions concerning the business shall be subject to consultations (negotiations) with the unions. This as well as all collective rights are vested with the unions and normally with the unions that actually have a collective agreement with the employer. The right of negotiation may be exercised either by an employer's organization or by the individual employer. An individual employee does not have any right to initiate negotiations or take part in a negotiation.

Upon request an employer is always obliged to consult (negotiate) with the union regarding any matter within the framework of the relationship between the employer and a union member who is or has been employed by the employer. The employer has the corresponding right vis-à-vis the union.

The employer is obliged to call for negotiations with the unions regarding all important decisions or changes prior to the decision being made (duty of primary negotiation). This applies inter alia to decisions concerning the extent and forms of operations such as expansion, reorganization, and closedown or reduction of operations, as well as terms of employment. Decisions regarding transfer of undertakings and layoffs due to shortage of work are always subject to consultations as a primary negotiation obligation. In this latter case, if the employer is not bound by collective agreement consultation shall take place with all affected unions.

The negotiations are to be a part of the employer's decision-making process. The employer is obliged to provide necessary information to enable the consultation process to be fruitful. There are several procedural rules and rights for the union designed to promote this interest. The employer is obliged to start the negotiations no later than when the employer has identified different paths of action. The relevant employer to call for negotiations is the employer that will make the decision in question. Normally this will not cause any problems, but in international organizations some concerns may be identified. When a decision-making process is taking place outside the legal entity of the employer, as is often the case when it comes to parent company decisions regarding the business of a subsidiary, the employer is obliged to call for negotiations as soon as it or any of its authorized representatives (such as board directors) becomes aware of the decision-making process. This means, for instance, that if a head office located outside of Sweden plans to close a Swedish subsidiary's facility and a board director of the Swedish subsidiary is participating in or is aware of this decision-making process, that knowledge will be attributed to the Swedish subsidiary and it is thus obliged to initiate negotiations or it will be liable for damages.

The negotiation process as such requires only that the employer and the union exhaust all arguments and points of view before the employer is entitled to make its decision. There is no requirement that the union has to agree to the decision. This is assumed to be the case when checked minutes from the negotiations are at hand. If one party contests this, the other may claim that it has fulfilled its obligation and retire from the negotiations. Whether or not this party is correct in its determination that there is nothing further to discuss will ultimately be tried by the Labor Court in the light of produced evidence such as minutes (if any), documents exchanged during the negotiations, and oral testimony. For completeness it should be noted that the union always has the right to call for negotiations with the employer in questions concerning the relationship between the employer and the employees.

The collective system provides for its own dispute resolution. Controversies of a legal nature are first to be discussed at the workplace or other local level. If not solved there, the matter may be brought to the parties to the nationwide agreement in question. Only once this latter negotiation has failed will the parties gain access to the Labor Court.

Share transfers are normally not a matter that would trigger any consultation obligations for the target company vis-à-vis its unions. The employer is still the same and normally there is no change at all for the target company as such and its internal relationships and benefits. Formally there are no changes nor decisions made in the subsidiary company when it is being transferred to a new company. However, the selling company as well as the buying company will normally be obliged to consult with the unions they are under collective agreement with. Following closing, the target company quite frequently will end up in a situation where it needs to call for negotiations with the unions. The share transfer may trigger a reorganization within the target and more likely the managing director and other business leaders may resign. The appointment of new business leaders is a matter for consultation if the company is under collective agreement.

An asset transaction will with almost no exceptions be seen as an event that should be taken to consultation with the unions. This will always be the case if the asset transaction qualifies as a transfer of undertaking. In situations of a mere sale of an important asset or machine (and thus not a transfer of an undertaking), both the seller and the buyer are obliged to negotiate provided they are under collective bargaining agreements.

Union Representation

The Union Representative Act is closely linked to the Act on Codetermination at Work. A union representative is a person elected by the union organization to represent the employees. The purpose of the Union Representative Act is to give union representatives enhanced job security. Under the Employment Protection Act, union representatives receive the same security against termination of employment as other employees, but through the Union Representative Act, a union representative is further protected against termination as a result of his or her union work. In the event of shortage of employees the representative also has priority to continue work if the union organization determines that the representative is needed at the workplace.

Board Representation

Employees in private companies with an average of at least 25 employees employed during the most recent fiscal year have the right to be represented on the board of directors by two directors (union representatives) and two deputy directors. If the company is operating in different trades and during the most recent fiscal year has employed on an average at least 1,000 employees, the employees are entitled to three seats on the board with the same number of deputy directors. The object is to afford employees information about and influence over the company's activities through representation on the board of directors. The employee representatives have the same rights and obligations as directors appointed by the shareholder(s). They are not, however, permitted to participate in matters regarding the relationship between employees and employers. The employee representatives on the board—as well as the directors elected by the shareholders—have a supervisory role. The one restriction for the employee representatives is that they are under law not allowed to participate in matters relating to collective bargaining agreements, industrial actions, or other matters where a trade union at the workplace has a significant interest that may conflict with the company's interest.

❷ SECTION II

My client is acquiring an existing business in Sweden. How do I assess the existing workforce and consider changes?

Share Deals Versus Asset Deals

Share Deals

There will be no effect on any employment-law-related matters when shares are transferred from one owner to another. Nor does the transfer of shares as such trigger any rights to terminate or change or alter conditions for the employees. The change does not trigger any consultation obligations for the target unless provided for to the contrary in local collective agreements.

To the extent the change in ownership affects existing contracts such as group company incentive plans, appointment of new management, and so on, consultations with the unions and renegotiations with the employees may need to take place.

From a practical perspective the due diligence in the presigning or preclosing phase may call for some concern. Although there are no legal requirements for the target to initiate consultation with its unions, it sometimes may choose to do so. Once the employees and the unions become aware of the due diligence investigation, they will be in a position to call for negotiations with the employer and thus influence the process. Sellers and buyers are well advised to take this aspect into consideration.

In a share transaction, standard practice is to have the board directors sign resignation letters and waivers of any claims against the target as a condition precedent to closing. Board members are typically not protected by the employment legislation system or regarded as employees. However, there may be situations where an acting chairperson has a specific contract that may be enforced against the target. This, of course, should be discovered during the due diligence process.

Asset Deals

In an asset transaction, board members, managing directors, and other employees outside the scope of the Employment Protection Act will not transfer to the purchaser.

Whether or not a transfer of assets can be seen as a transfer of undertaking is for the courts to decide. The courts take a comprehensive view on the purchase, and look at all the facts at hand, on the basis of criteria laid down by the European Court of Justice:

- The type of undertaking or business concerned;
- Whether tangible assets are transferred;
- The value of intangible assets at the time of transfer;
- Whether the majority of employees are taken over by the new employer;
- Whether customers are transferred;
- The degree of similarity between activities carried on before and after the transfer; and
- The period, if any, during which those activities are suspended.

Although several cases on this point have been decided, it is difficult to predict whether a specific transaction will be seen as a transfer of undertaking. Some guiding principles may be observed. One central issue is whether the buyer of the company actually will continue the same activity or an activity of the same kind. It is normally not enough that the assignment is taken over, for example, a cleaning business or a restaurant. In some cases it may be enough that the buyer takes over the main part of the staff. In labor-intense businesses this is normally the case. The opposite applies when the business is asset-intense.

If the asset transfer is seen as a transfer of undertaking, the rights and obligations in force at the time of the deal transfer by operation of law to the purchaser, except for pensions paid out by the company. Note that the collective agreements in many situations will also transfer pension rights. Individual employees may refuse to transfer and remain in employment with the seller.

A transfer of undertaking does not, in itself, constitute cause for termination, and dismissals for that reason are banned. The prohibition does not prevent terminations necessary for economic, technical, or organizational reasons. A necessary reduction of the workforce resulting from the transfer should be dealt with by the new employer. Employees transferred to the new employer are entitled to include their previous length of service when redundancies are selected in the combined workforce of existing and transferred employees.

Carrying Out a Workforce Reduction

If a workforce reduction is deemed necessary, the same rules apply whether the acquisition was of shares in the company or of assets regarded as a transfer of undertaking, with the obvious difference that the workforce in an asset transfer will be composed of both the acquirer's own workforce and the target's workforce. In this latter situation the matter could become complicated, especially if the acquirer and the target have different collective agreements or if only one of them has a collective agreement. However, the main principles will apply. Assuming that the reduction of workforce is not related to any employee's personal situation, the employer is free to decide (1) that a reduction shall take place and (2) the extent of the reduction.

Reduction of the workforce will always be a matter that the employer is obliged to bring to consultation with the unions. The employer is not entitled to make any decision prior to the successful conclusion of the negotiations with the unions. On the other hand, the unions have only consultation rights and thus no veto rights. Further, the reasons underlying an employer's decision to reorganize or reduce its workforce may not be tried in a court of law. However, the employer is obliged to follow seniority rules in making individual employees redundant. Small workplaces with 10 or fewer employees are allowed to exclude two employees that according to the employer's discretionary judgment are of specific significance for the continuing business from the termination process. Seniority lists for each and every separate workplace within the employer's business shall be made up. For employers under collective agreement, these lists may also be divided into separate lists for each and every applicable collective agreement area. Notice for termination of the employees is given in order of seniority, terminating the employees with the shortest term of employment prior to those with a longer term of employment. These seniority rules are mandatory and the employer may not deviate from them unless the employer is under a collective agreement allowing this. This means in most situations that the employer on the one hand and the employee with support of either the union or independent lawyers will negotiate individual agreements, giving the employee sometimes quite substantial severance compensation when the employer wants to cherry-pick.

Most collective agreements provide an opportunity for the employer and the union to deviate from the seniority rules. This flexibility is believed to be one of the strengths of the Swedish model in ensuring efficiency in business, as it enables the employer to keep the most valuable employees and at the same time, through the union's collaboration, to protect in particular older and less-qualified employees. The severance agreements are quite often far-reaching, particularly in large corporations. They tend to take a substantial social responsibility in providing for outplacement programs, training opportunities, and financial support for considerable periods of time. Employees terminated have a preference right to reinstatement for nine months after the day the employment expired.

Advance notification to the local county administrative board is required when 25 or more employees are laid off.

Workforce reductions can be speedy and effective and come at a reasonable cost. Under law there are no severance payments and consequently no employer severance cost. Collective agreements normally do not provide severance payments at a cost for the employer. The collective agreements normally provide an assurance solution in which the employer is obliged to pay annual fees to finance a severance pay system for all employees in the company bound by collective agreement.

Reorganizing the Workforce

An employee is obliged to perform all tasks that meet two standards: (1) the work must be part of the core work performed at the employee's place of work and (2) the employee must be qualified to perform these tasks. Stated differently, the principle holds that employees are obliged to perform all tasks covered by the applicable collective agreement.

Even though an employer in the private sector based on case law primarily may order an employee to perform new tasks, it may be restricted due to the individual employment contract. If the employee is hired for a specific job, it is that job the employee is expected to perform. Traditional contract interpretation will be used to resolve disputes concerning work tasks. Precise language may effectively stop individual changes, leaving the employer no other option than to make the employee redundant. The majority of white-collar employees are under contract, with varying language.

The employer is also restricted in transferring an employee to other positions. A Labor Court principle implies that the employer has to have acceptable reasons for a transfer of an employee, even if it is within the scope of the employment.

The employer has to state the reasons for the transfer, and those reasons have to be acceptable.

Changing the Wage and Benefits Structure

The new employer is bound by the terms of employment from the previous employer. Wages, vacations, and other conditions are therefore not subject to change as a consequence of the transfer.

Changes in wage and benefit structure may be feasible if treated as a reorganization matter. Provided that appropriate consultation takes place, the employer may dispose of certain positions and offer new positions at a lower salary. Those not prepared to accept the new positions may be made redundant observing consultation and seniority rules.

Consulting with Labor Unions

See "Labor Unions" in Section I.

Transfer of Collective Agreements

Not only will the individual employment contracts transfer under operation of law when an undertaking is transferred, but also the collective agreement of that business will transfer. Only if the acquiring company already has a valid collective agreement for its operations will the old agreement not transfer. On a personnel level, the terms and conditions of the old employer's collective bargaining agreement will apply for those employees that actually have been transferred up to one year from the transfer. Thereafter the terms of the new employer will apply.

⊕ SECTION III

My client wishes to sell its existing facility. What restrictions do we need to consider?

Assessing Employment Contracts

The key issues of importance to a buyer are the following:

- May key employees walk away in case of change of control?
- Are there fixed-term employment contracts of unexpected lengths? (Under Swedish law a fixed-term contract may not be terminated prior to the expiry of the term except for gross default.)
- Are incentive programs for management reasonable, effective, and in line with what the purchaser wants to achieve with this business for the future?
- Are there consultancy agreements or other agreements with legal entities that in fact are employment agreements?

- Are all pension obligations for current and previous employees and directors accounted for?
- Are all pension promises sufficiently funded and secured?
- Are there any collective agreements on a local level with far-reaching guarantees, restrictions on production intensity, and so on?

Negotiating with the Purchaser: Special Labor Issues

The negotiations with the buyer will, from the seller's perspective, normally be dominated by encouraging the buyer to audit as much as possible of the target and offering the opportunity to complete a full-fledged labor audit. The main objective is to reduce the necessity for far-reaching representations and warranties on the seller's side. The focus should be on creating incentives for key management to remain for a suitable time period after the transfer. Quite frequently a precedent to closing would be that the seller has no knowledge or reason to believe that any of the key management will resign as a consequence of the transfer. Sometimes the seller will assure that there will be no resignations between signing and closing. One intricate part of a negotiation representing the seller occurs when the buyer has specific requirements as to which employees should be part of the transfer. This will sometimes involve creative solutions on how to structure the actual transfer, either on the seller's side in order to transfer only the employees wanted or on the buyer's side transferring parts of the business into separate legal entities that could be effectively reorganized.

Consulting with Labor Unions

See "Labor Unions" in Section I.

🌐 SECTION IV

My client wishes to replace its senior manager(s). What restrictions do we need to consider?

To appoint a leader of a business is a decision of such importance that the employer has to initiate negotiations with the unions under collective agreement. In fact, employers are obliged to call for negotiations with such unions concerning all important changes to the business. Appointing a new leader of the business is an important change. Dismissing a managing director does not require consultation.

Unlike ordinary employees, a business leader is exempted and excluded from protection offered under the Employment Protection Act. (See "Employment Contracts" in Section I.) This means that the employer may terminate the employment contract without any penalties or severances by observing a not unreasonably short period of notice (six months is always acceptable). Due to this legal position, managing director contracts will normally specify personal arrangements and severances. As a standard practice, a managing director would be granted a 6–12 month notice period. A severance equivalent to 6–12 months of salary is sometimes issued as a guarantee payable only if the managing director does not obtain new employment during the same period of time.

To the extent a senior manager is protected under the Employment Protection Act and the dismissal is based on personal grounds, his or her protection may be quite small because of the importance of the position. The notice period has to be observed, the shortcomings evidenced, and a procedure observed. Determining whether or not objective grounds for dismissal exist begins with considering whether the employee was in breach of his or her obligations. Further, either the employee must have realized it was a breach or the employer must have made clear to the employee that the breach was unacceptable. It is a case-by-case assessment on the merits of the individual situation. Variations may occur. Once the employer has decided to terminate the employment, and after union consultations, if required, the employer is obliged to issue a note of its intent to dismiss the employee. This will afford the employee the opportunity to enter into formal negotiations with the employer regarding the intended dismissal. If the employee does not call for such negotiations or the negotiations do not affect the employer's decision, the employer will issue a notice of termination. This notice contains formal requirements, including an explanation of how the employee may take legal action if the employee objects to the dismissal.

The employee is entitled to take the dismissal to court; if the employee asks for reinstatement, the employment will normally not terminate at the expiry of the notice period but will continue in full force with full benefits and right (and duty) to work until the case is ultimately decided. This is obviously quite expensive for the employer, especially for a managerial position, as the legal process can take at least a year and sometimes even longer. Should the court decide that the dismissal was unfair, the employment will continue to be valid but the employer has the option of terminating the employment by paying a fixed severance to the employee. This severance is a fixed amount of 16 monthly salaries for an employment term of less than five years, 24 monthly salaries for an employment term of five to 10 years, and 32 monthly salaries for an employment term of more than 10 years. If the employer is willing to pay this severance, the employee has no means of staying employed. The employee may choose not to ask for reinstatement but only claim damages for loss of income after the expiry of the notice period. If successful in the suit, the employee will be entitled to the severance amounts outlined above, but only up to the difference, if any, between the old salary and the salary of any new employment. Ill health, pregnancy, race, ethnic origin, religious beliefs, sex, and the like will not constitute reasonable grounds for dismissal.

SECTION V

What prohibitions exist against discrimination on the basis of age, race, gender, disability, pregnancy, and other factors? What are the rights of employees, applicants, or former employees who believe that they have been discriminated against?

Gender Discrimination

The starting point of the protection against gender discrimination is a constitution provision found in Chapter 2, Article 16 of the 1974 Instrument of Government, which provides that "No act of law or other statutory instrument may entail discrimination of any citizen on grounds of sex, unless the relevant provision forms part of efforts to bring about equality between men and women or relates to compulsory military service or any corresponding compulsory national service."

Sweden's first legislation on gender discrimination was enacted in 1979. The present Equal Opportunities Act from 1991 was drafted to conform to European Union regulations.

The Swedish labor market is still segregated along gender lines, and women are underrepresented in higher positions. Additionally, jobs typically performed by women are paid less than typical male jobs. Women also earn less than men within the same sphere of business.

The Equal Opportunities Act prohibits sex discrimination in the labor market and requires that all employers, whether in the public or private sector, shall actively promote equal opportunities for men and women in the working environment. All employers with a minimum of 10 employees are required to prepare an annual equal opportunities plan as well as a plan or action for equal pay.

The Equal Opportunities Act prohibits both direct and indirect discrimination. For example, an employer may not place a job seeker or an employee at a disadvantage by applying a practice that appears to be neutral but which in practice is particularly disadvantageous to persons of one sex.

Discriminating against a pregnant woman is always considered as sex discrimination (according to both Swedish law and European Community law). The European Court of Justice has concluded that since only women can be refused employment because of pregnancy, such situations are always considered as cases of sex discrimination. Moreover, if the employer holds that a dismissal of a pregnant woman is based on economic considerations (caused by the pregnancy), the pregnancy as such should be considered as the main reason for the dismissal.

Gender-related and sexual harassment are also banned under the Employment Protection Act. Employers have an obligation to investigate and take action against harassment.

The prohibitions against sex discrimination apply when the employer makes a decision on an employment issue, selects a job seeker for an employment interview, or implements other measures during the employment procedure. The sanctions available under the Act are compensation for damages, invalidity (i.e., a contract shall be invalid to the extent that it prescribes or permits sex discrimination), and/or modification of a contract term or condition.

Some of the provisions in the Equal Opportunities Act, such as the prohibition of sexual harassment, have appeared rather insignificant in practice. It can, for example, be presumed that employees accused of sexual harassment often prefer to cease their employments voluntarily in order to avoid public attention.

Other Discrimination Grounds

In 1999, three new discrimination acts were adopted: the Measures to Counteract Ethnic Discrimination in Working Life Act (1999:130), the Prohibition of Discrimination in Working Life of People with Disability Act (1999:132), and the Prohibition of Discrimination in Working Life because of Sexual Orientation Act (1999:133).

These laws have to be observed by all employers and apply at all workplaces. Employees as well as employment applicants are protected under those acts. Both direct and indirect discrimination are banned. The sanctions available under the discrimination acts are the same as under the Equal Opportunities Act: compensation for damages, invalidity, and/or modification of a contract term or condition.

Since 2002, discrimination of part-time employees and employees whose employment is limited in duration is prohibited. An employer may not treat a part-time employee, or an employee with limited-duration employment, less favorably than a full-time employee. Indirect discrimination is also prohibited.

The Parental Leave Act (1995:584) prohibits unfair treatment of employees in connection with parental leave.

Antidiscrimination Act

The Prohibition of Discrimination Act (2003:307) prohibits discrimination on grounds of sex, ethnic background, disability, or sexual orientation in different areas of society such as employment policy (including employment agencies), social insurance, unemployment insurance, membership of trade union and employer's organizations, starting and running a business, and the professional provision of goods, services, or housing.

Ombudsmen

Four government officials are responsible for supervising the application of the discrimination laws and monitoring compliance. They are the Equal Opportunities Ombudsman, the Ombudsman against Ethnic Discrimination, the Ombudsman against Discrimination because of Sexual Orientation, and the Disability Ombudsman.

The Discrimination Committee

In distinction from many other countries, Sweden does not have any discrimination legislation of a general character. However, the government approved a new Discrimination Act on March 13, 2008, consolidating discrimination grounds in all areas of society. The proposed Act aims at counteracting discrimination and promoting equal rights and opportunities, irrespective of gender, gender identity, ethnic affiliation, religion, disabilities, sexual orientation, or age. The Act should, in principle, cover all areas of society. The government suggests two new grounds of discrimination, namely age and gender identity. Under this Act, the four agencies of ombudsmen will be consolidated into one Ombudsman against Discrimination. The new Act shall, if passed, enter into force on January 1, 2009.

⊕ SECTION VI

On the Horizon: What key labor and employment law developments should an employer doing business in Sweden anticipate occurring in the coming years?

There are no drastic development and changes to expect for the immediate future. Some things may, however, be worth mentioning.

The Swedish Labor Court has so far not recognized the principle of proportionality in industrial action cases. In a recent case, the European Court of Justice upheld the principle when a union activated a blockade against a foreign company posting workers in Sweden with the aim of forcing the foreign company to enter into collective agreement with the Swedish union. This should mean that the principle of proportionality now should be recognized.

A general but slow-moving trend is to reduce protection for older employees, enhancing flexibility on the labor market. Major efforts are made to take issue with misuse of social benefits and obstacles to enter and reenter the labor market.

A premium-based pension plan for white-collar employees will gradually replace the current benefit-based pension plan in the collective sector.

All in all, employers should expect improving conditions on the Swedish labor market, making investment in an already attractive market even more attractive.

CHAPTER 18

LABOR AND EMPLOYMENT LAW
IN SWITZERLAND

UELI SOMMER

SECTION I

My client wishes to establish a manufacturing facility in Switzerland and will need to hire a workforce. What are the key issues involved?

Employment Contracts: Who Receives Them and What Must They Include?

Mandatory Requirements

Under Swiss law, an individual employment contract may be made in writing, orally, or even implicitly. This contract is the cornerstone of the legal relationship between the employer and the employee. Within the bounds of mandatory law, the parties are free to define their rights and obligations as they see fit.

Article 319 *et seq.* of the Swiss Code of Obligations (SCO) (*Schweizerisches Obligationenrecht*) sets out the mandatory, semimandatory, and optional provisions relating to individual employment contracts. There must be no deviation from mandatory provisions (e.g., from the legally binding regulations on the right of termination or on prohibition against competition), either through separate agreement, standard employment contract, or collective agreement (see "Collective Agreements" on page 324) irrespective of whether it is to the employee's benefit or to his detriment. There must be no deviation to the detriment of the employee from semimandatory provisions (e.g., those relating to continued payment of salary following illness or to protection of individual inherent rights) either through separate agreement, standard employment contract, or collective agreement.

In addition, the Labor Act (Federal Act on Industrial, Trade and Commercial Labor, *Bundesgesetz über die Arbeit in Industrie, Gewerbe und Handel*) regulates employee protection in setting out working hours and stipulating special protective provisions for certain groups of employees (e.g., pregnant women). Employers and employees must adhere to the Labor Act, but it does not apply to senior management personnel. Senior management personnel are employees who are allowed to make important decisions that can affect the structure, the course of business, and the development of a business or a part of business.

Various other laws, especially the following federal acts, contain elements that also provide a legal basis for the rights and duties of employers and employees: Codetermination Act (Federal Act on Employees' Right to Information and Codetermination in the Workplace, *Bundesgesetz über die Information und Mitsprache der Arbeitnehmerinnen und Arbeitnehmer in den Betrieben, Mitwirkungsgesetz*), Data Protection Act (Federal Act on Data Protection, *Bundesgesetz über den Datenschutz*), and Equal Opportunities Act (Federal Act on the Equal Treatment of Men and Women, *Bundesgesetz über die Gleichstellung von Frau und Mann*).

Form of the Employment Contract

Employment Contract

An individual employment contract does not normally require a special form. In a few cases the written form is required (e.g., apprenticeship contracts), or expected though not absolutely required (e.g., traveling salesman's contract, subcontracted employment contract). In order to protect the employee, separate agreements (e.g., deviations from statutory notice periods) must be made in written form if they are to be valid. Collective agreements can also stipulate provisions relating to form.

Offer Letter

An offer letter signed by the employer and countersigned by the employee constitutes an employment contract. If a written employment contract is issued thereafter, the offer letter should be expressly rescinded.

Terms and Conditions

The employer may—but does not have to—issue general terms and conditions of employment (e.g., in the form of a staff handbook). In order to make such terms and conditions part of the employment contract, not only must they be stated unequivocally in the contract, but also employees must have had an opportunity to familiarize themselves with the details. Nonstandard provisions do not form part of the contract unless the employee is expressly told about these provisions.

The Labor Act stipulates that industrial businesses must issue internal company regulations. Industrial businesses are deemed to comprise undertakings with fixed installations of a permanent character for the production, processing, or treatment of goods or for the generation, conversion, or transmission of energy, insofar as (1) the work process or organization of work is determined by machines or other technical installations or serial operations and at least six employees are employed for the production, processing, or treatment of goods or for the generation, conversion, or transmission of energy; or (2) the work process or organization of work is substantially determined by automated processes; or (3) there are special hazards to the life or health of the employees. Such regulations must contain provisions on health and safety, accident prevention and, where necessary, on company rules and the conduct of employees within the company.

Required Information

The written form is usually recommended for individual employment contracts, even in cases where the law does not require it. It is also recommended that individual employment contracts include the following elements:

- Date of starting job;
- Function;
- Number of working hours;
- Term of the employment relationship;
- Salary (including bonuses, allowances, and other remuneration);
- Working time;
- Rules on probation and notice periods that deviate from the law;
- Vacations;
- Rules on continued payment of wages when ill or pregnant; and
- Other specific agreements made during contractual negotiations.

With the new Article 330b of the SCO, certain information is required by law. For employment relationships with an indefinite term or with a term of more than a month, the employer has to provide the following information in written form to the employee by one month after the starting date of the job at the latest:

- Names of the contracting parties;
- Starting date of the job;
- The employee's function;
- Salary (including nondiscretionary bonuses, allowances, and other remuneration); and
- Working time per week.

Language

Swiss law contains no rules on the choice of language. However, it needs to be ensured that the employees understand the employment agreement.

Timing Issues

Swiss law does not stipulate any time limits with regard to the conclusion of an employment contract. If a written offer is made in the form of an offer letter, a deadline should be set for acceptance.

Changes to the Terms and Provisions

Changes may be made to an employment contract by mutual agreement, by concluding a contract of alteration, or by termination. If the parties cannot agree, a notice of alteration is required. In a notice of alteration the employer gives the employee the choice of accepting a new contract or leaving the job after a standard notice period. It should be noted that in such a case the relevant provisions relating to right of notice apply (time limits, deadlines, and protection against unfair dismissal).

If the existing employment relationship continues in the meantime with different terms and conditions, this does not constitute a new employment relationship. It is simply the old relationship with new conditions.

Fixed-Term Employment

A fixed-term employment contract requires that a fixed term be defined. The contract ends when the agreed contractual term expires. No notice is required.

This contract may be terminated before the end of the fixed term only if there are exceptional reasons for doing so (e.g., summary dismissal for compelling reasons). If a fixed-term employment relationship is tacitly continued after the expiration of the agreed period, it is deemed to be an employment relationship for an indefinite period of time.

Under Swiss law it is possible to combine a fixed-term employment contract with a notice period.

A "chain contract," where a fixed-term contract is extended several times in order to evade statutory notice regulations (to the detriment of the employee), is deemed to be a circumvention of the law and the fixed-term contract shall consequently be treated as an indefinite-term employment. In this case, it can be terminated according to the rules that are applicable for indefinite-term employment (see "Carrying Out a Workforce Reduction" in Section II).

Wages and Benefits

Minimum Wage Requirements

There is no official minimum wage in Switzerland. However, a defined minimum wage is often a feature of collective and standard employment contracts. Wages paid by foreign employers to employees posted in Switzerland must comply with minimum wage requirements. In the case of foreign employees without Swiss residency, compliance with minimum wage requirements is checked when work permits are issued.

If the parties have not agreed on a wage, the employer must pay the usual wage paid in the same or similar industries in the same place. The law establishes that wages are to be paid at the end of the month, unless a standard or collective agreement stipulates a different date. In practice, payment of an additional month's wage, the so-called "13th-month wage," is often agreed.

Special Benefit Requirements

Ex Gratia Payments

An ex gratia payment is a special payment made on particular occasions or at particular times. It can either be a component of the contractual wage or a voluntary payment dependent on the goodwill of the employer. Ex gratia payments are by their nature and by virtue of the amount paid a special payment that the employer can make at its discretion. It should be noted that case law assumes that such a payment loses its voluntary character if it is paid several times without reservation. The recommendation is, therefore, that each time any ex gratia payments are made they are explicitly described as voluntary payments from which no legal claim can be derived.

Bonuses

There is no standard definition of the term "bonus" in Swiss law. If clear business results are stipulated as the determining factor for the size of the bonus, the bonus becomes a contractual element of the wage (often a variable element). If the employee achieves the targets set out in the relevant bonus regulations, he or she must be paid the bonus unless there are valid reasons for not doing so. However, if there are personal, unquantifiable performance targets that depend on the employer's subjective perception rather than objective standards, the bonus may not be a contractual element of the wage.

The general recommendation is to formally regulate details of the calculation and payment of bonuses.

Overtime

Extra hours worked in excess of the contractually agreed or standard hours, but not in excess of the weekly maximum hours set out in the Labor Act (45 or 50 hours depending on the industry), are known as additional hours. Time worked in excess of the maximum statutory working week is known as overtime. With the agreement of the employee, the employer may compensate for additional hours worked by granting free time of at least the same duration within an appropriate period. If additional hours are not compensated by free time and there is no other written agreement on the matter, the employer must pay for the additional hours at the standard wage rate plus a supplement of 25 percent (unless a different contractual arrangement has been made). The Labor Act states that overtime is usually compensated by a 25 percent wage supplement.[1] It should be noted, however, that the Labor Act does not apply to senior management personnel (see definition in "Employment Contracts: Who Receives Them and What Must They Include?"). Consequently, such senior management personnel are not eligible to receive overtime compensation according to the Labor Act. According to the SCO they may receive overtime premiums under specific circumstances (e.g., if the working hours are determined in the employment contract and nothing is otherwise agreed upon in writing).

Pensions and Social Insurance

The social security and retirement system in Switzerland is based on a three-pillar system.

1. The first pillar, state pension, insures the whole of the Swiss population (subject to qualification requirements) against the consequences of old age, death, and disability. This first pillar consists of the following:

    - Old-age pension (Old Age and Survivor's Insurance plus any supplementary benefits) and disability insurance (known respectively by their Swiss abbreviations, AHV and IV);

- Insurance for replacement income when performing military, civilian, or civil defense service, or after childbirth (EO);
- Family allowances; and
- Unemployment insurance.

2. The second pillar, occupational pensions, only insures working people, particularly those who are not self-employed. This pillar is governed by the Federal Act on Occupational Pension Plans (*Bundesgesetz über die berufliche Altersvorsorge*, BVG).

3. The third pillar comprises private pensions taken out by individuals.

In addition to paying the employee's basic wage, employers must make contributions to the first and second pillars. The employer's contributions to the first pillar are as follows (percentage of gross salary):

- 5.05 percent for AHV/IV/EO (the same amounts are also deducted from the employee's gross salary [employee contribution]).
- Up to 3 percent for family allowances (varies between cantons, no employee contribution).
- 1 percent for unemployment insurance up to a maximum salary of CHF 126,000 (about US $108,000) (the same amount is also deducted from the employee's gross salary [employee contribution]). There are no contributions on the part of salary that exceeds CHF 126,000.

According to the BVG, the employer's collective contribution must be at least as high as the employees' contributions. These amounts vary from business to business.

In addition, employees must be insured against accidents and may be insured against sickness (optional health insurance). Employers must continue to pay salary to an employee for a defined period if the employee is prevented from working through no fault of his or her own (e.g., because of illness, fulfillment of statutory obligations, exercise of a public office, or pregnancy). The law states that in the first year of service this continuation of salary payment shall last for three weeks. Thereafter, different regional practices have led to different salary continuation periods. In Berne, for example, salary continues to be paid to employees in their tenth year of service for 17 weeks, while in Zurich it is 16 weeks and in Basel 13. After this period, the employees themselves are responsible for compensating for the lack of wages, unless a daily sickness benefits insurance has been taken out for them.

In practice, daily sickness benefit insurance is often put in place to remove the employer's risk of having to continue to pay wages, while at the same time guaranteeing the employee longer protection against loss of wages.

Severance Pay

If an employee aged 50 or over leaves employment after 20 or more years of service, the employer must pay him or her severance compensation of between two and eight months' salary. If the employee receives benefits from a personal pension plan, these amounts may be deducted from the severance pay to the extent that these benefits are funded by the employer or, based on the employer's contributions, by the personal pension plan. Since pillar 2 was added to pension law, severance pay has become far less important, because the employer may deduct the contributions it has made to pillar 2 plans from the severance pay.

Paid Leave

Swiss law allows employees to stay away from work for a certain period if certain specified events occur. The permitted duration of absence depends on the event and it ranges from a few days (birth of a child, death of a close relative, wedding, moving into a new house) to several weeks (pregnancy). The obligation to continue to pay salary also varies from event to event.

Vacations

The employee is entitled to have one work-free day per week. However, the usual practice in Switzerland is for people to work a standard five-day week. In addition, employees are entitled to five weeks of vacation per year up to the age of 20, and four weeks thereafter. Employees must also be given days off on public holidays, though a distinction is drawn between federal holidays and additional cantonal (state) holidays. Not all cantons grant the same number of holidays.

Labor Unions

Establishment and Recognition Requirements

There is no standard definition of a labor union in Swiss law. "Unions" are considered associations that are dedicated to the employee's interests and that are empowered by their articles of association to conclude collective agreements. The law does not require that unions take an explicit organizational form, though they must be separate legal entities. Employee associations must also be independent from the employer in terms of personnel, finances, and philosophy.

Only about 30 percent of employees in Switzerland belong to labor unions.

Exclusive Bargaining

In Switzerland, nobody may be forced to sign a collective agreement, and nobody has an automatic right to participate in contractual negotiations beforehand. Nor may any employee be forced to join a union.

This contractual freedom means that parties may choose with whom and in what way they conclude agreements. Accordingly, even majority unions have no exclusive right to negotiate. Hence, employers are sometimes forced to negotiate with several unions but very often the parties try to agree upon one collective agreement. If this is not feasible, employers or employers' associations focus on the most important unions.

Collective Agreements

Duty to Bargain

In a collective agreement, employers or their associations and employees' associations set out agreed provisions on the commencement, content, and termination of the participating employers' and employees' individual employment relationships. It should be noted that on the employee's side, the contracting party must always be an employees' association. There is some dispute about whether this has to be a genuine labor union or whether an in-house association will also suffice. The provisions of the collective agreement concerning conclusion, content, and termination of the individual employment relationships are directly applicable during the collective agreement's duration to the participating employers and employees (member of the employees' association).

Generally, there are two different types of collective agreements. On the one hand, there is a "normal," standard collective agreement, which is typically concluded between a federation of employers and a trade union. On the other hand, there is a so-called "company collective agreement," which is a collective agreement between a single company and a trade union.

In Switzerland, collective agreements may also be declared by decree of the authorities to be generally binding. Such a decree serves to extend the collective agreement's scope of validity to all employees and employers in the profession or in a specific branch of the economy.

In Swiss law there is no obligation to conclude a collective agreement. If no collective agreement has been agreed in an industry, despite the fact that a collective approach to labor law would make sense, the authorities may issue a normal employment contract that sets out the directly applicable provisions on the commencement, content, and termination of an employment relationship. In particular a normal employment contract is often used to set out the regulations in areas where a lack of organization on the part of workers means that there is no collective agreement and consequently the rights of the employees are not adequately protected. However, the parties are free to amend the provisions of a normal employment contract, except for the provisions that the contract declares to be mandatory.

Form Requirements

Collective agreements must be in written form to be valid.

Mechanisms of Dispute Resolution

If there are disagreements about the rules pertaining to the conclusion of a new collective agreement, or disputes relating to regulations that are to be newly incorporated into an existing collective agreement, resolution is often, according to the terms of the collective agreement, the responsibility of a private arbitration tribunal, or if no agreement can be reached, a government conciliation service (compulsory mediation). In the event of legal disputes relating to the interpretation or application of the collective agreement, the matter shall be decided by an ordinary court, by a government conciliation service, or by a mutually agreed court of arbitration.

Changes and Termination

A collective agreement may be concluded for either a fixed or an indefinite period. A collective agreement may be changed or revoked by mutual agreement of the contracting parties (e.g., employers, employers' association, and labor unions) in writing. Unless the collective agreement is concluded for a fixed term, and unless stated otherwise, after one year it may be terminated on six months' notice by either contracting party.

Normal employment contracts may be changed or terminated only by the issuing governmental authority.

Works Councils

Mandatory Requirements

Employee representation is governed by the Codetermination Act. In companies with 50 or more employees, the employees may appoint one or more representatives from among their midst.

Functions and Frequency

Employees' representative bodies stand for the shared interests of employees in dealings with the employer. These bodies regularly inform employees about their activities. They are also entitled to receive from the employer prompt and comprehensive information about all matters that they need to know about in order to carry out their duties properly. The Codetermination Act also gives employees' representative bodies specific rights of codetermination in issues of legal security and employee protection as well as in cases where businesses or parts of businesses are transferred to a third party, where mass dismissals are proposed, and in issues relating to the conclusion or termination of contracts to transfer pension provision to an occupational pension plan.

According to Swiss law, employees' representative bodies have no entitlement to a seat on the executive board or board of directors.

National and Regional Groups

There is no particular interlinking of employees' representative bodies at the national or regional level. At the European level, reference should be made to the European guidelines on the makeup of a European Works Council. These guidelines can also indirectly affect Switzerland if Swiss companies with branches in Europe, or European companies with branches in Switzerland, are involved.

The standard surveys of employee representation vary greatly. Depending on the survey, between 30 percent and 70 percent of companies questioned in Switzerland have employees' representative bodies.

Relation to Labor Unions

Swiss law demands that employees' representative bodies and their members remain neutral with regard to labor unions when carrying out their role. They must not try to recruit for any particular union or ask anyone to join a particular union.

However, there is nothing to stop individual members of an employees' representative body from simultaneously being members of a union, provided the two activities are kept clearly separated.

SECTION II

My client is acquiring an existing business in Switzerland. How do I assess the existing workforce and consider changes?

Share Deals Versus Asset Deals

Due Diligence Requirements and Considerations

Swiss data protection legislation states that an employer may process data about an employee only to the extent that it is relevant to the person's suitability for employment or is needed for the implementation of the employment contract.

The Data Protection Act must be complied with when disclosing personal data as part of a due diligence process. Information may be disclosed as long as it is kept general and no personal data is disclosed. For example, average salaries and average ages may be revealed. It is also possible to disclose certain data on an anonymous basis. As part of a due diligence process, data may also be passed on to a prospective purchaser as long as the purchaser has signed a secrecy agreement and a commitment to restrict the use made of the information. This also applies to the disclosure of personal data as long as the data processing is proportionate and carried out in good faith. Whether data may be transferred to another country depends on whether that country provides a level of data protection equivalent to Switzerland's or whether there is a duty to report to the data protection authorities.

Statutory Regulations Concerning Transfer of Business

Asset Deal

If the employer transfers a business (being understood as an organizational unit and not as legal entity) or part of a business to a third party, the employment relationship, together with all rights and duties, is also transferred to the acquiring party, provided that the employee does not decline the transfer (SCO 333). A transfer of business occurs in particular when an organizational unit (and not the legal entity) with its assets and liabilities is transferred (or when companies merge). When this happens, there is a change in the legal entity holding the rights, in which case Swiss law stipulates a compulsory takeover of the employment contracts. Only the employee has a right to choose whether to accept or decline the takeover. If an employee refuses the takeover, the employment relationship ends at the next possible statutory termination date but still transfers across.

If the transferred employment relationship is governed by a collective agreement, the acquirer must adhere to this contract for one year unless it expires earlier or is terminated by notice being given (SCO 333).

When a business or part of a business is transferred to a third party, the employer must inform the employees' representative body, or if there is none, the employees themselves, about the reasons for the transfer and about the legal, financial, and social consequences of the transfer for employees (SCO 333a), and it must do this in good time before the completion of the transfer. If measures that will affect the employees are planned as a consequence of the transfer (e.g., layoffs), a consultation process must be initiated beforehand.

It should also be noted that, depending on the structure of the transaction and the organizational structure of the business being taken over, the acquiring party has to conclude new collective insurance policies to protect employees. An occupational pension provision for the employees transferred along with the business must also be arranged. Depending on the circumstances, employees may either stay with the existing pension fund or have their vested benefits transferred to a new pension fund.

Under Swiss employment law, the old employer and the acquiring party are jointly and severally liable for the employee's claims that fall due before the transfer or that will fall due up to the point at which the employment relationship could be ended or when it ends because the employee declines the transfer.

Share Deal

Purchase of a company in the form of a share deal does not alter the nature of the legal entity. At least initially, the transferred company retains its legal personality, thus leaving its position (and liability) as the employer of the employees unchanged.

Problems can arise, however, if companies are interrelated within a group and subsidiaries are spun off out of this group structure (e.g., insurance companies, pension funds). An assessment must be made of how best to deal in detail with an existing group arrangement (e.g., via subsequent insurance policies as an interim solution). In such cases the consequences can be the same as in an asset deal (e.g., exit from pension fund, partial liquidation of pension fund, new insurance policies).

Carrying Out a Workforce Reduction

Notice of Termination

Ordinary Notice of Termination

There is no notice of termination with a fixed-term employment contract. The contract ends when the fixed term expires.

With an indefinite-term employment relationship, notice within the probationary period, which may last no longer than three months, is seven days. After the end of the probationary period, the statutory period of notice is one month during the first year of service, two months during the second to ninth years of service, and three months thereafter. These periods may only be altered by written agreement, standard employment contract, or collective agreement, but in no circumstances may they be reduced to less than one month.

Termination Without Notice

The employment relationship may be terminated without notice at any time by either the employer or the employee if there are compelling reasons for doing so. A compelling reason is considered to be, in particular, the existence of any circumstance under which the terminating party cannot in good faith be expected to continue the employment relationship (SCO 337). This includes, for example, theft or embezzlement against the employer; violence or seriously insulting behavior against the employer, employee, or customers; and refusal to work or to carry out important instructions despite the express threat of termination without notice (also called summary dismissal).

Procedural Requirements

Procedural Rules

The notice period is calculated from receipt of the notice. Notice may be given in any form in principle, including orally. Both the employee and the employer may request that the reasons for termination be given in writing.

Procedure for Ordinary Termination

Anyone wanting to assert a claim for improper notice of termination must submit a written objection to the party who gave notice no later than by the end of the notice period. If the objection is made validly and if the parties cannot agree on a continuation of the employment relationship, the party that has received notice of termination may assert a claim for indemnity (through legal channels). The claim is forfeited if no legal action is taken within 180 days after the employment relationship has ended.

Procedure for Termination Without Notice

Summary dismissal (i.e., dismissal without notice) must be pronounced as soon as the compelling reason is known. A delay in summary dismissal shows that it was still possible for the employee to keep working for the business and that the dismissal could have been carried out using the normal period of notice. The rules on protecting employees from dismissal at improper times—as described below—does not apply in the case of termination without notice.

Layoffs

Layoffs are defined as notices of termination announced to the company by the employer within a 30-day period for reasons that are unrelated to the person of the employee and that affect

- At least 10 employees in businesses usually employing more than 20 and fewer than 100 persons;
- At least 10 percent of all employees in businesses usually employing more than 100 and fewer than 300 persons; or
- At least 30 employees in businesses usually employing at least 300 persons.

Special rules apply to collective redundancies. Employers first have to consult with the employees' representative body, or if there is none directly with the employees, and inform them in writing of the reasons for the layoff, the number of employees to be dismissed, the number of persons usually employed, and the time period within which the notification of the dismissals is to be given. Employers also have to inform the cantonal labor office of every planned layoff.

Statutory Protections

Swiss law includes two provisions to protect employees when dismissals are planned. One protects employees from dismissal at improper times, defining the specific periods during which an employer may not serve notice on an employee. The other relates to procedural matters, setting out the sanctions imposed if notice of termination is improper.

Notice of Termination at an Improper Time
After the probation period has expired, the employer may not terminate the employment relationship at the following times (SCO 336c):

- When the employee is performing military, civil defense, or civilian service;
- When employees are prevented from working through no fault of their own due to sickness or accident—for 30 days in the first year of service, for 90 days from the second to fifth year of service, and for 180 days from the sixth year of service;
- During pregnancy and for 16 weeks following the birth of the baby;
- When the employee is helping with an official aid effort in another country.

Any notice to terminate an employment contract during such periods is invalid. Any notice served before such periods is suspended when the period begins and then recommenced after it is over.

Improper Notice of Termination
There must always be a specific reason for serving notice of termination, but the law also lists certain specific actions that would render a termination improper. Notice of termination is improper if the notice is given for any of the following reasons:

- Because of qualities inherent in the personality of the other party, unless such quality relates to the employment relationship or significantly impairs cooperation within the business;
- Because the employee exercises a constitutional right (e.g., exercise of the constitutional right to freedom of religion);

- To frustrate the formation of legal claims;
- Because the other party asserts in good faith claims arising out of the employment relationship ("revenge dismissal");
- Because of other reasons given in the legislation (e.g., because the other party is performing military service; because the employee belongs to an employees' association; dismissal as part of mass dismissals that have not been discussed in advance with the employees' association).

If notice of termination is improper, it is not rendered invalid, but it does give rise to an obligation to pay compensation (SCO 336a). There is, therefore, no obligation to continue the employment relationship.

Legal Consequences of Unjustified Ordinary Termination

The compensation payable by the party that improperly gives notice of termination is set by the judge after assessing all the facts. It shall not, however, exceed the employee's wages for six months. In addition, compensation and recompense based on other legal grounds may also be claimed (including for reasons other than improper notice of termination).

In the context of a layoff, there is no automatic obligation to pay additional severance allowance if the dismissal is unlawful.

Legal Consequences of Unjustified Termination Without Notice

If the employee is dismissed without notice for no compelling reason, he or she may claim compensation to the amount he or she would have earned if notice had been given. A claim may also be made for additional compensation, though this compensation may not exceed the employee's wages for six months.

Reorganizing the Workforce

Statutory Protections

In principle, an employer is entitled to issue general rules for the employees regarding performance of work and the employee's behavior and is also entitled to give the employees special instructions. The employee must follow the employer's general rules and special instructions in good faith (SCO 321d). This duty exists for as long as the required action is not vexatious and is reasonable for the employee to perform it in terms of its nature and content. An action will be considered vexatious if, for example, it involves the use of skilled labor for tedious low-level work, unless such work is necessary under exceptional circumstances. The employer's right to issue instructions is also limited by individual arrangements contained in a given employment contract or in the wording of a collective agreement or standard employment contract. An employee who has been hired to carry out a particular type of work is under no obligation to accept an instruction to carry out a different type in the future. This also always applies to a situation where a newly allocated post is clearly inferior in hierarchical terms to an existing one. Similarly, a contractually agreed place of work may not simply be changed by instruction without any further agreement. In this case, dismissal with the option of altered conditions of employment must be considered.

Where there is a collective agreement, it may be amended or canceled only by mutual agreement in writing by the participating contract parties. Breach of a collective agreement, in addition to giving rise to a duty to pay compensation, may result in either termination without notice of the collective agreement or justified industrial action (e.g., a strike).

Procedural Requirements

Under Swiss law, it is permitted to reach an agreement to amend the employment contract, intended to take effect in the future. If the parties are unable to reach agreement, however, dismissal with the option of altered conditions of employment (notice of alteration) is required. In the case of the latter, the employer gives the employee a choice either to accept a new employment contract or to leave his or her post on expiry of the ordinary notice period. Here, it must be ensured that no new employment contract arises. Instead, the old employment contract must be continued under new conditions; and this is particularly relevant both to the duty to continue to pay salary in certain circumstances and to notice periods.

Protected Groups

In a number of situations, the employee enjoys time-based protection from dismissal. In this regard, see the remarks on procedural requirements in "Carrying Out a Workforce Reduction" in this section.

Changing the Wage and Benefits Structure

Statutory Protections

Essentially, during the term of the employment contract and for one month after it ends, an employee does not have the right to waive any entitlements arising under inalienable provisions of either general legislation or a collective agreement. Hence, the employee is protected from inadvertently recognizing—or being pressurized to recognize—claims of the employer.

Unilateral amendment of parts of the employment contract is deemed to be a dismissal with the option of altered conditions of employment. Nevertheless it is possible for the employer and the employee to reach an agreement on contractual amendments.

Procedural Requirements

In this regard, see the comments on staff reorganization, made previously.

It should also be noted here that the compulsory minimum or parity salaries set in the collective agreement, the normal employment contract, or the work permit in the case of foreign employees must serve as the relevant minimum pay.

Consulting with Labor Unions or Works Councils

Procedural Requirements

It is mandatory that unions be consulted whenever there are plans for restructuring personnel levels or working conditions that would require changes to the existing collective agreement; and the union must be a contractual party to the collective agreement.

The employer must always consult the employee representatives—or in companies where there are no such representatives, individual employees—on the following issues: questions of work health and safety; transfer of companies or parts of companies under an asset deal or merger that involves mass layoffs; and issues related to joining a pension institution and termination of an accession agreement to a pension plan (*Anschlussvertrag*).

Employees' representatives—and in companies with no employees' representatives, individual employees—must always be informed about the transfer of a business under an asset deal or the merger of the employer, in the following respects:

- The reasons behind the transfer; and
- The legal, economic, and social consequences of the transfer suffered by the employees.

The duty to consult the employees' representatives is expressly imposed on both the transferor and the transferee.

Transfer or Termination of a Collective Agreement

Where a collective agreement is applicable to an employment contract transferred as part of an asset deal (or a merger), the new owner of a company or part of a company must comply with the collective agreement for at least one year, unless it expires earlier or ends earlier due to the employee's resignation.

Consulting with the Government

The employer must notify the cantonal employment office in writing of every intended mass layoff and must also supply a copy of the relevant notice given to the corresponding employees' representatives, or if there are none, to the employees themselves. This notice must show the results of consultation with the employees' representatives and all relevant information regarding the intended mass layoff.

SECTION III

My client wishes to sell its existing facility. What restrictions do we need to consider?

Assessing Employment Contracts

Swiss employment law provides that whenever a company or part of a company is transferred to a third party, the employment contract is also transferred to the new owner, along with all its rights and duties, on the day of transfer. Swiss corporate merger legislation picks up and reaffirms this rule, so that it also applies to mergers, divestments, and asset transfers (see comments in "Share Deals Versus Asset Deals" in Section II). The employee has the right to reject the transfer of his or her employment contract. Provided the employee does not reject the transfer, the transferor is under absolutely no obligation to pay any special fee or compensation in addition to the contractually agreed salary and benefits (subject to any contrary arrangements contained in the corporate sale documentation). The employment contract is transferred to the new owner, along with all rights and duties.

For reasons of corporate efficiency and in order to retain key staff, it may be advisable to enter into specific agreements with such staff designed to ensure that they stay with the company being sold (see comments on retaining key employees in "Negotiating with the Purchaser: Special Labor Issues" in this section).

From the purchaser's point of view, clauses that give special financial advantages to employees in the event of termination after the sale are, of course, unwelcome (e.g., golden parachutes).

For the purchaser, the fact that key employees have entered into noncompete agreements and nonsolicitation agreements may prove to be decisive. This is possible under Swiss law, although subject to statutory restrictions.

Consulting with the Government

In this regard, see the remarks in "Share Deals Versus Asset Deals" in Section II on purchase of part of a company.

Consulting with Labor Unions or Works Councils

In this regard, see the remarks in "Share Deals Versus Asset Deals" in Section II on purchase of a company.

Negotiating with the Purchaser: Special Labor Issues

Use of Warranties in Transfer Agreement

In principle, the requirements of a contract always depend considerably on the kind of business that is transferred. The scope of relevant promises and warranties are a matter for negotiation and are heavily dependent on the purchasing situation that applies at the time. The following promises are generally required by purchasers to be included in a purchase contract:

- The seller has supplied the purchaser with true, correct, and complete information regarding the transferred employees, including their annual salaries, bonuses, and any other remuneration;
- All transferred employees are properly insured in accordance with applicable legislation and all employees are properly enrolled in a pension plan in accordance with applicable laws;

- The seller confirms that all pension contributions of transferred employees have been made in accordance with applicable laws;
- The seller confirms that no other employees than those agreed will be transferred to the purchaser as a consequence of the transaction, or undertakes to meet the costs of any employees transferred automatically by operation of law; and
- The seller confirms that all liabilities toward the transferred employee arising prior to the transfer will be paid off.

In order to avoid the need for a consultation, it is recommended that the sale documentation state that the purchaser undertakes to make no changes to employment conditions or to dismiss anyone for a specified time after the sale (e.g., by an undertaking or guarantee). Otherwise, it is important to be aware of the seller's plans, in order to find out whether a consultation will be necessary.

Means for Retaining Key Employees

In the case of a business transfer (via an asset deal or corporate merger), the employee is entitled to refuse transfer of his or her employment contract to the new owner. Here it should be noted that this right of refusal is not of a compulsory nature, which means that it is possible to insert a clause into an employment contract in which the employee waives such right.

If an employer wishes to ensure that an employee stays on in the company, it is recommended that a loyalty bonus system is agreed upon. Here, the employee is offered the prospect of a right to recurring bonuses of a set amount and lasting for a predetermined period, payable on condition that the employee does not resign. Retention agreements and retention bonus agreements are common in this area. This is the case, even though they can frequently be disadvantageous to the purchaser by providing a basis for legal claims in the event of employee dismissal carried out by the purchaser.

Further, the seller also has the option of concluding a fixed-tem contract with the employee, which would exclude the possibility of ordinary termination during a specifically agreed period; alternatively, indefinite-term employment contracts may be concluded that guarantee a minimum period free of employee termination.

Other Special Labor Issues

One issue that must always be dealt with is how to handle existing share participation agreements or share option programs, if the employee leaves a group.

The pension plan situation (defined contribution or defined benefits) must also be analyzed very carefully, because if an employee leaves the pension plan (e.g., by partial liquidation), this can have financial consequences for both the seller and the purchaser. For instance, the risk situation of a pension plan of the seller may change if a substantial portion of the active employees leave and consequently the percentage of the pensioners increases. Further, in case of an existing underfunding the purchaser will try to have the underfunding covered by the seller.

SECTION IV

My client wishes to replace its senior manager(s). What restrictions do we need to consider?

Employment Contracts

Statutory Protections

Fundamentally, with the exception of the terms of the Labor Act, senior management employees and senior directors are subject to the same provisions as discussed in relation to the individual employment contract in Section I. Collective agreements are not relevant to senior employees in practice, as they are generally not applicable in their case.

Common Contractual Protections

Frequently, executive employees are protected in relation to a possible transaction by means of incentive agreements. These agreements can be tailored to the specific needs of a company. First, there are agreements in particular that provide for fixed leaving payments. Second, it is also possible to agree on fixed-term contracts that do not permit ordinary termination within the relevant period or determine longer contractual (termination) notice periods than the statutory ones.

Procedural Requirements

See the comments on procedural requirements in "Carrying Out a Workforce Reduction" in Section II.

Protected Groups

See the comments on statutory protections in "Carrying Out a Workforce Reduction" in Section II.

The dismissal of an employee who is an elected employees' representative in a formal corporate arrangement or an institution linked to the company constitutes a special case. Swiss employment law states in this regard that such a dismissal will be abusive if the employer is unable to prove a justified reason for the dismissal.

Sanctions and Remedies

Breach of a contractual agreement always has consequences in terms of possible compensation. In addition, contractually agreed entitlements are also applicable.

Where it is the case that an individual is subject to time-based protection from dismissal, as described in "Carrying Out a Workforce Reduction" in Section II (e.g., due to pregnancy), any purported termination is void. The employment relationship would thus continue.

For the legal consequences of abusive dismissal, reference is made to the comments on statutory protections in "Carrying Out a Workforce Reduction" in Section II.

Statutory Severance Pay Requirements

Statutory Rules

See the discussion of special benefit requirements in "Wages and Benefits" in Section I. In general, there is no statutory right to severance pay.

Common Contractual Obligations

Frequently, senior managers have relatively long notice periods.

Quite often, change of ownership clauses can be found. These clauses are partly also to be found in long-term incentive, employee share option programs, and share participation programs.

Confidentiality and Nondisparagement Agreements

In the termination of employment contracts, detailed arrangements are regularly made governing confidentiality, nondisparagement, and press releases. Often, contractual severance pay is subject to compliance with certain rules (e.g., confidentiality, noncompetition).

Often, employment termination contracts also specify agreed wording of employee reference letters.

Statutory Restrictions on Dismissal Without Cause

Statutory Rules

A continuous employment contract may be terminated by either party. The terminating party must give written reasons for the termination, if the other party so requests. However, the law specifies no legal consequence, should this duty to give reasons be neglected. As a matter of principle, the party that fails to fulfill its duty of providing reasons will bear the risk of having to pay costs in any legal proceedings. In addition, academic literature on this topic contains calls for creation of a legal right to fulfillment (i.e., to be told reasons) and the consequential forcing of the terminating party to give an explanation.

Both the employer and the employee may terminate the employment contract without notice at any time, provided this is for compelling reasons. See the comments regarding procedural requirements for termination in "Carrying Out a Workforce Reduction" in Section II.

In principle, an employee who is dismissed by ordinary termination may be released from his or her duty to work (placed on "garden leave") at any time. The employee has no claim to continue actually working (one exception to this is the apprenticeship contract, under which the employer sometimes acquires a duty to continue working with the employee based on a duty of care). The employer must continue to pay salary until expiry of the ordinary termination period, but the employer may set off any income generated by the employee during the time of the release (if the employee was allowed to start a new job).

Sanctions and Remedies

See the comments on statutory protections in "Carrying Out a Workforce Reduction" in Section II. Unless the termination was either unjustified or occurred at improper time, the employee will have no legal claims.

SECTION V

What prohibitions exist against discrimination on the basis of age, race, gender, disability, pregnancy, and other factors? What are the rights of employees, applicants, or former employees who believe that they have been discriminated against?

Areas of Protection

The Equal Opportunities Act mainly concerns the prohibition of unequal treatment of employees and the resulting legal consequences. The protection afforded extends in particular to discriminatory failure to offer employment as well as discriminatory dismissal, due to gender, civil status, family situation, or pregnancy.

As regards any further antidiscriminatory provisions, it must be pointed out that Swiss employment law has not enacted any specific duty of equal treatment of employees.

Any claim to equal treatment will mainly rely on a single provision of the SCO. This provides that the employer must pay attention or sufficient attention to the personality and health of the employee and must also ensure that employees do not suffer sexual harassment.

Essentially, this means that the employer must not arbitrarily disadvantage individual employees within the same company, that is, without any valid objective reason. The Swiss Federal Court has ruled in this regard that even an irrelevant and arbitrary decision by an employer would only amount to character injury, and thus a breach of the individual discrimination prohibition, if it actually contains an element of disparagement of the employee's character. It should also be mentioned that racial discrimination is punishable under Swiss criminal law. In relation to employment law issues, any employer who refuses to hire a candidate due to race, ethnicity, or religion will be penalized.

Statutory Rules

The Equal Opportunities Act enacts a reversal of the burden of proof. This means that as soon as the court has ascertained that a substantial allegation has been brought up, the burden of proof is reversed. With regard to the allocation of tasks, configuration of working conditions, remuneration, initial and further training, promotion, and dismissal, there is a presumption of discrimination once it has been alleged by the affected person.

Swiss employment law does not reverse the burden of proof in any other cases. However, in employment disputes with up to CHF 30,000 (approximately US $25,000) at issue, the judge investigates the facts of the case ex officio and evaluates the evidence at his or her free discretion.

Further, it must be noted that organizations whose corporate statutes promote gender equality or preserve employee's interests may ask a court in their own name to find that discrimination has taken place; and this is so where the outcome of the proceedings is likely to impact on a large number of employment contracts.

Legal Effect of Nondiscrimination Policies

If the employer operates a nondiscrimination policy and implements the structures it requires, in an actual case of discrimination this would help to prove that the employer has met its duty of care and its other duties in full or even has done more than the minimum required by law.

In an individual case, however, issuing rules that go beyond the requirements of the general law may mean that the employee receives contractual protection that goes beyond available statutory protection. This could lead to additional compensation claims against the employer.

Venue and Procedure

Under the Equal Opportunities Act, the Swiss cantons must designate a special dispute resolution body (*Schlichtungsstelle*) for any arbitration proceedings. Arbitration proceedings are voluntary for the parties, though the cantons may stipulate that a legal action may be brought only after arbitration proceedings have run their course.

An action for compensation due to discriminatory refusal to offer employment, based on the Equal Opportunities Act, must be brought within three months of the refusal of employment by the employer. A court action for discriminatory termination must be brought before the end of the termination notice period.

Territorial and subject matter jurisdiction depend on the general provisions of employment law. In the case of facts falling exclusively within national law, territorial jurisdiction is governed by the Jurisdiction Act (Federal Act on Jurisdiction in civil court matters, *Gerichtsstandsgesetz*). For an employment-related action, the appropriate court is either the court at the residence or head office of the defendant or the court at the place where the employee normally carries out his or her work. This jurisdiction rule applies both to arbitration proceedings and court proceedings. Subject-matter jurisdiction is governed by cantonal law. In Canton Zurich, for example, there is an employment court located in two districts (Zurich and Winterthur), featuring either a single judge or a panel of judges, depending on the value of the subject matter. This is a court of first instance for employment disputes, with an oral hearing being the standard procedure. In other cases, the district court has jurisdiction (with either a single judge or a panel of judges, depending on the value of the subject matter).

Sanctions and Remedies

Anyone who has been affected by discrimination, as defined by the Equal Opportunities Act, is entitled to apply to either the court or the administrative authority for

- Impending discrimination to be prohibited or refrained from;
- Existing discrimination to be stopped;
- A finding that discrimination has taken place, if this continues to be disruptive;
- An order for payment of outstanding salary.

Where discrimination as per the Equal Opportunities Act consists in refusing employment or in terminating an employment contract governed by the SCO, the person affected by the discrimination is entitled to compensation, to be set under consideration of all the circumstances and to be based on either likely or actual salary.

In contrast, if an employment contract has been terminated in a discriminatory manner as per the Equal Opportunities Act, the employee may actually dispute the termination itself. Hence, the employee is entitled to continue the employment contract, although the employee may also renounce it and instead claim compensation for unjustified dismissal (regarding compensation, see "Carrying Out a Workforce Reduction" in Section II.). Where an employee has objected to a discriminatory act or acts, the Equal Opportunities Act provides additional protection against dismissal motivated by revenge. Throughout arbitration proceedings and the six months following, the employee may be dismissed only for a valid, explained reason.

In the case of discrimination falling outside the scope of the Equal Opportunities Act, the employee is entitled to compensation. There are also certain circumstances in which the employee is entitled to refuse to work or may claim justified summary termination (termination without notice) of the employment contract.

● SECTION VI

On the Horizon: What key labor and employment law developments should an employer doing business in Switzerland anticipate occurring in the coming years?

There are currently no major employment law revision projects in Switzerland. Nevertheless, the following projects affect subareas of employment law either directly or indirectly:

- A new tax law is currently being discussed for employee share and share option plans;
- Disability insurance is being revised in order to create incentives for, among other things, employers to hire people with health problems (e.g., initial work supplement for 180 days);
- There is a draft federal statute regarding the cancellation and simplification of permit procedures that would grant small firms certain concessions with regard to the documentation and organization of work safety; and
- There is a draft federal decree on the people's initiative for flexible AHV age requirements, which would enable the majority of the working population between 62 and 65 to draw a full AHV pension. The Swiss Federal Council has petitioned to reject this initiative.

🌐 NOTE

1. For overtime in excess of 60 hours per year.

CHAPTER 19

LABOR AND EMPLOYMENT LAW
IN THE UNITED KINGDOM

KATHLEEN HEALY

Preliminary remark: The principal rights and obligations imposed on employers and employees in the United Kingdom arise from three sources:

- Common law, which governs any contract of employment between employer and employee and includes the body of law created by earlier decisions;
- UK legislation; and
- European legislation and judgments of the European Court of Justice (ECJ).

In the UK, employers and employees are generally free to agree on whatever contractual terms they wish, provided certain statutory rights are complied with, including the right not to be discriminated against on grounds of age, sex, sexual orientation, race, religion, nationality, or disability. In the UK the main employment legislation is the Employment Rights Act 1996.

Common law implies certain general terms into contracts of employment, and employers must also comply with extensive health and safety regulations to protect the health of their employees.

SECTION I

My client wishes to establish a manufacturing facility in the United Kingdom and will need to hire a workforce. What are the key issues involved?

Employment Contracts: Who Receives Them
and What Must They Include?

A contract of employment need not be in writing, although senior executives' contracts commonly are.

However, as a matter of statute, all employees have the right to receive a written statement of the main terms of employment within two months of starting employment. The statement must provide the following information:

- The identity of the parties;
- The date employment began and the date of continuous employment (if different from the start date);
- Salary;
- Hours of work;
- Place of work;
- Vacation entitlement;
- Sickness provisions;
- Any provision in respect of pension;
- Length of notice;
- Job title;
- Disciplinary rules and grievance procedures; and
- Whether any collective agreements apply to the employment.

Employees have a right to a minimum notice period from their employer, which is one week per year of service up to a maximum of 12 weeks. Senior executives typically have longer notice periods of between six and 12 months.

Change to Terms and Conditions of Employment

Employees must be notified in writing of any changes in these particulars as soon as possible and, in any event, within a month. Employers often reserve the right in a contract to vary terms and conditions of employment. In practice changes may be made unilaterally only if they are minor. Material changes may be made only with the consent of the employee in question.

Language

There is no specific requirement for the written statement to be in English, but it would be unusual for a statement of terms to be provided in a language other than English.

Fixed-Term Contracts

An employment contract may be for a fixed term. However, the inclusion of an express agreed expiry date does not mean that the employer may simply allow the contract to expire without following any procedure in connection with the expiry of that contract, as the expiry of that contract counts as a dismissal for UK statutory purposes. Note also that fixed-term employees have the statutory right not to be treated less favorably than comparable permanent staff.

Wages and Benefits

A national minimum wage (NMW) applies to all workers. The NMW is currently GBP 5.52 and will increase to GBP 5.73 in October 2008. A lower rate applies to young workers (18–21). Employees who are not paid the NMW may bring a claim before an employment tribunal. It is a criminal offense for employers willfully to refuse to pay the NMW.

It is also unlawful for employers to make deductions from employees' wages (other than where required to do so by statute) unless the employees have either expressly authorized the deduction or the deduction is provided for by a term of the employment contract and the employees have confirmed the term in writing.

Employers must give employees itemized pay statements specifying, among other things, gross and net wages or salary and the amount and purpose of deductions.

Pensions

State Pensions

As well as being entitled to the flat-rate, old-age state pension, employees may build up a state earnings-related pension (State Second Pension). Entitlement to both pensions is based on payment of national insurance contributions (social security contributions) by the employer and employee.

Private Pensions

Many employers provide an occupational pension to supplement or partially replace the State Second Pension. Such plans are subject to a wide range of regulations.

Individuals may also establish personal pension arrangements directly with a bank or an insurance company. An employer is not necessarily involved in such arrangements, although it may choose to contribute.

Stakeholder Pensions

If an employer with five or more employees does not offer an occupational pension plan or contribute at least 3 percent of basic pay on behalf of employees to a personal pension plan, it must allow employees access to a stakeholder pension plan. An employer must nominate a plan to which employees can make contributions through the payroll. The employer does not have to make a contribution itself.

Sickness Absence and Pay

Subject to certain qualifications, employees are entitled to receive statutory sick pay (SSP) during periods of incapacity for work. The maximum entitlement to SSP is 28 weeks in any period of entitlement. Broadly the entitlement period starts with the first day of absence and ends (as a maximum) three years thereafter. The current weekly amount payable for those who earn more than the lower weekly earnings limit for national insurance liability (GBP 84) is GBP 70.05.

Vacation Leave and Working Hours

Employees have a number of rights in relation to working time. Broadly, workers have a right to:

- Four weeks' paid annual leave;
- Work no longer than an average 48-hour week;
- A daily rest period of 11 hours;
- A daily rest break of 20 minutes;
- A weekly rest period of 24 hours; and
- Restrictions on the amount of night work they perform.

Labor Unions

Employees have the right to join an independent trade union. Those who do so benefit from certain bargaining rights if their union is recognized by their employer.

An employer with 20 or more workers is obliged to recognize a trade union where there is majority support among the workforce for recognition. Where an employer does not recognize a union voluntarily, the union may follow a statutory procedure to obtain recognition. Recognition obtained through the statutory procedure entitles the union to bargain collectively on pay, hours, and vacation.

If an employer recognizes a trade union, a union may have a right to be informed and consulted on a number of issues, including redundancies, health and safety, and business transfers. An employer may withdraw voluntary recognition from a trade union at any time, but an employer has to follow a specific derecognition procedure if recognition was originally granted under the statutory procedure.

The employer and trade union may enter into a collective agreement covering matters such as terms and conditions of employment, conditions of work, disciplinary procedures, and hiring and removing employees. Collective agreements are generally not legally enforceable unless they state expressly that they are intended to be legally binding. Nevertheless, employers with such collective agreements tend to observe their content, as from an industrial relations perspective, this assists in maintaining a good working relationship with the union.

There is no legal right to strike in the UK. Employees who participate in industrial action are usually in breach of their contracts of employment. However, where an employee takes part in official industrial action (industrial action taken after a number of conditions set out in legislation have been complied with), it will be automatically unfair to dismiss such an employee for taking action within 12 weeks of action starting. More limited protection against dismissal is provided after the initial 12-week period (although the period in which enhanced protection applies may be extended in some cases).

Collective Agreements

Where a union is recognized, the employer and the union will negotiate an agreement as to the method by which they will conduct collective bargaining. If the parties are unable to agree on a method for collective bargaining, then one will be imposed on the parties by the Central Arbitration Committee (CAC) and in those circumstances the method has effect as if made in a legally enforceable contract between the parties. Otherwise the method is not presumed to be legally enforceable, but the parties can apply to the CAC for assistance if one or more of the parties fails to comply with the agreed method of collective bargaining.

Works Councils

As a result of the introduction of the Information and Consultation of Employees Regulations 2004, employees in organizations with 50 or more employees have a right to request that their employer set up a works council so that they can be informed and consulted on a regular basis about issues in the organization in which they work.

In addition, companies with more than 1,000 employees in the European Economic Area are subject to the European Works Council Directive. Employers with 1,000 workers in the EEA and with at least 150 workers in each of at least two member states may be obliged to set up an information and consultation procedure if employees request it.

⊛ SECTION II

My client is acquiring an existing business in the United Kingdom. How do I assess the existing workforce and consider changes?

Share Deals Versus Asset Deals

Share Deals

Where a business is to be acquired by way of a share sale, the process will be fairly straightforward as regards employment issues. There is no change in the entity employing the workforce and therefore no statutory employment framework that applies to the transaction.

There are no information and consultation obligations on a share transfer unless (1) the employer has an agreement with or a custom and practice of informing and consulting with a recognized union on such matters; or (2) there is a works council in place that has the right to be consulted in respect to share sales (relatively rare in the UK).

Business Sale

Where the business is to be acquired as a going concern (i.e., not a share sale) then the position is more complex as a result of the application of the Transfer of Undertakings (Protection of Employment) Regulations 2006 (TUPE).

The broad effect of TUPE is to transfer practically all the rights and obligations relating to employees from the seller to the buyer. This includes collective agreements that apply to the workforce that is transferring. There are limited exceptions to this principle, including in particular accrued rights in relation to occupational pension plans, which do not transfer.

Dismissals that are in connection with a TUPE transfer will be automatically unfair unless there is an economic, technical, or organizational reason entailing changes in the workforce (ETO reason) for those dismissals.

On a business transfer, both the seller and the buyer will be obliged to inform and consult with appropriate representatives of affected employees. Certain prescribed information must be given to the employee representatives, and where there are "measures" envisaged in connection with the proposed transfer, the seller/buyer must consult with the employee representatives. The buyer must provide the seller with a "measures letter" in which the buyer sets out any measures that are envisaged in relation to the seller's workforce after the transfer. There is no fixed period for the information/consultation exercise—it must be long enough before the transfer is to take place to allow that consultation to take place on any measures envisaged.

Failure to inform and consult on a TUPE transfer can result in a penalty of 13 weeks' pay per affected employee. Liability is joint and several as between the buyer and the seller.

Due Diligence on Acquisitions

As part of the due diligence exercise on any business or share acquisition, the seller will provide the prospective buyer with information relating to the workforce in the business. Information will usually be redacted to avoid any breach of the Data Protection Act of 1998 principles in relation to the processing of personal data.

The information provided will allow the buyer to assess the number of staff it is inheriting, their terms and conditions, whether there are unions or collective agreements in place, and what other liabilities in relation to the workforce may exist in order to assess what types of warranty and indemnity protection may need to be sought.

Where TUPE applies, the seller is obliged to provide the buyer with "employee liability" information no later than 14 days before the transfer.

Carrying Out a Workforce Reduction

When an employer is proposing to make collective redundancies (layoffs), depending on the number of proposed dismissals, obligations may arise to consult with recognized trade unions/employee representatives. Failure to comply with the obligations can result in court action and lead to substantial awards being made against the employer.

It should be noted that the statutory duty of consultation is in addition to any obligations that the employer may have under a preexisting agreement, a collective agreement with a trade union, or under the Information and Consultation of Employees Regulations 2004. If the redundancy program is part of a wider European plan, there may also be obligations to consult with European Works Councils.

When Does the Duty to Consult Arise?

An employer must enter into consultations with appropriate representatives if it proposes to lay off 20 or more employees at one establishment within 90 calendar days.

The legislation does not contain a definition of what is meant by an "establishment," but case law has given some guidance. In very general terms, the test is whether each site has a significant degree of autonomy. A court will look at "the unit to which the workers made redundant are assigned to carry out their duties" when determining what amounts to an establishment.

Note that the emphasis on "site" does not necessarily apply just to a physical site. In one case a sales team based in different locations around the country was found to be an "establishment" because it was treated as a distinct entity by the company.

Who Should Be Consulted?

The employer is obliged to consult with appropriate representatives of the employees "who may be affected by the proposed dismissals or may be affected by measures taken in connection with those dismissals." This may clearly include those employees who are not at risk of dismissal themselves but who will be affected by the dismissals that will take place, for example, because certain duties will be reallocated to them.

If there are recognized trade union representatives already in place, the employer must consult them. It may not bypass the union by choosing to hold elections for and consult with nonunion employee representatives only.

If trade unions are recognized only in respect to part of the affected workforce, the employer will therefore need to hold elections to appoint employee representatives for the remainder. There is a statutory process that must be followed in order to elect representatives; depending on the size of the proposed workforce reduction, such an election process in practice will take between two and six weeks.

When Must Consultation Start?

The legislation states that the consultation must commence "in good time" once the employer has proposals. Consultation should therefore begin as soon as layoffs become a real possibility, with minimums as follows:

- If the employer has proposals to lay off between 20 and 99 employees in a 90-calendar-day period at one establishment, the consultation must commence at least 30 calendar days before the first of the dismissals takes effect;

- If the employer has proposals to lay off 100 or more employees in a 90-calendar-day period at one establishment, the consultation must commence at least 90 calendar days before the first of the dismissals takes effect.

Proposals to Dismiss

There is some uncertainty about what actually amounts to a proposal to dismiss. Taking a purposive approach, it could be said that an employer will have a proposal when its plans are still at a formative stage and representatives still have an opportunity to influence the outcome.

However, it has been held by a UK court recently that simply having formulated a plan that may have the consequence of layoffs does not amount to a proposal. It only becomes a proposal, the court said, when it is "[laid] before another or others as something that one offers to do or wishes to be done."

What Information Needs to Be Provided?

For the purposes of commencing the consultation process, the legislation requires the employer to provide the appropriate representatives with the following information in writing:

- The reasons for the proposed layoff;
- The number and descriptions of employees whom the employer is proposing to dismiss as redundant;
- The total number of employees of each description employed by the employer at the relevant establishment;
- The proposed method of selection for dismissal;
- The proposed method of carrying out the layoff with due regard to any agreed procedure, including information as to the proposed period over which the layoff will be carried out; and
- The proposed method of calculating any enhanced severance payments.

Since the above are the crucial matters on which the consultation will take place, this information needs to be provided at the outset of the consultation process (although the topics may be dealt with sequentially during consultation rather than all being covered at the outset).

In addition to the above information to be provided to the representatives, the employer must also submit certain information to the government on Form HR1. Failure to comply with this obligation can result in a fine (although this is rare for a first offense).

What Is the Nature of the Consultation?

The employer is obliged to consult with the appropriate representatives about the dismissals. The legislation states that this must include consultation about ways to

- Avoid the dismissals;
- Reduce the number of dismissals; and
- Mitigate the consequences of dismissals (e.g., possible redeployment or retraining).

Recent case law in the UK has made it clear that the employee representatives have the right to be consulted on the business reason for the proposed workforce reduction.

Consultation must be conducted "with a view to reaching agreement" on the above matters.

For any employer working on plans for redundancies, it is important that any documentation produced by a working group is clearly marked as a "proposal" or "draft" or "subject to consultation" and cannot be viewed as a firm decision having been taken by the employer. Such documents would have to be disclosed in a tribunal action alleging failure to consult.

What Payments Are Due on Redundancy?

An employee who is terminated by reason of redundancy and who has two or more years' continuous service is entitled to a statutory redundancy payment. There is a prescribed formula for calculating the statutory redundancy payment. The formula is set by statute and is based on the age of the employee, length of service, and weekly salary (capped). An employee with less than two years of continuous employment is not entitled to any statutory redundancy payment. The statutory formula is exempt from the UK legislation on age discrimination.

An employee will lose the right to receive a statutory redundancy payment if the employee has unreasonably refused an offer of suitable alternative employment by the employer.

Protected Categories of Staff

Certain categories of staff enjoy special protection and may not be selected for redundancy if the reason for their selection is linked to or as a result of their special circumstances. Any such dismissals will automatically be unfair. These include dismissals where the statutory disciplinary procedure has not been followed and dismissals relating to pregnancy, health and safety, trade union membership or activities, an employee's position as pension plan trustee or employee representative, the making of a protected disclosure, or asserting a statutory right. In some of these circumstances, special awards apply. There is usually no qualifying period of employment for bringing such a claim.

Reorganizing the Workforce

Assuming that the employer does not necessarily wish to downsize the workforce but may wish to make other changes (e.g., reorganizing the workforce, relocating staff, changing terms and conditions), then other considerations arise.

Any proposals that involve staff being required to relocate are likely to trigger redundancy information and consultation requirements, as a redundancy situation is deemed to arise where the requirements for employees "in the place in which they are employed" diminishes or reduces. Therefore the above requirements as to information and consultation (depending on the total numbers involved) are likely to apply.

Changing Terms and Conditions of Employment

Contractual terms and conditions may be changed only with the consent of the individual employee. Alternatively, the employer could seek to give notice of termination under the existing contract of employment and at the same time offer a new contract on the revised terms and conditions of employment. However, doing so would amount to a dismissal for which there would be no fair reason, and therefore a possible statutory claim of unfair dismissal might arise (leaving aside the obvious industrial relations issues that might also arise with such a course of action).

Where terms and conditions have been negotiated in accordance with a collective agreement, changes will similarly need to be collectively negotiated (assuming the same collective rights of the union are still in place).

The question of how to change discretionary terms is more difficult. Often the question arises as to whether a discretionary benefit has become contractual over time or whether it has become contractual as a matter of custom and practice. Determining whether this is the case involves looking at how the term (e.g., a discretionary bonus plan) has been applied in the past, to whom it has been applied, and what has been said to employees about the particular benefit.

Changing Terms and Conditions Following a TUPE Transfer

There is an additional layer of complication to changing terms and conditions of employment following a TUPE transfer. Terms and conditions of employment may be varied only if the proposed changes are either (1) not connected with the transfer or (2) connected with the transfer but for an ETO reason. Otherwise any change is void.

In practice it is difficult for employers to show that changes following a transfer are unconnected to that transfer, not least because the primary reason employers wish to make changes is to harmonize the terms of the incoming workforce with those the employer already employs. Often incoming employees are therefore "red-circled"—that is, their terms and conditions are preserved in the short term until the employer can establish a reason for the change that is unconnected with the earlier TUPE transfer. Such red-circling is not, however, a long-term option and it may give rise to discrimination or equal pay issues over time.

⊕ SECTION III

My client wishes to sell its existing facility. What restrictions do we need to consider?

Assessing Employment Contracts

The first step for an employer considering selling its existing facility is to gather data on the workforce. Any potential buyer will expect detailed information on the current workforce, that salary and benefit structure, what collective employee representation is in place, what severance arrangements may apply in the event that layoffs are made, whether current disputes are ongoing, threatened, or pending, and so on.

Buyers will be particularly alert for the following types of terms:

- Change-of-control provisions (often found in senior executive contracts, such clauses allow the employee to resign on short notice and claim a compensation payment);
- Enhanced severance terms;
- Generous bonus plans that may be contractual;
- Restrictive covenants (to restrict employees' activities after they leave employment); and
- Any collective agreements that may apply.

Consulting with Labor Unions, Works Councils, and the Government

Depending on the structure of the proposed disposal (whether it is a share or a business transfer), the seller may have information and consultation obligations. See above for a summary of the obligations that apply.

Unless layoffs are contemplated in connection with the proposed disposal, there is no obligation to notify any governmental authority.

Negotiating with the Purchaser: Special Labor Issues

On a share sale, the buyer will expect a comprehensive set of warranties to give comfort on a range of employment-related matters. In particular, the buyer will want warranties that provide that all data disclosed in relation to the workforce is complete and accurate in all respects and that all information relevant to terms and conditions of employment has been disclosed. A compliance warranty to give reassurance as to how the business has been run in the past is common. In addition the buyer may seek a warranty that all wage and other payments are up to date, that any material employee litigation has been disclosed, and that no key manager intends to resign as a result of the proposed transaction.

The retention of key senior executives is often a significant issue. It is not uncommon for a buyer to negotiate new contracts with such employees prior to the implementation of the sale. Alternatively, the buyer may look to the seller to put appropriate retention provisions in place to ensure that key staff members do not simply leave on completion of the transaction. Such arrangements will often be a mix of a cash bonus payment and/or equity that will often be subject to a vesting period of, for example, three years as a lock-in mechanism.

On a business sale in addition to the above, a buyer will seek indemnities from the seller, giving the buyer protection in relation to acts or omissions in relation to the employees prior to the business transfer.

SECTION IV

My client wishes to replace its senior manager(s). What restrictions do we need to consider?

Employment Contracts

There are two types of claim that may arise on the termination of an employee's employment: claims arising from a breach of contract (known as wrongful dismissal) and statutory claims (such as unfair dismissal, redundancy, and discrimination). The main points to be aware of in each case are outlined below.

Wrongful Dismissal

This claim will usually arise where an employer terminates the employment in breach of its contractual obligation to give notice. Unless the employer has terminated in circumstances in which it was entitled to do so without giving notice (for example, where the employee has committed an act of gross misconduct), damages will be awarded to put the employee in the position he or she would have been in had the contract been terminated in accordance with its terms. Damages will therefore reflect the net value of the salary and other contractual benefits that the employee would have received if the notice period (or the unexpired portion of a fixed term) had been observed.

An employee may also be able to bring a wrongful dismissal claim if the employer has committed a repudiatory breach of contract that the employee accepts. This is generally referred to as a constructive dismissal. To be a repudiatory breach of contract, a breach must be so serious that it "goes to the root of the contract of employment or shows that the employer no longer intends to be bound by one or more of the essential terms of the contract." For example, changes to terms and conditions relating to pay will normally amount to repudiatory breaches of contract. If the employer commits such a breach, the employee is entitled to resign in response and does not have to work through the notice period. The employee could claim wrongful dismissal and damages would again reflect the net value of the salary and other benefits the employee would have received during the notice period.

Alternatively, the employment contract may contain a clause specifying payment in lieu of notice. If it does, then the employer may exercise its rights under the clause to terminate the employment with immediate effect by paying the prescribed amount.

Statutory Claims

Unfair Dismissal

The main claim that the senior executive may have is a statutory unfair dismissal claim that may arise where an employer terminates the employment without good reason and/or without following a fair procedure. An employee may also bring an unfair dismissal claim if he has been constructively dismissed. An employee will generally need one year's continuous service to bring a claim of unfair dismissal, and the claim must be brought within three months of the effective date of termination.

There are six potentially fair reasons for a dismissal: conduct, capability, redundancy, illegality, some other substantial reason, and retirement. If the employer cannot show one of these reasons, the dismissal will be unfair. Assuming the employer can point to a potentially fair reason, the employer must also show that it acted reasonably in all the circumstances in treating the reason as a fair reason to dismiss and that it followed a fair procedure. For example, in a conduct dismissal, an employer will need to conduct a fair investigation, hold a disciplinary hearing, and allow the employee a right of appeal if a dismissal is to be fair.

In a constructive dismissal situation (i.e., where the employee has resigned in response to some action on the part of the employer) it is for the employee to show that he or she has in fact been dismissed. The employee will need to demonstrate that the employer committed a repudiatory breach of contract and that the employee resigned in response to the breach and did not affirm the contract by remaining in employment for too long after the breach had occurred. If the employee shows that he or she was dismissed, the employer will have to show the reason for the dismissal and that it acted reasonably in all the circumstances of the case. Typically it is difficult for an employer to show that a constructive dismissal was nonetheless fair.

If the employee is successful in an unfair dismissal claim, he or she is entitled to receive a compensatory and a basic award. The basic award is calculated on the basis of age and length of service (broadly an employee will receive a week's pay, capped at GBP 330 a week, for every year's service) to a maximum of GBP 9,900 (as of February 1, 2008). The compensatory award is such amount as the tribunal considers just and equitable, having regard to the loss suffered by the employee as a result of the dismissal, up to a maximum of GBP 63,000 (as of February 1, 2008).

Employers should also be aware of the statutory disciplinary procedure that came into force in October 2004. This provides for notification of the events that could lead to dismissal, a disciplinary hearing, and a right of appeal. If the procedure is not followed, a dismissal will be automatically unfair and compensation increased by between 10 and 50 percent (although compensation is still subject to the overall cap as referred to above).

Note that dismissals on certain grounds are regarded as "automatically unfair." For example, if an employee is dismissed for making a protected disclosure (whistleblowing) or for reasons related to pregnancy or maternity leave (among other things) the dismissal will be automatically unfair. There is no service requirement to bring a claim about an automatically unfair dismissal—an employee is protected against such a dismissal from the start of employment. In certain situations (for example, dismissals for making a protected disclosure) there is no limit on the compensation that can be awarded and it may be possible for an employee to obtain an interim award of compensation pending the full hearing.

Discrimination

A discrimination claim will arise where an employer terminates the employment for a reason that relates to the employee's age, sex, race, disability, religion or beliefs, or sexual orientation. It is also unlawful to discriminate on grounds of part-time or fixed-term status. There is no cap on the compensation that may be awarded for discrimination claims.

Note that the burden of proof provisions in the relevant statutes and regulations only require an employee to point to facts from which the employment tribunal could conclude that the employer had committed an act of discrimination. If the employee satisfies this burden of proof, the tribunal "shall uphold the complaint" unless the employer proves that it did not commit the act.

If the employee may have grounds to bring a discrimination claim, the employer will want to give careful consideration to how the termination is documented and the procedure it adopts when carrying out the dismissal, to enable it to show that there has been no discrimination. The statutory disciplinary and grievance procedure applies where the employee argues that the dismissal was an act of discrimination. If the employer has failed to follow the procedure, any compensation subsequently awarded will be increased by between 10 and 50 percent.

Negotiating a Settlement with the Senior Manager

There are no statutory rules as to how severance with a departing employee is to be negotiated and paid. The exception to this is if the employee is being made redundant. If this is the case, and the employee has two or more years of continuous employment, then the individual will be entitled to receive statutory redundancy pay (such pay is based on a formula of age, length of service, and capped weekly salary).

In addition if the employer operates an enhanced severance pay plan, the individual may be entitled to a payment in accordance with such plan.

In circumstances where there may be no fair reason for the dismissal, it is therefore common for the employer to seek to negotiate a termination package with the employee (particularly a senior employee).

Various types of information will be needed to calculate the compensation to which an employee is likely to be entitled for breach of contract and/or unfair dismissal as follows:

- A copy of any service agreement and any amendments, any terms and conditions of employment, staff or other handbooks, any letters or memoranda promising promotion or mentioning prospects, and the employee's replies;
- Relevant documents relating to pension arrangements, life insurance benefits, and share option plans, including details of all of the employee's entitlements under such plans;
- Confirmation of the employee's current salary and details of all other benefits, including bonus arrangements, car, arrangements under which the employer pays the employee's home telephone bill or rent (in full or part), commission plans, and profit-sharing plans;

- Whether there is any scope for benefits such as medical or life insurance to be continued for a period post-termination;
- Whether the employee works abroad and if so, details of time spent abroad, and, if there are split contracts, duties and salary under each agreement;
- Age of the employee;
- Whether the employee has obtained new employment and, if so, the date on which the employment commenced or will commence, and details of terms and conditions of new employment, or if the employee has not yet obtained alternative employment, his or her prospects of doing so;
- Whether the employee has any company credit cards or other credit facilities, including loans from or arranged by the company;
- Whether the employee has any accrued but untaken vacation, and if so, the number of days outstanding;
- Whether the employee is a director of associated companies or of other companies as nominee for the company; and
- Whether the employee holds any shares as nominee or for qualification purposes.

Negotiations should always be conducted on a without-prejudice basis, bearing in mind that at any time an "agreed" termination may cease to be agreed and an employee may seek compensation for wrongful dismissal, unfair dismissal, and/or discrimination if appropriate.

The company should be aware that as far as the statutory claims are concerned, a "full and final settlement" that purports to preclude any person from bringing tribunal proceedings will not waive an employee's statutory claims unless the employee takes independent legal advice on the effect of the agreement and its impact on the individual's ability to pursue his or her rights before an employment tribunal. This means that an agreement not to take proceedings will not be enforceable unless the settlement agreement complies with the prescribed provisions of the relevant statute. The employer would usually make a contribution toward the costs incurred by an employee in seeking such advice, as it is in the employer's interest that an employee's waiver of claims is fully effective.

Restrictive Covenants

Under UK law, it is permissible for the employment contract to contain various post-termination restrictive covenants. Provided that the employer has a legitimate business interest to protect and the restrictive covenant goes no further than is reasonably necessary to protect that legitimate business interest, it should be capable of being enforced. Common restrictive covenants would seek to prevent an employee from soliciting or dealing with the employer's clients, from poaching its key staff, and from engaging in a competing business. The maximum period of post-termination covenant that is usually enforced by a UK court is 12 months (and courts often adopt a restrictive approach to the enforcement on noncompete provisions, as they are the most restrictive of post-termination covenants).

If the contract does not contain appropriate restrictive covenants (or if the employee's employment has been terminated in breach of contract, in which case the covenants would not apply), then as part of the settlement negotiation the employer may wish to agree new post-termination restrictions with the individual. As with all elements of a negotiation, the departing employee is likely to want to be remunerated for any new restrictions.

Other Common Terms

In addition to post-termination restrictions, it is common for the parties to negotiate nondisclosure wording in relation to the terms of the settlement, mutual nondisparagement wording, internal/external announcement wording, and the wording of any reference.

SECTION V

What prohibitions exist against discrimination on the basis of age, race, gender, disability, pregnancy, and other factors? What are the rights of employees, applicants, or former employees who believe that they have been discriminated against?

Areas of Protection

Discrimination in the employment field is prohibited in the UK on the following grounds:

- Sex (under the Sex Discrimination Act 1975 and the Equal Pay Act 1970);
- Pregnancy or maternity;
- Marital or civil partnership status;
- Gender reassignment;
- Age;
- Race or ethnic or national origins;
- Color or nationality;
- Religion, religious beliefs, or philosophical beliefs;
- Sexual orientation; and
- Disability.

Statutory Rules

A claim for discrimination may be brought before an employment tribunal if all of the following conditions are met:

- The case falls within one of the legally protected areas (as described above).
- The claimant has suffered one of the relevant classes of discrimination (direct discrimination, indirect discrimination, victimization, harassment, or disability-related discrimination).

- The discrimination has taken place in circumstances that are actionable in the employment field. (Discrimination is not, in itself, actionable, but must occur in circumstances that are protected by the discrimination legislation.)
- The claimant is a class of person protected by discrimination law. (Discrimination legislation in relation to employment extends to employment at an establishment in Great Britain. It covers applicants for such employment, persons in such employment, and persons who have left such employment.)
- The employer or other respondent is liable for the discrimination. (Discrimination law allows an employee, job applicant, or former employee to bring claims not only against employers but also against a manager, fellow employee, or other individual who is responsible for the discrimination or harassment.)
- The respondent does not have a defense.

The task of proving a discrimination case lies initially on the claimant. It is now the case in all employment cases under the discrimination legislation (with a limited exception under the Race Relations Act 1976) that when the claimant has established a prima facie case of discrimination, the burden of proof then formally shifts to the respondent to prove (on the balance of probabilities) that its treatment of the claimant was not for a prohibited discriminatory reason.

Legal Effect of Nondiscrimination Policies

Nondiscrimination policies are generally not legally binding. However, they may be produced as evidence that an employer has taken practical steps to prevent employees from committing discriminatory acts (and so potentially assist with an employer's defense in a discrimination claim).

Venue and Procedure

The main method of enforcement of discrimination law is through individual claims brought by employees in employment tribunals. Employment tribunal practice and procedure differs from that in other civil courts, and is governed by its own set of rules.

A person may present the complaint to an employment tribunal that another person has committed an unlawful act of discrimination or harassment against the claimant (the principal or employer will also be treated as having committed the discrimination) within three months of when the act complained of was done.

All strands of the discrimination legislation provide for a claimant or potential claimant to be able to submit a questionnaire regarding their allegedly discriminatory treatment to a respondent or potential respondent. Failure of the respondent to respond adequately to a questionnaire will in many cases (subject to the "just and equitable" requirement) be sufficient to establish a prima facie case and place the burden of proof on the respondent to prove that there was no unlawful discrimination.

Sanctions and Remedies

Where an employment tribunal finds that a complaint is well founded, it may make a declaration that the claimant has been discriminated against, a recommendation as to action the respondent should take to obviate or reduce the adverse affect on the claimant of the act of discrimination complained, and/or an order requiring the respondent to pay compensation[1] (discrimination disputes can be costly because there is no upper limit on damages). Successful claimants in discrimination cases may also be awarded compensation for injury to feelings (indeed, it is possible to succeed in a claim and obtain a remedy even if the only "loss" suffered is injury to feelings). Although cost orders are sometimes made in the employment tribunal, they are only made in very limited circumstances. Therefore, an employee is usually not at risk of having to pay the employer's costs if their tribunal claim is unsuccessful.

SECTION VI

On the Horizon: What key labor and employment law developments should an employer doing business in the United Kingdom anticipate occurring in the coming year?

The Equality Act 2006 introduced a new limb of employment protection—that of protection against age discrimination. The Equality Act has already had its first anniversary, but as yet there have been very few reported decisions. Employers should therefore monitor developments in discrimination law generally, but in age discrimination cases in particular.

Amendments to the Sex Discrimination Act of 1975 to ensure that the amended Equal Treatment Directive (76/207/EEC) is implemented correctly did not come into force on October 1, 2007, as planned. According to the Women and Equality Unit, the amendments are now due to come into force "at the earliest possible opportunity." The changes will include the elimination of the statutory requirement for a comparator who is not pregnant or on maternity leave when a woman brings a claim for pregnancy or maternity leave discrimination.

The Corporate Manslaughter and Corporate Homicide Act 2007 came into effect on April 6, 2008. It creates a new criminal offense of corporate manslaughter. It does not apply to individuals, but convicted companies will face an unlimited fine as well as a possible "remedial order" and "publicity order."

Employers concerned about the implications of the extension to statutory leave entitlement have until April 1, 2009, before the leave becomes 28 days (it increased to 24 days on October 1, 2007). Some time the same year, the government is expected to extend paid maternity leave to 12 months, some of the latter part of which will be transferable to the father.

NOTE

1. The compensation ordered by the tribunal will take account of the financial loss resulting to the claimant due to the discrimination complained of. In general, the tribunal will seek to assess the financial compensation necessary to put the claimant back into the position he or she would have been in were it not for the discrimination.

CHAPTER **20**

LABOR AND EMPLOYMENT LAW
IN THE UNITED STATES

PHILIP M. BERKOWITZ
ANDERS ETGEN REITZ

SECTION I

My client wishes to establish a manufacturing facility in the United States and will need to hire a workforce. What are the key issues involved?

The labor and employment laws of the United States are regulated on both federal and state levels. Thus, in many cases, relevant labor and employment issues differ from state to state.

Unlike most other countries, there is a general presumption of "at-will" employment in all states with the exception of Montana. At-will employment means that either the employer or the employee may terminate the employment relationship without notice or cause (see "Statutory Restrictions on Dismissal Without Cause" in Section IV).

Employment Contracts: Who Receives Them and What Must They Include?

There is no general obligation in the United States for the employer to issue employment contracts. As the at-will employment is only a presumption that may be rebutted by other circumstances, it is generally recommended that the employer use caution when drafting an employment contract, as this may imply more protection than available under the at-will doctrine.

Employment contracts are more frequently used in situations where special terms and conditions not covered by the company's general employment policies apply. This could be the case if the employer wishes to impose a noncompetition clause or fixed-term employment, or if the employee is awarded more favorable terms such as severance pay or a change-of-control clause.

Senior executives and management level employees are far more likely to be subject to a formal employment agreement than are general line and nonmanagement employees. These agreements will likely cover such complex issues as deferred compensation and bonus arrangements, noncompetition agreements, and provision of severance in the event employment is terminated without cause.

Notwithstanding the general rarity of employment agreements, at least among nonexecutive employees, employers are making more frequent use of offer letters, which employees are expected to countersign. These offer letters may state some essential terms of employment, including an acknowledgment that employment is at will and that the employees will respect confidential trade secret information, and they may even incorporate a noncompetition agreement.

If an employment contract is issued, it is important to carefully consider the language to avoid unintended implied rights such as termination for cause requirements, special grievances procedures, and probation periods.

There is no legal requirement that an employment agreement must be in a particular language. Naturally, for the purposes of enforcement, it is important that any agreement between the employer and employee, and indeed any written policies, be written clearly and in a language that the employee understands.

It is generally recommended that the employer issue general employment policies stating the terms and conditions of the employment relationship. Such policies may include rules of conduct, disciplinary actions, safety rules, harassment policies, substance abuse policies, discharge or grievances procedures, vacation regulation, and sickness procedures. When drafting such employment policies, it is important to consider the language carefully because it may provide a basis for implied rights. It is for this reason that the policies generally state that they do not constitute a contract, and that the employer reserves the right to modify or even deviate from them.

Changes in employment contracts generally require acceptance from the employee unless the changes can be reasonably justified or the employer previously has reserved the right to change the contract. The same may be the case with employment policies. However, here the courts are more willing to accept unilateral changes, as the terms often also have been introduced unilaterally. In both cases, it is recommended that the employer reserves its right to make future changes. If the employer contemplates changes it is advised that reasonable notice be given, as this will allow unsatisfied employees to voice their concerns and may influence the courts' view on the enforceability of the changes.

Fixed-term contracts are generally considered to be terminable only "for cause." It is therefore advised that such agreements be phrased carefully to avoid unintended employee protection. Alternatively, they may provide for termination at will, and set forth the employee's specific rights in those circumstances—which may include payment of less severance than would otherwise be implied by the term of the contract.

Arbitration agreements are most common when hiring managerial employees. In some companies, they are also part of the general standard employment contracts. The advantage of arbitration, besides costs, confidentiality, and duration, is that it may lessen the likelihood of an award of punitive damages claims. The courts generally accept such clauses if they are procedurally fair and not in violation of public policy.

The issue of whether to require arbitration of disputes is a complex one that goes beyond the scope of this chapter. The principal advantage to arbitration is that the employer can avoid a jury trial, and juries are notoriously sympathetic to employee plaintiffs. Nevertheless, many employers disfavor arbitration, despite its varied advantages, because the employer may not have access to the same level of discovery, and because of the limited ability to have the arbitrators decide dispositive motions, among other reasons. Additionally, the arbitration process is becoming less streamlined and more like a traditional litigation, and so employers are increasingly abandoning the arbitration process as an alternative to litigation.

Hiring Managerial Employees

Managerial and supervisory personnel are excluded from the protection of the National Labor Relations Act (NLRA) (see "Labor Unions" in this section) and most often also from federal statutes such as the Fair Labor Standards Act (FLSA). This gives the parties more freedom to determine the terms and conditions of the employment. However, such employees will most likely not be considered independent contractors and will still be protected by the antidiscrimination statutes (see Section V). It is important to remember that even though managers may not be protected by some of these statutes, lower-level employees applying for a managerial position may be still be covered. In addition, it is somewhat disputed whether some groups such as partners in accounting and law firms are independent contractors or employees.

When hiring managerial employees, it is more common to draft employment contracts, as the need for special provisions is likely to be higher. Examples of such provisions could be restrictive covenants, conflict-of-interest clauses, arbitration agreements, and confidentiality provisions.

Restrictive covenants, such as noncompetition clauses, are generally enforceable in most states. However, overbroad clauses may be denied enforcement by the courts. Therefore, it is important when drafting such provisions to consider the reasonable necessity of the imposed restrictions regarding the duration and the geographic scope.

When hiring managerial employees, it is often common to grant some form of financial participation plan, such as bonus plans, stock option plans, or other types of financial instruments. There is generally freedom of contract when drafting such plans. However, as the plans may fall under the complicated requirements of the Employee Retirement Income Security Act (ERISA), the language of such plans should be carefully considered.

Wages and Benefits

Minimum Wages

Under the FLSA, most companies are required to pay a minimum wage to the employees, and the salary must be paid on time. Along with minimum wage requirements, the employees covered under the FLSA must be paid at time and a half for each hour worked over 40 hours a week, irrespective of whether the overtime was requested by the employer. The FLSA sets standards for working time and time off that should be followed carefully. Additionally, many states have their own parallel laws that may even exceed the requirements of the FLSA and give employees even greater rights.

There are a number of exceptions or exemptions to the FLSA, depending generally on the employee's level of education and responsibility. This is a highly complex area that has resulted in significant litigation in recent years, with recoveries and settlements for groups of employees who claim that they were improperly classified as nonexempt, or denied overtime and other wage payments, in the tens and even hundreds of millions of dollars. Penalties include not only the unpaid wages but additional liquidated damages and attorneys' fees. In some states, violation of wage-and-hour laws is criminal and may result in fines or imprisonment (although criminal prosecution is rare and is limited to only the most egregious cases of exploitation).

Employers must be sure to put in place policies and procedures to assure that their employees are properly classified as exempt or nonexempt under the FLSA, and that their nonexempt employees are properly paid for time worked.

Holidays and Vacation

Private companies are not required to grant paid vacation or holidays. In many cases, employees are not granted paid vacation the first year. Thereafter, the amount of paid vacation may vary from two to four weeks per year. If the employee is granted vacation or holiday with salary, specific rules may apply. In some states, vacation entitlement becomes vested as it accrues and will be payable upon termination. Other states may accept forfeiture provisions in the employment policies.

Leave

Under the Family and Medical Leave Act (FMLA), employees with more than 12 months' seniority may be entitled to 12 weeks' unpaid leave per 12-month period for a number of family- and medical-related matters, including the birth or adoption of a child or a serious medical condition of the employee or someone with whom the employee is "associated," such as a family member. The employer is required to hold the job or a similar position during FMLA leave.

Under the Uniformed Services Employment and Reemployment Rights Act, employees may be entitled to up to five years' unpaid leave to serve in the military. The federal Jury System Improvements Act also requires employers to provide leave for employees who are called to serve on a jury; in some states, the leave must be paid.

Illness

Employers are not legally required to pay salary during illness. Most employers do offer paid leave for a limited period of time, ranging from less than full salary to full salary, and others allow a certain number of paid sick days per year. Under certain state laws, the employer may be required to insure the employee against short-term illness.

Pension and Insurance

The employer is not required to offer pension or other retirement benefits to the employees. However, if the employer does provide a pension plan it may fall under the complicated provisions of ERISA, which requires that the pension plan be in writing. Some pension plans are subject to favorable tax treatment, such as the so-called 401(k) plans. For that reason, ERISA plans are most often carefully drafted by tax and "ERISA" attorneys.

Employers are not legally obligated to offer health insurance from the employer. However, as health insurance is costly and the employer may get better rates by grouping the employees, these kinds of insurance plans are often offered as a valuable employment benefit. Employers that do provide health insurance may be required to continue the benefits under the federal Consolidated Omnibus Budget Reconciliation Act (COBRA) for a certain period after termination of the employment relationship. Special discrimination issues should also be considered (see Section V), as the pension or insurance plan may indirectly disfavor a protected group of employees.

Labor Unions

Under the NLRA, which covers companies engaging in interstate commerce, a labor union may seek to establish support by the majority of workers in an appropriate unit. This is usually done through elections among the employees or by the employer's voluntary recognition. The cases regarding establishing and recognizing unions mostly concerns the issue of what constitutes an "appropriate" unit. In cases where more than one union seeks to represent the employees, the employer should be careful when considering to voluntarily recognize one of the unions, as this may violate the rights of the employees to choose their own representative.

If a union is successful in obtaining certification as the majority representative, the employer is obliged to recognize its authority as the exclusive bargaining agent of so-called mandatory subjects of bargaining, which are wages, hours, and terms and conditions related to wages.

Regardless of the presence of a union, employees are generally protected from reprisal for engaging in concerted activities with the purpose of establishing better terms and conditions of employment. The employer is prevented from interfering with these rights and any defensive actions should be considered carefully.

Collective Agreements

As the exclusive bargaining agent, the employer must bargain in good faith with the certified union on matters related to wages, hours, and terms and conditions of employment. The employer is not required to enter into a collective bargaining agreement, but the employer must have a good-faith intention to reach an agreement. This may require the employer to participate in a minimal number of meetings with the union, to provide sufficient information, to consider proposals, and not to take unreasonable positions solely to avoid an agreement.

When the parties have exhausted their abilities to reach an agreement, the parties are at "impasse" and unilateral terms and conditions may be implemented by the employer, with the risk of strikes, lockouts, and the like. During a strike, the employer is permitted to hire permanent replacements unless the strike is the result of an employer's unfair labor practice, in which case it can only hire temporary replacements during the length of the strike.

If a collective bargaining agreement is signed, the employer is generally prevented from unilaterally changing the terms and conditions of employment as set forth in the collective bargaining agreement for the duration of the agreement. Should the parties wish to change the agreement, specific procedures apply, which, among others, require the party requesting renegotiations to issue a written notice 60 days prior to the expiration. Matters reflected in the collective bargaining agreement or discussed substantively in negotiations may not be changed without the agreement of both parties. However, the employer may change terms and conditions of employment that were neither discussed nor reflected in the agreement. Moreover, no-strike clauses are enforceable if they are made explicit in the collective bargaining agreement.

There are no statutory requirements of what must be in a collective bargaining agreement. However, besides mandatory and permissive subjects of bargaining, the parties may wish to include terms and conditions that are deemed "unlawful" subjects. The nature of the contemplated terms should therefore be examined carefully before signing.

There is no permanent arbitration institution for labor disputes in the United States. However, arbitration clauses are common in collective bargaining agreements. The courts generally accept such clauses if they are procedurally fair and not in violation of public policy.

Works Councils

Works councils generally do not exist in the United States in the known form introduced by the European Union (EU), where employees and management are required to meet and consult about day-to-day issues arising in the organization. Such consultation bodies are generally not allowed under the NLRA if the purpose of the meetings is to "deal" with working conditions. As such activities may be viewed as unlawful interference by the employer, it is recommended that the purpose and content of any such meetings between management and the employees be carefully monitored to include only exchange of information, brainstorming, suggestions, and other unilateral mechanisms.

SECTION II

My client is acquiring an existing business in the United States. How do I assess the existing workforce and consider changes?

As in most other countries, it is common to carry out a due diligence procedure to assess the existing workforce in a target company. This is especially the case in a stock deal where the buyer generally assumes all employer liabilities, but also in an asset deal where the buyer may assume liability for the seller's conduct before the closing. The personal data protection in due diligence procedures is generally not nearly as strong as in the EU, for example, and therefore the buyer may request detailed information about employees. However, employers need to be aware of privacy protection granted to employee medical information under the federal Health Insurance Portability and Accountability Act of 1996 (HIPAA), which ensures the privacy and security of health information.

Generally, there are no federal statutes regulating transfer of business as known in other countries; however, some states have enacted regulations in this regard for specific industries, such as New York for building service workers. In most other situations, the courts have developed certain protections of employees in target companies, but the general rule is still at-will employment, which entitles both seller and buyer to terminate employees without notice or cause.

Making Changes to Key Managerial Positions

As a result of the at-will employment doctrine, the buyer is generally not required to hire the employees in the target company if the sale is carried out as an asset deal. In a stock deal, the buyer generally assumes all liabilities as a successor employer and any change in management must be done through terminations. The NLRA does not protect managers and supervisors (see "Hiring Managerial Employees" in Section I). However, the application of these exclusions should be considered carefully on a case-by-case basis. Individual contracts and employment policies may also protect the managerial employees from termination due to change of ownership, which makes the due diligence process crucial to the success of the takeover.

Any discussions with senior management regarding their role in the company going forward should be carried out with care to avoid an implied protection against termination. When contemplating termination of senior management it is important to avoid conflicts with the Age Discrimination in Employment Act (ADEA), which protects employees over 40 years old (see Section V); ERISA, which protects employees from termination close to vesting of employment benefits; and the Older Workers Benefit Protection Act (OWBPA), which protects older workers from losing their retirement benefits.

Carrying Out a Workforce Reduction

As most employees are subject to at-will employment, the buyer is generally free to carry out a workforce reduction in the acquired company regardless of whether it is an asset or a stock deal, provided that the buyer is not acting in bad faith or violating antidiscrimination statutes (see Section V). Unless otherwise agreed, the employees are generally not entitled to special notice or severance, with the exception of particular federal or state notice statues as discussed next.

The Federal Workers Adjustment and Retraining Notification Act (WARN) applies to reductions that result in plant closing or that exceed 50 employees within a 90-day period in companies with (1) 100 or more full-time employees or (2) 100 or more full- or part-time employees, who aggregately work at least 4,000 hours per week exclusive of overtime.

Under WARN, the employer is required to give a minimum of 60 days' notice before terminating the employment relationship, unless the layoffs were caused by unforeseeable events, natural disasters, or similar exceptions in the Act. Unlike the NLRA (see "Hiring Managerial Employees" in Section I and "Making Changes to Key Managerial Positions," previously), WARN also covers management and supervisors.

The employer is required to give notice to (1) the affected nonunion employees, (2) representatives of affected unionized employees, (3) the state's dislocated-worker unit, and (4) the local government where the layoffs are executed. Each of the notices is subject to specific requirements.

According to WARN, the employer's obligation to provide 60 days' notice is transferred to the buyer at the date of sale. Any employees who are still employed with the seller at the effective date of the sale shall be considered an employee of the buyer. This means that if the buyer does not wish to hire all the seller's employees and is not able to have the seller perform the terminations before the sale, the buyer will be required to follow the WARN procedure.

Violation of the employer's duties under WARN may result in civil penalties for each day of violation. In addition, the employer may be forced to pay back pay and benefits to the affected employees for the 60-day period. It is therefore recommended that the duties and liabilities under WARN be considered in the transfer agreement. Employees may waive their rights under WARN in exchange for adequate consideration. Some states have enacted their own WARN statutes, which may provide for better protection of the employees.

In a stock deal where the employees are represented by a certified union, the buyer may be forced to recognize the union and bargain over the effects of the contemplated reduction in workforce. This may also be the case in an asset deal if the majority of employees in the target company are transferred to the buyer. If the target company has entered into a collective agreement, this may prevent a reduction in workforce.

Aside from the general concerns regarding termination of employees in protected groups (see Section I), no employees enjoy special protection against workforce reductions. Union-represented employees are not immune from termination, but the collective agreement may require the employer to show legitimate business reasons for the terminations and some collective agreements may expressly prevent reductions in workforce.

Reorganizing the Workforce

The buyer's contemplation to reorganize the workforce leads to many of the same considerations as changing employment contracts and employment policies (see "Employment Contracts" in Section I) and as reductions in the workforce (see

"Carrying Out a Workforce Reduction" in this section). There is generally no statutory protection against the buyer's unilateral changes in employment terms and conditions.

In a stock deal, the buyer should carefully consider the existing employment contracts and employment policies to determine whether unilateral changes are permitted (see "Employment Contracts" in Section I). If the employees are covered by a collective agreement, the employer will be required to follow the special procedure for renegotiating the terms with the union (see "Collective Agreements" in Section I). If no collective agreement has been reached but a certified union exists, the employer may be required to recognize the union as the exclusive bargaining agent and may have a duty to bargain in good faith about the proposed changes.

In an asset deal, the employer is generally not required to offer the same terms or conditions, but should the employees be covered by a collective agreement, the buyer may be expressly required to assume the seller's obligations under the agreement.

Relocating the workplace generally does not require acceptance from the employees. However, relocation resulting in plant closing or mass layoffs may be subject to a special WARN procedure (see "Carrying Out a Workforce Reduction") unless (1) the employer offers to transfer the affected employees to another location within a reasonable commuting distance with no more than a six-month break in employment or (2) the employer offers to transfer the affected employees to a more distant site within the same time and the employees accept the offer within 30 days of the offer, the closing, or the layoff, whichever occurs later. There may be additional requirements under state law.

Of course, there exists the risk that relocating the workplace would be challenged as an unlawful excuse to eliminate employees in a particular protected group such as age, race, or gender.

Changing the Wage and Benefits Structure

Unlike reorganizations of the workforce, the wage and benefits structure may be considered contractually protected terms. The employer may be required to give proper notice in order to change the wages and employment benefits. If the employees are protected against dismissal, this may prevent unjustified changes in the employees' compensation. Employers may, however, lawfully reserve to themselves the right to make unilateral changes in compensation or benefits.

In a stock deal, this means that the buyer is recommended to seek consent from the employees before introducing wage and benefit plans to the target company's employees or otherwise ensure that proper notice is given. If the employees are covered by a collective agreement, the same issues arise as with reorganizations. Consent, however, is implied by the employees' decision to remain employed after notice is given.

If the benefit plan is covered by ERISA or OWBPA, the employer may be forced to follow special procedures contained in the plan documents, which should be followed carefully.

In an asset deal, as with reorganizations in workforce, the buyer is not generally obligated to offer the same terms and conditions as the target company, unless such rights are expressly or impliedly agreed by the seller.

Consulting with Labor Unions or Works Councils

There is generally no special requirement that the buyer must consult with the unions or employee representatives due to the purchase of assets or stocks in a target company.

In an asset deal, collective agreements do not transfer automatically unless expressly provided in the collective agreement. The buyer may therefore generally introduce new terms and conditions to the seller's employees. However, the buyer may be required to recognize the union and bargain in good faith over the terms and conditions if a majority of the seller's employees is transferred (see "Making Changes to Key Managerial Positions"). If the buyer contemplates major restructurings or reductions in workforce, the buyer may be required to bargain over the effects of these changes (see "Reorganizing the Workforce") and to give notice to the union representatives under WARN (see "Carrying Out a Workforce Reduction").

In a stock deal, the buyer is generally obligated to assume all obligations of the target company, and any change in collective terms and conditions must be bargained over with the union (see "Collective Agreements" in Section I).

Regarding works councils, see "Works Councils" in Section I.

Consulting with the Government

There is generally no obligation to consult with the authorities regarding the employees about the transfer of business irrespective of whether a stock or an asset deal.

Should the transfer of business result in reductions in workforce, the buyer may be required under WARN to give notice to the local government where the layoffs take place (see "Carrying Out a Workforce Reduction").

✪ SECTION III

My client wishes to sell its existing facility. What restrictions do we need to consider?

Assessing Employment Contracts

The most important consideration for a seller of a target company with employees is usually the ability to transfer all of its liabilities and obligations toward these employees.

In a transfer of assets, the liabilities generally transfer at the time of closing, unless otherwise agreed. The seller may in some cases also be liable for events after closing, such as the buyer's obligations under WARN to notify the employees of mass layoffs (see "Carrying Out a Workforce Reduction" in Section II) and under antidiscrimination statutes when hiring employees from the target company (see Section V). It is therefore recommended that the seller ensure the indemnification for such claims with warranties and preclosing conditions.

Consulting with the Government

See "Consulting with the Government" in Section II.

Consulting with Labor Unions or Works Councils

The seller is not generally required to notify the unions of the contemplated sale of the target business, regardless of whether it is carried out as a stock or an asset deal unless otherwise provided in a collective agreement.

An asset deal resulting in reduction in the seller's workforce or other material changes in working conditions may require the seller to negotiate with a certified union over the effects of these changes (see "Carrying Out a Workforce Reduction" in Section II).

If a collective agreement exists and is not transferred to the buyer, it may continue to run regardless of the transfer of employees. The employer is therefore recommended to contact the union to dissolve the agreement.

In a stock deal, there is principally no change in the identity of the employer and therefore no grounds for consultation unless the buyer introduces changes. If the seller assumes preclosing obligations to reduce the workforce, the same rules apply as to the buyer (see "Carrying Out a Workforce Reduction" in Section II).

A collective agreement would, in a stock deal, transfer to the buyer, unless expressly provided otherwise in the agreement. If the seller remains obligated under the agreement, it is recommended that the transfer agreement include a provision for indemnification by the buyer.

Negotiating with the Purchaser: Special Labor Issues

In a stock sale, the buyer may want to ensure that the seller guarantees that all conduct prior to the closing has been lawful and that any claims arising from the preclosing period will be carried out by the seller, who will indemnify the buyer of any such claims. If a reduction in workforce is foreseeable, the buyer may request that this reduction be done by the seller, who then bears the risk of discrimination and other claims. In contrast, the seller may wish to transfer all liabilities to the buyer and avoid liability for conduct postclosing.

In an asset transfer, the buyer generally would only assume liabilities toward the employees that the buyer hires, and then only for postclosing events. The seller may be interested in ensuring that it is not held liable for the buyer's hiring of employees in violation of antidiscrimination statutes (see Section V) and perhaps even require the buyer to offer all employees a position to avoid possible exposure of liability in a termination process. The buyer may be interested in retaining maximum flexibility in determining which employees to offer a position and at the same time avoid any liability as a result of the seller's termination of the remaining employees. The buyer may wish to have the seller carry out the necessary reduction in workforce prior to closing to avoid any exposure. Often, the target company's key employees are vital for the future business and so it may be important to the buyer to require the seller to make certain efforts to ensure the retention of these employees up to closing. This is often done by having the seller introduce bonus plans and the like, subject to a successful transfer.

SECTION IV

My client wishes to replace its senior manager(s). What restrictions do we need to consider?

Employment Contracts

In general, replacing senior managers imposes the same concerns as making changes in key managerial positions (see "Making Changes to Key Managerial Positions" in Section II). As the managers are excluded from the NLRA (see "Hiring Managerial Employees" in Section I), there is no concern of union interference or protection of (concerted) management activities. Employment of managers is presumptively at will, and there is no general statutory protection against replacing managers (see "Statutory Restrictions on Dismissal Without Cause" in this section).

Nevertheless, it is very common that senior managers have some protection in their individual employment contracts (see "Hiring Managerial Employees" in Section I). Contractual protection includes clauses like period of notice and just-cause requirements, grievances procedures, exit clauses, transfer of control, severance pay, and so on.

In cases where the contract requires breach or similar justified cause to terminate the contract, it is important to note that senior management may be protected to some extent by a business judgment rule and that poor business decisions may not necessarily entitle termination unless bad faith is established.

Discrimination Issues

Management is also protected under the antidiscrimination statutes (see Section V), and the employer should carefully consider the reasoning for the replacement. Statutes particularly relevant to management include ADEA, which protects employees over 40 years old; ERISA, which protects employees close to vesting of employment benefits; and Title VII, which protects against, among other things, sex and race discrimination.

Statutory Severance Pay Requirements

Generally, senior managers are also subject to at-will employment (see "Statutory Restrictions on Dismissal Without Cause," next) and there is no statutory requirement to pay severance unless the employer is contractually obligated to do so.

Often the employer has good reason to ensure the amicable exit of senior management to avoid any external exposure. In such cases, severance pay is often combined with confidentiality agreements. The employer may want to arrange for agreed press releases, and the manager may be interested in a reference. It is generally recommended that a severance agreement be drafted reflecting the final settlement of all claims.

Statutory Restrictions on Dismissal Without Cause

Under the at-will employment doctrine, there is presumptively no requirement to justify the dismissal of senior management.

This presumption is very strong and deviated from only in specific circumstances, such as (1) situations where an explicit or implied contract or collective agreement states otherwise, (2) situations where the employer is preventing the employee from engaging in protected concerted activities, or (3) to exercise rights under statutes such as

- NLRA
- FLSA
- ERISA
- FMLA
- WARN
- Consumer Credit Protection Act
- Civil Service Reform Act
- State and federal whistleblower statues (see "Whistleblower Protection" in Section VI)

In addition, under court-developed common law, the employment relationship does imply an obligation of good faith and fair dealing. If the termination is a result of bad-faith motivation, the employee may claim breach of contract or tort (depending on the state in which the employee works).

Should the courts find the dismissal to be unlawful or wrongful, the manager may claim back pay, compensatory and punitive damages, or front pay depending on the basis for the claim. Reinstatement claims are rare in senior management claims, as the company may have justified business reasons to refuse reinstatement.

❂ SECTION V

What prohibitions exist against discrimination on the basis of age, race, gender, disability, pregnancy, and other factors? What are the rights of employees, applicants, or former employees who believe that they have been discriminated against?

Statutory Rules

There are a number of federal, state, and local laws protecting minority groups against discrimination in the United States. The dual system may cause conflicts between federal and state regulation. In some cases, state regulation offers less protection than the federal statutes, and in those situations federal regulation should be followed. On the other hand, state and local laws may, in some cases, offer greater protection (e.g., prohibiting discrimination on the basis of sexual orientation), in which case state law should govern. The most common federal statutes protecting against discrimination are the following:

- Americans with Disabilities Act (ADA), protecting discrimination of employees with disabilities.
- ADEA, protecting employees age 40 and over from discrimination because of age.
- Title VII of the Civil Rights Act (Title VII), protecting employees from discrimination because of race, color, religion, national origin, sex, or pregnancy.
- Equal Pay Act (EPA), protecting employees from wage discrimination because of sex.

Discrimination cases are generally divided into

- *Disparate treatment cases*: Intentional discrimination based on illegal or pro- tected criteria.
- *Disparate impact cases*: Unintentional adverse effect on protected group due to a neutral employer practice.
- *Harassment cases*: Harassment based on the characteristics of a protected group.
- *Retaliation cases*: Retaliation for asserting protection under discrimination and harassment law.

Disparate Treatment Cases

Disparate treatment generally requires that the employee initially produce sufficient evidence of the employer's unlawful intention. However, circumstantial evidence is often sufficient. In a failure to hire case, the employee must further establish that he or she (1) is within the protected group, (2) applied for the job, (3) was qualified for the job, (4) was denied the job, and (5) the employer continued to accept applications for the job. This evidence requirement has been applied with natural modifications to other employer decisions such as discharges and denial of promotion. Disparate treatment cases may also include situations where the employee has been forced to resign due to the employment practice of so-called "constructive discharge," which is recognized by some states.

The employer may rebut the presumption of discrimination by showing (1) the employee was treated the same as employees outside the protected group, (2) the employee would not have been hired due to other nondiscriminatory factors, or (3) the employer's action was justified by the so-called bona fide occupational qualification (BFOQ) defense. To establish a BFOQ defense, the employer must prove (1) a relationship between the job requirement and the job performance, (2) the necessity of the job requirement for successful job performance, and (3) that the job performance affected is the essence of the employer's business operation. The BFOQ defense is very limited and the burden of proof is on the employer.

Disparate Impact Cases

Disparate impact requires the employee to show that a neutral employment practice adversely affects members of a protected group. Cases often involve employment requirements such as height, weight, education, standardized tests, or other seemingly neutral practice that presumably gives a valid prediction of the necessary employee characteristics, but that due to social, cultural, or historical reasons affect one minority group significantly differently from the majority.

The employer may rebut the presumption of discrimination by showing (1) that the neutral employment practice did not adversely affect the protected group or (2) that the neutral employment practice was justified by business necessity. The first defense often involves a battle of statistics to find the relevant group of affected persons. Regarding the second defense, the courts require significant proof of the necessity once the employee has established that the employment practice adversely affects a protected group. (However, in age-discrimination cases, the employer need show only that the practice was based on a "reasonable factor other than age.")

Harassment Cases

The discrimination statutes also protect members of the protected groups from harassment in the workplace based on the characteristics of the group. The employee must establish that one or more supervisors engaged in harassment that resulted in demotion, termination, or denial of benefit or that the harassment has created a hostile work environment. In hostile working environment cases, the employer may have an affirmative defense to liability if the employer has exercised reasonable care in attempting to prevent, and promptly correct, workplace harassment, and the employee unreasonably failed to take advantage of such opportunities. For this reason, it is recommended that the employer put into place sufficient antiharassment policies.

Retaliation Cases

Most discrimination laws, as other employment protection statutes (see "Statutory Restrictions on Dismissal Without Cause" in Section IV), contain provisions that protect employees in asserting their rights under the act. Retaliation cases generally fall under employee opposition or participation cases. In opposition cases, employees are generally protected from retaliation for complaining or protesting against an employer practice if they had reasonable and good faith to believe that the employer's practice was unlawful under the act. In participation cases, employees are generally protected when filing charges, testifying, and so on against the employer in a discrimination case, even if the charge is later shown to be without merit.

Enforcement

Discrimination cases are enforced by the Equal Employment Opportunity Commission (EEOC) or by private actions. Before bringing a lawsuit under Title VII, the employee must exhaust his or her administrative remedies through EEOC. A charge of discrimination must be filed with the EEOC (or a local state or municipal agency) within 300 days of the act of discrimination. The EEOC has no authority to impose remedies. However, some state and local agencies do have the power to award relief.

Discrimination cases are often subject to so-called class actions where a few individuals bring the case on behalf of a larger group. As Title VII and ADEA allow the employee to demand a jury trial, these factors significantly increase the potential exposure of discrimination disputes. Mandatory arbitration covering discrimination cases is generally permitted. The employer may consider imposing arbitration on its employees, as arbitration limits the risk of exposure and punitive damages claims are generally not awarded. The courts generally accept such clauses if they are procedurally fair and not in violation of public policy.

The discrimination statutes may provide for back pay, compensatory damages, punitive damages, reinstatement, or front pay. Punitive and compensatory damages are available only for disparate treatment cases under Title VII and the ADA and are capped to a specific amount dependent on the size of the company. Under ADEA, the employee may instead be awarded liquidated damages up to the same amount as back pay.

Whistleblower Protection

In recent years, the right of employees to complain about allegedly unlawful or unethical conduct, whether to their employer or to government officials, has expanded tremendously. These rights are guaranteed under federal and state laws, but the issue was greatly expanded by passage of the Sarbanes-Oxley Act (SOX).

The Sarbanes-Oxley Act

SOX was passed in the wake of the Enron scandal and similar events. It is intended primarily to make companies more accountable to shareholders for their internal financial controls. However, along with imposing quite substantial internal corporate governance obligations on publicly traded companies, the law also provides a remedy for employee "whistleblowers."

The antiretaliation protections of SOX apply to employees who work for public companies, that is, companies with a class of securities registered under Section 12 of the Securities Exchange Act of 1934, or required to file reports under Section 15(d) of the Securities Exchange Act of 1934. SOX also protects employees from retaliation by "any officer, employee, contractor, subcontractor, or agency of such company." Accordingly, individuals can be held personally liable for retaliatory conduct. This broad coverage differentiates SOX from many other whistleblower statutes, which generally only apply to employers.

An employee is not required to demonstrate that a violation has actually occurred. Rather, to be protected, an employee must only demonstrate that he or she "reasonably believes" that a violation has occurred. Employees have been found to have engaged in protected activity even where the conduct about which they complained was later determined to be legal.

State Whistleblower Protection Laws

Along with SOX, many states have enacted their own laws providing whistle-blower protections. These laws provide a myriad of protections for employees on a number of different subjects, and may vary significantly from each other and from SOX. As an example of those laws, we briefly discuss New Jersey, California, and New York.

The New Jersey Conscientious Employee Protection Act prohibits an employer from taking any retaliatory action against an employee because the employee discloses (or threatens to disclose), to a supervisor or public body, an activity, policy, or practice of the employer (or another employer with whom there is a business relationship) that the employee "reasonably believes" is in violation of "a law, or a rule or regulation" or is "fraudulent or criminal." It also provides protection to employees who object to, or refuse to participate in, any such conduct or who object to, or refuse to participate in, any conduct that the employee reasonably believes "is incompatible with a clear mandate of public policy concerning the public health, safety or welfare or protection of the environment."

California law provides for a number of protections for whistleblowers. First, an employer may not "retaliate against an employee for disclosing information to a government or law enforcement agency, where the employee has reasonable cause to believe that the information discloses a violation of state or federal statute, or violation or noncompliance with a state or federal regulation."[1] The law also prohibits an employer from retaliating against an employee for refusing to participate in an activity that would result in a violation of a state or federal statute.[2]

The law also requires the office of the Attorney General to maintain a whistleblower hotline to receive calls from persons who have information regarding possible violations of state or federal statutes or "violations of fiduciary responsibility by a corporation or limited liability company to its shareholders, investors or employees."[3] The Attorney General is then required to refer such calls to the appropriate government authority for review and possible investigation. Employers are also required to "prominently" display a written notice that lists the hotline telephone number and the employee's rights and responsibilities under the state's whistleblower laws.[4]

The New York whistleblower laws are relatively limited in scope, compared to New Jersey and California. New York Labor Law Section 740 prohibits employers from taking "any retaliatory personnel action" against an employee because the employee discloses, or threatens to disclose, to a supervisor or to a public body, information involving "an activity, policy or practice of the employer that is in violation of law, rule or regulation which violation creates and presents a substantial and specific danger to the public health or safety, or which constitutes health care fraud." The law also protects employees who (1) provide information to, or testify before, any public body conducting an investigation, hearing, or inquiry into any such violation of a law, rule, or regulation, or (2) object to, or refuse to participate in, any such activity, policy, or practice in violation of a law, rule, or regulation. Courts have construed the public health and safety requirement narrowly. Alleged fraudulent economic practices do not constitute a danger to public health or safety.

New York Labor Section 741 provides health care service employees employed by health care service providers with additional whistleblower protection. This section prohibits employers from taking retaliatory action against an employee for (1) disclosing or threatening to disclose, to a supervisor or public body, an employer activity, policy, or practice that the employee, in good faith, reasonably believes constitutes "improper quality of patient care," or (2) objecting to, or refusing to participate in, any employer activity, policy, or practice that the employee, in good faith, reasonably believes constitutes "improper quality of patient care." Notably, employee whistleblower protection is not available under this section unless the employee has first brought the matter to the attention of a supervisor and afforded the employer a reasonable opportunity to correct the activity, policy, or practice, unless there exists an imminent threat to public health or safety or to the health of a specific patient and the employee reasonably believes in good faith that reporting to a supervisor would not result in corrective action.

In the wake of SOX's passage, employers are renewing their attention to internal corporate compliance programs that provide employees (all of whom are, after all, potential whistleblowers) an avenue for bringing alleged wrongdoing to the company's attention so that it may be investigated and remedied.

"Qui Tam" Lawsuits

Another extraordinary federal statute, the federal False Claims Act (FCA), has received renewed attention from employers. The FCA prohibits making fraudulent claims for payment or approval to the U.S. government or to the armed forces of the United States, and further prohibits related activities such as conspiracy to receive payment for a false or fraudulent claim and participating in such a fraud.

Lawsuits brought under the FCA, called "qui tam" cases, may have even broader significance to employers for potential liability and adverse publicity. The FCA does not merely provide whistleblowers with a cause of action; it goes far beyond that, making whistleblowers potential partners with the U.S. Department of Justice, which prosecutes the action on behalf of the employee and shares in the recovery.

Under the FCA, whistleblowers may recover between 15 and 25 percent of the amount recovered against their employer, whether by settlement or otherwise, depending on the extent to which the employee "substantially contributed to the prosecution of the action."

Consequently, recoveries to individual plaintiffs in cases like these, given the extraordinary way in which they may be awarded, are often in the tens of millions of dollars.

Like SOX, the FCA prohibits retaliation against whistleblowers and permits a civil action to recover back wages as well as "any special damages sustained as a result of the discrimination," including attorneys' fees and costs.

The potential liability presented by the FCA, as well as SOX's whistleblower provisions, are more than ever the focus of in-house counsel. Counsel are reviewing their internal practices to assure zero tolerance for fraudulent business practices. Companies are also establishing policies and procedures to encourage employees to complain about any adverse employment action based on protected conduct, to report internally any alleged violations of law, and to assist in any investigation of alleged violations.

SECTION VI

On the Horizon: What key labor and employment law developments should an employer doing business in the United States anticipate occurring in the coming years?

Electronic Discovery and Obligations of Counsel

The explosion in the use of e-mail has created tremendous burdens on companies, and on employment counsel in particular, in the conduct of labor- and employment-related litigation.

In the United States, the courts permit broad discovery of documents, as well as taking depositions and other quite burdensome and expensive disclosure. Thus, any foreign employer should expect that its documents and databases may be subject to broad disclosure, if the employer maintains documents or other materials, electronic or otherwise, that are relevant to the matter.

The seminal case *Zubulake v. UBS Warburg LLC,*[5] described by the court as "a relatively routine employment discrimination dispute," foreshadowed important new rules concerning the preservation and production of electronic discovery in civil litigation.

There, the court ruled that once a party *reasonably anticipates litigation*, it must *suspend* its routine document retention and destruction policy and put in place a "litigation hold" to ensure the preservation of relevant data. However, that is only the beginning of counsel's obligations. Indeed, counsel must oversee compliance with the litigation hold, actively monitoring the client's efforts to retain and produce relevant documents.

The court makes clear that counsel must take a hands-on approach to overseeing these obligations. This, according to the court, will invariably involve speaking with information technology personnel. It will also require that counsel interview key witnesses to determine how they stored information. For example, some employees may print out relevant e-mails and retain them as hard copies, while others may create separate computer files. As the court states: "Unless counsel interviews each employee, it is impossible to determine whether all potential sources of information have been inspected."

While the client "must bear responsibility for a failure to preserve," nevertheless, the court pronounces that counsel is more likely than the client to be "conscious of the contours of the preservation obligation." To assure the client's compliance, the court rules, counsel must actively supervise the client's activities in this regard.

In this case, the court decided that the employer had failed to preserve e-mail records, and issued an "adverse inference" instruction: that is, the jury was to be instructed to draw an inference adverse to the employer in determining why the e-mails were not retained. In April 2005, the jury returned a verdict in favor of the employee in the amount of $29 million.

New Discovery Rules Following Zubulake

In December 2006, the Federal Rules of Civil Procedure (FRCP), which govern discovery in federal courts, were revised to address electronic discovery issues. Among other things, the new rules:

- Require the parties to provide the court with early notice of potential electronic discovery issues;
- Establish a procedure for addressing the risk of inadvertent transmission of *privileged and protected materials* during electronic discovery;
- Permit the *production* of "documents, electronically stored information, and things" and adds provisions specifically addressing the form in which electronic data is to be provided;
- Provide a *safe harbor* for "routine, good-faith" loss of data; and
- Provide that *subpoenas* may demand the production of electronically stored information, and may specify the form(s) in which electronically stored information is to be produced.

New Proposed Legislation

As of summer 2008, the U.S. Congress is in the virtual control of the Democratic Party, but the margin is too narrow for much legislation to pass. This margin may grow after the 2008 elections—when, many pundits predict, the Democrats will retake the White House. Thus, an examination of new and proposed legislation from Congress offers a glimpse of what life may be like after the 2008 presidential elections.

Discrimination on the Basis of Sexual Orientation

In September 2007, Congress held hearings on the Employment Non-Discrimination Act (ENDA). This bill would prohibit discrimination against employees because of sexual orientation and gender identity. It would prohibit discrimination against gay, lesbian, bisexual, and transgender employees.

The law would prohibit discrimination not only because of protected status, but also because of perceived protected status. Thus, it would seem to explicitly prohibit discrimination based on sexual stereotypes.

ENDA goes beyond the protection offered by the numerous states whose laws have already addressed discrimination against homosexuals. For example, the New York Sexual Orientation Nondiscrimination Act prohibits discrimination only on the basis of sexual orientation. Currently, 13 states have policies prohibiting both sexual orientation and gender identity discrimination in employment, seven states including New York have state laws that prohibit discrimination based on sexual orientation only, and 15 states have laws that have been interpreted to protect transgender persons.

Arbitration Fairness Act

The Arbitrations Fairness Act (AFA), introduced in August 2007, would prohibit predispute arbitration agreements that require arbitration of employment, consumer, or franchise disputes. The bill's authors believe that mandatory arbitration of employment disputes inevitably favors the more powerful party—namely, the employer—because it allegedly favors repeat players (companies), is expensive and time consuming, imposes a shroud of secrecy over employment disputes, and is virtually devoid of judicial review. The AFA would overturn 15 years of Supreme Court precedent that has repeatedly favored arbitration of employment disputes, including claims of discrimination.

Fair Pay Restoration Act

The Fair Pay Restoration Act (FPRA), introduced in July 2007, would amend several federal employment discrimination statutes to specify that an unlawful job practice occurs each time an employee receives pay resulting from an allegedly discriminatory compensation decision. The bill seeks to supplant the U.S. Supreme Court's 2007 decision in *Ledbetter v. Goodyear Tire & Rubber Co.*,[6] which held that the time limit for filing a discrimination charge starts to run only when the employer makes a discriminatory decision about the employee's compensation.

The FPRA would amend federal antidiscrimination laws to provide that the time limit would be triggered each time wages, benefits, or other compensation is paid, resulting in whole or in part from an unlawful discriminatory decision.

Employee Free Choice Act

In March 2007, the House passed the Employee Free Choice Act, which aims to amend the National Labor Relations Act (NLRA). The Act would require the National Labor Relations Board to certify a union without an election as the exclusive representative of employees if a majority of the employees in an appropriate unit has signed valid authorizations.

EEOC Guidance on Family Caregivers

One recent development shows an increased interest in enforcement of prohibitions of discrimination against individuals because of their family responsibilities. In April 2007, the Equal Employment Opportunity Commission (EEOC), which enforces federal antidiscrimination laws, issued "Guidance on Family Responsibilities Discrimination." The guidance draws attention to the possibility that increased discrimination claims may arise from the increase in dual-income households and the conflict between balancing work and family obligations.

The guidance points out how sex- and age-based notions of family obligations may violate existing laws, and even constitute a hostile environment. While hardly groundbreaking, it reflects an increased focus by the EEOC on this important area. Employers would be well advised to pay attention to their policies, particularly in the areas of leaves of absence and reasonable accommodation for disabilities.

NOTES

1. Cal. Labor Code Section 1102.5 (2008).
2. *Id.*
3. *Id.* Section 1102.7 (2008).
4. *Id.*
5. 229 F.R.D. 422 (S.D.N.Y. 2004).
6. 127 S. Ct. 2162 (2007).

INDEX